Leaders of the Church of England

LEADERS OF THE
CHURCH OF ENGLAND
1828-1944

David L. Edwards

London
OXFORD UNIVERSITY PRESS
NEW YORK   TORONTO
1971

Oxford University Press, Ely House, London W.1

GLASGOW NEW YORK TORONTO MELBOURNE WELLINGTON
CAPE TOWN SALISBURY IBADAN NAIROBI DAR ES SALAAM LUSAKA ADDIS ABABA
BOMBAY CALCUTTA MADRAS KARACHI LAHORE DACCA
KUALA LUMPUR SINGAPORE HONG KONG TOKYO

ISBN 0 19 213110 9

Printed in Great Britain by
Western Printing Services Ltd, Bristol

Contents

List of Illustrations

Preface

These essays in biography have a practical purpose. The history of the Church of England since about 1828 is a subject which we can now begin to see in perspective, and a number of us guess that we should be both entertained and instructed if we knew more about it. Students of history or literature, and general readers, including those who view the Church of England with amusement or nostalgia only, can share this subject with students of theology, and those interested in it need not be Anglicans or Englishmen. Yet many of us who are willing to explore the period have too many other interests to work through all the biographies, the other narratives, and the specialist studies, if we can get hold of them; and when we do open these books, we find at least the older among them intolerably over-solemn and un-critical. These biographers were widows, children, or hero-worshippers. Many of their books read like the obituaries in *The Times*; and about the latter, Somerset Maugham remarked that if men were so good he wondered why the other pages of the newspaper were the records of folly.

Here, then, are fresh portraits of twenty English churchmen from Thomas Arnold to William Temple, together with a few sketches of lesser characters and a short epilogue taking the story down to 1970. I have included three laymen, and I regret that no woman seemed prominent enough to merit inclusion. The men are studied two by two: Thomas Arnold with his son, William Temple with his father, some with friends, others with rivals. The pairing of them like Noah's animals does, I hope, illustrate the comprehensiveness of the Church of England, where these strikingly varied temperaments were all at home and afloat, even Cardinal Newman being in some vital characteristics always an Anglican. Indeed, in a remarkable number of cases they shared loyalties to a small number of very English places: Canterbury and York, Oxford and Cambridge, Westminster and Durham, Rugby School and King Edward's School, Birmingham. My own interest in them is, I trust, not sentimental, but it has been aroused by the years when I have lived as a schoolboy in Canterbury, as an undergraduate in Oxford, as a Fellow of All Souls College, Oxford, and of King's College, Cambridge, and as a Canon of Westminster.

Although the decision had to be taken not to clutter these pages with footnotes, I am of course indebted and thankful to the many scholars on whose researches my narrative was built, and particularly to Michael Hennell, David Newsome, and Charles Smyth, whose comments improved it. The volume on the twentieth century which I hope to contribute to Black's *Ecclesiastical History of England* is intended to be a work of research, but here my purpose has been almost entirely confined to a study of other men's books. I dare not dedicate such a work to a learned body, but more informally I offer it to my colleagues and audiences in the Cambridge Divinity Faculty, whose kindness encouraged me to write it.

Westminster Abbey,   D.L.E.
Christmas 1970

Prologue

It is roughly true to say that the revival of English religion in the nineteenth century corresponded with the power of the middle classes. Going to church or chapel was an important part of being respectable. Sociologically speaking, the only other cause of widespread religious observance in Victorian England was going to Mass, which was an important part of being Irish. People below or above respectability were not so ecclesiastical. Since the 1810s a constant theme to be heard in all the English Churches except the Roman Catholics and some Nonconformist quarters such as the Primitive Methodists has been a lament for the absence of the working classes. The small upper class often went to church in Victorian times, when even Eton College Chapel witnessed scenes of devotion, but with a few outstanding exceptions it was not so creative religiously as the classes immediately below it.

However, it would be a travesty of the historical facts to think of all the Victorian Churches as temples of a crude middle-class self-interest. While they inevitably reflected many of the social and mental habits of the people who supported them in such numbers, part of their function as teachers of respectability was to raise the attention of the middle classes above money-getting, at least on Sundays. The entirely voluntary efforts of the Nonconformists held up some kind of a vision in ten thousand chapels; this was the age of Robert Browning. The Church of England slowly got to work on the evangelization of the lower middle classes, and even tried to preach to the people; and its message, although not normally a social gospel with the full courage of the Christian Socialists, was also not usually a completely simple manifestation of class snobbery. 'Duty' was a word constantly repeated, and it was a duty that could cut across self-interest. Of course there was a great deal of hypocrisy in all this respectability; hypocrisy must accompany any great effort by human societies in the sphere of religion or in any other enterprise calling for nobility. Such is the way of all flesh.[1] But that is not the whole truth.

[1] Written in 1873–84, and published posthumously in an expurgated version in 1903, Samuel Butler's *Ernest Pontifex or The Way of All Flesh* should be read with Richard Hoggart's Introduction (Penguin Books, 1966).

When Anthony Trollope thought about the Church, he thought of the cathedrals and rectories where so much pettiness and injustice flourished among so much dignity and beauty, or of his father who amid the ruins of his life had contracted religious mania trying to compile something to be called the *Encyclopaedia Ecclesiastica*. It all seemed comically, or tragically, irrelevant to an age when Trollope had to proclaim that he manufactured words for money. But others believed that the Church would survive the fall of Barchester. Trollope hit off so neatly the various clerical types as the Victorians knew them. But his should not be taken as the last word on the Victorian Church. His first-hand acquaintance with the ecclesiastical scene was small; London was, as he said, the only cathedral city he knew from the inside; and 'most of Trollope's characters are incapable of connected thought on religious questions'.[2]

What religion was to millions of Englishmen in the nineteenth century is shown by a story then widely circulated about Bishop Joseph Butler's death in 1752. According to this edifying tale, for which there is no authentic foundation, when the great philosopher-bishop was in his last sickness in Bath he summoned his chaplain to his bed, and said to him: 'Though I have endeavoured to avoid sin, and to please God, to the utmost of my power, yet, from the consciousness of perpetual infirmities, I am still afraid to die.' The anecdote continues that the chaplain replied: 'My lord, you have forgotten that Jesus Christ is a Saviour.' Religion, a feeling for the mystery around human life, and a fear of it, was also a response to the figure of Christ who had dominated the imagination of England and Europe for more than a thousand years. And it is reported that the bishop said to his chaplain: 'True, but how shall I know that he is a Saviour for me?'[3]

Many Englishmen in the nineteenth century thought that they needed 'a Saviour for me'. In a famous outburst against Butler's successors (such as Archdeacon Paley) who had tried to prove the designing power and benevolence of the Creator from the 'evidences' of nature as well as of the Scriptures, Coleridge exclaimed: 'Evidences of Christianity! I am weary of the word. Make a man feel the want of it; rouse him, if you can, to the self-knowledge of his need of it; and you may safely trust to its own Evidence. . .' Many Englishmen felt this need with a special intensity because a process of secularization, going deeper than the intellectual enlightenment which had confronted Bishop Butler, was gradually penetrating the foundations of personal

<hr/>

[2] A. O. J. Cockshut, *Anthony Trollope* (Collins, 1955), p. 79. See also R. M. Polhemus, *The Changing World of Anthony Trollope* (University of California Press, 1968).

[3] The chaplain comforted the bishop by quoting the text: 'Him that cometh unto me, I will in no wise cast out'. Thomas Bartlett, *Memoirs of the Life, Character and Writings of Joseph Butler* (Parker, 1839), pp. 221–2.

confidence and of the social order. If God was not in his heaven (not even the Deists' God to whom Tom Paine and Robert Owen clung), what was right in the world? And what was the point of setting the world right? And what remained for anyone at the end of the road?[4]

Such ultimate questions threatened the young John Stuart Mill with a breakdown, until he turned to the poetry of Wordsworth and to his marriage. But others, who included Wordsworth, turned with a new earnestness to the possibility gaining evidence of 'a Saviour for me' within the community of faith. To some observers, the new zeal for doctrine and the Church exposed traditional Christians all the more pathetically to the climate of the modern age—like men caught in a thunder-storm, flying for refuge to a tree which only the more certainly would attract the lightning.[5] But many people in the nineteenth century did sincerely believe that when the lightning of modernity struck the Church, not everything would be consumed.

All over Europe the nineteenth century saw a rally in the Christian forces, while the Christian advance in North America, Africa, Asia, and Australasia made the century the greatest era ever known in missionary expansion. In many places the energy of the rival churches produced both conversions and controversies. In Scotland, for example, the Established (Presbyterian) Church was torn asunder by questions which were basically similar to those which agitated England under Victoria: questions about the presentation of the Gospel in an age of new knowledge (in Scotland the Evangelical and Moderate parties were well organized), questions about the relation of Church and State in an age of new energy and danger (in the Church of Scotland, where of course no bishoprics were available to serve as the flashpoints of the conflict, there was a bitter dispute about the rights of patrons over the parish churches). In Scotland, Thomas Chalmers, a figure as remarkable as any south of the Border in his time, an Evangelical of Moderate origins and lingering habits, a pastor, professor, and statesman, led the Disruption of the Church in 1843.[6] No less dramatic was the conflict in France, for example, where some great Christian men wrestled with the Papacy on the one hand, and the People on the other, until the first decade of the twentieth century saw the complete separation of

---

[4] The anxiety of the age was well presented by Walter E. Houghton, *The Victorian Frame of Mind* (Yale University Press, 1957).

[5] So J. A. Froude thought, looking back on the 'Oxford Counter-Reformation' in the last of his volumes of *Short Studies of Great Subjects* (Longmans, Green, 1883). See W. H. Dunn, *James Anthony Froude: A Biography*, 2 vols. (Clarendon Press, 1961-3).

[6] See Hugh Watt, *Thomas Chalmers and the Disruption* (Nelson, 1943); and for some biographical essays, *Fathers of the Kirk*, ed. R. Selby Wright (Oxford University Press, 1960).

Church and State and the apparently final divorce of Catholic faith from modern knowledge.[7]

In England, the Nonconformist bodies and the Roman Catholics also experienced great tensions and some triumphs.[8] The Church of England did, however, come to possess a special significance in the nineteenth century, accounting in part for the intensity of the passions displayed by its chief actors and for the almost insatiable enthusiasm of their audiences.

When the century began the Church of England was, proportionately to the population (all of which it married and buried), the richest religious body seen anywhere since the Middle Ages. It was able to dispose of handsome endowments to promote religion in Ireland and Wales, without any very noticeable effort to be Irish or Welsh. Its higher clergy received stipends for being connected with a splendid collection of cathedrals and other great churches, and if individual stipends were not splendid enough they held two or more together. A quarter of the Justices of the Peace in 1832 were clergymen. Comfortable parsonages belonged to the Jane Austen landscape, however great was the scandal of non-resident incumbents (about a quarter of the incumbents were pluralists), and however deep the poverty of many of the curates who did most of the work. Such a profession was attractive, more so for peaceable gentlemen than the Law, Medicine, the Army, or the Navy. Three-quarters of the undergraduates who rowed in the first boat race, in 1829, became parsons. The college chapels in Oxford and Cambridge, the city churches in London, and the elegant pulpits in the spas spoke of the consecration or the humbug of learning, wealth, and fashion. Compulsory tithes to maintain the clergy, and compulsory rates to repair the churches, were very practical expressions of the obligations acknowledged, however unwillingly, in the parishes. The attachment of the Crown to the National Church, at least nominally, had been maintained since the flight of James II. Protestants not prepared to receive Holy Communion in the Church of England were in theory excluded from public life until 1828 (al-

---

[7] An Anglican scholar, A. R. Vidler, has provided three studies in *Prophecy and Papacy: A Study of Lamennais, the Church and the Revolution* (SCM Press, 1954); *A Century of Social Catholicism, 1820–1920* (SPCK, 1964); and *A Variety of Catholic Modernists* (Cambridge University Press, 1970). See also W. G. Roe, *Lamennais and England* (Clarendon Press, 1966).

[8] An historian with a Congregationalist background enables us to sense the atmosphere in all the denominations, in two volumes of his history of worship and theology in England. See Horton Davies, *From Newman to Martineau, 1850–1900*, and *The Ecumenical Century, 1900–1965* (Princeton University Press, 1962–5). For the conflicts within nineteenth-century Methodism, see John Kent, *The Age of Disunity* (Epworth Press, 1966), and Robert Currie, *Methodism Divided* (Faber & Faber, 1968). J. W. Webster has outlined the story of *Free Churchmanship in England, 1870–1940* (Independent Press, 1962).

though annual Indemnity Acts made it possible for some of them to hold office), and the small Roman Catholic minority was not emancipated politically until 1829. Parliament acknowledged this work for religion, or for the class system, when it handed over more than a million pounds to the poorer clergy in 1809–29, and a million and a half pounds for new churches in 1818–24; and worried bishops assumed that things would get better if only more seats could be provided in more churches. The National Society, founded in 1811, attempted to promote 'the education of the poor in the principles of the Established Church'.[9]

This stately home of official England had many claims to be considered the most abuse-ridden Church in the world. 'The Church, as it now stands, no human power can save', wrote Thomas Arnold in 1832, knowing how the mobs had rioted against the bishops. John Stuart Mill reckoned that the only question delaying its abolition was the question what to put in its place. The Reformation of the sixteenth century had left the National Church's medieval structure virtually intact. In the next century the new discipline which swept through Catholic Europe as the Counter-Reformation was known in Protestant England mainly through the rival efforts of Archbishop Laud, who was beheaded, and the Puritans, who failed with Cromwell. The Methodist movement of the eighteenth century had been forced out of the National Church. Its shrewder friends, and all its foes, therefore now argued that if the Establishment was to survive, its many corruptions must be purged and its prevailing slackness must be invigorated. But if the Church of England was to be given a new structure and a new spirit, if it was to be no longer the Church 'as it now stands' in 1832, who was to control the reform? That seemed to be a question of consuming interest, for with all its defects the Established Church remained a rich prize.

Ecclesiastical parties manoeuvered in order to capture this prize, with propaganda such as the militant Evangelical weekly, the *Record*, or on the other wing, the Anglo-Catholic *Tracts for the Times* which gave rise to the name 'Tractarians' and to much else. Those who refused to support the theology or the tactics of the Low Church, or High Church, party found themselves classified as 'Broad Church', however indignantly they protested that they were not a party. In October 1853 an article in the *Edinburgh Review* by W. J. Conybeare attracted wide attention as the clearest analysis to date of these competing factions.[10]

9 The most active leader in good works for the Church in this period was a layman. See A. B. Webster, *Joshua Watson* (SPCK, 1954). For the social attitudes of the bishops from 1783 to 1852, see R. A. Soloway, *Prelates and People* (Routledge & Kegan Paul, 1969).

10 After the deletion of some personalities, it was reprinted in W. J. Conybeare, *Essays Ecclesiastical and Social* (Longmans, Green, 1855). It popularized

Conybeare estimated that the clergy of the Church of England (including Wales but excluding Ireland and Scotland) were about 18,000 in number in a population of about eighteen millions, and he guessed that they could be classified as follows:

Low Church	Normal type ('Evangelical')	3,330
	Exaggerated type ('Recordite')	2,500
	Stagnant type ('Low and Slow')	700
High Church	Normal type ('Anglican')	3,500
	Exaggerated type ('Tractarian')	1,000
	Stagnant type ('High and Dry')	2,500
Broad Church	Normal type	2,800
	Exaggerated type (concealed infidels)	20(?)
	Stagnant type	700

Two further groups were mentioned by Conybeare: 'about 1,000 peasant clergy in the mountain districts', largely Welsh, and 'twenty-eight bishops and archbishops . . . thirteen belonging to various shades of High Church, ten to the Broad Church, and five to the Evangelical parties.' Conybeare admitted that all this was 'an approximation', but it does give us some idea of the groups arranged in the background behind the leaders whose portraits we are to paint. And we must add that in 1859 the High Church forces were mobilized—they claimed, defensively—in the English Church Union, to be followed in 1865 by the Church Association for the Low Church party. The battlefield was set.

One reason why the Church of England was a valuable prize was that the island where it had slumbered was now the world's first industrial state, while the Royal Navy commanded the seas. For all its isolation and casualness, nineteenth-century England could not avoid a role in the world; it continued to influence the American ex-colonies, and as the century progressed it became the centre of a vast new imperial system. Religious ideas exported by Englishmen went all over the world, and the Church of England itself slowly and reluctantly ceased to be insular. We shall find Thomas Arnold, John Keble, Samuel Wilberforce, and successive Archbishops of Canterbury all aware of a global setting for the particular theologies and ecclesiologies which they favoured, and had our study begun at an earlier date we should have paid special attention to the Evangelicals' enthusiasm for the

---

the transfer of the label 'Low Church' from the successors of the earlier 'Latitudinarians' to the Evangelicals. The term 'Broad Church' had only recently begun to be used by Arthur Stanley and others, and during the 1870s the tendency grew to replace it by 'Liberal Churchmen'.

work of the Church Missionary Society, founded in 1799. These religious ideas, when they had been exported, often returned to England in the lives or legends of men who had become apostles while building the Church on new ground overseas; and England was influenced. Still one comes across churches or monuments which are visible reminders of that world-wide achievement, and still the great libraries contain some faint echoes of the excitement. Thus Bishop Samuel Wilberforce, in addition to compiling a large memoir of the Evangelical missionary hero Henry Martyn, who had died in Persia in 1812, wrote another book (in 1844) which drew the attention of his fellow-countrymen to the history of the Protestant Episcopal Church in the United States. In 1864 Samuel Adjai Crowther, who had been rescued from slavery forty years before, was consecrated as bishop of his native Nigeria—*The Black Bishop* as Jessie Page's account of his long life proclaimed (1908). From 1867 onwards the Lambeth Conference of bishops, normally held once every ten years, acted as the focus of what came to be called the Anglican Communion. And so the Book of Common Prayer, with some local adaptations, was used in worship

> From Greenland's icy mountains,
> From India's coral strand,
> Where Afric's sunny fountains
> Roll down their golden sand . . .[11]

In 1841 an Etonian who had been a curate in Windsor sailed to New Zealand as its first Anglican bishop, at the age of thirty-two. In 1844, at Waimate, he summoned a synod of three archdeacons, four other priests, and two deacons. It was the first experiment in corporate action by nineteenth-century Anglicans outside the United States; for at this date the ancient Convocations of the clergy in the Church of England were silenced. That experiment was accompanied by others, in the course of which Anglicanism was strongly renewed. Even before his enthronement as Bishop of Lichfield in 1868, this architect of Anglicanism in New Zealand, George Selwyn, taught the lessons which England could learn.

The experience of a new colony [he declared in 1847] convinces me that the Church of England system fully worked: 1. Under an able and pious head; 2. With sufficient clergy of one mind; 3. With no pecuniary basis; 4.

[11] From one of the many hymns written by Reginald Heber, a Fellow of All Souls College, Oxford, who at the age of forty in 1823 abandoned one of the most charming parishes in England and certain prospects of literary and ecclesiastical distinction to become the second of the short-lived early Bishops of Calcutta. His story, which made a great impression after his death in 1826, was retold for the Victorian missionary public by George Smith, *Bishop Heber* (John Murray, 1895).

With no State interference; 5. With free power of expansion . . .; 6. With a *sacramentum* [oath] of obedience; 'Here am I, send me'; 'I go, sir'; as well understood as in the army and navy. . . . That, these postulates granted, the Church of England would speedily become a praise upon the whole earth.

Here Selwyn underrated the strength of habit and prejudice in England, but his words illustrated the new spirit of world-wide Anglicanism. Those who had found 'a Saviour for me' in England might find themselves supporting missionaries, or actually themselves preaching in the southern seas, or even being murdered there, as John Coleridge Patteson, the first and saintly Bishop of Melanesia, was in 1871; and so they might find an unexpected vitality in their Christian faith, as when the news of Patteson's death stirred all England.[12]

In one respect, indeed, these builders of the new Anglicanism at home and overseas were more significant than could be known by anyone at the time. In efforts towards religious peace in England, the Tudor architects of the National Church had made it as comprehensive as possible. That was the reason why in the nineteenth century the Church was the battleground of rival theologies, perhaps more conspicuously than it was an army against unbelief. But most of the theological rivals were still yoked together by the system of the Church of England, which seemed to hold for them even more blessings than curses; and the system of the Established Church of England came to have a more and more distinctly ecclesiastical basis. At home and overseas, as the Tudor arrangements fell away Anglicans were stimulated to serious thought about what were the essentials and inessentials in the constitution of the Christian Church. Controversy was inevitable once this problem had been set, but when the modern ecumenical movement, which is generally regarded as having started at the Edinburgh Conference of 1910, tried to move towards an ideal of unity which would include much diversity within a bond of charity, Anglicans naturally found themselves involved in the reconciling trend; and when in the 1960s after the Second Vatican Council a new era opened in the attitude of Roman Catholics to other Christians, Anglicans were eager for this dialogue also. Thus the tensions within Anglicanism could be regarded as a training-ground for the tensions and hopes of

[12] H. G. G. Herklots has introduced the story of the making of the Anglican Communion in *Frontiers of the Church* (Benn, 1961), and Stephen Neill the wider story in his *History of Christian Missions* (Penguin Books, 1964). There is a modern biography of Selwyn: J. H. Evans, *Churchman Militant* (Allen & Unwin, 1961). Charlotte Yonge wrote a biography of Patteson, who had been influenced by Selwyn at Eton, and recruited by him in 1855 to found the Melanesian Mission. For other episcopal martyrdoms, in Africa, which caught the imagination of the Victorians, see E. C. Dawson, *James Hannington* (Seeley, 1887), and Owen Chadwick, *Mackenzie's Grave* (Hodder & Stoughton, 1959).

the ecumenical struggle for Christian renewal and reunion around the world.

Its ability to produce missionaries such as Selwyn and Patteson was one of the most important of the strengths which enabled Victorian England to stumble into its imperial role. There were many more like them at home. The Church of England was then proud to have heroes, captains of a new empire of Christ. This was in the Carlylean style of the period. Nonconformist congregations were built around their preachers, and basked in the glory of princes of the pulpit such as R. W. Dale in Birmingham or Joseph Parker or Charles Spurgeon in London.[13] Methodism produced in Jabez Bunting an administrator who was more of a dictator than any bishop, and later in Hugh Price Hughes a publicist whose commanding enthusiasm was able to create a newspaper, a network of central halls, and a whole 'Forward Movement'.[14] Most astonishing of all was the meteoric career, flaming across darkest England, of William Booth, the ex-Methodist founding General of the Salvation Army.[15]

The leading Anglican ecclesiastics, however, definitely belonged to the ruling class—even if some far-seeing men such as Thomas Arnold and George Selwyn had begun to say that the Church of England must broaden the social basis of its clergy and forget the 'Gentleman-Heresy'. In the shires the clergy prospered financially and socially in the Victorian age more than at any other time in English history; they were helped, rather than hindered, by the commutation of agricultural tithes in kind for money payments in 1836, since these easily collected payments provided many handsome incomes for the parsons until the whole of English agriculture began to suffer through foreign competition in the 1870s. The higher clergy of the Established Church were educated alongside the other leaders of the national life. They were nominated to their posts by the Crown on the recommendation of the government of the day. It was a convention surviving from the old days of the unity of Church and State. Although indefensible theologically, this was convenient for the time being, in that it enabled the Crown to push to the top some able men who were unpopular with, or unknown to, the parochial clergy. In the colonies,

[13] His son Arthur wrote *The Life of R. W. Dale of Birmingham* (Hodder & Stoughton, 1898); he was pastor of Carr's Lane Chapel, 1853–95. Both Parker, who was Minister of the City Temple, 1874–1902, and Spurgeon, whose preaching drew large crowds at the Metropolitan Tabernacle and elsewhere in the period 1854–92, wrote autobiographies.

[14] See John Kent, *Jabez Bunting: The Last Wesleyan* (Epworth Press, 1955). His daughter Dorothea wrote a *Life of Hugh Price Hughes* (Hodder & Stoughton, 1904).

[15] A good short presentation of Booth's work is to be found in Richard Collier, *The General Next to God* (Collins, 1965).

where the Crown's control of the Church was gradually weakened by geography as much as by theology, the quality of the bishops became all the more important; in the development of the Anglican Communion, few things mattered more than the Colonial Bishoprics Fund in London. And in the colonies the clergy and lay missionaries, however poor, were the recognized ambassadors of a proud 'Christian civilization'.

Were such churchmen truly eminent? They were not so eminent as their contemporaries believed. No one today could read with entire conviction such Victorian works as Frederick Arnold's two volumes on *Our Bishops and Deans* (1875), or the quarrelsome Dean Burgon's *Twelve Good Men* (1888); and no one today could plausibly write in that style about later churchmen. But it is equally true that no student of the largely frustrated life of Lytton Strachey can help wondering whether a man such as that was right to assume an air of bland superiority to the bishops, the deans, the parsons and the earnest laymen of the Victorian Church and its aftermath.[16] For one thing, the Victorians were far more critical of their own failings than Strachey and other intellectuals of that generation were of theirs. Frederick Arnold in the course of his chatter observed that 'the crying necessity of our times is a sweeping Ecclesiastical Reform Bill, and unless reform is adopted we shall have Revolution or Destruction.'[17] The Victorian churchmen at whom Strachey sneered did reform, although not enough. They fought the battles of faith, and won some of them. They led a large religious body into a new style of life. They influenced a great—by many standards, the greatest—age in English history, for 'no one will ever understand Victorian England who does not appreciate that among highly civilized . . . countries it was one of the most religious that the world has known'.[18] And they did this at a time when the Church of England was significant to other countries and to other Churches. It is true to say about them what has been said about the great Anglican who stood behind them. 'John Wesley had not indeed been able to stem the process of secularization and dechristianization, but he had none the less played a very significant part in seeking to combat it. He could not change the march of history but there can be little doubt that he left his mark on it.'[19]

---

[16] See Michael Holroyd, *Lytton Strachey: A Critical Biography*, 2 vols. (Heinemann, 1967–8). Strachey's *Eminent Victorians* was published in 1918.
[17] *Our Bishops and Deans* (Hurst & Blackett, 1875), vol. i, p. 41.
[18] R. C. K. Ensor, *England 1870–1914* (Clarendon Press, 1936), p. 137.
[19] V. H. H. Green, *John Wesley* (Nelson, 1964), p. 160. Wesley was converted in 1738, and died in 1791.

FOR FURTHER READING

The best history of *The Victorian Church* is by Owen Chadwick, in two volumes (Black, 1966–70). The best survey of nineteenth-century English religious thought is B. M. G. Reardon, *From Coleridge to Gore* (Longman, 1971). Earlier narratives which have retained their high value include S. C. Carpenter, *Church and People 1789–1889* (SPCK, 1933), and V. F. Storr, *The Development of English Theology in the Nineteenth Century, 1800–1860* (Longmans, Green, 1913); and the two books by L. E. Elliott-Binns, *Religion in the Victorian Era* (Lutterworth Press, 1936), and *English Thought, 1860–1900: The Theological Aspect* (Longmans, Green, 1956). The best brief guide to the movement of thought remains G. M. Young, *Victorian England: Portrait of an Age* (Oxford University Press, 1936). Basil Willey, in his *Nineteenth Century Studies: Coleridge to Arnold* and *More Nineteenth Century Studies: A Group of Honest Doubters* (Chatto & Windus, 1949–56), has connected the development of religious thought with the cultural background. Some documents illustrating *Religious Controversies of the Nineteenth Century* have been edited by A. O. J. Cockshut (Methuen, 1966). A companion volume is *Church and State in Britain since 1820*, ed. David Nicholls (Routledge & Kegan Paul, 1967). K. S. Inglis has researched into some of the social background in his *Churches and the Working Classes in Victorian England* (Routledge & Kegan Paul, 1963). *The Oxford Dictionary of the Christian Church*, ed. F. L. Cross (Oxford University Press, 1957, subsequently revised), is specially strong on Anglican history.

1

Thomas and Matthew Arnold

1

When Thomas Arnold began to reign as Headmaster of Rugby School in 1828, he was thirty-three years old and full of the ambition to educate. 'My object will be, if possible, to form Christian men, for Christian boys I can scarcely hope to make.' His own eldest son Matthew, then aged almost six, was a problem. When barely six months old he had already seemed 'backward and rather bad-tempered'. Matt had to wear irons in order to straighten out his legs; his father nick-named him 'the Crab'. The boy was not permanently lame, but he was awkward and a stammerer. He alarmed his father by being a dreamer. 'Matt does not know what it is to work, because he so little knows what it is to think.' Was his moral influence on the other children all that it might be? As a precaution, he was for a time separated from them.

Amid 'trembling' at home, Matthew Arnold was sent off to his father's old school at Winchester. His father had been happy there, but now he feared that the son might fall into vice—although the son wrote one of his first poems about the moral issues involved in entry into a public school. However, what happened was that some of the boys heard him telling a master that the work was 'quite light', and Matt was teased brutally; so, after a year, he was recalled and placed under his father's care at Rugby. When told to stand behind the Head-master's throne for being unsatisfactory in the Sixth Form, he made funny faces at the class. His father was 'astonished' when the boy won a scholarship to Balliol College, Oxford; and Oxford was no less astonished to find Thomas Arnold's son totally unlike the young prigs emerging from Rugby. Matt was a dandy, conspicuous for the length of his hair, the colour of his waistcoats, the sophistication of his know-ledge of French literature, and his habit of calling his friends 'my darling'.

Oxford meant much to father and son, the countryside even more than the colleges. The father loved that country because in it he could work off some of his energy. He took to the river, he went for immense walks, and he specially enjoyed 'skirmishes' which involved plunging over, or through, hedges and streams. For the son, however, delight in the country around Oxford was not an athlete's pleasure; Matthew Arnold sought relief from mental exhaustion. His reading in Oxford had contributed to his virtual rejection of his father's religion. For a time, he found a substitute in the religion of beauty, 'all the live murmur of a summer's day'. But in the end, beauty was not enough. Was it merely that Matthew Arnold grew middle-aged? Already in 1853 he wrote to Clough: 'I am past thirty, and three parts iced over'. Or was he turning from the country to the town, from poetry to prose, because of his inheritance? Or was it the fault of a 'deeply unpoetical' age? He asked himself such questions many times, and there is no reason why we should give a clearer answer than he did.

At any rate, Matthew Arnold expressed the dilemma of his age better than anyone else—and it was a talkative age. As the key image of the eloquence, he immortalized the Oxford (or, to be more accurate, the Cumnor) countryside by painting it in an atmosphere which he himself described in self-criticism as 'a pleasing melancholy'. 'The Scholar-Gipsy' (1853) was based on the seventeenth-century story of the Oxford man who had gone into the country in search of a secret, in his case the gipsies' skill in hypnotism. As the seasons came and went, this scholar still awaited the great secret.

> Thou waitest for the spark from heaven! and we,
> Light half-believers of our casual creeds,
>   Who never deeply felt, nor clearly will'd,
> Whose insight never has borne fruit in deeds,
>   Whose vague resolves never have been fulfill'd; . . .
> Ah! do not we, wanderer! await it too?

'Thyrsis' (1866) was another lament, set amid the 'high Midsummer pomps' of the same country. It was a lament for his schoolfellow Arthur Hugh Clough, who at Rugby had been heartily admired among the heroes of the Sixth Form. Oxford and the world had proved too much for Clough, and he had become a poet of the vanished faith, the full tomb.[1] Matthew Arnold had disapproved of this withdrawal from duty and this surrender to anxiety; 'Thyrsis', despite its melancholy, ended on a distinctly religious note. And in his poem 'Rugby Chapel' (1867), he strained language as far as it would go in order to identify himself with his father's faith. Thomas Arnold was now remembered from the days when he had led his children ('the Dogs') for walks up the fells in the Lake District; and he was imagined among

---

[1] See Katherine Chorley, *Arthur Hugh Clough: the Uncommitted Mind* (Clarendon Press, 1962). Matthew Arnold's *Letters to Arthur Hugh Clough* were edited by H. F. Lowry (Clarendon Press, 1932).

the dead whose courage had somehow earned immortality and who had taken lesser men into regions which, however misty, were higher than the workaday plain.

> Languor is not in your heart,
> Weakness is not in your word,
> Weariness not on your brow. . . .
> Eyes rekindling, and prayers,
> Follow your steps as ye go.

Matthew Arnold wrote 'Rugby Chapel' because in his own inner life he had been reconciled with the memory of 'dear papa'. He himself said that he wrote the poem as a result of the novel by Thomas Hughes, *Tom Brown's School-days*, published in 1857; he dated the poem 'November 1857' although he did not visit Rugby in that month. The novel moved Matthew Arnold, and a hostile review by Fitzjames Stephens, leaving the impression that the Headmaster of Rugby had been a narrow, bustling fanatic who spread gloom, made him indignant. The son knew, better than anyone else, how clumsy and oppressive his father could be. But he also knew—and he could say it better than any of his father's adoring pupils—how Arnold of Rugby deserved more than a chance patronizing notice. This 'strong soul' still had a message of high seriousness to deliver, while nature itself proved powerless to solve the spiritual problems which emerged as the old order of mind and society declined, while

> Coldly, sadly descends
> The autumn-evening. The field
> Strewn with its dank yellow drifts
> Of wither'd leaves, and the elms,
> Fade into dimness apace,
> Silent; —hardly a shout
> From a few boys late at their play!

2

There were many shouts when Thomas Arnold began his work at Rugby in 1828; and not only shouts of pain from the fags being bullied, or shouts of battle as Rugby football worked off young male instincts less sadistically. Thomas Arnold did much of the shouting himself. He was then at the height of his manhood, and his reputation rested on his energy. While running a small private school in the Thames-side village of Laleham, he had shared the work and the sports of his pupils with equal ardour. At Rugby he still needed hard exercise, and particularly enjoyed swimming and jumping. Although the public school cult of compulsory games was not introduced in his time, it was an important part of his policy to encourage innocent recreations, knowing that the alternatives had made public school life notorious. He also insisted, for the first time in the school's history, that the boys should sleep in separate beds.

The school was made into something more like a family. At Laleham his pupils spent their evenings in his drawing room. At Rugby he was a more remote figure, but favourites such as Arthur Clough would find themselves often with Matt and the Headmaster's other children, and the system by which the boarders at the school in fact boarded in Dames' Houses in the town was abolished in favour of having the boys in School House under the Headmaster or in other houses under assistant masters. Although the boys were still allowed far more freedom than would have been tolerated under the later development of the house system in public schools, they were now under closer supervision than before. In order that they might supervise, the masters were both ordered and enabled to give up their part-time curacies in parish churches. Schoolmastering was now seen as a full-time profession, for the schoolmaster's role was parental. A flag would often fly over the Headmaster's study. It was an invitation to any boy to call and discuss anything. Other masters were expected to be similarly available.

Thomas Arnold had a lively sense of the financial implications of his policy. His insistence on adequate salaries for his staff would entitle him to be the patron saint of the National Union of Teachers, and what he demanded for his staff he was not too shy to obtain for himself: he received the then enormous salary of over £3,000 a year together with a free house. Although he entered the post in debt and brought up nine children, he reckoned that fifteen years as Headmaster of Rugby would enable him to retire for the rest of his life to the family home which he now built, Fox How, in the heart of the Westmorland fells, on a site chosen by Wordsworth. These larger salaries for himself and his staff came partly from the increase in the number of boys (he was paid per head), but mainly from raising the fees. The parents of boarders paid thirty guineas a year when he arrived. By 1834 they were complaining that they had to find at least £130 a year. Arnold did not hesitate to change the intention of its Elizabethan founder for Rugby School; at the beginning, in 1567, the school had provided education for a small village, but during Arnold's reign poorer boys were effectively excluded from its benefits, despite local indignation. A local school emerged to take care of those who could not afford Rugby School's new fees.

One of the reasons why it was easier for Arnold to recruit the sons of the upper middle class on a national basis was that this was the railway age. *Tom Brown's School-days* was deliberately nostalgic in its opening chapters about Squire Brown staying at home in Wiltshire and then sending his son off to school by the stage coach. In real life the Doctor welcomed the railway to Rugby, and took regular services for the railwaymen at the new station. He also saw the railways' unification of England as part of a new age for the world. He was the son of the chief customs officer in the Isle of Wight, and his boyhood at Cowes had been spent in sight of ships and the sea. As soon as he had any money he began touring Europe with a gusto rare in his time; he made twelve European expeditions, and later his travel diaries were published. Matthew Arnold thought that this European outlook was as important as anything else in his father's legacy. At the time it seemed bold that the form masters at Rugby should be required to teach French as well as the classics, and bolder still when a man was appointed to the staff who spoke French as a native. The wandering headmaster also thought much about remoter horizons. He spoke of crossing the Atlantic if Revolution came at home, or of becoming a colonial bishop, or of teaching in Tasmania or New Zealand, or at least of sending Matt out there so that he might learn how to work. One of his disciples was his son Willy, who became the educational pioneer of the Punjab.[2]

Thomas Arnold's formula can be made to sound like the privileged being politer to each other in a more prosperous world. But he did not regard the public school system as a bastion of privilege. The boys who flogged the guilty and used the fags as slaves were not given such rights because of their physical strength. On the contrary, boys whose physical development had outpaced their minds found themselves quickly removed from the school. 'The Doctor', we recall from *Tom Brown*, 'who had long had his eye on Flashman, arranged for his withdrawal next morning.' Nor did a boy's status in Rugby School depend on his parents' status in the world. The Doctor himself had not come from the top of the social tree. The clever boys of the Sixth Form were the 'praepostors' to whom these privileges were entrusted. And Rugby School was viewed by its headmaster as part of a system which depended on the upper middle class making itself useful. Arnold had no respect for a selfish cleverness, and he applied to a public school the principles which he had shown in action at Laleham. A pupil of his from those days, who subsequently joined the Rugby staff, wrote: 'Dr. Arnold's great power as a private tutor resided in this, that he gave such an intense earnestness to life. Every pupil was made to feel that

[2] He was commemorated by Matt after his death at sea in 'Stanzas from Carnac'. F. J. Woodward told the story of William Arnold, together with Stanley, Clough, and J. P. Gell, in *The Doctor's Disciples* (Oxford University Press, 1954).

there was work for him to do—that his happiness as well as his duty lay in doing that work well.'

A boy such as Arthur Clough, then a thorough convert, worked and lived in order to add to the moral glory of Rugby School. The other senior boys were all expected to share the same attitude. Many of them did, or at least they learned to echo their formidable headmaster's idealism; for one of Arnold's policies was to use to the full his right to require the parents of boys who were unsatisfactory for any reason at all to remove their offspring before they corrupted the school. It came to feel like a compliment to be asked to pay the Rugby fees. Once a boy had conformed to the system and had earned promotion to the Sixth, he seemed morally mature enough to act as judge and executioner over younger boys. There were public outcries against flogging in the school during Arnold's time, but the Headmaster refused to appease outsiders. Another reaction came from the senior boys themselves, who would often retire to the sick room with 'fatigue', but the moral pressure was maintained when the Doctor and his wife paid pastoral visits to the bedside.

The course of duty was overtly Christian. Indeed, the religious atmosphere of the whole of life in Rugby School, at least in its headmaster's eyes, was its most significant challenge to other schools. This was what 'spoiled the public schools' (in Clough's phrase, for once playful). Previously, good headmasters had been expected to concentrate on the production of classical scholars for the universities, and during the 1840s some still insisted that Greek, not morality, provided their role. While the scholars were being coached, the other boys could toughen each other up for their future lives as squires or soldiers. If in the process they hurt each other, their elders remembered how the Englishman's freedom had been defended on the playing fields of Eton. At Rugby Arnold's priorities were new: 'first religious and moral principle; secondly gentlemanly conduct; and thirdly intellectual ability'. The flogging was as religious as the preaching. The expulsions, as much as the Communions, made Rugby a school for Christian gentlemen.

At the time, Thomas Arnold's religion was hard to classify. 'But is *he* a Christian?' was Newman's reaction when someone quoted his views on the Old Testament prophets—whom Arnold regarded not as foretellers of the future but as proclaimers of good and evil. Doctrinal difficulties, particularly over the Athanasian Creed, had made him hesitate about entering the ordained ministry as a young Fellow of Oriel College. When friends headed by John Keble (an Oriel colleague) had persuaded him to become a deacon, he had still jibbed at taking responsibility for a parish or for the priesthood. Since he could not continue to reside as a Fellow of Oriel if he married, schoolmastering seemed the obvious profession. He never worked out a satisfactory system of beliefs. He would advise young clergymen to read the Bible, Bunyan, and the classics of Greece and Rome; the only English theologians for whom he expressed any admiration were Richard Hooker and Joseph Butler. He was one of the first to apply the Victorian remedy for doubt: work.

However, Lytton Strachey in *Eminent Victorians* may have confused Thomas with Matthew Arnold when he ascribed to the Doctor a 'puzzled mind'. Thomas Arnold experienced enough of the religious crisis to reject, or to feel uneasy about, a number of traditional dogmas, but it is impossible to read his sermons and letters with a modicum of sympathy and still to doubt his piety. Any boy's approach to irreligious levity or impertinence was checked with a glance, or a white face, or if necessary a terrible word or a judicial blow. Even adults who could not be treated in such a way sensed that the Doctor wrestled with the Devil. Keble was probably right to refuse to take his doubts seriously, and the Provost of Oriel, Edward Hawkins, probably had his religious stature in mind when he supplied the testimonial which won the headmastership for him, prophesying that if elected Thomas Arnold would 'change the face of education all through the public schools of England'.

Although still only a deacon when appointed, he promptly became a priest and a Doctor of Divinity, and he had not been at Rugby for long before he got himself made chaplain to the school. Sunday by Sunday he preached to the boys, sometimes weeping in the pulpit, sometimes denouncing their faults, sometimes warning them of death and hell, sometimes proclaiming Christ as the only Saviour for them, sometimes holding up the vision of a nobler life for man and nation. It was all in the mood of warm Evangelical seriousness, even if his desire to talk the language of common life and his independence of mind prevented him from echoing all the slogans of the Evangelical party. His sermons were authoritarian, even if his insistence on moral power and on preaching drove him to say that 'to revive Christ's church is to expel the antichrist of priesthood'.[3] Although he wanted commentaries to be written which would apply criticism to the Bible, he had little sense of the destructive power of the new sciences on religious faith. He fell out with the one visitor who had lectured on science to the Rugby boys under his predecessor. When he published an essay 'On the Right Interpretation and Understanding of the Scriptures', it was in a volume of 1832 containing twenty-nine intensely practical sermons to the Rugby boys, whose difficulties were clearly believed to be more moral than intellectual.

[3] Thomas Arnold, *Christian Life: Its Course, its Hindrances and its Helps* (Fellowes, 1841), p. lii.

Any theological hesitations got little attention in Rugby Chapel, and child psychology less.

There always are boys scattered up and down the School [Thomas Hughes remarked] who in heart and head were worthy to hear and able to carry away the deepest and wisest words there spoken. But these were a minority always, generally a very small one, often so small a one as to be countable on the fingers of your hand. What was it that moved and held us, the rest of the three hundred reckless, childish boys, who feared the Doctor with all our hearts, and very little besides in heaven or earth. . . .?

Hughes answered his own question by remembering 'the warm living voice of one who was . . . calling on us to help him and ourselves, and one another'. The Doctor who preached to them was 'a man who was striving against whatever was mean and unmanly and unrighteous in our little world'. Not all the boys responded even in this way, but there was enough response to entitle Arnold to be indignant when Newman's foolish little joke was repeated to him. His sermons, published in six volumes (two of these posthumously), enabled him to appeal over the heads of his enemies to more impressionable readers including Queen Victoria. It was a prophecy turned towards secular affairs (but was there a real difference between secular and sacred?); towards unrighteousness in the school, but also towards the economic and political problems of the nation. He would quote Francis Bacon: 'In this world, God only and the angels may be spectators.' When one reads about the very full life which he led with his family and his school, one is further exhausted to discover that Thomas Arnold's most passionate interests lay in the social crisis of the time. 'I must write or die' was his motto, for as he told the boys in a sermon 'this is a marked time—a time such as neither we, nor our fathers for many generations before us, have experienced'.

He was far from being a sophisticated statesman. Matthew Arnold was to recall, in the first edition of *Culture and Anarchy*, how his father had advocated flogging rioters. It had worked in Ancient Rome; it was working at Rugby, where the boys called him 'Tiger Tom' and learned to fear the bulging of the blue vein on his forehead. But because Thomas Arnold's ardent sympathies in the theory of politics were with the poor, his fellow-gentlemen regarded him as a radical. In 1831 he started his own newspaper, the *Englishman's Register*, to warn the country of the great evils which he saw coming imminently from a selfish aristocracy and a class of managers who treated workers as 'hands'. The newspaper was a flop, but other journals, in Sheffield and Hertfordshire, printed other controversial political letters which he did not sign, but which he also did not disown. His convictions about politics made him unpopular among the gentry around Rugby. At a banquet in 1835 some shouted 'No insult to the Doctor!'—but more took up the Tory cry, 'Church and King!' This partly explains his many complaints about Warwickshire and the joy with which he would leave the school for Westmorland on the first day of the holidays twice a year, postponing his return until the last possible moment—although he once broke into a Lakeland holiday, making the long and expensive journey back in order to vote against the Tories.

Friends, including Provost Hawkins, deplored his entanglement in public controversies, for it was bound to offend those on whose good will and fees Rugby School depended. Observers thought his habit of seeing Antichrist in his opponents ridiculously unworldly if not intolerably arrogant. Sydney Smith was to call him 'a learned, pious, virtuous person, without five grains of common sense'. In 1836 resentment at the well-paid headmaster's social radicalism and over-zealous indiscretions came to a head because Arnold published in the *Edinburgh Review* a bitter attack on 'the Oxford Malignants and Dr. Hampden' (a title supplied by the editor, but fair enough). These 'malignants' included other Fellows of Oriel such as Newman; naturally their colleagues crowded round in nervous curiosity when Arnold dined at Oriel College in 1842, and Provost Hawkins had to say hurriedly, 'Arnold, I don't think you know Newman?' The 'malignants' also included Keble, Thomas Arnold's intimate friend when they were both undergraduates at Corpus Christi College and now Matthew Arnold's godfather. These men were denounced for their 'moral wickedness', and a comparison of them with the Jews who crucified Christ seemed to exceed even the harsh conventions of theological controversy. The article was written because Newman and others had been protesting— also in an extravagant style—against the Whig government's appointment of an excessively broad-minded theologian, Renn Hampden, as Regius Professor of Divinity. The article's passionate indignation appears to have sprung partly from Arnold's suspicion that Hampden's real offence had been to want Dissenters admitted to Oxford, and partly from his belief that by insisting on reading the worst possible meaning into Hampden's benevolent-minded ambiguities the Tractarians were throwing away the Church's best chance of survival in the new age. But one result of this article's unbalanced tone was that the Doctor nearly lost his own appointment. Of the eight trustees who voted as the governing body of Rugby School, four now wanted his dismissal.

He was already in trouble in the Church because of a pamphlet written at Fox How during the Christmas holidays of 1832–3 on *Principles of Church Reform*. This was one of a spate of pamphlets about the ecclesiastical crisis at the time of the First Reform Act of 1832, when it looked as if the Church of England might be reformed violently and destructively. Thomas Arnold's purpose was conservative; indeed, he wrote in reply to a pamphlet by the Evangelical Lord Henley urging the radical remedy of virtual disestablishment as the only medicine for the Church's ills. Arnold wanted to see the establishment of the Church of England secured. However, he was at that stage convinced, as many others were, that 'no human power' could save the Establishment as it then was. His remedy was to broaden the Church's basis in the national life. There should be more (but poorer) bishops, each surrounded by an advisory council and a diocesan conference. Parishioners should have a say in the appointment of rectors or vicars, and working-class men should be ordained as deacons. The doctrinal comprehensiveness of the Church, already large, should be widened so as to include all Christians in England except the Roman Catholics and the Quakers. Perhaps the creeds might be revised. Presumably the sweeping legislation needed could come only from Parliament. Such proposals alarmed the Lord Bishops in their palaces, the incumbents in their freeholds, all the clergy who valued their middle-class self-satisfaction, all who feared Parliament, and all who despised Dissent as being socially inferior as well as religiously erroneous. Even the Dissenters were not flattered; they were to be extinguished by comprehension. It was now clear that Arnold could not be made a bishop, despite the shortage of clergymen acceptable to the Whig government. 'What have Tory churchmen ever done for me,' asked the Prime Minister, 'that I should make them a present of such a handle against my government?'[4]

Arnold was not even allowed to preach at another's consecration to the episcopate. When Edward Stanley—a liberal, but a Whig aristocrat to his fingertips—was nominated as Bishop of Norwich, and invited his friend Arnold to be preacher, the Archbishop of Canterbury vetoed the idea on the ground that it would anger the clergy. The only post which the Liberals could safely produce for their champion was a non-theological professorship. Accordingly he was appointed Regius Professor of Modern History at Oxford in 1841. He had confessed to being 'one of the most ambitious men alive', but had tried to

---

[4] Lord Melbourne's attitude to the Church was epitomized by the monologue which he addressed from his bed to a scholar to whom he had just offered the Bishopric of St. David's, in 1840. 'Very glad to see you; sit down, sit down, hope you are come to say you accept. I only wish you to understand that I don't intend if I know it to make a heterodox bishop. I don't like heterodox bishops. As men they may be very good anywhere else, but I don't think they have any business on the bench. I take a great interest in theological questions [pointing to a pile of folio editions of the Fathers]. They are excellent reading, and very amusing; some time or other we must have a talk about them.' *Letters Literary and Theological of Connop Thirlwall*, ed. J. J. S. Perowne and L. Stokes (Bentley, 1881), pp. 160–1.

take his disappointment in the Church as a chastisement from God; and he was delighted at this new and more scholarly opening for his energies. When, as he planned, he resigned from Rugby in 1844, he would sit in his study at Fox How and write history, visiting Oxford in order to lecture. Meanwhile he gave away his Oxford salary while he received his Rugby income and his first lecture in the university was a triumph. Although only a handful of undergraduates regularly studied modern history, his admirers claimed that this was the largest audience which Oxford had provided for any lecture since the close of the Middle Ages.

It is, indeed, possible that had he lived Thomas Arnold would have become a considerable historian. It is true that he wrote little about the time between the fall of Rome and the nineteenth century, although he did announce plans to cover the modern world in future lectures. But his imagination had been seized by history, and his view of the contemporary drama had been coloured by the great narratives of the social crises of the ancient world. They appealed to the preacher in him. In an essay on 'The Social Progress of States' appended to the first volume of his edition of Thucydides, he compared states with the childhood, youth, manhood, and decay of individuals; and, viewing his own age as an age of decay, he believed that Providence had acted in history like a schoolmaster. But he also loved history for its own sake. He had learned German in 1824 in order to read Niebuhr's work and thus benefit his own *History of Rome*; and he sympathized strongly with Niebuhr's interest in institutions as well as heroes. When he published the first volume of this *History*, in 1838, he announced his hope to carry it on to the coronation of Charlemagne, although his last words, written a month before his death, were about Hannibal. His *Thucydides* in three volumes (1830-5) was one of the real beginnings of English study of Greek history, despite signs of haste inevitable in the work of a busy schoolmaster. His Sixth Form at Rugby was deeply impressed by his teaching of history, and it is possible that, given time, he might have matured sufficiently to be taken seriously by adults, ordering the past if he could not order the 1850s and 1860s.[5]

It is also possible that he would have lived down the unpopularity of the 1830s, and would have been taken from his literary labours to pour his zeal into the work of a bishop. John Keble was going to spend some of the summer holidays of 1842 at Fox How for a reconciliation. But Thomas Arnold did not live. Almost on the eve of his forty-seventh birthday, on a Sunday morning in June 1842, he died after an attack of *angina pectoris*, from which his father had also died. He took the pain as from God, quoting the text: 'But if ye be without chastisement,

---

[5] Duncan Forbes, *The Liberal Anglican Idea of History* (Cambridge University Press, 1952), studied Thomas Arnold, Arthur Stanley, and H. H. Milman.

whereof all are partakers, then are ye bastards and not sons.' He was buried in front of the altar of Rugby Chapel.

3

His family and his pupils were stunned. When Matthew Arnold saw the dead body, the thought crossed his mind that the head had been the family's one source of information. When Rugbeians at Oxford and elsewhere heard that the Doctor was dead, an important part of their world died; and for some, nothing ever took its place. But the nation took little notice until two years later one who had been (even more than Clough) favourite among all the Rugby boys, Arthur Stanley the Bishop of Norwich's son, published *The Life and Correspondence of Thomas Arnold, D.D.* Through that book, and through the Tom Brown novels (there was a sequel, *Tom Brown at Oxford*, in 1861), the life of this frustrated and pessimistic schoolmaster, a life ended prematurely, was prolonged to form one of the major influences in the making of Victorian England.

Few biographies, if any, have been so well adjusted to their purpose as was Stanley's. The letters were printed with a minimum of editorial comment, which added to the impression that the plain truth was being told: on the surface there was scarcely a touch of emotion. But with his editorial skill, and some vivid words of his own, the young Arthur Stanley proved himself a first-class publicist. Arnold's words were selected in order to adorn a theme. References to embarrassing matters were left unexplained. Local, political, and religious storms were played down. Enough opposition was mentioned rather vaguely, and only enough, to enable Stanley to present his headmaster as a crusader. The only long chapter in his own words was a eulogy of the Rugby system. The whole book was dominated by the courage and piety of the deathbed, which was described minutely. The man who had been known nationally as a controversialist, and locally as a boy-flogger and fee-raiser, was transfigured, as he had been when the candles shone on him in the pulpit. Rugby School now felt that it was the centre of the moral universe, and parents became anxious to include their boys in the saga. Masters and Sixth Formers in other schools studied the book and resolved to make their schools more like Arnold's—or at least Stanley's—Rugby. The teaching profession found itself heroic.

Of course historians have added their notes to the legend. Some religion, as well as Latin and Greek, must have been communicated by some of the many thousands of clergymen who taught English schoolboys before 1828. Thomas Arnold's own predecessor at Rugby, John Wooll, is one of those who do not deserve total oblivion. He had built the chapel where Arnold preached; Arnold added only stained glass and burial vaults. Wooll had in fact transformed the appearance of the school, to house numbers which grew under his early rule and diminished only with his own decline. As headmasters, both Wooll and Arnold rose with the rising market of the new classes given money by the industrial revolution, wanting their sons to be made gentlemen alongside Squire Brown's son, and prepared to see them Christians too because that was better than the French Revolution. Some of Arnold's distinctive characteristics were handicaps in appealing to this market, which did not like the overflow of his exuberance into radical talk about Church and State. Certainly the popular image of the Doctor as spread by Arthur Stanley and Thomas Hughes had to suppress some aspects of the complicated reality of the living Thomas Arnold.

Historians also stress how the impact of the legend of the Doctor was not complete. Many schoolmasters resented the Rugby ideas; many parents thought them not practical enough for a commercial life; many boys carried on as before. Even at Rugby, vast tracts of boy-life remained impervious; *Tom Brown's School-days*, although it ended in tears over Arnold's grave, indicated as much, and went far to justify Arnold's sermons against public school vice. And, despite the Doctor of Divinity in the centre of its background, it was from first to last an anti-intellectual book. When Stanley read it, he commented: 'It is an absolute revelation to me: opens up a world of which, though so near to me, I was utterly ignorant.'

Yet the legend was powerful. It probably owed its initial impact to one and a half pages contributed to Stanley's *Life* by George Moberly, then Headmaster of Winchester. Moberly had taught Stanley and other Rugbeians at Oxford, and had been impressed by the school's elevating influence on them. He knew, as he confessed, 'but little' of Arnold. He was a generous, rather sentimental, man who was writing to console the mourners. He referred to the deep 'delinquencies' of the old days at Winchester and to an Oxford where 'a religious undergraduate was very rare, very much laughed at when he appeared'. He added that 'a most singular and striking change has come upon our public schools', and he attributed this mainly to Arnold's influence on Rugbeians who became 'thoughtful, manly-minded, conscious of duty and obligation'.

It was an oversimplified picture. How had a handful of Rugbeians been able to change the scene within a few years from darkness to light? Even as headmasters—and a remarkable number of pupils and colleagues did become headmasters—the Doctor's disciples could not have effected the transformation by moral force alone.[6] Yet the picture

[6] For the facts, see T. W. Bamford, *The Rise of the Public Schools* (Nelson, 1967).

was painted by the most acceptable kind of artist. Moberly was at the head of a famous school. He was also a High Churchman, the intimate friend and spiritual director of John Keble himself; his name carried weight in circles where Tom Arnold had been a figure of fun. The fact that Moberly was prepared to accept the Doctor impressed many who were looking for a hero; and there was enough truth in his tribute to make Arnold of Rugby a major influence in actually changing the schools after his death and the appearance of the books by Stanley and Hughes. His death was essential to his legend—how could a Professor Stanley have written so movingly about a Professor Arnold who had given up schoolmastering as soon as he had made enough money? And his legend made him a maker of history; for 'without Rugby it may be doubted whether the public schools would have survived'.[7]

This history, made within the very small world of the public schools, also spread into the national life. The essence of Thomas Arnold's theories about Church and State was that England should be made more like Rugby School. It should be changed by moral preaching and example. One defect of this approach was that the preacher never stopped to argue details, but such an approach had the merit of being usable by men who believed that the original preacher had got some of the details wrong. The aim was clear. It was to make the holders of power more conscious of their duties. Arnold felt that he had to some extent succeeded in this aim with the boys of the Sixth, and wrote his pamphlets in the hope of persuading adults such as their parents to behave themselves. There was no need to be ashamed of possessing privilege, or to be hesitant in expecting respect and conformity. But the power was to be exercised within a community, and for its benefit, under the eye of God.

Thomas Arnold's schemes to make Church and State more communal, in a sacred order, were a mixture of the shrewd and the crazy. As his friends begged him to remember, his personal experience was limited to schools and Oxford. For all his sympathy with it, the industrial revolution was what lay between School House and Fox How. (When he was offered a post in Manchester, he said that he could not afford to accept it.) This lack of realism about the social structure of the nation blinded him to the sociological necessity of Dissent, and of working-class movements. He did not see that society had changed so that there were now millions of Englishmen who did not want to be comprehended in an enlarged National Church, because they did not want leadership from Thomas Arnold and his like. However, to be fair we must add that before the 1851 religious census few English-

---

[7] G. Kitson Clark, *The Making of Victorian England* (Methuen, 1962), p. 268. For George Moberly, whom Gladstone made Bishop of Salisbury in 1869, see C. A. E. Moberly, *Dulce Domum* (Murray, 1913).

men realized quite how popular Dissent was. We must also add that history showed abundantly that the basic principles of Rugby could be asserted by men eager to be involved more deeply than the Doctor in the day-to-day work of Church and State: men such as the author of *Tom Brown's School-days*, and subtler men.[8]

One historian of the Victorian Church has, indeed, picked on this as the central thread. 'This was the great accomplishment of the Church in Victorian England. Through the writing, teaching, and preaching of its creative minority, it gave to the powerful new middle classes an ethic of "service", based upon Christian principles.'[9] Thomas Arnold helped to falsify the prediction of Marx and Engels that the English middle classes would act more and more selfishly, and bring Church and State down in their ruin. For he did as much as any man to teach that stern sense of duty which was regarded as sacred even by Victorian agnostics such as George Eliot, Leslie Stephen—and Matthew Arnold.[10]

Gradually the moral development of a more democratic, and far more heavily populated, England was seen to involve the necessity of primary schooling for all. Secondary education, and even the universities, had also to be expanded. Who was to be responsible? Almost into the last quarter of the nineteenth century, many Englishmen still assumed that the Established Church must be the nation's schoolmaster, and others added that Nonconformity must educate its own. When the twentieth century began, there were still more English children in church than in state schools. The principle that Roman Catholic children should be taught in Roman Catholic schools was still scarcely questioned in the middle of the twentieth century. But the growth of the population in the nineteenth century, and the practical demands of commerce and industry, defeated the ambitions of churchmen. Heroic sums of money were raised for church schools, the most dramatic example being the work of Nathaniel Woodard in providing a chain of schools for the middle classes, with the great chapel at Lancing on the Sussex coast as the spiritual centre.[11] Woodard

[8] Thomas Hughes was equally unconvincing as an M.P., as a judge and as the founder of Rugby, an idealistic colony in Tennessee. But he practised the social creed which he glamourized in the novel: a patriotic, paternalistic creed of fighting for justice to the grateful workers. He came to rely for his theology on F. D. Maurice, and taught boxing at the Working Men's College under him. A biography has been written by E. C. Mack and W. H. G. Armytage (Benn, 1952).
[9] Desmond Bowen, *The Idea of the Victorian Church* (McGill University Press, 1968), p. 258.
[10] The best biographies are G. S. Haight, *George Eliot* (Clarendon Press, 1968), and Noel Annan, *Leslie Stephen* (MacGibbon & Kee, 1951).
[11] For the Woodard schools, see Brian Heeney, *Mission to the Middle Classes* (SPCK, 1969).

argued that, given enough money, clergymen with devout assistants could educate all the middle classes. However, despite his genius for fund-raising, his hope was wild. Replying to Woodard in *A French Eton* (1864), Matthew Arnold gradually presented an eloquent, unanswerable, and influential case for massive intervention by the State; and he was strengthened in this case by some rather vague words written by Arnold of Rugby as he looked towards the nation's educational future.

Thomas Arnold also bequeathed a more direct legacy to the nation's schools. His fatal heart-attack seems to have been hastened by the emotions which arose in School House when his favourite daughter, Jane, the 'dearest K' of Matthew Arnold's letters, was jilted by one of the Rugby masters within three weeks of the wedding; the young man went on to become Bishop Cotton of Calcutta. Jane was heartbroken by this insult, followed so soon by her beloved father's death, and Matthew Arnold's 'Resignation' records the sombre emotions with which she and her brother now retraced the old walks from Fox How. But Jane survived, and she married a Liberal politician, William Forster. She remained very much an Arnold: indeed, her distinguished family took the name of Arnold-Forster. And the instrument by which the English State assumed its responsibility for the schooling of the people was Forster's Education Act of 1870.

What of the Church? Thomas Arnold's *Principles of Church Reform* had for the most part not been translated into effective reforms by 1970. The idea that deacons and other clergy could in large numbers continue to earn their livings by secular occupations, and thus remain close to the people, was as slow to appeal as the idea that Dissenters could hold their services in the parish church on a Sunday afternoon, and thus return to the National Church. Although a greater participation by the laity at every level of church government had gradually led to the creation of councils and conferences, a National Assembly and a General Synod, the Church of England in 1970 still retained many traces of the older theory that power descended from on high through the Crown and the patron, or perhaps through the bishop and the priest. Bishop E. R. Wickham, the pioneer in industrial mission in twentieth-century Sheffield, could say: 'Thomas Arnold out-thought the Church of his day by generations, and not yet have we matched his teaching.'[12]

Yet the fact remains that during the middle years of the nineteenth century, the Church of England *was* changed. Thomas Arnold's death

[12] Quoted by M. J. Jackson and John Rogan at the end of their Introduction to a new edition of Thomas Arnold, *Principles of Church Reform* (SPCK, 1960). E. R. Wickham, *Church and People in an Industrial City* (Lutterworth Press, 1952), analysed the Church's pastoral problems in nineteenth-century Sheffield.

was followed by an outburst of energy which saved the Establishment by putting it to work. Parsons like Arthur's father in *Tom Brown's School-days* did battle in the industrial towns.[13] When Bishop Selwyn returned from New Zealand to preach at Cambridge in 1854, he declared: 'a great and visible change has taken place in the thirteen years since I left England. It is now a very rare thing to see a careless clergyman, a neglected parish or a desecrated church.' Much of the credit was due to the Tory reformer, Sir Robert Peel, whose determination to start and staff new parishes for the new population was practical and effective, largely at the expense of the rich and idle clergy in the cathedrals. Peel saved the Church of England in one sense.

In another sense, Thomas Arnold saved it. In the 1830s he had to use the argument that 'the sight of a church tower . . . is an assurance that everything has not been bought up for private convenience or enjoyment'. Arnold had to confess that a closer inspection of this building was not so encouraging. 'The very church itself, closed during the greater part of the day, perhaps of the week, is opened only for the performance of the uniform service, never to be added to, never to be varied'—and never to be *shared*, for 'the people are, as members of the Church, wholly passive'. Accordingly he could preach about Whitsunday, the Festival of the Spirit in the Church, as 'the birthday of a dead friend'. But the ecclesiastical history of the Victorian age is the story of a resurrection.

Obviously Thomas Arnold's part in this revival of the Church was as limited as was his direct influence on education, but this book will show the infection of his example. When Conybeare came to describe the ecclesiastical parties in 1853, he found that although the Broad Churchmen were not well organized,

the Broad Church are, to the middle of the nineteenth century, what the Low Church were to its beginning—the originators of ecclesiastical reform, and the pioneers of moral progress. Regarded as a whole, the comprehensive party in the Church cannot be accused of coldness or want of energy. Arnold was no indifferentist, and his followers have been no Epicureans.

Many of the facts bear out that judgement. Here only the Church of England's top post can be mentioned. C. T. Longley died in 1868; he had been Headmaster of Harrow and then the first Bishop of Ripon, a man admired by Arnold and aware of industrial realities, but without drive in his latter years. The next three Archbishops of Canterbury

---

[13] The greatest example in real life was Walter Hook, the bookworm of Winchester and Oxford who became the heroic Vicar of Leeds, 1837–59. See C. J. Stranks, *Dean Hook* (SPCK, 1954).

had been on the Rugby staff and were full of the Rugby gospel. The Archbishop who came immediately after them was the beloved disciple of Arnold's successor at Rugby. The greatest of this line at Canterbury was a Rugbeian who in his youth boasted that he was a disciple of Thomas Arnold.[14]

4

Matthew Arnold was pleased when bishops spoke to him in the Athenaeum Club, and although he was known to shirk churchgoing the biblical or ecclesiastical images or quotations to be found everywhere in his poetry and prose show the religious atmosphere in which he lived and thought habitually. His wife used to dismiss talk about his heresies by saying that he was at bottom a good Christian. His inclusion in a small portrait gallery of leaders of the modern Church of England would, no doubt, have surprised him no less than his father. 'Institutions are to be judged by their great men; in the end, they take their line from their great men,' he wrote. 'The Christian Church, and the line which is natural to it and which will one day prevail in it, is to be judged from the saints and the tone of the saints.'[15] He was not of that company. But a layman may articulate the feelings of many of his fellow-laymen in the religious community, and may more widely influence the attitudes of his fellow-countrymen. The distinction of Matthew Arnold as a writer entitles us to include him in this book as a layman through whom we may get in touch with levels of religion liable not to be noticed if we fix our attention entirely on ecclesiastics (or an ecclesiastic *manqué* such as Thomas Arnold) and theologians. The churches of Victorian England were revived, but a study of Matthew Arnold is the best way possible of entering into the subtler question of what was really happening in the Englishman's view of God.

The legacy of Arnold of Rugby helped to kill his eldest son as a poet. 'Sohrab and Rustum' put Matthew Arnold's personal story into a poem which, when completed in 1853, was reported to his mother as 'I think by far the best thing I have yet done. . . . I have had the greatest pleasure in composing it—a rare thing with me. . . .' The style was influenced by Homer and Virgil; the material was gathered from fragments of the geography and legends of Persia; but the passion and dignity welled up from the poet's experience, for it was the story of a father who unintentionally killed his son.

Sohrab, the son, had been brought up far from Rustum, so that he must say

14 William Temple: see below, p. 301.
15 *Last Essays on Church and Religion* (Smith, Elder, 1877), p. 119.

'I seek one man, one man, and one alone—
Rustum, my father; who I hoped should greet,
Should one day greet, upon some well-fought field,
His not unworthy, not inglorious son.'

And Matthew Arnold is known to have been shocked by the early
death of his father, particularly since it came before he had achieved
a real understanding with him. His letters contain a number of confessions of his desire to vindicate himself after his father's distrust.
This desire was all the stronger because he retained a great love for
his mother, who survived until 1873.

When Rustum does meet Sohrab in single combat, neither recognizing the other, they talk of the possibility of reaching an understanding. Although the main purpose of this talk in the poem may be
to maintain the dramatic suspense, there is at least one reference,
when death has been inflicted, to the distant happiness which father
and son had shared.

The castle, and the dewy woods, and hunt
And hound, and morn on those delightful hills . . .

And Matthew Arnold never forgot how with their father 'the Dogs'
had walked the fells. For all his sensitivity to his father's insensitivity,
for all the impatience which he would sometimes betray when people
quoted the Doctor's verdicts, for all the dislike (dare we say it?) which
he largely suppressed, he was never finally alienated from his father,
or willing to condemn him. In the poem Sohrab spares Rustum when
he might have killed him, and he drops his shield fatally when at last
Rustum announces who he is.

What finally angers Rustum, and drives him into the duel, is an
effeminate appeal for peace from Sohrab. Rustum thunders:

'Girl! nimble with thy feet, not with thy hands!
Curl'd minion, dancer, coiner of sweet words!'

But when Sohrab has received the mortal blow, his dying eloquence
makes his father weep. Did Matthew Arnold as a boy dream of con-
verting the angry father by his poetic sweetness and light? We may
guess so; yet we know that as a man, he was himself slowly converted
back to what his father had taught. In a poem where glimpses of the
story of a heart mingle with sonorous lines of 'orientalizing', Sohrab
finally dies because he chooses to draw his father's spear out of his
side. For Matthew Arnold's were poems of a growing resignation: first
a resignation to the loss of belief in the precise gospel preached by his
father, and then a resignation to a destiny to preach a revised version
of this gospel. When the poet finally acknowledged that he was a

prophet's son, and accepted his destiny as being the work of education in his father's steps, the poetry more or less ceased. As his family had seen with surprise when they had opened his first book, *The Strayed Reveller* (1849), Matt's had been a poetry of pain.

For a time the pain would be eased by nature, and his collection of poems in 1852 included very lovely examples of how the sight of the moon over a city street, or of the grass in a London park, would calm his heart.[16] But his 'Calais Sands', a poem of waiting in agitation for 'my darling', was significantly different from Wordsworth's evening walk on those same sands, in the quietness half-hearing the pagan gods of nature. Nature did not have consolations enough for Matthew Arnold—whom Quiller-Couch aptly called Wordsworth's widow—but then, pantheism did not have enough religious value to be the permanent satisfaction of Wordsworth himself.[17]

For a time Matthew Arnold seemed about to find a new strength in his emotional life from the love of women. While on a Swiss holiday in 1848 he was conquered at the Hôtel Bellevue, Thun, by 'the blue eyes of one of its inmates', as he told Clough. The infatuation lasted barely a year, and, seeing 'Marguerite' as impossible in the role of Thomas Arnold's daughter-in-law, the poet gradually declined into speculations about how many lovers she had already enjoyed, and whether she had become a prostitute. But his poems testify to the intensity of what seems to have been his first serious love-affair. On the rebound from Marguerite, and after the further shock of his sister Jane's marriage in 1850, he fell in love with a judge's daughter, Frances Lucy Wightman, 'Flu', whom he married in 1851. It was almost certainly to her that he wrote:

> Ah, love, let us be true
> To one another! for the world, which seems
> To lie before us like a land of dreams,
> So various, so beautiful, so new,
> Hath really neither joy, nor love, nor light,
> Nor certitude, nor peace, nor help for pain . . .

But help for the heart's pain in the love of women did not lead Matthew Arnold to write poetry with the theme of Robert Browning or Coventry Patmore, successful as his marriage with his 'Flu' was. The lines just quoted may have been composed before 'Dover Beach', and added to it although they contain no reference to the sea; but al-

---

[16] 'A Summer Night' and 'Lines Written in Kensington Gardens'.

[17] The best biography of William Wordsworth is by Mary Moorman, in two volumes (Oxford University Press, 1957–64). On religion and the romantic movement, see Thomas McFarland, *Coleridge and the Pantheist Tradition* (Clarendon Press, 1969).

ready in them the religious scene, however forlorn, was getting more attention than nature or love. The heart's ultimate questions were too insistent. Where was the 'bright and tranquil' sea glimpsed at the end of 'Sohrab and Rustum'? How was the individual to enter its peace? Or was it really 'the unplumb'd salt, estranging sea' of one of his poems to Marguerite?

> Dotting the shoreless watery wild,
> We mortal millions live *alone*.

It was probably from the description of the attack on Epipolae by moonlight in Thucydides (translated by Thomas Arnold) that Matthew Arnold drew the conclusion to 'Dover Beach':

> And we are here as on a darkling plain
> Swept with confused alarm of struggle and flight,
> Where ignorant armies clash by night.

And the religious confusion implied in those lines was what enabled them to be linked with the great image of 'Dover Beach':

> The Sea of Faith
> Was once, too, at the full, and round earth's shore
> Lay like the folds of a bright girdle furl'd.
> But now I only hear
> Its melancholy, long, withdrawing roar,
> Retreating, to the breath
> Of the night-wind, down the vast edges drear
> And naked shingles of the world.

No countryside and no lover could permanently calm grief of the depth described in 'To a Gipsy Child by the Sea-Shore'. No mortal man could possess the ultimate meaning attributed to 'the Tree' in 'Thyrsis'. The sense of 'the burthen of the mystery' was too great for his heart to rest without a religion. He had felt with a cruel intensity:

> Resolve to be thyself; and know that he,
> Who finds himself, loses his misery!

This self-conscious, self-torturing young man had then answered his own anxiety:

> Live by thy light, and earth will live by hers!

And he had rebuked Clough for being too worried about the riddle of the universe. But who *was* he? What *was* his light?

For a time he was impressed by Hindu mysticism, but in the end Matthew Arnold's light had to be a moral tradition going back to Christ, and all his questions could be concentrated on the nineteenth-century question: was the Saviour dead?

> 'While we believed, on earth he went,
> And open stood his grave.
> Men call'd from chamber, church, and tent,
> And Christ was by to save.

> 'Now he is dead! Far hence he lies
> In the lorn Syrian town;
> And on his grave, with shining eyes,
> The Syrian stars look down.'

Was that verdict in 'Obermann Once More' final? One of the dramatic poems, 'Empedocles on Etna', was about a despairing philosopher's suicide, and the spiritual misery of some of the other poems do suggest that Matthew Arnold (like John Stuart Mill or Thomas Carlyle) may have contemplated suicide as an end to the enigma of existence, when very near to the complete breakdown of his inner life. But if he needed a religion, the religion could not be conventional. In his pencilled notes for poems to be composed during 1849, he jotted down: 'Empedocles—refusal of limitation by the religious sentiment'. And the religious sentiment in its traditional form was never strong enough to heal Matthew Arnold's hurt. He had enjoyed the style of Newman's sermons while an undergraduate, and later he went out of his way to pay compliments to him, but the alleged discovery of the living God in the living Church always struck him as revived medievalism, and so as 'impossible' for free, modern minds. 'For God's sake, believe it then!' was the most he could say (in his poem 'Pis-Aller') to those who, like Newman, declared that life could not be lived without belief in a supernatural grace. For him the romance of the Grande Chartreuse was a retreat from reality:

> Here leave us to die out with these
> Last of the people who believe!

But one of the companions of Empedocles, Pausanias, leaves him on the mountain before the philosopher's leap into the volcano. Pausanias returns to work in the cities of the plain; and the only solution of his own dilemma that Matthew Arnold achieved was to identify the living Jesus with the 'sweet reasonableness' of a sober gospel of daily righteousness. It was not a strongly traditional, doctrinal, articulate sentiment of Newman's kind; but it seemed enough, for thus Matthew Arnold returned to the Christ at the centre of his father's religion.

In a poem first published in 1867 under the title 'Anti-Desperation',
he answered the question which had paralysed Clough:

> 'Sits there no judge in Heaven, our sin to see?—
>
> *'More strictly, then, the inward judge obey!*
> Was Christ a man like us? *Ah! let us try*
> *If we then, too, can be such men as he!'*

Another short poem of 1867, 'East London', was about the Reverend
William Tyler, a Congregational minister. Tyler had moved Arnold
by being, while

> the fierce sun overhead
> Smote on the squalid streets of Bethnal Green . . .
> 'Much cheer'd with thoughts of Christ, *the living bread.'*

This was the spear of Rustum, *alias* Thomas Arnold.

In 'Obermann Once More', which seems to have been written in
1865–6, a revelation comes to replace the vanished certainty of the old
religion. The agitation which had set up in Matthew Arnold's loyalties
when he had first read in Oxford de Senancour's seductive novel of
ennui in 1804, *Obermann*, was now at least more or less resolved in mid-
Victorian energy.

> *'Unduped of fancy, henceforth man*
> *Must labour!—must resign*
> *His all too human creeds, and scan*
> *Simply the way divine!'*

But 'the morning' does not 'break' until the poet has accepted the commission to preach this gospel of the simple way:

> 'Though late, though dimm'd, though weak, yet tell
> Hope to a world new-made!'

And having glimpsed the glory of the sun

> Across the glimmering lake,

the poet does turn to encourage others along the way. As he remembered in 'Rugby Chapel':

> But thou would'st not *alone*
> Be saved, my father! *alone*
> Conquer and come to thy goal,
> Leaving the rest in the wild.

5

But was Matthew Arnold a Christian? His prose usually leaves a first impression of sunshine, happiness, clarity, assurance—of 'sweetness and light' in the one phrase of his (borrowed from Dean Swift) which all the reading public regarded as typical. His books are much more tranquil than his father's sermons, or his own poems; they seem like the books of a man who has found peace, because they charm like the glimmering lake. He winks while preaching. Even the rebukes seem to come from a weary teacher who will not disturb himself enough to flog us. This mood was, indeed, what the ex-poet wanted. He wanted to be a sage; more authoritative because calmer, less easy to ridicule or hurt, than Arnold of Rugby. When a sister complained that he was becoming as dogmatic as Ruskin, he pointed out in high good humour that Ruskin was dogmatically *wrong*. A more serious reply would have been that Ruskin was, in comparison, dogmatically graceless. When the remark went round that he was a Jeremiah in kid gloves, he only commented that Jeremiah was the Old Testament prophet whose style he admired least.[18]

This appearance of a tranquil authority succeeded because the reading public was then ripe for it, and because some readers ever since have treated this prose as one of the strengths of a great age. Of course, the religious books have not been so popular as the literary criticism. Some friends doubted whether 'Flu' Arnold had ever read them, and he himself complained in 1881 that 'whoever treats religion, religious discussions, questions of churches and sects, as absorbing, is not in vital sympathy with the movement of men's minds at present'. However, Arnold set a new standard in the assessment of literature, a new standard of knowledge, discernment, and elegance, with the result that some of his *Essays in Criticism* were being studied in English schools a century after their writing. The religious books of such an eminent critic were given special sympathy, and the irony was that the prestige of the prose stimulated the sales of the poetry at a time when the poet could only edit, revise, and add inferior pieces.

His was a time which knew that it needed guides, because it knew that a new day was dawning; and its major guides left room for Matthew Arnold. Tennyson and Browning, far greater and more popular as poets, had no comparable achievement in prose. Carlyle and Ruskin, far louder prophets in prose, were known outside the ranks of their disciples to be on the brink of insanity. Although Newman fascinated, his theology was not taken very seriously. Although George

[18] John Holloway has a good chapter on Matthew Arnold's tone in his *The Victorian Sage* (Macmillan, 1953).

Eliot, the preacher of unbelief, was a grave and penetrating moralist, she was, no less than Newman, in conflict with the Victorian Establishment. Behind such mid-Victorian sages stood the figure of another pontifical poet-theologian, Samuel Taylor Coleridge, but Coleridge's addiction to opium had been one of the reasons why his work was fragmentary, and among many Victorians his character inspired (the word was Matthew Arnold's) 'repugnance'.[19]

Matthew Arnold with his many compromises may be viewed as the secular Newman, as the churchgoer's George Eliot, or as the respectable man's Coleridge. But his was, after all, a great moral achievement, and that mattered to a generation which shared his own view of conduct as 'three-fourths of life'. Shaken as much as anyone by the spiritual problems resulting from the collapse of the old Christian framework, he had not allowed himself to be either paralysed or attracted into an escape which would have meant the suppression of his intelligence. That moral victory in his 'buried life' runs through his poems, while the more obvious respectability of his working and domestic life was implied by his prose. His workaday morality was published to the edification of many when some of his letters to his mother, sisters, and wife were edited after his death with an admiring memoir by Mr. Gladstone's friend, G. W. E. Russell. (This Christian statesman, who specialized in graceful studies of eminent churchmen, loftily remarked in his Prefatory Note about Matthew Arnold that 'his theology, once the subject of some just criticism, seems now a matter of comparatively little moment'.) Matt was a model of loyalty as a son, brother, husband, father, and friend; and of industry as one of Her Majesty's Inspectors of Schools for thirty-one years from 1851.

People often complained that he gave himself superior airs. They ought to have considered what arrogance an Arnold could show—as when Matthew's brother Thomas, a man of painful integrity, criticized the social work of Thomas Hughes as 'too democratic, too content with commonplace strivings after comfort and recreation'.[20] As it was,

---

[19] See C. R. Sanders, *Coleridge and the Broad Church Movement* (Duke University Press, 1942); J. D. Boulger, *Coleridge as Religious Thinker* (Yale University Press, 1961); J. R. Barth, S. J., *Coleridge and Christian Doctrine* (Harvard University Press, 1969). There is, however, no evidence that Matthew Arnold made any close study of Coleridge's prose. See Leon Gottfried, *Matthew Arnold and the Romantics* (Routledge & Kegan Paul, 1963).

[20] Thomas Arnold, *Passages in a Wandering Life* (Edward Arnold, 1900), p. 34. 'To provide more pleasure for those in narrow circumstances, by sending them on cheap trips, assembling them at soirées, concerts, exhibitions, flower-shows, long vacation lectures, and so on, is indeed most praiseworthy in the providers, but is not the way to change and uplift the souls of the provided,' he explained. But his own 'wandering life' showed the Arnoldian courage. He went out to build a school system in Tasmania, and was converted to Roman Catholicism. He returned home to poverty, although Newman used him as a professor

Matthew Arnold, when already one of the most distinguished literary figures of the day, toiled at the constant travel and petty detail of school-inspection. For his first twelve years he was almost entirely restricted to inspecting Nonconformist primary schools, and later, when allowed to visit a wider variety, he was compelled to preside over mechanical tests of reading, writing, and arithmetic. The wonder was that he did it so competently, with so few complaints; and the result was that he could appeal to the public as one of them. A family man, he could make wry jokes about going to work on suburban trains. It was a miracle of self-discipline, because many hours of boredom must have inspired his dictum that 'to the middle class, the grand aim of education should be to give largeness of soul and personal dignity'— and his sly question whether Shakespeare or Virgil would have enjoyed crossing the Atlantic in the company of the Pilgrim Fathers.

This miracle appealed to the clergy; for his involvement in their work of social uplift, together with his literary prestige, made Matthew Arnold less unpopular with parish priests than his father had been. The clergy who invited him to address them in Sion College in London could applaud his admiration of three-fourths of their work, because it was the patently sincere tribute of a lay fellow-worker.

A man who has published a good deal which is at variance with the body of theological doctrine commonly received in the Church of England cannot well, it may be thought, stand up before the clergy as a friend to their cause and to that of the Church. . . . Perhaps that opinion is shared by some who now hear me. I make bold to say that it is totally erroneous. . . . I regard the Church of England as, in fact, a great national society for the promotion of what is commonly called *goodness*, and for promoting it through the most effectual means possible, the only means which are really and truly effectual for the object: through the means of the Christian religion and the Bible. This plain practical object is undeniably the object of the Church of England and of the clergy.[21]

Another virtue which communicated itself to the Victorians was his courage in maintaining his intellectual activities. He said in his Preface to *Literature and Dogma* that

the plea that this or that man has no time for culture, will vanish as soon as we desire culture so much that we begin to examine our present use of time . . . Give to any man all the time that he now wastes, not only on his

---

in Dublin and as a schoolmaster in Birmingham. He then lost his Roman Catholic faith, scraped a living as a private tutor in Oxford, and was reconciled to Rome before the end. His daughter, Mrs. Humphry Ward, was the author of popular novels about the ebb and flow of religious faith.

[21] *Last Essays on Church and Religion*, p. 110.

vices (when he has these), but on useless business, wearisome or deteriorating amusement, trivial letter-writing, random reading, and he will have plenty of time for culture.

And he practised what he preached. He not only read; he made notes, and meditated on them until they became parts of his own mind. It was the reason why his books contained so may texts, biblical or secular, although these might hold less meaning for his readers.[22] The Inspector of Schools also lectured on Homer, or Celtic literature, or 'the grand style' in general, as Professor of Poetry at Oxford; and the prophet of a new religious understanding edited Isaiah for schools. One fruit of his application to his duties and books was his zeal in reconsidering educational policy. When he began inspecting he seems to have regarded it merely as a rather better-paid job than being Private Secretary to Lord Lansdowne; he wanted to marry. In 1856 he confessed to his brother Willy that he was always tempted to say to people when asked about education: 'My good friends, this is a matter for which my father certainly had a *specialité*, but for which I have none whatever.'[23] But unlike Clough, who also drew an income at the Education Office, he came to regard it as something more than a subsidy to a poet. He gave his mind to education.[24]

Having seen so much, read so much, and thought so much, and having transformed the distress of his soul into the eloquence of a moralist, Matthew Arnold was able to make his own brand of dogmatism almost convincing. When he defined culture as 'the acquainting ourselves with the best that has been known and said in the world', and when he said that those who had put themselves under this discipline would show it by being 'disinterested', 'calm', and 'mild', he was able to illustrate his precepts from his own behaviour. When he extolled the culture of France or Germany, his own intellectual habits were those of a European.[25] When he admired the standards which had been set through the influence of the French Academy and its

[22] His *Note-books* were edited by H. F. Lowry, K. Young, and W. H. Dunn (Clarendon Press, 1952). His reactions to the Greek and Latin authors with whom he lived habitually have been studied by Warren D. Anderson, *Matthew Arnold and the Classical Tradition* (University of Michigan Press, 1965).

[23] *Unpublished Letters of Matthew Arnold*, ed. A. Whitridge (Yale University Press, 1923), p. 31.

[24] W. F. Connell has studied *The Educational Thought and Influence of Matthew Arnold* (Routledge & Kegan Paul, 1950), and a selection of documents illustrating *Matthew Arnold and the Education of the New Order* has been edited by S. Smith and G. Summerfield (Cambridge University Press, 1969).

[25] See Iris Sells, *Matthew Arnold and France* (Cambridge University Press, 1935). But after his youthful intoxication with Goethe and Schiller, he was equally enthusiastic about the German literary tradition.

equivalents on the Continent, he seemed to be constituting himself as a one-man academy, to be inviting the British public to see things as they really were. When he denounced the barbarism of the aristocracy, the Philistinism of the middle classes, the near-bestiality of the Populace, and the dogmatism of the National Church, he was stating both the spiritual needs of England and the superficiality of its official pastors; he was stating what the whole romantic protest had tried to say; and he was stating these things persuasively.

Yet Matthew Arnold was in his own way both as dogmatic and as unconvincing as the enemies on whom he waged war. The glimmering wit was the dance of the sunshine on a shallow lake. Take, for example, his famous parody of the Evangelical creed.

In imagining a sort of infinitely magnified and improved Lord Shaftesbury, with a race of vile offenders to deal with, whom his natural goodness would incline him to let off, only his sense of justice will not allow it; then a younger Lord Shaftesbury, on the scale of his father and very dear to him, who might live in grandeur and splendour if he liked, but who prefers to leave his home, to go and live among the race of offenders, and to be put to an ignominious death, on condition that his merits shall be counted against their demerits, and that his father's goodness shall be restrained no longer from taking effect, but any offender shall be admitted to the benefit of it on simply pleading the satisfaction made by the son; —and then finally, a third Lord Shaftesbury, still on the same high scale, who keeps very much in the background, and works in a very occult manner, but very efficaciously nevertheless, and who is busy applying everywhere the benefits of the son's satisfaction and the father's goodness; —in an imagination, I say, such as this, there is nothing degrading, and this is precisely the Protestant story of *Justification*. And how awe of the first Lord Shaftesbury, gratitude and love towards the second, and earnest co-operation with the third, may fill and rule men's hearts so as to transform their conduct, we need not go on to show, for we have all seen it with our own eyes.[26]

There are two possible interpretations of that passage. The first is that Arnold was protesting against the crudity of the Evangelical slogans and of other popular religion. The great Christian symbols of the infinite and inexhaustibly mysterious God as Father, Son, and Spirit had been taken by the Barbarians, the Philistines, and the Populace, and had been dragged down to their level; and preachers willing to pander to this religious market had debased the currency of serious theology. Any man who has acquired some insight into the depths of religious experience, and who has preserved some integrity in the use of religious language, is bound to protest against such triviality. Thomas Arnold's son was under a special obligation to prophesy, and the

26 *Literature and Dogma* (Smith Elder, 1873), pp. 306–7.

weapon of sarcasm might be legitimate. He might even be entitled to attack Joseph Butler as shallow.[27] But the second possible interpretation is that Arnold by telling the 'fairy tale' of the three Lord Shaftesburys was ridiculing any attempt to use analogies drawn from human experience in order to struggle to speak of that tremendous and fascinating mystery, the ineffable; and he was doing this because he did not think that it was at all possible to talk about, or to know about, any reality beyond our experience of this world. Thus any awe, gratitude, or love felt for a transcendent God was misplaced. If this second interpretation is correct, then the help which is given to 'conduct' through the imagination by the use of Christian symbols may be regarded as help which could be discarded in a happier time, in a fuller light, when men would be able to understand, accept, and enjoy their true condition without recourse to the remnants of Christianity; and the best hope of man becomes not a return to Bible reading but the growth of a new poetry to replace the Bible.

Which interpretation best represents Matthew Arnold's thought? Almost certainly the second. Arnold was shrewd enough to know why he was so often pressed from the Right and the Left, but he never offered a clear, systematic exposition of his religious thought. He excused himself charmingly by saying that he was no metaphysician, and that after his *Last Essays on Church and Religion* (1877) he would be relieved to return to the study of literature. He placated the pious by referring to their faith as 'extra-belief', as '*Aberglaube*, the poetry of life'; their preference seemed to be optional or not verifiably certain, rather than clearly wrong. He also consoled them by pointing out that he was reckoned a religious conservative on the Continent and in the United States. Above all, he identified himself with clerical conservatism in England. His *Culture and Anarchy* (1869) echoed the alarm of the upper middle class about the advent of democracy; he was suspicious of the scheme to revise the translation of the English Bible; he was opposed to the clamour for the disestablishment of the Church of England; he was contemptuous of the style of the burial services which Nonconformist ministers were at last allowed to conduct in parish churchyards. He amused his readers by more little jokes at the expense of those who were crudely orthodox or crudely atheistic, and he impressed them temporarily by repeating his favourite phrases in the context of his favourite quotations, thus making it clear that his intention was to edify as well as to entertain. His readers gathered that religion was closer to literature than to science, but they did not gather precisely what was the status of religious knowledge—nor what

[27] 'Bishop Butler and the *Zeit-geist*' in Matthew Arnold, *Last Essays on Church and Religion*, may be contrasted with the tribute paid to Butler by Dean Church in his *Pascal and Other Sermons* (Macmillan, 1895).

were its contents. At the very moment when he would seem to be con-
tradicting talk (such as Bishop Butler's) about the 'moral and intelligent Governor of the universe' as contrary to the modern mind, he
would find a place for it in the modern heart. 'We do not think that
it can be said that there is even a low degree of probability for the
assertion that God is a person who thinks and loves, properly and
naturally though we may make him such in the language of feeling;
the assertion deals with what is utterly beyond us.'[28]

He preferred to speak about God as 'the Eternal', airily claiming
that this was the name used by the Hebrews. God was 'the stream
of tendency by which all things strive to fulfil the law of their being',
or more significantly God was 'the Eternal Power, not ourselves, which
makes for righteousness'. But what did the capital E signify? Did 'the
Eternal' lie beyond time, or was the phrase a way of describing the
universe? As F. H. Bradley asked, could one equally well speak about
'the Eternal not ourselves that makes for cleanliness'? Or might 'Early
to bed and early to rise' be presented as 'the Eternal not ourselves that
makes for longevity'?[29] All that Arnold said very clearly was that men
have experienced something more than themselves. 'The grandeur of
the spectacle given by the world, the grandeur of the sense of its all
being *not ourselves*, being above and beyond ourselves and immeasur-
ably dwarfing us, a man of imagination instinctively personifies as a
single mighty and living power; as Goethe tells us. . . .' The contribution of Israel was the emphasis on the moral sense, even more than on
the imaginative feeling, as the most important element in this experience. 'To one who knows what conduct is, it is a joy to be alive; the
not ourselves, which by revealing to us righteousness makes our happiness, adds to the boon this glorious world to be righteous in. That is
the notion at the bottom of the Hebrew's praise of a Creator; and, if
we attend, we can see this quite clearly.'[30]

What is evident is that Matthew Arnold brought a fine spirit and
a subtle mind to the discussion of abiding mysteries. In the words of a
twentieth-century philosopher, 'his keen insight into the imaginative
and poetic element in religious belief as well as his insistence that
religion is primarily concerned with guiding conduct make him a profound philosopher of religion as well as a Christian teacher full of the
"sweet reasonableness" he attributed to Christ'.[31] But we cannot be so
clear about the relevance of Matthew Arnold's philosophy to any

[28] *God and the Bible* (Smith, Elder, 1875), p. 108.
[29] F. H. Bradley, *Ethical Studies* (Henry S. King, 1876), p. 283.
[30] *Literature and Dogma*, pp. 33–4.
[31] R. B. Braithwaite in *Christian Ethics and Contemporary Philosophy*, ed.
I. T. Ramsey (SCM Press, 1966), p. 69. Professor Braithwaite's own position
and theological reactions to it printed in the same volume recall Matthew
Arnold and his critics.

tradition which regards religion as primarily the worship of the ultimate. Matthew Arnold's 'patronage of a Christianity fashioned by
himself is to me more offensive and trying than rank unbelief', Mr.
Gladstone told the Duke of Argyll in 1895. His two great successors
as the critic-moralists in England, T. S. Eliot and F. R. Leavis, have
united with the professional theologians to dismiss his theology.[32]

There was a perpetual ambiguity in his use of the word 'God', an
ambiguity which became all the stronger as he clarified and simplified:

> God's wisdom and God's goodness! —Ay, but fools
> Mis-define these till God knows them no more.
> Wisdom and goodness, they are God!—what schools
>
> Have yet so much as heard this simpler lore?

The ambiguity is there, we may conclude, in Matthew Arnold's
heart. However nostalgically he may admire the wisdom and goodness of the Christian past, and however prophetically he may look to
the spark from heaven in the new age of science, the one thing that he
cannot say is: God is real. 'Arnold's final platform', it has been observed, 'is the absence of God.'[33]

Since every living theology is an autobiography, Matthew Arnold was
perfectly entitled to say what he knew from his own life to be true.
He had found his 'best self' and his happiness through the 'not ourselves' which, by proclaiming duties, makes for righteousness; and one
aspect of this discovery had been his acceptance of his status as the
natural heir of one of the great Christians of the nineteenth century.
He could justly say that he had striven to fulfil the law of his being.
What was more open to objection was his claim that nothing more
had ever really existed in Christianity. For in his *St. Paul and Protestantism* (1870) he seemed to assume that Spinoza, the seventeenth-
century pantheist who was prepared to bless a warmer religion for the
benefit of weaker intelligences, had thought out what St. Paul had
really meant. When Jesus prayed *Abba*, Father, he meant 'the best self',
and any other teaching arose because Jesus was over the heads of his
reporters. The religion based on Jesus could be satisfactorily rendered
as 'morality touched by emotion', with the result that 'the peace of
God' became 'the Christian phrase for civilization', and the following
formula became the proper statement of 'the essential facts and truths'
behind the legends:

What then is the miracle of the Incarnation? A homage to the virtue of pure-
ness, and to the manifestation of this virtue in Jesus. . . . What does Easter

[32] See, e.g., Vincent Buckley, *Poetry and Morality* (Chatto & Windus, 1959).
[33] J. Hillis Miller, *The Disappearance of God* (Harvard University Press,
1963), p. 268.

celebrate? Jesus . . . dying to re-live. To re-live in Paradise, in another world? No, in this. But if in this, what is the Kingdom of God? The ideal society of the future. Then what is immortality? To live in the eternal order, which never dies.[34]

Such a free translation of Christianity was, surely, a sublime example of the very tendency that he denounced in *Culture and Anarchy* as 'Doing as One Likes'.

Matthew Arnold claimed that only by his method of interpretation could the Bible be retained as the basic book of English morality.

The great danger to the Bible at present [he wrote] arises from the assumption that whoever receives the Bible must set out with admitting certain propositions, such as the existence of a personal God, the consubstantiality of Jesus Christ with this personal God who is his Father, the miraculous birth, resurrection and ascension of Jesus. Now, the nature of these propositions is such that we cannot possibly verify them.[35]

It was a debatable claim when it was made, and the debate has continued. During his lifetime criticism of the Bible was already going deeper than could be shown on the glimmering lake of his religious books, and the formation of a Christian answer to that criticism—if such an answer was possible—was increasingly seen to be a task involving not only more careful and honest scholarship but also a more profound experience of the God 'utterly beyond us' and the Saviour's 'open' grave, among the 'people who believe'. Thus the challenge to Anglican complacency, thrown down by Thomas and Matthew Arnold, was being taken up by churchmen and theologians more conscious than either of them was of the complexities of the spiritual situation, and more alert to the dimensions of religion beyond righteousness.

Matthew Arnold died of a heart-attack in Liverpool in 1888, and was buried at Laleham. On his grave it is recorded not that he wrote poetry or prose, but whose son he was.

FOR FURTHER READING

The Life and Correspondence of Thomas Arnold, D.D., by A. P. Stanley in two volumes (Fellowes, 1842), ran into many editions. Stanley also edited a volume of Arnold's *Miscellaneous Works* (Fellowes, 1845), including his contributions to the *Sheffield Courant* and *Hertford Reformer* but tactfully suppressing his most famous article, on the 'Oxford Malignants'. Modern studies include R. J. Campbell, *Thomas Arnold* (Macmillan, 1927), in the series on 'Great

[34] *Irish Essays* (Smith, Elder, 1882), pp. 139; *Irish Essays and Others* (Macmillan, 1904), pp. 322–3.
[35] *God and the Bible*, p. 6.

English Churchmen'; Norman Wymer, *Dr. Arnold of Rugby* (Robert Hale, 1953), with new detail about his personal life; T. W. Bamford, *Thomas Arnold* (Cresset Press, 1960), drawing on hostile contemporary newspapers, and *Thomas Arnold on Education* (Cambridge University Press, 1970); E. L. Williamson, *The Liberalism of Thomas Arnold* (University of Alabama Press, 1964), a study of his religious and political writings.

Matthew Arnold forbade an official biography. His *Letters, 1848–88*, were edited by G. W. E. Russell in two volumes (Macmillan, 1895). There have been many critical studies, of which the most useful were by three North American scholars: Lionel Trilling, *Matthew Arnold* (Allen & Unwin, rev. edn. 1949), William Robbins, *The Ethical Idealism of Matthew Arnold* (Heinemann, 1959), and A. Dwight Culler, *Imaginative Reason: The Poetry of Matthew Arnold* (Yale University Press, 1966). A suggestive short book was D. G. James, *Matthew Arnold and the Decline of English Romanticism* (Oxford University Press, 1961). The *Poetical Works* were edited by C. B. Tinker and H. F. Lowry, who also wrote a commentary on *The Poetry of Matthew Arnold* (both Oxford University Press, 1950). Kenneth Allott has annotated Arnold's *Poems* and arranged them chronologically (Longmans, Green, 1965). The best edition of the *Complete Prose Works*, ed. R. H. Super, was inaugurated in 1961 by the University of Michigan Press.

2

Newman and Keble *1792-1866*

1

When John Keble preached the Assize Sermon in the university church of St. Mary the Virgin, Oxford, on 14 July 1833, his protest against government policy in Ireland provided the occasion for John Henry Newman to begin leading a religious movement. Keble's views on Ireland did not really matter. He never went there. Even he did not find it very easy to defend the particular abuse in Ireland which had attracted the attention of the reforming government in West-minster: the financial support required by twenty-two Anglican bishops in a country consisting largely of Roman Catholic peasants. ('What are the Protestants of Ireland', as Thomas Arnold had indiscreetly asked in a pamphlet four years before, 'but military colonies planted by the conquering nation who can only have a distinct existence so long as the evils of conquest are unatoned for . . . ?') On that Sunday morning in Oxford, the government's plan to suppress ten of these dioceses was mentioned as the main item in a list of national sins by the preacher, who was a Tory country clergyman.[1]

Newman, who had a passion for anniversaries, kept 14 July as the beginning of the Oxford Movement, although curiously enough he left behind no account of hearing the sermon. In 1833 he had just re-turned from six months abroad, his health having broken down after years of academic overwork. While in Europe he had thought con-stantly of England, of himself, and of his mission to England. For many years already he had felt himself to be a man set apart by God. When alone in Sicily, ill with fever, his assurance that he had a work to do had reached a new power of introspection and self-dedication. He could not die until his work was done; he had not sinned against the light. When he returned home, his friends did not recognize him. His body was now brown and muscular, his energy exuberant. He was determined that men should know that he was back. Keble's sermon gave him his cause.

There were, of course, many others connected with the movement

[1] Keble's sermon was printed in, for example, *The Oxford Movement*, ed. E. R. Fairweather (Oxford University Press, New York, 1964), pp. 34–49.

of 1833. Edward Pusey was to give his name to the movement, although apparently he never cut the pages of the copy of Keble's sermon sent to him when it was printed. Hugh James Rose, a Cambridge theologian more learned and even more conservative than any Puseyite, had a name to rally the High Church party until he died prematurely in 1839. But none of these possessed Newman's flair as a journalist. It was he who conceived the idea of *Tracts for the Times*, and who wrote the first: '*Choose* your side . . .'. None of the others had quite his sense of a campaign; he once said that he burned to be a soldier. Perhaps none had quite his personal reasons for fighting in defence of the Church; and certainly none had his power to fascinate both his contemporaries and the future.

Twelve years later he was at the feet of the rain-soaked Father Dominic, asking to be received into the 'One Fold of the Redeemer'. Thirty-two years from 1833, he walked towards a front door where another old man, white haired and almost deaf, stood talking. The other looked at him in puzzlement. Newman silently produced his visiting card. The old man was John Keble, who grew agitated. His wife was ill (both the Kebles were to die within a year). They already had one visitor, Pusey. But Keble invited Newman into Hursley Vicarage, and the three men dined together for the first time in their lives. Pusey dominated the meal with talk, but went off to take Evensong in the village church. Newman and Keble walked in the garden, and had just begun to resume something of their old intimacy when a sound of wheels on the drive joined the sound of church bells. Father Newman's gig had come to take him on his journey.

2

It is one of the most discussed questions in church history, why Newman and Keble parted in 1845. Newman was unable to find peace outside the Roman Catholic Church, while Keble remained a country parson. The question was intensely debated at the time. England, secular as it seemed to the Oxford apostles, was still excitable by ecclesiastical controversies. Oxford was then England's most lively centre of religious thought, and Newman had cast a spell over it. For Newman to become a Roman Catholic was somewhat like a prominent Conservative becoming a Communist in the twentieth century. And Newman, knowing how many eyes were upon him, feeling in every fibre (and how many fibres he had!) that the decision would be momentous, fasting and weeping, studying and praying, kept himself and his audience in an agony of suspense, although after 1841, if not before, it was reasonably clear that this was to be the outcome of his religious development. One by one the steps were taken: Oxford abandoned for the village of Littlemore (then part of the parish of St. Mary's), the vicarage of St. Mary's resigned (but an informal kind of monastery continued in the stables which he owned in Littlemore), past attacks on Roman Catholicism publicly recanted, the Fellowship at Oriel given up, the young men allowed to make their submission, finally— as a sign that he no longer considered himself a clergyman of the Church of England—grey trousers worn. At each stage letters of advice flooded in from friends such as Keble; at each stage his explanations flooded out. Which among all these actions was decisive? Where among all these words was the vital truth?

While he was 'on his death-bed' as an Anglican, Newman wrote and rewrote a book which was to show why he was becoming a Roman Catholic, and which was to persuade others to follow. The book was broken off because he felt that he had to submit to Father Dominic and to leave Littlemore and his library. It had this address to the reader as its conclusion:

Put not from you what you have here found, regard it not as a mere matter of present controversy; set not out resolved to refute it, and looking about for the best way of doing so; seduce not yourself with the imagination that it comes of disappointment, or disgust, or restlessness, or wounded feeling, or undue sensibility, or other weakness. Wrap not yourself round in the associations of your past, nor determine that to be truth which you wish to be so, nor make an idol of cherished anticipations. Time is short, eternity is long.

But *An Essay on the Development of Christian Doctrine* was not, in fact, a defence of nineteenth-century Roman Catholicism. That was a subject about which Newman at the time knew very little, although he devoted some pages to analysing a collection of popular tracts recently sent to him. He used to say that he had never met a Roman Catholic in England before becoming one. The book was about the Church fourteen or fifteen centuries before: the Church of the Fathers. It was an essay in theology, with the thesis that the history of Christianity was the history of a great idea's development; and no thorough explanation was offered to convince critics that Roman Catholicism was the only development which passed the proper tests.

In 1850 he did publish *Lectures on Certain Difficulties felt by Anglicans in Submitting to the Catholic Church*. He had delivered the lectures in London, and the audience had been impressed, but the book has not retained a place in literature. It was rhetorical and rambling. As many debating points as possible were made against 'the movement of 1833' as being 'uncongenial to the National Church' and therefore barren except as a path to Rome. As many debating points as possible were made in defence of 'the Catholic Church'—almost as effectively as that same Church had been denounced by the same author in the 1830s. A few pages were autobiographical, but Newman seemed to stand too close to his conversion for the full magic of his nostalgia to be evoked. Only occasionally do his words to Anglicans sound as if spoken in a dress-rehearsal for the coming triumph of remembrance. 'Can I wipe out from my memory, or wish to wipe out, those happy Sunday mornings, light or dark, year after year, when I celebrated your communion-rite in my own Church of St. Mary's; and in the pleasantness and joy of it heard nothing of the strife of tongues which surrounded its walls?'[2]

In 1864, while he was close to despair about his work, Newman wrote a far more personal book in order to vindicate his motives in his submission to Rome. Charles Kingsley, a clergyman in the Thomas Arnold tradition and a popular novelist, who was then Professor of Modern History at Cambridge, reviewed a volume in the *History of England* by James Anthony Froude. In the course of the article, three fatal sentences slipped from his pen.

Truth, for its own sake, has never been a virtue with the Roman clergy. Father Newman informs us that it need not, and on the whole ought not to be; that cunning is the weapon which heaven has given to the Saints wherewith to withstand the brute male force of the wicked world which marries and is given in marriage. Whether his notion be doctrinally correct or not, it is at least historically so.

Such an insult might have been ignored. But it gave Newman the opportunity to explain and justify himself to his fellow-Catholics as well as to Anglicans, and he interpreted this opportunity as an obligation. The material lay ready to hand, in the letters and journals; it was already in his mind, in the memories. Once again he threw himself into writing a book, sacrificing all comfort to it as he had done to the *Essay on Development*, and to *The Arians of the Fourth Century* which had brought about the breakdown before the foreign tour of 1832–3. He wept as he wrote. The result was one of the immortal autobiographies: *Apologia pro Vita Sua*.[3]

Its immediate consequence was to transform Newman's place in public opinion by vindicating his integrity. Yet even this was not a complete self-portrait. As the sub-title made clear, it was *A History of*

---

[2] Yet even the generosity of this memory of religious experience in the Anglican Church (p. 69) is soon qualified by the point that the same must be true about experience in Methodism, and 'are you willing to place yourself on the same footing with Wesleyans?' (p. 74).

[3] Edited by Martin J. Svaglic (Clarendon Press, 1967). See also Walter E. Houghton, *The Art of Newman's 'Apologia'* (Yale University Press, 1945), and G. Egner, *Apologia pro Charles Kingsley* (Sheed & Ward, 1969).

His Religious Opinions. It proved that he had sincerely sought religious truth, which was all that he thought he had to show against Kingsley. It proved that he still believed that he had found it, which was all that he had to prove against his critics within the Roman Catholic Church. But it was not an account of all the influences which had made his mind such an extraordinary mixture of courage and 'undue sensibility', shrewdness and credulity ('If I am to bandy words it must be with sane persons', wrote Kingsley, refusing a publisher's invitation to reply to the *Apologia*); it was not a full confession. More may be gleaned from a number of other fragments of autobiography.[4]

Later books have attempted to fill the gaps. Some of them have concentrated on the Newman family, telling the unhappy stories of the father, a bankrupt who sank to keeping a public house in Clerkenwell; of the brother Francis who, abandoning his prospects in Anglican Oxford, became a learned eccentric in London; of the other brother Charles, who became an embittered recluse in a Welsh cottage (and refused to see John before he died, for he was an atheist). When John Henry Newman deviated from the *via media*, the safe middle way of Anglican conventionality, did the explanation lie in the unusual psychology of the whole family? And was the devout John simply softer than his brothers? 'You are encouraging a nervous and morbid sensibility and irritability of mind', his harassed father had warned him back in 1822. 'Religion, when carried too far, induces a softness of mind. Take care, I repeat.' And when John inclined towards religious authoritarianism rather than his brothers' scepticism, did another bitter taunt come true? When the young John had defended the conduct of George IV, the father had sneered: 'Always stand up for men of power! And in time you will get your promotion!'[5]

John Henry Newman's emotions have been probed from other

---

[4] Newman's *Autobiographical Writings* have been edited by Henry Tristram (Sheed & Ward, 1956).

[5] In 1850 Francis Newman published his own apologia, *Phases of Faith, or Passages from the History of My Creed*. In it he traced the development of his quest for a more spiritual religion since the day in 1821 when, as a schoolboy being confirmed, he had thought the Bishop of London (Howley) 'a made-up man and a mere pageant'. In 1830 Francis Newman had left his fellowship at Balliol in order to join an extremely Protestant mission in Baghdad. Returning in 1833 just as his brother was returning from Italy, Francis had continued his spiritual pilgrimage until by 1850 he was in a position close to Matthew Arnold's. 'Religion was created by the inward instincts of the soul: it had afterward to be pruned and chastened by the sceptical understanding.' He became Professor of Latin at University College, London, but some of Matthew Arnold's most effective ridicule, in his lectures at Oxford, was expended on this crank's attempts to translate Homer. In 1891 Francis Newman published a savage little book about his brother. See *Newman Family Letters*, ed. Dorothea Mozley (SPCK, 1962), and William Robbins, *The Newman Brothers* (Heinemann, 1966).

angles. In his lifetime men detected a feminine quality in his sensitivity and in his very looks. One visitor thought of him as an old lady washed in milk. As a boy he vastly preferred his mother, who could be idealized, to the blundering father. When he was a young man, the only woman who meant much to him was, so far as we know, his sister Mary, who was aged nineteen when she died. Towards men he had a great gift for friendship; one scholar has reminded us of this by a delightful study of the men to whom Newman dedicated his books, and another by editing his devotional addresses to his brethren in the Oratory.[6] But the truth must be faced. Some of the Oxford friendships with men were passionate, although all the evidence suggests that he had an innocence perhaps possible only in that pre-Freudian time. He was devoted to John Bowden, Hurrell Froude, Henry Wilberforce, and Frederic Rogers, one after the other. But Bowden married and died, Froude grew consumptive and died, Wilberforce married, Rogers (later Lord Blachford) grew alarmed at Newman's intensity. Each parting was bitter. When Henry Wilberforce hoped that their friendship might continue, Newman wrote back that 'you ask me to give you my heart, when you give yours to another', and that he was resolved 'to make my own mind my wife'. Fortunately he had the sense not to send the letter (although he kept it), and they remained friends. When Newman became a Roman Catholic, it was always clear that he would live surrounded by a community of younger admirers; his entourage went with him. In this circle one emerged prominently, and not only because he helped Newman by translating German or was in mind as Newman's eventual biographer; he was the best friend. The *Apologia* ended with a tribute to 'dear Ambrose St. John; whom God gave me, when He took everyone else away'. When Ambrose St. John died, Newman is said to have spent the whole night on the bed beside the corpse, sobbing; and when Newman died he was buried in the same grave. It was a generation which accepted friendships between men as friendships; these were a mark of the Evangelicals as well as of the Oxford Movement. The death penalty for sodomy remained on the statute book until 1861, and the word 'homosexual' was not coined until 1897. In such circumstances Newman's nature, which all acknowledged to be pure, was left in some obscurity. But it was no accident that Kingsley's attack included the two words 'male' and 'marriage'.[7]

[6] See Henry Tristram, *Newman and His Friends* (Bodley Head, 1933), and Placid Murray, *Newman the Oratorian* (Gill & Macmillan, Dublin, 1969).

[7] A study of 'virginity and friendship' in the Oxford Movement was made by Sir Geoffrey Faber in his *Oxford Apostles* (Faber & Faber, 1933). Charles Kingsley's psychology has been presented by R. B. Martin, *The Dust of Combat* (Faber & Faber, 1959). Kingsley was ashamed of the licence of his youth and of his liability to nervous breakdown; marriage seemed the only safe outlet

What, then, was Newman's secret? He refused to put his 'reasons for becoming a Catholic in a teacup'. He recorded parts of the intricacy in his journals, and hoarded every kind of souvenir. He communicated aspects of his personality to correspondents—more easily, it would seem, than in conversation; and about twenty thousand of his letters were preserved. He, of all men, knew that the truth about him could never be presented simply. The only book apart from his novels which he ever wrote without a driving controversial necessity, his *Essay in Aid of a Grammar of Assent* (1870), was a subtle analysis of the complexity of the forces behind 'real apprehension' of a living religion and 'real assent' to it. In the course of that book Newman quoted some of his own words, written in 1841: 'Life is for action. If we insist on proofs for everything, we shall never come to action: to act you must assume, and that assumption is faith.' The truth about his faith and action must be complex—and more complex than even he knew. He should not be taken solely as he put himself on the printed page; that would be like the mistake, which he came to acknowledge, of believing in Anglicanism as a paper religion. But in the final analysis Newman's genius was religious, so that his psychology should be explained in terms of the thirst for God as well as in reductionist categories. Sixty years later Newman still remembered 'with what feelings I went up . . . in November 1817 for my first communion—how I was in mourning for the Princess Charlotte, and had black silk gloves—and the glove would not come off when I had to receive the Bread, and I had to tear it off and spoiled it in my flurry'.[8] Richard Church, Dean of St. Paul's, wrote in an obituary that Newman had wanted a New Testament kind of holiness—and had not found it in the Church of England. If a single explanation has to be offered as the key to Newman, that surely must be it.[9]

---

for his passionate masculinity, and a muscular Protestantism the only faith to inspire an active life. He was probably at his best when under the influence of F. D. Maurice, a theologian who did not threaten his defences as Newman did.

[8] Thomas Vargish, *Newman: The Contemplation of Mind* (Clarendon Press, 1970), p. 187.

[9] R. W. Church, *The Oxford Movement* (Macmillan, 1891), has remained the best short history, although it was written when Church was an old man, and was never finally revised.

3

Lead, Kindly Light, amid the encircling gloom,
Lead Thou me on!

So Newman prayed in his famous poem, written when becalmed on his homeward voyage from Sicily, a month before Keble's Assize Sermon. This light came to him as the inner light of conscience. It cannot be emphasized too much that what ended in Rome and ecclesiastical miracles began for him at the same tribunal that was revered by the moralists who wished to stay within the limits of reason. In the *Grammar of Assent*, he took the religious witness of the conscience for granted. 'Even philosophers, who have been antagonists on other points, agree in recognizing the inward voice of that solemn Monitor, personal, peremptory, unargumentative, irresponsible, minatory, definitive. This I consider relieves one of the necessity of arguing with those who would resolve our sense of right and wrong into a sense of the Expedient or the Beautiful, or would refer its authoritative suggestions to the effect of teaching or of association.' Here, in every child, was the 'external Master'. In the pamphlet where he defended the infallibility of the Pope against Mr. Gladstone in 1875, he could still remark that if he had to give a religious toast at the end of a dinner, he would propose Conscience before the Pope. In his *Apologia* he recalled how as a boy his mind had already rested 'in the thought of two and two only absolute and luminously self-evident beings, myself and my Creator'.

He could never remember a time when he had not felt certain about the reality of the Creator, although he often spoke about this as the most difficult part of the Christian creed. 'I know that I know.' He seems to have been naturally religious, influenced by his mother's simple Bible piety but chiefly by his own conscience and imagination: 'I thought life might be a dream, or I an Angel, and all this world a deception, my fellow-angels by a playful device concealing themselves from me, and deceiving me with the semblance of a material world.' The experience which came to him when he was fifteen, in 1816, the experience sometimes referred to as his 'conversion', was the direct connection of this early religious sense with life's moral drama, under the influence of a schoolmaster, Walter Mayers, who had himself recently become a convinced Evangelical. But Newman's was not the full Evangelical conversion. For better or for worse, it left him still seeking. Evangelical readers wrote to point this out when he told the story in his *Apologia*, but any perceptive student of his *Justification* could have seen it some thirty years before. For Newman in that theological treatise showed no sympathy with Luther. The essential Protestant idea of 'justification by faith' seemed a psychologically meaningless formula, because he had never had Luther's experience of finding peace with God through trust in him. Not faith, placed in God once and for all, but the Church's sacraments must be the key to Christianity, for they at least were objectively real while the experience of faith was an unreliable condition. Because the heart was deceitful, its conversion could not be enough.[10]

When he was elected a Fellow of Oriel at the age of twenty-one, he seemed a priggish, narrow-minded, tongue-tied Evangelical, and Richard Whately, the endlessly argumentative logician and hearty dog-owner, was entrusted by the Common Room with the task of bringing their new colleague out of his shell.[11] Whately succeeded; so much so that Newman became his factotum and Vice-President of Alban Hall under him, adding up his accounts, drafting a book on logic for him, and running around like one of his dogs. But no logic could efface Newman's sense of the presence of God, or his wish to obey the will of God. Indeed, the study of logic only served to increase his emphasis on the role of the will in the formation of opinions and lives. He was ready to risk or to sacrifice all, and he knew that there was for him no guarantee of earthly comfort—or of transcendent assurance. In a conversation with Wilfrid Ward in 1885, he could look back and allow himself to half-wonder: 'Is not the ideal Christian life a very risky venture, based perhaps on a conclusion due to prejudice and fanaticism?' But after 1816 it was his way, his life.

> And with the morn those angel faces smile
> Which I have loved long since, and lost awhile.

He first saw the angels in the gardens of Grey Court House in Ham. All through his life he dreamed about those gardens and about the beautiful house. They were always his image of heaven. His father was then a banker, able to afford two elegant homes, at Ham and nearer the centre of London, for his pretty wife, his three sons and his three daughters. The children seem to have enjoyed an exceptionally happy childhood, although John, the eldest, was his mother's favourite. But the bank was ruined in March 1816. The father then tried to manage a brewery in Hampshire, but his self-confidence was gone—and was not restored on the many occasions when his wife urged him to follow John's advice in money matters. The family's status sank until all

---

[10] For an assessment of the Oxford Movement by a Lutheran scholar, see Yngve Brilioth, *The Anglican Revival* (Longmans, Green, 1925).

[11] *The Life and Correspondence of Richard Whately, D.D., late Archbishop of Dublin*, was compiled by his daughter Jane (Longmans, Green, 1866).

their furniture, including John's music, had to be sold. When John graduated at Oxford, it was to the immediate need to earn enough to give Frank a university education. So the 'conversion' a few months after bankruptcy was, in part, the turning of an ultra-sensitive adolescent from his feckless, now shabby-genteel, family, from the ruins of his childhood, to the Communion of Saints. Those who supported the Church, but who had their own families, could never understand the passion of Newman's devotion. As Richard Church noted: 'With Mr. Newman, his cause was identified with his friendships and even his family affections'.

The books which Mr. Mayers lent him shaped his mind for ever. Joseph Milner's *History of the Church of Christ*, with its extracts from the Fathers, introduced him to the fourth and fifth centuries, always his sacred age—a 'paradise of delight' as he wrote in 1850. Thomas Newton's *On the Prophecies* stamped Rome on his imagination, for Newton argued that the Pope was the prophesied Antichrist. Other Evangelical books showed the boy what serious, personal religion was, and he now grew convinced that he was called to lead a single life. From one of these authors, Thomas Scott, Newman drew the essence of Trinitarian orthodoxy ('Manhood taken by the Son'), and with it two proverbs which expressed the pattern of his own search until it ended on a summer's evening in 1890: 'Holiness rather than peace' and 'Growth the only evidence of life'.

> The night is dark, and I am far from home—
> Lead Thou me on!

His real home was now the holy city of his imagination and of the theology which he began to learn, but Newman gradually abandoned the Evangelical simplicity of the schoolboy under the pressure of Oriel College. Oriel was then the cleverest college in England, for it threw open its fellowships to examination on intellectual merit alone and not on parentage. If Oriel thought that they possessed the promise of intellectual excellence, it was prepared to elect as fellows even young men, such as Newman himself, who had failed to gain Firsts in the university's examinations. (Newman's own failure came because of unwise overwork—and also perhaps because the private school at Ealing had not been as efficient as Winchester or Rugby.) Newman's colleagues, almost without exception, became devout clergymen; the college was no hotbed of heresy. But in that firmly clerical Oxford the Oriel circle which included Richard Whately and Thomas Arnold was thought to be daringly liberal and reforming, and was dubbed the 'Noetics', from a Greek word suggesting 'Intellectuals'. Under Whately's tutelage the young Mr. Newman forced himself to argue as they did, and to read and write more than they did.

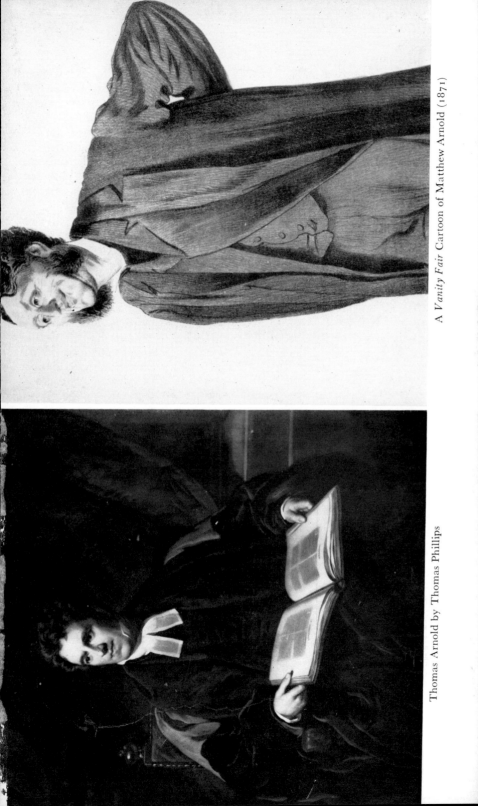

A *Vanity Fair* Cartoon of Matthew Arnold (1871)

Thomas Arnold by Thomas Phillips

FAR FROM THE MADDING CROWD.

A *Judy* Cartoon of Gladstone (1875)

Manning, Pusey, Newman, Keble, Wilberforce

The college made Newman a thinker—and a pastor, for it was Provost Hawkins who persuaded Newman to gain some parish experience as a curate among the poor around St. Clement's in Oxford. Hawkins and other Fellows of Oriel explained the real Church to the young man. The Evangelicals tended to view the Church as an invisible society of saved individuals. All other men were outside; there were, as Newman noted, 'two classes, the one all darkness, the other all light'. Oriel showed Newman the visible Church, a society with a long history, a 'mixed multitude' of good and evil. It was a great corporation, responsible for the moral education of the country; but Thomas Arnold's teaching that this was its chief role—'like a Mechanics' Institute' in Newman's phrase—could, Newman came to think, be avoided. From Whately's own (but anonymous) *Letters on the Church by an Episcopalian*, in 1826, he learned that Church and State should be independent of each other, and that in separation the Church should retain not only its mission but even its property. From other Fellows of Oriel, principally Keble and Froude who had at first been suspicious of him as an Evangelical or (worse) a Noetic, he learned to see the Church as a society of saints and sinners, believers and doubters; a society recruited and united not by its feelings or opinions but by its sacraments and creeds. His rejection of the Noetics' Protestantism in the end set up echoes far beyond the Oriel Common Room. One who looked back on the Noetics' Oxford many years later sadly concluded: 'Newman beat and supplanted them, winning the great majority of the clergy and through them of the devout but half-instructed laity, by his maintenance of a sacerdotal as against a national Church'.[12] Not the intellectuals but the priests should decide the faith of Christians.

In his lectures published as *The Idea of a University*, Newman was to put into urbanely splendid prose, transmuted by the tears of an exile, the spell cast by Oxford through a quarter-century. It was a vision of a complete civilization with a rational and humane, but authoritative, theology at its centre; a vision of a university which was a community of talk between equals preparing to seek God as gentlemen in Church and State. But if as a Fellow of Oriel he was drifting into liberalism, preferring intellectual to moral excellence as he himself put it, his sister Mary's death in 1828 recalled him to his own vision of life. 'What a veil and curtain this world of sense is', he wrote to another sister some months later; 'beautiful, but still a veil'. His vocation was, after all, to pierce the veil, not to study the world's beauty; to be a priest, not a scholar; to renew the Church in holiness, not to reform Oxford. Years afterwards truly academic minds such as Mark Pattison's would still grow bitter with the thought of how irrelevant the whole Oxford Movement had been to the true business of a

[12] William Tuckwell, *Pre-Tractarian Oxford* (Smith, Elder, 1909), p. 260.

university. Oxford, Pattison held, should be dedicated to teaching, and above teaching to research in order that there might be more knowledge to teach. But what was all this to Newman? 'Now by Liberalism', he explained in the *Apologia*, 'I mean false liberty of thought, or the exercise of thought upon matters, in which from the constitution of the human mind, thought cannot be brought to any successful issue, and therefore is out of place. Among such matters are first principles of whatever kind; and of these the most sacred and momentous are especially to be reckoned the truths of Revelation.' His heart lay behind the veil—and that was one of the secrets of his fascination. Mark Pattison, now a sceptic who faced death, wrote to him in 1883: 'I can still truly say that I have learnt more from you than from anyone else with whom I have ever been in contact.'[13]

The world always lay in darkness for Newman; or rather, the world was unreal in comparison with the Creator and the soul. The soul was purged by the Creator's holy love, and finally sent by the Creator to endless bliss or endless torment behind the veil. Nothing else mattered ultimately. That was why 'I have never seen Oxford since, excepting its spires, as they are seen from the railway' (as he wrote at the end of the *Apologia*). Richard Whately, who became Archbishop of Dublin but remained a formidable Noetic, used to say that Newman had become a Roman Catholic because the alternative for him was to have no religion at all. Whately considered such a sacrifice to be treason to the mind, and refused to meet Newman during all the time when the two men were in Dublin. Of the two men, however, it was Newman to whom his own proud words, preached before the University of Oxford on 22 January 1832, could be applied: 'A few highly-endowed men will rescue the world for centuries to come'.

> I loved the garish day, and, spite of fears,
> Pride ruled my will: remember not past years.

Newman remembered that once, when his mother had pointed out that he had not got his way over some triviality as a child, he had replied: 'No, but I tried very hard!' Many noted that as an adult his will was imperious. That was why he so enjoyed organizing the Tractarians, with what he called 'a mixture of fierceness and sport'. The strange truth about this man who wrote so exquisitely was that he thought of himself as an activist. His grief in the Roman Catholic

[13] The best study of Newman's educational ideal is A. Dwight Culler, *The Imperial Intellect* (Yale University Press, 1955). John Sparrow, *Mark Pattison and the Idea of a University* (Cambridge University Press, 1967), should be contrasted with it. For Pattison, see V. H. H. Green, *Oxford Common Room* (Edward Arnold, 1957). Newman visited the dying Pattison; with what result, we do not know.

Church was that he was not given 'work' to do; he was doomed to spend his life 'indoors'. As an old man he put up a newspaper map of General Gordon's journey in the Sudan on the wall of his Birmingham room, and there it remains to this day. The general *manqué*, the donnish Caesar: that was the old Adam in him, and he knew it. Knowing the temptation, his crucial objection to 'popular Protestantism' was that it encouraged 'private judgement'. It failed, as he claimed in his lectures on *Justification*, to subdue the soul 'to receive the Divine Presence . . . and to be made a Temple of the Holy Ghost'. Often in his early and best years as a preacher, he preached against pride.

His sermons while Vicar of St. Mary's were mostly addressed in theory to his parishioners, a few shopkeepers and college servants in the centre of Oxford. But he always found it difficult to talk with lower middle class people as contrasted with visiting the grateful poor, and everyone including Newman admitted that 'I do not know my Oxford parishioners' (as he wrote to Keble in 1840). The response came gradually, from undergraduates and young men recently elected to fellowships. They heard the message; it was so simple, but it was so tense because heartfelt, so eloquent because austerely restrained. A sentence would rush out; then a pause; then another sentence, like a nail hammered into the heart. Pride was sin. Christians must be humble before the Church. Christians must be humble before Christ, the incarnate God who had humbled himself to the death of the cross.[14]

Like other preachers, Newman did not always find it easy to hear his own message. When he was so ill with his fever in Sicily in the spring of 1833, he reproached himself with being in Sicily at all. It was an example of his remaining wilfulness, for it had been wrong to insist on exploring Sicily instead of returning to England from Rome with his companion Hurrell Froude (and with Froude's father, a grim archdeacon). The need to obey was bound up with Newman's very idea of God, apprehended by the conscience. On his return to Oxford and the *Tracts*, he often professed his devotion to the Bishop of Oxford, Richard Bagot. 'My own Bishop was my Pope', he recalled in his *Apologia*. When Bishop Bagot criticized Tract Ninety, Newman's whole position in the Church of England was shaken, and he began to move on.

> So long Thy power hath blest me, sure it still
> > Will lead me on
> O'er moor and fen, o'er crag and torrent, till
> > The night is gone.

[14] Extracts from his sermons have been selected and systematically presented to form *A Newman Companion to the Gospels*, ed. A. J. Coupet (Burns, Oates, 1966). The more philosophical *Newman's University Sermons* have been reissued, ed. D. M. MacKinnon and J. D. Holmes (SPCK, 1970).

Newman felt deeply that the man of God must grow in holiness; everything except this road was a waste. When he was made a tutor of the Oriel undergraduates, he taught his favourite students with a devoted care but made no secret of his contempt for the rowdies—who were still making a noise when Thomas Hughes arrived from Rugby, as *Tom Brown at Oxford* shows. However, this intensely pastoral conception of a don's duty alarmed Provost Hawkins, who in 1828 refused to send Newman any more pupils; and Renn Hampden took over the tutorship. St. Mary's, Tractarianism, and theology became the only outlets for Newman's energies, and he hoped that his writing might earn a professorship. When the chair of Moral Theology fell vacant in 1834, he was so confident that he recorded his appointment in the title page of a new volume of sermons, but Hampden was appointed and Newman again turned back to stony paths.

But *was* the Church of England the road to holiness? It was all very well to say that an individual or a religious body must depend on creeds and sacraments, not on feelings, but as Newman's knowledge of the Establishment grew he saw to the full its weakness. Few of the clergymen who after some years adorning the university progressed with their brides to country vicarages had much of Newman's otherworldliness. In his first tract, he put to them a serious, practical question. 'Hitherto you have been upheld by your birth, your education, your wealth, your connexions; should these secular advantages cease, on what must Christ's minister depend?' His immediate answer was that they depended on 'our apostolical descent'; they were 'assistants, and in some sense representatives' of the bishops who were successors to Christ's apostles. But few of the bishops of England in 1833 were amused when Newman in that Tract wished for them the 'blessed termination' of the first apostles: 'the spoiling of their goods, and martyrdom'. (The fate which came to Bishop Bagot was a nervous breakdown resulting from the unprecedented excitements of the Oxford Movement.) Nor were they much more attracted by the theological role in which Newman had cast them. They were the spiritual lords of a Protestant country; mitres were on their silver spoons in palaces, not on their heads in parish churches. And the reluctance of the bishops to see themselves in the mirror held up by Newman was matched by the refusal of others to agree with Newman's episcopalian challenge. Evangelicals, and even liberals such as Arnold, showed that they, too, had ideas to offer.

As the contemporary scene grew more alarmingly confused, the Tractarians penetrated more deeply into the past for the ideal of the Church. Pusey's historical scholarship changed the *Tracts* from pamphlets into treatises, and he first made his mark by citing the Fathers of the Church to show that all sin after Baptism was very grave. Pusey had already bought copies of the works of the Fathers for Newman in Germany, at a shilling a volume, and Newman's *Arians of the Fourth Century*, dedicated to Keble, had attempted to display the purity of doctrine from the beginning. It was the traditional High Anglican line: orthodoxy had been accepted always, everywhere, by everyone until heretical minorities had challenged it and had evoked its definition by the great councils. It echoed the boast of Lancelot Andrewes about 'two Testaments, three creeds, four general councils, five centuries'. But gradually Newman found himself less able to take refuge from his disillusionment in the pure womb of the Patristic past. The Tractarians launched an immense series to bring back the Fathers in translation. But nowhere in these volumes did Newman find what his heart needed. The Church of the Fathers turned out to be full of controversy and confusion, like the Church of England; and Antiquity had the further disadvantage of being dead.

In the Introduction to his lectures on *The Prophetical Office of the Church* (1837), Newman wrote: 'We travel by night; the teaching of the apostles . . . which once, like a pillar in the wilderness, was with the children of God from age to age continually, is in good measure withdrawn; and we are, so far, left to make the best of our way to the promised land by our natural resources.' All his arguments against Rome in those lectures crumpled under the impact of his religious need. For he came to believe that he needed a pillar of fire by night, that it was not enough that the light had once shone in the darkness. There were too many quarrels in the nineteenth century about who held the light, and what it was; and dead men, as he used to say, could not decide the quarrels of the living. That applied even to his beloved Fathers; it applied also to the Anglicans whose teachings about the Church of the Fathers he attempted to bring into a synthesis in *The Prophetical Office*. 'It still remains to be tried whether what is called Anglo-Catholicism, the religion of Andrewes, Laud, Hammond, Butler, and Wilson, is capable of being professed, acted on, and maintained on a large sphere of action and through a sufficient period, or whether it be a mere modification or transition-state either of Romanism or of popular Protestantism, according as we view it.'

It was to be Newman's own developing view that Anglicanism was a transition-state—but not to popular Protestantism. As he said in *The Prophetical Office*, 'the essence of revealed religion is the submission of the reason and heart to a positive system, the acquiescence in doctrines which cannot be proved or explained'. He wanted 'an infallible oracle of truth' teaching a dogmatic system, but always the truth he wanted was a truth supporting a holy life. He edited yet another series, this time of the lives of the English saints. But those volumes could not make him a saint. He needed a living voice which he could venerate as Christ's own; a pillar moving on through the wilderness.

4

We can trace the path to Rome at two levels, emotional and intellectual. When he first saw Rome on 2 March 1833, it fascinated him more than Oxford itself. He still disapproved of its religion. Lecturing on *Justification* in 1838, he thought that the charge was 'not unfounded as regards popular Romanism, that it views or tends to view the influences of grace, not as the operation of a living God, but as something to bargain about, and buy, and traffic with, as if religion were, not an approach to things above us, but a commerce with our equals concerning things we can master'. But he slowly grew out of the idea that the Pope was Antichrist; and from his travels in Sicily he remembered a crowded village church at Mass early one morning, or the cool, dark peace of the churches in sunbaked Palermo. It has been suggested that the course of religious history might have been different, had Newman known German. He was cut off from the most important theology of his time by this lack; for example, Schleiermacher's *The Christian Faith*, first published in German precisely when Newman was forming his mind, was not to be translated until 1928, although it related Evangelical feelings to the formal Christian doctrines and to the culture of the world at a level deeper than any nineteenth-century book in English. Yet it seems improbable that the thought of Schleiermacher, or any other variety of Protestantism, would have satisfied Newman's dependence on the Holy Church—or that Germany would have satisfied his highly visual imagination. There was only one place in the world with the religious authority and glamour which he needed.

> Oh that thy creed were sound!
> For thou dost soothe the heart, thou Church of Rome,
>   By thy unwearied watch and varied round
> Of service, in thy Saviour's holy home.

His friendship with Hurrell Froude at Oriel drove deeper into Newman the religious spell of Rome. Froude was clever and energetic, 'bright and beautiful' as he was remembered by his friends. He was also a dying man, in a hurry to do battle for his chosen cause. And he was odd. He brooded secretly over the sins of youth: sado-masochism appears to have been among these. He found consolation in romantic thoughts about the Church of the Middle Ages. 'Really I hate the Reformation and the Reformers more and more.' The Reformation was 'a limb badly set, it must be broken again to be righted'. In 1838–9 Newman and Keble published Froude's *Remains*, including a number of such quips amid more innocuous letters and sermons. The spiritual journal now given to the world showed that Froude was ashamed because he enjoyed being admired for his bold sailing and other athletic vigour; so he slept on the floor. He was ashamed because he liked roast goose or buttered toast; so he fasted in his college room. He wanted to impress a companion on a walk, he pretended to have read a book, he could not keep his mind fixed on the chapel services; he accused himself of many faults. Newman and Keble seem to have cut out the graver sins, which might have explained the pervading sense of guilt, but the general verdict was that they had betrayed their friend's memory by not burning the morbidly scrupulous confessions which remained.

Newman continued to brood over the mystery of Hurrell Froude. Had he or the Reformers been right? If the Reformers had been wrong, could grace still be left in the Church of England, grace which had nourished Hurrell Froude himself, grace such as that still given to the ten rebellious Northern tribes of Israel? James Anthony Froude also thought and re-thought about his dead brother, whose bullying had made his boyhood miserable. His *Nemesis of Faith* (1849) was an incoherent but moving novel about a clergyman's loss of faith. In a Preface to the second edition, he insisted that the story was not auto-biography (he had never been ordained), but he added his own poignant cry: 'We seek for God, and we are sent to find Him in the words and thoughts of other nations and other ages about Him. . . .' Eventually he tore himself away, to become the disciple and biographer of Carlyle and the historian of the English Reformation. William Froude, the youngest brother, became a leading scientist and agnostic. He would say that he had been taught by Hurrell to apply a bold mind to Butler's *Analogy*, and had reached the conclusion that the truth of Christianity was improbable.

Newman's own thoughts went another way. He carried on an argument by letter with William Froude over thirty-five years, and rejoiced when William's wife and son (named Hurrell) were received into the Roman Catholic Church.[15] An accident at the beginning seemed to show the path. Asked to choose a book from Hurrell Froude's library as a keepsake, he wanted Butler's *Analogy*, but it was already taken. He chose instead the Roman Catholic *Breviary*, and was so impressed that he published a translation as Tract Seventy-five. In 1841 he published Tract Ninety, which argued that the doctrine of the Church of England had not been changed fundamentally at the Reformation,

15 See *Cardinal Newman and William Froude, F.R.S.: A Correspondence*, ed. G. H. Harper (John Hopkins Press, Baltimore, 1933).

despite the evidence printed in every Prayer Book: the Thirty-nine Articles. He sought to persuade others (and himself) that the Articles, although 'the offspring of an uncatholic age', had not been intended to exclude the Catholic doctrines which he had come to regard as parts of Christian holiness. He did this by applying his logical and debating power to the Articles. Could they not be stretched to include much in Catholicism? Indeed, had not the framers of the Articles intended this in order to include Catholic-minded Englishmen in the National Church? 'The Protestant Confession was drawn up with the purpose of including Catholics; and Catholics now will not be excluded.' Almost half a century later, Gladstone—who took more trouble than Newman did to investigate the history of the Elizabethan settlement of religion— remarked to Lord Acton that Tract Ninety had been basically correct. 'The *general* argument of that tract was unquestionable, but he put in sophistical matter without the smallest necessity.'[16]

The condemnation of Tract Ninety by the heads of the Oxford colleges, and later by the bishops, awoke Newman to the unreality of his version of Anglicanism. The Oxford Movement since 1833, he now saw, had been a defence of a Church which did not wish to be defended by his arguments. Like an indignant *prima donna*, he recalled in his *Apologia:*

I was quite unprepared for the outbreak, and was startled at its violence. . . . I saw indeed clearly that my place in the Movement was lost; public confidence was at an end; my occupation was gone. It was simply an impossibility that I could say any thing henceforth to good effect, when I had been posted up by the marshal on the buttery-hatch of every College of my University, after the manner of discommoned pastry-cooks, and when in every part of the country and every class of society, through every organ and opportunity of opinion, in newspapers, periodicals, at meetings, in pulpits, at dinner tables, in coffee-rooms, in railway carriages, I was denounced as a traitor who had laid his train and was in the very act of firing it against the time-honoured Establishment.

This was Newman's way of acknowledging that Oxford now held little or no scope for his spiritual and intellectual ambition. To be sure, he was still Vicar of St. Mary's; but he had never deceived himself about his effectiveness in his parish, and his prestige with the undergraduates seemed to have been broken. The defeat of Isaac Williams as a candidate for the Professorship of Poetry in succession to Keble (on the ground that he was a Tractarian) was now a reminder to Newman that he was unlikely to receive academic promotion or to be reinstated as a tutor in his college. He had assumed that he would

[16] For selections from, and comments on, Tract Ninety, see, e.g., *The Oxford Movement*, ed. E. R. Fairweather, pp. 144–156.

'live and die a Fellow of Oriel', and seems never to have seriously considered any post in the Church of England outside Oxford. In his life the Oxford chapter, and with it the Anglican chapter, seemed to be closing. At bottom the necessity which drove him to challenge the Church of England with Tract Ninety was suicidal.

The ambition, however, was very far from being crude. He had been purged. On 8 April 1843 he was meditating in his journal

that God put into my heart, when 5 or 6 years old, to ask *what* and *why* I was, yet now I am forty-two, and have never answered it in *my conduct*; that if disobedience is *against nature*, I am, in the sight of Angels, like some odious *monster* which people put out of sight; that I have acted hardly ever for God's glory, that my motive in all my exertions during the last 10 years, has been the pleasure of energizing intellectually, as if my talent were given me to play a game with (and hence I care as little about the event as one does about a game). . . . Various great trials struck me, 1. the having to make a General Confession to some one in our Church, I not having full faith that our Church has the power of Absolution. 2. having to join the Church of Rome. 3. having to give up my Library. 4. bodily pain and hardship. I considered that God is used to accept offers, but I think He will not exact such.

Why, then, did he delay until 9 October 1845 his submission to the Rome where he could find light? Why in April 1842 did he retreat to Littlemore? Perhaps he was sulking; certainly he was watching. What he saw confirmed the Protestant character of Anglicanism. The Church of England co-operated with the Prussian Lutherans, who were undeniably Protestants, to sponsor a joint bishopric in Jerusalem. To Newman it seemed a move in power politics; and it was the kind of thing Thomas Arnold would have liked. In Oxford Pusey was dropped from the list of university preachers and a dramatically public and vindictive move was made to strengthen the university's formal condemnation of Tract Ninety, although the move was vetoed by Richard Church as one the proctors for the year. And part of the explanation of the years in Littlemore is that Newman was praying for light; no longer in a game.

Although he had never talked with a Roman Catholic in England, he knew enough about their communion to be realistic. In a few years' time, in his *Lectures on the Present Position of Catholics* (1851), he would show why 'we Catholics are so despised and hated by our countrymen'. His mood would then be defiant; and his hectic gaiety nearly landed him in prison, for a jury held that he had libelled the ex-priest, Achilli. But to decide to adopt this despised and hated position was not easy for a Fellow of Oriel. In the 1840s he knew well that the Roman Catholic gentry had been excluded from higher education for centuries, and that Roman Catholicism in England was unlikely to attract many fresh recruits except from Ireland, and that if illiterate and drunken Irish peasants were driven by hunger to make roads, canals, railways, and slums in a Victorian England full of prejudice against them the result would not be beneficial to the old Catholic gentry. In the summer of 1845, as Newman prayed and read at Littlemore, the future of Roman Catholicism in England was largely hidden from him, for it was the failure of the Irish potato crop through disease that autumn (and in 1946–7) which decided that future. But by the summer of 1845 the unpopularity of the Roman Catholic Church in England was already great enough to draw the heart of England's most accomplished theologian.[17]

Had the Roman Catholic Church been more successful in England, it would have been less attractive to Newman. For its very weakness could now be taken as showing that it was no idol. In his lectures on *The Prophetical Office of the Church*, the danger of idolatry had been his key argument against Rome. The heart of Lecture III, on 'Doctrine of Infallibility Morally Considered', had been this sentence: 'When religion is reduced in all its parts to a system, there is hazard of something earthly being made the chief object of our contemplation instead of our Maker.' Released from this fear by the thought of the Church of Rome's ill-repute, Newman now found what he needed in his longing for self-sacrifice as the gate to holiness. He had found the humble Body of Christ, to be adored because thus the Maker might be worshipped. He had ended his articles which were reprinted as *The Church of the Fathers* (1840) with a story about St. Martin. The saint saw a vision of Christ; he knew it to be a false vision, when this Christ failed to show the print of the nails.

In the *Essay on the Development of Christian Doctrine*, there are three magnificent paragraphs which compare the Roman Catholic Church of the 1840s with the Church of the Fathers. These paragraphs were necessary to explain why if St. Athanasius and St. Ambrose were to come to Newman's Oxford, that 'fair city, seated among groves, green meadows and calm streams', they would 'turn from many a high aisle and solemn cloister which they found there, and ask the way to some small chapel where mass was said in the populous alley or forlorn suburb'. Two of these paragraphs provide the climaxes to Sections II and III of Chapter VI. The first comes at the beginning of the chapter.

There is a religious communion claiming a divine commission, and holding all other religious bodies around it heretical or infidel; it is a well-organized, well-disciplined body; it is a sort of secret society, binding together its members by influences and by engagements which it is difficult for strangers to

[17] See *The English Catholics, 1850–1950*, ed. G. A. Beck (Burns, Oates, 1950), and *Anti-Catholicism in Victorian England*, ed. E. R. Norman (Allen & Unwin, 1968).

ascertain. It is spread over the known world; it may be weak or insignificant locally, but it is strong on the whole from its continuity; it may be smaller than all other religious bodies together, but is larger than each separately. It is a natural enemy to governments external to itself; it is intolerant and engrossing, and tends to a new modelling of society; it breaks laws, it divides families. It is a gross superstition; it is charged with the foulest of crimes; it is despised by the intellect of the day; it is frightful to the imagination of the many. And there is but one communion such.

However, Newman himself possessed one of the best intellects, as well as the most magical style, of his day. Much of his time in the late 1830s and early 1840s was spent on the academic study of the Fathers; much of his *Development* was occupied by the assembly of this historical material, and by its adjustment to the central theme of the 'one communion'. His intellectual need was to show that the Rome of the 1840s was a legitimate, and indeed the best possible, development of the doctrine and holiness entrusted by Christ to his apostles. He began where his Anglican reading of the Fathers had left him: with the truth that if one confined oneself to what all the Fathers had taught, one was left with a creed which was too brief if one had developed a strong taste for dogma. The shrewder Anglican apologists, acknowledging this, had argued that matters such as the government of the Church by bishops had been left by the apostles for decision by others, but the absence of a strong link with the apostles had proved religiously intolerable for Newman and other High Churchmen. Newman's studies had increased the problem by revealing to him a lack of a clear agreement among the earlier Fathers—whatever the older Anglican theologians, such as Bishop Bull, had pretended. 'They make mention indeed of a Three; but that there is any mystery in the doctrine, that the Three are One, that They are coequal, coeternal, all increate, all omnipotent, all incomprehensible, is not stated and never could be gathered from them.' The Fathers, then, were inadequate guides not only to ecclesiastical government but also to the most important mystery in Christianity—unless the Fathers could be interpreted by being developed. So the whole Church had in practice acknowledged by accepting the decrees of the Ecumenical Councils beginning with Nicaea. But if the earlier councils were obeyed, why not the Council of Trent which had defined modern Roman Catholicism?

The standard Anglican answer to this last question was that Rome had developed the tradition too enthusiastically and in the wrong direction. As he looked back over the pilgrimage of his own life, Newman was able to suggest a new mood by writing a general chapter on the development of ideas. He was wiser now than as a schoolboy; growth was the evidence of intellectual life.

It is indeed sometimes said that the stream is clearest near the spring. Whatever use may fairly be made of this image, it does not apply to the history of a philosophy or belief, which on the contrary is more equable, and purer, and stronger when its bed has become deep, and broad, and full. . . . In a higher world it is otherwise, but here below to live is to change, and to be perfect is to have changed often.

Of course not all change led to perfection: Newman knew how his own brothers Charles and Francis had developed away from orthodox Christianity. He thought he knew how his rival, the Professor of Divinity in Oxford, was going the same way without being aware of it; that had been the theme of his pamphlet of *Elucidations* of Renn Hampden's theology. But at least it could be agreed, after this introductory discussion, that all bodies of Christians, whether orthodox or not, in practice develop the doctrines of Scripture. Since the good development must be distinguished from the bad—*must*, because the soul of religion demanded it—Newman could invite all readers to agree also that 'there is a strong antecedent argument in favour of a provision in the Dispensation for putting a seal of authority on those developments'.

It must be a very strong authority, for Newman's studies of the history of the Church had shown him what a battle had been necessary to defend Christian doctrine and holiness against human error. Christianity might easily have been lost. 'If Christianity is both social and dogmatic, and intended for all ages, it must humanly speaking have an infallible expounder.' Anglicans solved this problem by pointing to the authority of the Church represented by the bishops assembled in Ecumenical Councils. But the Thirty-nine Articles had declared that great churches such as Antioch or Alexandria might err, and Newman's historical researches had confirmed the point. The Articles had added that the Church of Rome had also erred; this Newman could not now grant. His argument included emphasis on the importance of the representatives of the Popes, and of the Papacy's one theological treatise in the ancient doctrinal controversies, the short *Tome of Leo* of 446. Anglican theologians admitted that high honours had been paid in the Church of the Fathers to the see of Rome as the custodian of the memories and teachings of Peter and Paul; Newman turned the admission of Papal dignity into an insistence on Papal supremacy (although this had in fact only clearly developed from the time of Pope Leo the Great—and then only in the West). But was obedience to the nineteenth-century Papacy the right development of such early honours? Newman appealed to Butler: probability had to be the guide where conclusive proof was impossible. He found enough probability by pointing to the evidence of the holiness bred in the Church of Rome, before moving on to the more intellectual arguments that a true development of doctrine must not contradict itself and must exhibit certain 'notes': preservation of type, continuity of principle, power of assimilation, logical sequence, anticipation of its future, conservative action on its past, chronic vigour. These 'notes' could all be found in Rome.

How far, then, had the Papacy made *additions* to the creed of the apostles? Newman avoided the sharp questions about innovation, partly because the Roman Catholic definition of Papal infallibility was not clear until the Vatican Council of 1870, and partly because his style was more rhetorical than logical. But the second half of the book, unclear as it was, was definite enough that any changes in Rome had not distorted the tradition. An exhausted author broke off his discussion: 'Doctrine is where it was, and usage, and precedence, and principle, and policy; there may be changes, but they are consolidations or adaptations. . . .'

Newman did not think that the question of the extent of the 'consolidations or adaptations' developed in Rome was crucially significant. After all, as an Anglican he already held almost all Roman Catholic doctrines, and used many Roman Catholic customs; and even in 1845 he did not intend to break completely with the spirit of Anglican Oxford. As a Roman Catholic the reserve which he felt towards Italianate or 'Ultramontane' teachings and devotions was enough to make him suspect as a crypto-Anglican, so that for years his reputation lay under a cloud in the Vatican. Newman, who would declaim that 'you must accept the whole or reject the whole', liked to speak about throwing himself into the Anglican or the Roman Catholic system, but as his critics noted in practice he largely chose what to believe and to do, after as well as before 1845; his quest for authority stopped just short of fundamentalism. His choice was for the Church of the Fathers, brought alive by the 'chronic vigour' of the Church of England or of Rome. What was crucial in his decision between England and Rome was a factor which, curiously, was not listed among the 'notes' of true development. It was the factor of Catholicism, or universality.

When studying the history of the fifth century, Newman was struck by the thought that most of the bishops had wished to compromise while rejecting the heresy of Eutyches about the nature of Christ. They had made the damaging admission that Christ had only one nature; in a word, they were Monophysites. Rome had been a stronghold of the doctrine, later judged to be orthodox, that two natures, divine and human, were united in Christ. Newman asked himself: in that summer of 1839 might not Anglicans be imitating the compromising bishops, backed as those had been by political forces, instead of the orthodox Pope? 'I saw my face in that mirror, and I was a Monophysite.' That September an article by Nicholas Wiseman, later Cardinal Archbishop of Westminster, was put into Newman's hands.

The article compared the Anglicans not with the heretical Mono-physites, but with another ancient movement, the Donatists who were Puritans guilty of the sin of schism; and it included an anti-Donatist quotation from St. Augustine, *Securus judicat orbis terrarum*: 'The world judges safely'. As Newman later recalled, these four words 'absolutely pulverized' the Anglican appeal to Antiquity. If an infallible expounder was needed to preserve and develop Christian doctrine and holiness, his basis must be global. Authority would not be safe in the hands of local bishops in the East, who might be heretical; or in North Africa, who might be schismatic; or in England.

It would be possible, but pointless, to protest that Anglicans were not officially Monophysites or Donatists; that the Church of England did not stress too exclusively the divine nature of Christ or the holy nature of the Church. It would also be possible to remark that *Securus judicat orbis terrarum* was, on the face of it, not a defence of the Vatican but a call for a public opinion poll, which Newman would have derided. Newman knew very well that men could interpret history differently; he knew his Gibbon.[18] It was enough for him that historical study provided a mirror, to help him to see his nineteenth-century face with its puzzlement and its belief. It was enough for him that history could add precedents, when he had decided that the authority of his Anglican bishop was uncertain in comparison with the authority of the Bishop of Rome. His story, he knew, was the story of his heart, and the motto which he chose when he was made a cardinal summed up both his prayer to God and his influence on men: *Cor ad cor loquitur*, 'Heart speaks to heart'. He wrote in his own *Apologia*: 'It was not logic that carried me on. The whole man moves; paper logic is but the record of it.'

5

Newman in 1845 did not see the distant scene. He believed that at the age of forty-four his creative days were over. Now that he had submitted to the teachings of 'the Church of Christ', for some years he had no thought of writing another book of theology. Who was he, to teach the teachers? If he was to lecture in public, it would be in order to ridicule the Church of England as the creature of the State, as hopelessly worldly and compromising, and in order to vindicate the Roman Catholic Church in the face of Protestant ignorance and prejudice; here he could speak out of experience, and he enjoyed doing

[18] A reasonably objective presentation of the evidence to which Newman appealed has been provided by H. Burn-Murdoch, *The Development of the Papacy* (Faber & Faber, 1954).

so, publishing three books based on such lectures in 1849–51. He also wrote two propagandist novels, one (*Loss and Gain*, 1848), a narrative of an Oxford man's conversion to Rome, the other (*Callista*, 1856), a romance about a third-century martyr. His chosen work was that of an educational organizer. With other Oxford converts he founded in Birmingham a centre for prayer and study, an Oratory of St. Philip Neri (a seventeenth-century saint who reminded Newman of Keble). A school was attached to it, 'on the plan of the Protestant public schools, Winchester, Rugby, etc.' Neither the Oratory nor its school grew large, and neither escaped personal tensions around Newman; but here in Birmingham was his home.

He undertook two other adventures. Both of them were failures, both of them parts of this convert's martyrdom that gradually refined his thought until it reached the pure essence of the *Apologia* and the *Grammar*.

He became rector of a new Catholic university in Dublin, envisaging it as a centre for the higher education of Roman Catholics from all over the English-speaking world. It was to be another and better Oxford, to teach 'all knowledge' while retaining the Lord as its light and theology as its queen. It was to be an 'Alma Mater, knowing her children one by one, not a foundry, or a mint, or a treadmill'. He worked for the success of this idea of a university, with a command of detail which astonished. But the idea was stillborn. The Irish bishops had no intention of blessing the debates of another Oxford; the parents of young Irishmen wanted them to be equipped with some of the 'utilitarian' skills upon which the rector of this new university poured such elegant scorn; and the English and American Catholics saw little reason to go to Dublin. Newman received the insignia of a bishop from enthusiastic friends, for he had been promised this status, but the final appointment never arrived from Rome. This university, although equipped with a university church, with many regulations, with many inspirations from Newman's eloquence, and with the nucleus of its future buildings and professoriate, never attracted more than a hundred students at a time and was not chartered to award a degree. A medical school remained from the wreckage.[19]

His second adventure was the editorship of the *Rambler*, a magazine dedicated to the encouragement of culture among the English Catholics. When he had edited two numbers, bishops fearful of its unsettling effect persuaded him to resign. He was as helpless in this controversy as he had been in the battle of Dublin, for while believing that it was his mission to edify and educate Catholics he had no stomach for a fight with the reactionary bishops and no aptitude for intrigue. A

[19] For a detailed study of this tragi-comedy, see Fergal McGrath, *Newman's University: Idea and Reality* (Longmans, Green, 1951).

cold dislike existed between him and Henry Manning, another Oxford convert, who became Archbishop of Westminster in 1865; but Newman was unwilling to lend his support openly to the opposition to Manning's religiously reactionary and socially progressive policies. When Manning twice frustrated a plan for Newman to open a branch of the Oratory House in Oxford, his victim kept silence although he had confessed to dreaming of another Oxford Movement. Newman had said when the Roman Catholic hierarchy was restored in 1850, 'we want theology, not bishops'—and now they had Manning. When Manning's insistence that the infallibility of the Pope should be decreed carried the day at the Vatican Council in 1870, Newman's attitude was that this doctrine was true, but that it was not expedient to proclaim it. He refused to be a consultant at the council, but in a private letter which was leaked to the press he branded the party demanding the decree as an 'insolent and aggressive faction'. He also let slip a complaint about the 'Roman malaria' at the foot of the rock of St. Peter.[20]

A vague idea that Newman might supervise a new translation of the Bible came to nothing because the bishops declined to be sponsors. Meanwhile Newman did not produce any major defence of Christianity against the new secularism. He was sensitive to the censorship, or at least displeasure, of Rome; 'it is like the Persians driven to fight under the lash'. He wrote privately in 1864 that 'unless one doctored all one's facts one would be thought a bad Catholic', and his cowardice in accepting this situation angered Lord Acton, the English historian who led the fight against his fellow-Catholics' dishonesty.[21] Part of the trouble was that, unlike Acton, he was not really in touch with the best thought of the day on an international basis, although his praises of Christian scholarship were sincere enough. His *Essay in Aid of a Grammar of Assent*, although it appeared in the same year as the in-

[20] Newman's contempt for Manning went back to the time in 1843 when as Anglican archdeacon the latter preached in St. Mary's a violent sermon against Popery, and then walked out to Littlemore to see his old friend Newman. Newman was 'not at home', believing that the sermon had resulted merely from ambition. J. A. Froude had to walk the humiliated archdeacon back to Oxford. After that Newman spoke to Manning no more than a dozen times, although their mutual antipathy did not come to a head until a hostile review of one of Manning's books appeared in the *Rambler* and Manning blamed Newman. Manning's life was written in two fascinating volumes by the inaccurate and splendidly indiscreet journalist E. S. Purcell (Macmillan, 1896), whom Lytton Strachey used. Later books have to some extent restored his reputation. See *Manning: Anglican and Catholic*, ed. John Fitzsimons (Burns, Oates, 1951), and V. A. McClelland, *Cardinal Manning: His Public Life and Influence, 1865–1892* (Oxford University Press, 1962). E. E. Reynolds, *Three Cardinals* (Burns, Oates, 1958), tried to do justice to all, while preferring Newman.

[21] See Hugh MacDougall, *The Acton-Newman Relations* (Fordham University Press, 1962).

fallibility decree, could be published because in it Newman did not need to get involved in too many embarrassing discussions of specific dogmas. The book had an inner integrity; he had been saying much the same thing while an Anglican, and the developed form of the *Grammar* was the emotion of his successive religious crises recollected in the tranquillity of his mature philosophy. He pondered it, and struggled to write it, at intervals over twenty years. It had two targets. On the one hand, it rebuked sceptics who refused to acknowledge the seriousness and subtlety of religious decisions; and on the other hand, it rebuked theologians who fancied that the acceptance of a creed was a simple matter of logical inference—because they, too, had never been through the slow pain of making such a decision. Yet, for all the force of its analysis of 'real assent' to religious doctrines, it was not a definitive work of philosophical theology. It would be more accurate to classify its exposition of the 'illative sense' under 'psychology' or 'phenomenology' of religion. It was not likely to exert a profound influence on the revival of deep studies of St. Thomas Aquinas which began in the Roman Catholic Church after Newman's day. Nor was it likely to convince the sceptics, for they would dismiss Newman as a man credulous from boyhood. It cannot be denied that Newman gave his real assent to legends which most educated Roman Catholics a century later would despise.[22]

It is a record of disappointment after the brilliant promise of the 1830s. Pusey commented shrewdly that the Church of England had not known how to employ Newman, and if we take 'employ' in the rather subtle sense which Pusey must have intended we can see that the Church of Rome was equally at a loss. We cannot be surprised that before the *Apologia* the rumour spread that Newman was about to become an Anglican again. He contradicted this report, adding for good measure that 'the thought of the Anglican service makes me shiver'. Such bitterness came, however, from unhappiness. Newman wrote in his journal for 15 December 1859:

I am writing on my knees, and in God's sight. . . . When I was young I thought that with all my heart I gave up the world for Thee. . . . When I was older and in Anglican Orders I prayed absolutely and without condition against rising in the Church. . . . I knew what I was saying, and how it is Thy way to grant, to fulfil such petitions and to take men at their word. . . . O my God, not as a matter of sentiment, not as a matter of literary exhibition, do I put this down. O rid me of this frightful *cowardice*, for this is at the bottom of all my ills. When I was young, I was bold, because I was ignorant—now I have lost my boldness, because I have advanced in experience. I am able to

---

[22] Studies of the *Grammar of Assent* and its background include David Pailin, *The Way to Faith* (Epworth Press, 1969), and Thomas Vargish, *Newman; The Contemplation of Mind* (Clarendon Press, 1970).

count the cost, better than I did, of being brave for Thy sake, and therefore I shrink from my sacrifices.

Next month he again wrote at length in his diary about his failures and his loneliness. 'O my God, I seem to have wasted these years that I have been a Catholic. What I wrote as a Protestant has had far greater power, force, meaning, success, than my Catholic works, and this troubles me a great deal. . . .'

The success of the *Apologia* four years later brought him out of that particular depression, but it is worth noting that Thomas Arnold's biographer was among the Anglicans who renewed their contacts with Newman as a result of the self-disclosure and the charity of that book; and Stanley recorded a long conversation with Newman in the autumn of 1864.

It left the impression, not of unhappiness or dissatisfaction, but of a totally wasted life, unable to read, glancing at questions which he could not handle, rejoicing in the caution of the Court of Rome, which had (like the Privy Council) kept open question after question that he enumerated as having been brought before it; also, although without the old bitterness, still the ancient piteous cry. 'O my mother! why dost thou leave us all day idle in the market place?' Studiously courteous, studiously calm.

Even when Stanley's touch of complacency as the literary and popular Dean of Westminster has been discounted, this impression remains representative of the thoughts of observers who remembered the past (as Newman himself did so thoroughly). And the disappointment remains for those who have experienced that world-wide crisis of religion which Newman expected. 'My apprehensions are not new, but above 50 years standing', he wrote in a letter of 1877. 'I have all this time thought that a time of widespread infidelity was coming, and through all those years the waters have in fact been rising as a deluge. I look for the time, after my life, when only the tops of the mountains will be seen like islands in the waste of waters.' Against that day, what had Newman done?

In 1879 he was made a cardinal by Pope Leo XIII; Leo was an imaginative aristocrat who had quietly groaned under the rule of St. Pius IX. A last-minute manœuvre by Manning to prevent the honour failed. Newman was allowed to remain at the Birmingham Oratory and was too old to play any part in the politics of the Church, but he was delighted, feeling that 'the cloud is lifted from me for ever'. Two years previously he had been made an Honorary Fellow of Trinity College, Oxford, which pleased him almost as much.

Even now, however, Newman did not foresee the nature of his posthumous destiny. When he received the red hat of a cardinal in Rome, he restated the purpose of his life. 'For thirty, forty, fifty years

I have resisted to the best of my powers the spirit of Liberalism in religion.' He explained such liberalism as

the doctrine that there is no positive truth in religion, but that one creed is as good as another. . . . . Revealed religion is not a truth, but a sentiment and a taste; not an objective fact, not miraculous; and it is the right of each individual to make it say just what strikes his fancy. If a man puts on a new religion every morning, what is that to you? It is as impertinent to think about a man's religion as about his sources of income or his management of his family. Religion is in no sense the bond of society.

Newman saw that education was spreading this attitude. It was 'a universal and thoroughly secular education, calculated to bring home to every individual that to be orderly, industrious, and sober is in his personal interest', instead of being based on the supernatural sanctions or religion. And Newman concluded by bidding his hearers not to fear this movement. 'Christianity has been too often in what seemed deadly peril, that we should fear for it any new trial now. . . . Commonly the Church has nothing more to do than to go on in her own proper duties, in confidence and in peace; to stand still and to see the salvation of God.'

This was a suitable speech for an old man on being made a cardinal. It was a suitable speech for a Christian who was a lifelong conservative. But it was not a speech which hearers in Rome would regard as special for anything more than its beauty. Its dogmatism was precisely the cause which had been invoked against the new cardinal by Manning and the other fanatical or foolish guardians of religion; and outside Manning's Church, it was a lost cause in England. When he had regarded Rome as Antichrist, Newman had been logical in believing that an Englishman should not be allowed to vote if he was of the Roman Catholic religion; but even in 1829 Newman had reluctantly accepted Roman Catholic emancipation, and religious liberty and toleration were now established. Back in 1841, Newman had written seven long letters to *The Times* brilliantly ridiculing Sir Robert Peel's support of popular education when opening the Tamworth Reading Room, on the ground that Sir Robert had not mentioned God enough, and had trusted in education to improve the morality of the people; but history had not laughed at Peel. Was Newman, then, merely trying to put the clock back? Was his nostalgia irrelevant to the hard questions which Thomas and Matthew Arnold had asked (if not answered): what kind of a truth was in religion, and how should the Churches while trying to teach it, view each other, and how was it to be apprehended by the conscience, and how was it to be related to a democratic society? If the speech at Rome in 1879 had represented Newman's only contribution to the coming Catholicism, the opening sentence of Chapter V of his *Apologia* would have had a truth fatal to his significance for the future: 'From the time that I became a Catholic of course I have no further history of my religious opinions to relate.'

As it was, Newman was able to add immediately in the *Apologia*: 'I do not mean to say that my mind has been idle, or that I have given up thinking on theological subjects.' And that was one of his winsome understatements. It was true that he could write in complete sincerity: 'I never have had one doubt.' But he did not attempt to maintain a rigid dogmatism, at least not by Roman standards; and his degree of flexibility was to be influential precisely because his intention to submit his mind to the mind of the Roman Catholic Church without one doubt could be questioned even by the malignant, because his achievement of orthodoxy could not be assailed except in details or by the ignorant, and because no one could look on his old age without realizing that here was a man who, mistaken or not, lived for God. His legacy thus remained available to those whose task in the twentieth century would be the updating of the Roman Catholic Church, to the delight of the 'separated brethren' of other Churches. The *aggiornamento* around the Second Vatican Council, with all its ecumenical fruit, grew from loyally Catholic roots, and it would be both an insult and an error to call it a concession to Protestantism. However, among all the theologians of the Roman Catholic past John Henry Newman seemed most symbolic of the spirit of that Council of Renewal, Aquinas himself being read in his light; and those accused of innovating could always appeal to his name. We may conclude that although he so dramatically left the Church of England, and so eloquently and so often denounced it, John Henry Newman always embodied, and in the end spread, much of what was best in the spirit of Anglicanism. It was his destiny that he, who depicted the chasm between the devout and the liberal, was to be valued later by his fellow-Catholics as a bridge-builder; that he, who came to be at ease only among the faithful in Birmingham, was later, after his death, to be admired widely as the voice of Oxford in Rome.[23]

An article by Newman in the *Rambler* in 1859, which was delated to Rome for heresy (without result), advised the bishops to consult the faithful in matters of doctrine. Newman did not completely explain

[23] Christopher Hollis, *Newman and the Modern World* (Hollis & Carter, 1967), and John Coulson, *Newman and the Common Tradition* (Oxford University Press, 1970), were English laymen's essays on Roman Catholicism in terms of ecumenical renewal and reunion after Vatican II. Examples of the international study which was filtered into the council included, from Belgium, J.-H. Walgrave, *Newman the Theologian* (Geoffrey Chapman, 1960), and, from Germany, Gunter Biemer, *Newman on Tradition* (Burns, Oates, 1966). See also the tribute by the French scholar, Louis Bouyer, *Newman: His Life and Spirituality*. The English translation (Burns, Oates, 1958) was commended by H. Francis Davis, 'though books on Newman appear almost monthly'.

what he meant by 'consult', but the principle that the laity as well as the hierarchy could, and did, guard the faith was a principle to be acknowledged by the Second Vatican Council.[24] The importance of sober and honest theology, for which Newman contended in his day according to his lights, was acknowledged by that council's method of work, involving consultations between the bishops and distinguished and articulate theologians—who, unlike Newman, did not refuse to be consulted. The *Development*, which no theologian in Rome could understand when Newman took it there in 1846, was being widely used in a theological renaissance more than a century later to show Catholics how it was not heretical to suggest that doctrine had indeed developed—and might develop again, for even orthodoxy must be seen as coloured by its historical background, and thus opened to future change.[25] The *Grammar of Assent*, which had survived the reign of the scholastic textbooks with their cold 'proofs' of the faith, was being expounded in order to show that some men's minds could be profoundly aware of the mystery of religion, and aware of the difficulties involved, and yet could hold Christianity as true. Newman's attitude to the Bible, where he acknowledged human elements but found the source of the river of tradition and the food of prayer, was being studied to inspire both the scholarship and the devotion of the biblical revival.[26] *The Idea of a University*, all that survived from the dream of Dublin, now provided a golden text preaching the freedom and vitality of man's mind to Christian humanists. Even where men did not read any of his books, Newman's name was invoked as patron by graduates.[27] It could even be pointed out that Newman was not a complete Tory in politics. He was cynical about all states, whether Liberal or Papal; his name could be cited by those who wanted a renewed Catholic Church to stand on its own spiritual feet.[28]

The name of Newman also became acceptable to Anglicans. One day in 1862 he met in a London street a former curate of his, a priest who was still an Anglican, W. J. Copeland, and pressed him to talk

[24] *On Consulting the Faithful in Matters of Doctrine* has been reissued with an Introduction by John Coulson (Darton, Longman & Todd, 1961).

[25] For a study of the idea of development in Roman Catholic theology by an Anglican scholar, see Owen Chadwick, *From Bossuet to Newman* (Cambridge University Press, 1957).

[26] Two essays of 1884 were reprinted with a useful Introduction by J. D. Holmes and R. Murray, in J. H. Newman, *On the Inspiration of Scripture* (Geoffrey Chapman, 1966). J. Seynaeve has provided a thorough study of *Cardinal Newman's Doctrine of Holy Scripture* (Blackwell, Oxford, 1953).

[27] An illuminating essay on Newman's idea of an educated laity was contributed by John Coulson to *Theology and the University*, a symposium which he edited (Darton, Longman & Todd, 1964).

[28] See Terence Kenny, *The Political Thought of John Henry Newman* (Longmans, Green, 1957).

at the Oratory: he did not wish to convert, but to remember. Out of
their renewed friendship came the idea that Copeland would edit
anew Newman's *Parochial and Plain Sermons*. As a Roman Catholic
Newman had tinkered with them, but in vain: they had stopped
selling. Now republished without censorship, they—or extracts from
them, or the vague reputation of them—recovered for Anglicans the
sense which undergraduates had felt in St. Mary's: the sense that
through Newman the Christ of the gospels spoke, and through the
Christ of the gospels the eternal God. Stanley said about these sermons:
'They belong, not to provincial dogma, but to the literature of all
time.' Gladstone, although he considered Newman 'no philosopher' in
comparison with Bishop Butler, said boldly in 1866 that 'since the
days of Butler the Church of England has reared no son so great as
Newman', and gave the style of Newman's sermons as his reason. 'I
find myself constantly disposed to cry aloud. . . . It is like the very
highest music, and seems sometimes in beauty to go beyond the
human.'[29] In his tribute at his death, Richard Church could 'almost
say' that Newman was 'the founder of the Church of England as we
see it'. This direct influence of Newman the preacher on Anglican
spirituality—or the more blurred image of Newman the man on the
Anglican imagination—was part of the whole triumph of the Oxford
Movement, which raised the spiritual level of parochial, diocesan, and
national life, and expanded the Anglican Communion in prayer as
well as geography. The fiftieth anniversary of Thomas Arnold's death
found the Archbishop of Canterbury, E. W. Benson, reflecting in his
journal: 'It is impossible not to see that everything almost which distressed Arnold in Church life is changed for the better, but mainly
by the agency of the Oxford Movement which he opposed.'[30]

On Monday 25 September 1843 Newman preached his last Anglican
sermon, in the little church which he had built at Littlemore. Twenty-
five years later, a passer-by found Newman at the same church, 'leaning
over the lych gate crying. He was to all appearances in great trouble.
He was dressed in an old grey coat with the collar turned up and his
hat pulled down. . . .' But in 1843 his congregation did the weeping,
as they heard:

And O my brethren, O kind and affectionate hearts, O loving friends, should
you know any one whose lot it has been, by writing or by word of mouth, in
some degree to help you; if he has ever told you what you knew about your-
selves, or what you did not know; has read to you your wants or feelings, and
has comforted you by the very reading; has made you feel that here was a

[29] *Correspondence on Church and Religion of W. E. Gladstone*, ed. D. C.
Lathbury (John Murray, 1910), vol. ii, pp. 300–1.
[30] Anglican tributes have included R. D. Middleton, *Newman at Oxford*
(Oxford University Press, 1950).

higher life than this daily one, and a brighter world than that you see; or encouraged you, or sobered you, or opened a way to the inquiring, or soothed the perplexed; if what he has said or done has ever made you take an interest in him, and feel well inclined towards him; remember such a one in time to come, though you hear him not, and pray for him, that in all things he may know God's will, and at all times he may be ready to fulfil it.

In the Church of England as in the Church of Rome, many have granted that request.

6

There have been some who have remembered Newman's disclosure of the secrets of human hearts and his pointing to a 'higher life', without thinking the nineteenth-century dogmatism of the Roman Catholic Church an absolutely necessary safeguard.

In 1876 a religious novel by a Birmingham manufacturer of chemicals became a best-seller. The author of *John Inglesant*, J. H. Shorthouse, was an Anglican, and his book ended with a discussion about the Church of England, set by the river in Worcester one evening in the seventeenth century. John Inglesant expounded the Anglican position to a doctor, Valentine Lee.

I am not blind to the peculiar dangers that beset the English Church. I fear that its position, standing, as it does, as a mean between two extremes, will engender indifference and sloth, and that its freedom will prevent its preserving a discipline and organizing power, without which any community will suffer grievous damage; nevertheless, as a Church it is unique: if suffered to drop out of existence, nothing like it can ever take its place.

His companion protested that such a compromise was not enough. 'If there be absolute truth revealed, there must be an inspired exponent of it, else from age to age it could not get itself revealed to mankind.' 'That is the Papist argument', answered John Inglesant; 'there is only one answer to it—Absolute truth is not revealed.' 'But if absolute truth is not revealed', Dr. Lee inquired, 'how can we know the truth at all?' Inglesant gave a long answer, in which the key quotation was: 'the Kingdom of God is within you.'[31]

John Keble was not among the Anglicans who accompanied Newman to Rome, and his loyalty to the Church of his baptism and ordination because the Kingdom of God was in it became, even more than Pusey's refusal to move, the symbol of a rootedly English variety of

[31] For a study of J. H. Shorthouse among other literary results of the Oxford Movement, see Raymond Chapman, *Faith and Revolt* (Weidenfeld & Nicolson, 1970).

Catholicism. The popularity of his *Christian Year* in his lifetime made him the most humanly appealing exponent of this happy Anglicanism, for Victorians at many different heights of churchmanship and social status loved and used the book—'without equal, the Bible excepted, in the English language', as Thomas Arnold roundly declared. The most popular poems in that collection were harvested for the hymnals, so that since Keble's death innumerable Anglican congregations have continued to sing his explanation of where his heart found peace and the Kingdom:

> Old friends, old scenes, will lovelier be,
> As more of heaven in each we see. . . .
>
> We need not bid, for cloistered cell,
> Our neighbour and our work farewell,
> Nor strive to wind ourselves too high
> For sinful man beneath the sky:
>
> The trivial round, the common task,
> Would furnish all we ought to ask,—
> Room to deny ourselves, a road
> To bring us daily nearer God.

It was a domestic creed. Keble's father was altogether more stable than Newman's; he had the same name as his son, and much the same nature. Born at Court Close, Fairford, in one of Gloucestershire's most delightful small towns during the year of the last Jacobite rising, John Keble senior died in the same house in 1834, having married a parson's daughter who bore him five children, and having done his own duty as a clergyman by ministering as the incumbent of the village of Coln St. Aldwyn, two or three miles away. For a time he was also a Fellow of Oriel. This tranquil life was a glimpse of heaven to John Keble junior, and nothing broke his loyalty to it. He remained at heart what he was as a boy, never seeking the second birth of the Evangelicals, never tempted towards the modernism of the liberals. He was one of the most elegantly accomplished scholars in the university, but his education had been entirely at home until he had won a scholarship to Oxford at the age of fourteen, and his heart never left home. He gave the best years of his life, 1823–35, during which by his own account there was a major crisis in Church and State, to looking after his father and Coln St. Aldwyn. One of the most influential priests in Anglican history, in his maturity he used to say about a theological proposition with which he agreed that it was exactly what his father had taught him.

Some letters, and some poems in *The Christian Year*, hint at moods when the son contemplated the possibility that he might be wasting his life in his father's house, and when the round in Gloucestershire seemed too trivial. But such depressions were soon brought under his dominant feeling that by denying any worldly ambitions—by refusing the Archdeaconry of Barbados which was offered to him in 1824 and which was then worth '2,000 a-year, &c., &c.', and by so behaving that no official dignity was even offered to him in England—he would be brought nearer to God amid old scenes. Newman, on the other hand, could never get back to that security after the loss of the angelfaces in the garden of Ham. When Newman stayed with the Kebles in 1828 (the visit had been arranged by Hurrell Froude) he saw 'Keble's verses, as it were, written on all their faces'; but he saw this family life as an outsider. When Keble published a book of poems about children in order to raise money for building a new church at Hursley (*Lyra Innocentium*, 1846), Newman never acknowledged the copy which the 'always your affectionate and grateful J. Keble' sent him, but instead published in the *Dublin Review* an article in which he argued that a man of Keble's poetic temperament should not rest content with the dreary scenes of Anglicanism, where the royal arms had replaced the crucifix. 'Poetry is the refuge of those who have not the Catholic Church to fly to and repose upon; the Church itself is the most sacred and venerable of poets.'

Another contrast between Newman and Keble arose from Keble's dependence on women. Keble did attract sensitive men; there was a beauty in his looks and his whole life, and he could be light-hearted (but so could Newman). But he never needed the devotion of men. He fell in love with a young lady in Devon; later he set his heart on Cornelia Cornish. His 'humdrum marriage' (Newman's phrase) with Charlotte Clark after his father's death in 1835 may have begun as an affair of convenience (Charlotte's sister had married his brother Tom), and they had no children; but his love for her deepened as he nursed her through various illnesses, until by the 1860s it had become all that a Christian marriage should be. He was also devoted to his sisters; one of them who had an artificial leg lived gently in his vicarage. A very frequent visitor to his vicarage, and to the homes of deserving poor in his parish, was Charlotte Yonge, whose novels were to do almost as much as his poems to spread the aroma of Tractarian piety. These women in Keble's life were delicate creatures, spending much time on the sofa, but to see them in church for daily Evensong when they were able to manage the little excursion meant more to Keble than to see the Fellows of Oriel polishing their logic over their port.[32]

[32] Charlotte Yonge put together *Musings over the Christian Year and Lyra Innocentium, together with Gleanings of Recollections of the Rev. John Keble* (Parker, Oxford, 1871), and wrote another book about *John Keble's Parishes* (Macmillan, 1898).

Continuity marked his affections to the moment when he was wheeled silently away from his wife's sickbed because his own time had come to die, and his spirituality never wavered. In Holy Baptism, the baby was filled with a supernatural life; in Holy Communion, as the little congregation held out empty hands Christ was really present (in the heart and, as he came to add after a long conservative hesitation, also in the hands). The whole countryside was an extended church, where nature preached. The bishops were remote from this idyllic scene, and Keble never bothered much about them; when his bishop refused to ordain his curate as a priest because the young man's theology was suspect, Keble carried on with him as a deacon. But the absent bishops could be regarded through the golden haze as in some sense heirs of the apostles, and therefore their defence against the politicians seemed part of one's religious duty. What mattered here was not so much episcopacy as the belief that the Church depended on Christ's presence, not the State's favour. John Keble used to say that, whatever happened outside, the Church of England would always be found in his parish.

For almost twenty years he had no full-time job of his own, but alternated various curacies with periods in Oxford (where he was Professor of Poetry, 1831-41, lecturing in Latin, praising Wordsworth but disparaging Shelley, Byron, and even Milton on moral grounds). As a position to take in nineteenth-century life, it was too mild even for the Fellows of Oriel, who did not elect Keble when the provostship fell vacant in 1827. 'We are not electing an angel but a provost', remarked Newman, for whom Keble resembled 'something one put under a glass case and kept on one's chimney-piece for one's children to admire'. The parish where Keble settled instead was not a complete paradise; the Baptism registers show how many of the girls were pregnant as they came to be married, and some of the boys delayed touching their caps to the Vicar until they received his stick across their shoulders. And he was not completely content. His lack of theological power during what he habitually referred to as the Church of England's 'very great and continued distress' grew painfully apparent, to himself as to others (when presenting the correspondence to Keble College, Oxford, Newman censored as too embarrassing the many passages where Keble blamed his own inadequacies). But as Vicar of Hursley for thirty years, he still lived under something like a glass case, for the squire, Sir William Heathcote, who had been one of Keble's most admiring pupils, virtually owned the village and would allow no Dissenter, let alone an atheist, among his tenants.[33]

[33] See Frances Awdry, A Country Gentlemen of the Nineteenth Century (Warren, Winchester, 1906).

Keble refused to expose himself either to Oriel (where Newman learned the logic which he was to deploy in Tract Ninety and the *Apologia*) or to Birmingham (where, at least in his early years, Newman spent a good deal of his time hearing the confessions of the poor). And Keble paid a price. He became the editor of Richard Hooker, the compiler of a life of the saintly Bishop Wilson, an unwearying student of the Fathers; but he was incapable of intellectual creation. In handling his own time, his ignorance of the world crippled his judgement. He would refuse to discuss 'infidelity', saying briefly to a young inquirer in 1851 that most of the men who had difficulties as to the inspiration of Holy Scripture were 'too wicked to be reasoned with'. He even lacked insight into how the minds of other Oxford clergymen were likely to react to theological events. His advice was often sought by the young Newman, who took a long time to get over his sense of awe on that first evening as a Fellow of Oriel. How difficult it was to call the great Mr. Keble by his mere surname! But how charming he was to the gauche newcomer at dinner! On at least two occasions, however, Keble's advice to Newman proved disastrous: when he strongly encouraged the publication of Froude's *Remains* and of Tract Ninety, apparently not expecting the indignation which would be aroused by these major indiscretions. We cannot wonder that Newman, while he wrestled with the Fathers and his own soul at Littlemore, depended no longer on Keble, although they exchanged friendly letters; nor that the two men, once such intimate allies, ceased to correspond after the crisis of 1845.

Why, then, was Keble College founded as a national monument to this escapist country priest? Because many believed that the system of values illustrated by Keble and his parish ought to be preserved in an Oxford dominated by Matthew Arnold and worse. Because Keble's stability at Hursley symbolized what was steady in the Anglican revival of clerical duty and church life; he fasted and was humbly penitent, he happily saw God in the countryside and the villagers, he was constant at daily services in church, he prayed for his people and 'waited on' them in their homes regardless of his personal convenience, he prepared young people for Confirmation in twenty or thirty classes for each, he taught for two hours a day in the village school. Because his quiet work as a director of souls made it less thinkable for another devout Anglican soul such as Hurrell Froude (or Newman) to struggle for Catholic holiness without a guide.[34] And because it all added up to a spiritual revival. The Tractarians, as has been well said,

weakened the church in politics by dividing; and in dividing, by loosening its grip on the Tory party and the crown . . . [and] weakened the church in

[34] Some of Keble's *Letters of Spiritual Counsel* were edited by R. F. Wilson (Parker, Oxford, 1880).

popular esteem by making laymen suspicious of clergymen. . . . But beneath the popular disesteem and public weakness they strengthened the soul of the Church of England.[35]

Keble's sermon had been the beginning, and his *Christian Year* had been the poetry, of this movement; he had been its saint. Accordingly Richard Church, who eyed with alarm some of the strange men coming as mourners and claiming a share in the legacy, found his funeral 'more like a festival than anything else, with the sun and the fresh keen air, and the flowers just coming out, and the beauty of the place and the church, and the completeness of that which had come to its last stage here'.

FOR FURTHER READING

Wilfrid Ward compiled *The Life of John Henry Cardinal Newman*, based on the private journals and correspondence, in two volumes (Longmans, Green, 1912), and his daughter Maisie Ward added *Young Mr. Newman* (Sheed & Ward, 1948). Meriol Trevor wrote a modern life including many vivid details culled from the primary sources but lacking a critical approach: *Newman: the Pillar of the Cloud* and *Newman: Light in Winter* (Macmillan, 1962). Father C. S. Dessain of the Birmingham Oratory, the editor of *The Letters and Diaries of John Henry Newman* (a complete edition published by Nelson and inaugurated in 1961), has written an excellent short study of *John Henry Newman* (Nelson, 1966), which includes a bibliography. *Letters and Correspondence of John Henry Newman during his life in the English Church*, ed. Anne Mozley (Longmans, Green, 1891), and *Correspondence of John Henry Newman with John Keble and Others, 1839–1845*, edited at the Birmingham Oratory (Longmans, Green, 1917), provide material for a period not yet covered by the Dessain edition. Glimpses of recent Newman studies were provided by the ecumenical symposium, *The Rediscovery of Newman*, ed. John Coulson and A. M. Allchin (published jointly by Sheed & Ward and SPCK, 1967).

Sir John Coleridge wrote an official but rambling *Memoir of the Rev. John Keble* (Parker, Oxford, 1869). Georgina Battiscombe, *John Keble: A Study in Limitations* (Constable, 1963), contains additional material, and W. J. A. M. Beek, *John Keble's Literary and Religious Contribution to the Oxford Movement* (Centrale Drukkerij, Nijmegen, 1959), is an objective analysis of his thought.

An illuminating selection of documents is *The Mind of the Oxford Movement*, ed. Owen Chadwick (Black, 1960).

[35] Owen Chadwick, *The Victorian Church*, Part I, p. 230.

3

1805-73,   181-82.

Wilberforce and Tait

1

As is well known, Anthony Trollope's *Barchester Towers* (1857) began with speculation around a bishop's deathbed. 'The illness of the good old man was long and lingering, and it became at last a matter of intense interest to those concerned whether the new appointment should be made by a conservative or liberal government.'

There was such an incident in 1868, when *The Last Chronicle of Barset* had only recently come out with its hints that Archdeacon Grantly or his successors would probably not be dominating many more dinner tables in the county, and that the hidden influence of the saintly Septimus Harding was also in jeopardy. In such a time of crisis, the mortal illness of an Archbishop of Canterbury aroused interest; for it was an age of 'improvement' in response to the crisis, and such energy as had been displayed by recent archbishops had not been enough to remove the impression that there was room for improvement at Lambeth Palace—even if not everyone shared Newman's belief about the Anglican Church that 'as her prospects have opened and her communion extended, the See of Canterbury has become the natural centre of her operations'.[1]

Who, then, would make the new appointment?

As Archbishop Longley lingered with bronchitis, Disraeli's Conservative government was tottering under the impact of Gladstone's new cry that the Church of Ireland must be disestablished. If Gladstone became Prime Minister in time, it was understood that he would move Samuel Wilberforce, Bishop of Oxford, a moderate High Churchman, to the Primacy. But Disraeli had in mind Charles John Ellicott, Bishop of Gloucester and Bristol, a moderate Evangelical. He was an industrious pastor, and healthy enough to work as a bishop until 1904. A Cambridge scholar, and the tireless chairman of the company of the scholars revising the English version of the New Testament from 1870 to 1881, he obstinately upheld the infallibility of the Bible in its original tongues. And he was a Conservative, strong in the defence of

---

[1] *Essay on the Development of Christian Doctrine*, IV, iii, 8, drawing the conclusion that 'no Church can do without its Pope'.

the Church of Ireland and likely (Disraeli reckoned) to rally to the Conservative candidates in the forthcoming general election all who distrusted Gladstone either as a Liberal or as a High Churchman. He struck most men of the world as a talkative ass. Could he be as silly as he seemed? 'He has a foolish voice and manner which make him appear weaker than I believe he really is', Lord Derby wrote. Disraeli, who did not care for clerical society, had not taken the trouble to get to know him.

In the end, neither Wilberforce nor Ellicott was promoted. Archbishop Longley died on 27 October. Disraeli remained Prime Minister until 1 December, but Queen Victoria refused to consider Ellicott or Disraeli's other ideas. Only one man was possible in her eyes: Archibald Campbell Tait, Bishop of London, 'an excellent, pious, liberalminded, courageous man, who would be an immense support and strength to the Church in these times', as she told Disraeli on the day when she heard of the death of the 'worthy and amiable' Longley. Disraeli did his best to persuade her that Tait was too Broad Church to be a strong churchman, and too sympathetic to be a leader.

Acknowledging his abilities and virtues, Mr. Disraeli finds him as an Ecclesiastical statesman obscure in purpose, fitful and inconsistent in action, and evidently, though earnest and conscientious, a prey to constantly conflicting convictions. . . . This is to be observed of the Bishop of London, that, though apparently of a spirit somewhat austere, there is in his idiosyncrasy a strange fund of enthusiasm, a quality which ought never to be possessed by an Archbishop of Canterbury, or a Prime Minister of England. The Bishop of London sympathises with everything that is earnest; but what is earnest is not always true; on the contrary, error is often more earnest than truth. . . . Is this the Prelate who can lead the Church? The Church *must* be led: gently, but firmly and consistently. It will not do any longer merely to balance opposing and conflicting elements.

Privately he lamented that Tait's appointment 'will please only a few clerical freethinkers' and 'some Romanisers'. Was it not a tragic waste of a political opportunity? But Disraeli had already betrayed his ignorance of ecclesiastical personalities by his suggestion of Ellicott. He had no convincing alternative to offer ('I could win if I had a man'); and he had to give way to the insistent Queen.[2]

On 13 November 1868, therefore, Tait received Disraeli's 'desire, if it meet your own wishes, to recommend Her Majesty to elevate you to the Primacy'; and he promptly replied with an acceptance. Wilberforce did not even get the vacant London; any question of a move

2 *The Letters of Queen Victoria*, second series, ed. G. F. Buckle, vol. i. (John Murray, 1926), pp. 544–51. See also G. F. Buckle, *The Life of Benjamin Disraeli, Earl of Beaconsfield*, vol. v (John Murray, 1920), pp. 57–73.

for him was settled at this point by the announcement that his daughter was becoming a Roman Catholic. Disraeli moved the colourless Jackson to London from Lincoln, and Wilberforce contented himself with writing about Disraeli as 'a master of selfish cunning and unprincipled trickery'—and with advocating concessions to Gladstone's ecclesiastical policy.

Tait had been almost certain that Disraeli would choose William Thomson, Archbishop of York, for Canterbury, and would send Samuel Wilberforce to York. And this forecast reveals his opinion of Disraeli, for Thomson's career had been an example of energy rather than earnestness. While an undergraduate William Thomson wrote a textbook on philosophy which compensated for his Third in the examinations and ensured his return to the Queen's College, Oxford, after brief curacies. As a don he was a success: he was Tutor, Chaplain, Dean, Bursar, Provost, active and reforming. He was also much in demand as a preacher in London. He was consecrated Bishop of Gloucester and Bristol at the age of forty-two in 1861, and his first episcopal act was to preach about the death of Prince Albert. Within a year he was telling his handsome wife, 'My dear, I am the Archbishop of York'. She replied: 'Oh, *do* go and lie down.'

He was an active archbishop for more than a quarter of a century, promising to hold a confirmation in any village which could muster ten candidates, consecrating a hundred new churches, and specially liking to deliver vigorous, common-sense addresses to the working men of Sheffield. (Sheffield did not have its own bishop until 1913.) He certainly did better than, for example, Vernon Harcourt, who was Archbishop of York for forty years from 1807. But despite all his pleas for the reconciliation of religion and science, it could not be pretended that he had any very convincing theology of his own. Nor, for all his addresses in Sheffield, could it be pretended that he had a clear view of the emerging democracy. In 1886, four years before his death, he plunged into a major controversy with the churchwardens of St. Mary's, Beverley, who wanted to open all the seats in the church to all parishioners. This shocked Archbishop Thomson, who threatened legal proceedings and invited the parishioners to inform him of their social status so that he could personally distribute the seats in their parish church 'according to their degree'. Neither Ellicott nor Thomson as Archbishop of Canterbury would have been reckoned among Disraeli's more brilliant coups.[3]

[3] See H. Kirk-Smith, *William Thomson, Archbishop of York* (SPCK, 1958). But it is fair to remember tributes such as Frederick Arnold's: 'He is the one prelate on the bench, before any other, who is familiar with all the intellectual phenomena of unbelief, and encounters them with honesty and sympathy and real intellectual force.' *Our Bishops and Deans*, vol. i, p. 339.

Wilberforce and Tait deserve our study, for they were better examples of the industrious clergyman in Victorian England. Tait himself quoted Wilberforce's example when he spoke to the clergy: 'No men have greater means of guiding their fellows than we have, if we learn from those who have gone before us to sanctify whatever gifts God has bestowed upon us, by devotion to His service, by making the study of His Word the great object of our lives, and by giving ourselves to unwearied toil.' On that occasion, Tait could not resist adding a jab at his dead rival. 'He had doubtless his faults—some say they were grave ones—but who has not?'[4] This was more than an unkind aside. Wilberforce and Tait, united in their power of self-dedication, were dedicated to different policies.

An important issue was decided for the time being when the powerful Tait was preferred above Ellicott or Thomson; and another issue when Wilberforce was defeated by Longley's bronchitis. For Tait, now the Primate of All England, believed in liberty for Protestants, under the protection of the Crown and the law. He adhered to the Reformation of the sixteenth century, and was sympathetic with those who wanted a second Reformation to respond to the new knowledge and the new society. He regarded the work of the Church as a work of quiet education and moral improvement, and in order to preserve the Christian character of England wanted good relations with Nonconformity. In more ways than one, he was the successor of Thomas Arnold. His own speciality in this work was influence on Parliament in order to secure ecclesiastical legislation and to counteract the secularizing tendency of the age. He partly succeeded, because he had learned the art of managing men, and because the Queen and many of her people thought him wise; but the majority of the clergy in the parishes distrusted him as being too liberal, and it may be doubted whether he ever really understood clergyman any more than Thomas Arnold understood boys.

Wilberforce, on the other hand, believed in the faith and order of the Catholic Church, safeguarded by the bishop. He exhibited an apostolic zeal which made the House of Lords nervous. Gladstone warned him in 1862: 'I seem to observe that the character you have got with politicians among whom I live is that of a most able Prelate, getting all you can for the Church, asking more, giving nothing.' But the clergy became fascinated by the energy and eloquence which he threw into their favourite causes. Men who were opposed to him, or embarrassed by him, wished to emphasize a flaw in him, and they found it easily enough in his snobbery—which they attributed to ambition, and connected with a basic humbug. When Disraeli came to

---

[4] *Some Thoughts on the Duties of the Established Church of England as a National Church* (Macmillan, 1876), pp. 38–40.

John Keble by George Richmond

F. D. Maurice by Samuel Laurence

A *Vanity Fair* Cartoon of A. C. Tait

An 'Ape' Cartoon of Lord Shaftesbury

portray an Anglican ecclesiastic in his novel of 1870, *Lothair* (which he wrote to relieve his financial problems on his fall from power), he had Wilberforce in mind.

The Bishop was high-church, and would not himself have made a bad cardinal, being polished and plausible, well-lettered, yet quite a man of the world. He was fond of society, and justified his taste in this respect by the flattering belief that he was extending the power of the Church; certainly he was favouring an ambition which could not be described as moderate.

More soberly, Dean Wellesley, her confidential adviser on ecclesiastical personalities, told the Queen that 'there is a want of moral strength in Wilberforce which prevents him being really dangerous in the Church whilst his brilliant and popular talents prevent him being hated in the country'.[5]

The fatal nickname stuck to Wilberforce, in his lifetime and later: 'Soapy Sam'. He was not, however, a hypocrite. Gladstone was not easily fooled by clergymen, and Gladstone always treated him as a serious Christian, although he disapproved of some aspects of his complex character. The remarkably frank biography, using indiscreet journals and letters, which shocked many when it appeared in the 1880s, was judged by Gladstone to be 'edifying'. It seemed to confirm what Gladstone had written to the living bishop in 1869. 'Thank God it has not been in the power of jealousy or cowardice or spite, or any other evil creature, to detract one jot from the glory of that truly great episcopate, the secret of which you have written alike in the visible, outward history of the Church and in the fleshly tablets of the hearts of men.' Samuel Wilberforce had distinct thoughts of becoming Archbishop of Canterbury on Howley's death in 1848, and recorded them in his journal. He wanted to be Bishop of London in 1856; he wanted to be an archbishop again in 1862; he would have liked Canterbury or London in 1868. What happened was that Gladstone made him Bishop of Winchester in 1869. But he left behind the memory of a man who put all his many talents into the renewal of the parish and the diocese.

⁵ Robert Blake, *Disraeli* (Eyre & Spottiswoode, 1966), p. 510. Wellesley, who was Dean of Windsor 1854–82, wielded immense influence behind the scenes. Gladstone 'reckoned his life the most precious in the Church of England' and the Queen depended on his shrewd judgement, particularly after Prince Albert's death. When Tait was wrongly thought to be dying, Gladstone secured the Queen's agreement to the nomination of Wellesley to the Archbishopric of Canterbury—which suggests the mistakes which might have been made, had the Queen not been guided by Wellesley's common sense in considering other ecclesiastical appointments. See Georgina Battiscombe, 'Gerald Wellesley: a Victorian Dean', in *History Today* (March 1969).

2

Samuel Wilberforce was the son of William Wilberforce, the Member of Parliament for Yorkshire famous for his leadership of the campaign which led to the abolition of the slave trade in 1807 and of slavery in the British Empire in 1833, the year of his death. William Wilberforce, this Great Emancipator, was also famous as the author of *A Practical View of the Prevailing Religious System of Professed Christians in the Higher and Middle Classes in the Country, contrasted with Real Christianity*. When published in 1797, this at once became the Evangelical manifesto against the eighteenth century—and against the French Revolution which did much to encourage the higher and middle classes in England to look with favour on this call for personal loyalty to Christian doctrine, morality, and stability. William Wilberforce was a leader in Parliament by his eloquence and his intimacy with the younger Pitt, a leader in society by his charm and wealth, earned from trade in the Baltic; and a leader in the Church by the zeal with which he organized evangelistic and philanthropic societies, converted individuals, and spread 'seriousness'. But he was nowhere more remarkable than in his home. He resigned his seat in the Commons in order to devote himself to the education of his four sons and two daughters, and when his unsatisfactory eldest son got into financial trouble he produced the money and did without a home of his own.[6]

Such a devoted father inevitably aroused some rebellion, despite his sons' gratitude and the willingness of three of them to be ordained. Henry, the youngest, was a vicar in Anglican parishes and married (to Newman's dismay, as we saw), but he became a Roman Catholic and an ecclesiastical journalist. Robert, who had been Archdeacon of the East Riding in Yorkshire and an impressive theologian, followed Henry; had he not died in Rome in 1857, Newman would have been less isolated.[7] Samuel's only deviation from his father's position was to embrace moderately High Church views—and that was not a real deviation, for his father was responsible for enrolling him at Oriel

[6] Sir Reginald Coupland's *Wilberforce* (2nd ed., Collins, 1945) has been supplemented by Oliver Warner, *William Wilberforce and His Times* (Batsford, 1967). Studies of his circle include E. M. Howse, *Saints in Politics* (Allen & Unwin, 1952); Michael Hennell, *John Venn and the Clapham Sect* (Lutterworth Press, 1958); and Ford K. Brown, *Fathers of the Victorians* (Cambridge University Press, 1961).

[7] Robert Wilberforce's writings of 1848–53, systematically linking the Incarnation with the Church, are summarized in *The Oxford Movement*, ed. E. R. Fairweather, pp. 283–367. They anticipated the themes of Charles Gore, and as a theological basis for the Church were outclassed only by F. D. Maurice.

College in 1823. Samuel's ambition was in keeping with William Wilberforce's precepts, for the father ended many of his letters to him with the single word REMEMBER. It had been the last word of Charles I, but William Wilberforce meant by it 'all a father's (let me say a Christian parent's) wishes and prayers for a dearly-loved child's temporal and eternal happiness'.

The very temporal tinge in Bishop Wiberforce's ambition was also not totally opposed to his inheritance, for his father, although he sacrificed public office to his causes and refused a peerage, taught the young Samuel the social arts as part of his duties in the Lord's temple. He urged him to bring together

all Men who are like-minded, and who may probably at some time or other combine and concert for the public good. Never omit any opportunity, my dear Sam¹, of getting acquainted with any good man or any useful man (of course, I mean that his usefulness, in any one line, should not be countervailed by any qualities of an opposite Nature from which defilement might be contracted). More perhaps depends on the selection of acquaintances than on any other circumstance in life, except, of course, still more close and intimate Unions. Acquaintances are indeed the raw Materials from which are manufactured friends, wives, husbands, &c. . . . O my dearest Boy, *Aim high*. Don't be satisfied with being hopeful, still less with being merely 'not vicious'. How little do you know to what Services Providence may not call you.

Samuel aimed; and twenty years later, he wrote the outcome in his journal. 'Afternoon at 6, while sitting with Mrs. Sargent, arrived a messenger from Sir R. Peel, with offer of Bishopric of Oxford. I had wished for this, and now that it comes it seems *awful*. Wrote to Sir R., whose letter was remarkably cordial, and accepted.'

Samuel Wilberforce confided to his journal about the prospect of episcopal work: 'My soul is penetrated with a thrilling sense of it.' It was more than the thrill of a clerical Disraeli at the sweet smell of success. The sons of William Wilberforce belonged to a generation, the generation of Arnold and Newman, which was fascinated by the mixture of glamour and slovenliness in the Established Church. Six months before offering him Oxford, Sir Robert Peel had made him Dean of Westminster. Instantly the young man's mind had been filled by the excitements of reform. 'The school is in a dreadful state . . . the choristers are a grief of heart to me . . . the openings for exertions all round are most numerous.' In Samuel Wilberforce's itch to reform the Church of England, as in Newman's zeal to defend it, we can see the touch of Gladstone's mixed metaphor: 'The Evangelical movement filled men so full with the wine of spiritual life that larger and better vessels were required to hold it.'[8]

[8] Gladstone's shrewd article on 'The Evangelical Movement, its Parentage, Progress and Issue' was reprinted in his *Gleanings of Past Years*, vol. vii (John

The Evangelical societies of William Wilberforce's day, associations of pious and moral people in order to make others more like them, became less attractive as the objects and instruments of 'exertions' once the possibility really arose of influencing or capturing the parishes and dioceses of the Established Church itself. William Wilberforce's campaign for the abolition of the slave trade set a new moral tone, and gave a new example of efficiency, for the whole of English politics; but almost as important was its sequel in opening a new career of effectiveness to the leaders of the Church of England and in liberating them from mere place-seeking. Had not Charles Simeon, the greatest name among the Evangelical clergy (who died in 1836), set the example by his firm loyalty to the Church of England and by his enterprise in buying up advowsons (the right to appoint clergy to parishes)? And many self-effacing Evangelicals were now at work in the parishes; one had even been made a diocesan bishop in the year of Waterloo. Yet precisely because he grew to be so fascinated by the Church, and by himself as an agent of its revival, Samuel Wilberforce grew dangerously apart from Protestant Englishmen who distrusted bishops as well as priests; and he came to reflect that his Catholic conception of the Church and the episcopacy had cost him the supreme honour of the clerical profession. In 1857 he burst out to a correspondent, Golightly: 'You do not suppose that I am so blind as not to see perfectly that I might have headed the Evangelical party and been seated by them at Lambeth.' But, he went on, he believed in 'the Spiritual presence of Christ and the Personal presence of God the Holy Ghost' in the Church of England.

However, we have first to glance at Samuel Wilberforce's years of preparation. After taking a First at Oxford and a tour of Europe, he failed to join his brother Robert as a Fellow of Oriel. Instead he was married (by Charles Simeon) to Emily Sargent, with whom he had been in love since he was a boy of sixteen. After a curacy in a pretty village by the Thames, in 1830 he moved to the pleasant rectory at Brightstone in the Isle of Wight, and remained there for ten years of great happiness. With Robert he compiled his father's *Life and Letters* in seven volumes; but like his brother he was already a man with his own opinions, so much so that the seven volumes failed to make clear exactly what his father's Evangelicalism had been. He rejected

---

Murray, 1879). For a recent study by a German scholar, see Dieter Voll, *Catholic Evangelicalism* (Faith Press, 1963).

[9] See Charles Smyth, *Simeon and Church Order* (Cambridge University Press, 1940). The influence of Simeon at Cambridge and Newman at Oxford has been assessed in V. H. H. Green, *Religion at Oxford and Cambridge* (SCM Press, 1964).

Newman's attempt to dominate, but Hurrell Froude was an intimate friend. It was equally in accordance with the trend of the time that Henry Manning, the curate from Oxford who lived in Lavington Rectory in Sussex (Emily Wilberforce's old home), also became a High Churchman in the 1830s—and married Emily's equally devout, equally beautiful, and equally delicate sister, Caroline. It was natural, too, that the two other Sargent girls were carried off by two young clergymen who were Newman's disciples, George Ryder and Samuel's own youngest brother, Henry—although old Mr. Sargent had been an Evangelical.

Unlike Keble, Samuel Wilberforce rapidly attracted attention as a fluent speaker, pleading for new churches or missionaries. At one meeting in Winchester he thought that a speech by the great Palmerston was insufficiently enthusiastic about the Church, and he said so with such passion that the Duke of Wellington, who was also present, observed that he would sooner face a battery. (Thereafter Palmerston never liked Wilberforce.) Offers of larger parishes came in, and he shared none of Keble's hesitations about preferment; but he was not willing to leave his base in the Isle of Wight until, during 1839–40, he was made a Canon of Winchester, Archdeacon of Surrey, and Rector of Alverstoke. Despite his many outside interests, he was diligent both in organizing his curates and in paying warmly personal visits to his parishioners. In January 1841 he was also appointed Chaplain to Prince Albert, and while looking forward with pleasure to his future sermons at Court he settled down to write Bampton Lectures for delivery in Oxford, on the Holy Spirit. He was as happy as could be.

Then the blow fell. His Emily had given birth to a fourth son, Basil, later the eloquent Archdeacon of Westminster. Her many pregnancies cannot have helped her weak heart, and she now developed a fever. He held her through the night in his arms, thinking that the deep breaths might mean sleep. She died, and the next evening he wrote up his journal:

March 10, 1841. A day of unknown agony to me. Every feeling stunned. Paroxysms of convulsive anguish—and no power of looking up through the darkness which had settled on my soul. O Lord have mercy upon me. *March 11.* In some degree, yet but little, able to look to God, as the smiter of my soul for healing. Oh, may HE enable me to lead a life more devoted to His glory and my Master's work. May ye utter darkening of my life, which never can be dispelled, kill in me all my ambitious desires and earthly purposes; my love of money and power and place, and make me bow meekly to Christ's yoke.

Again and again around Good Friday 1841 he told himself that his Emily had been taken away because the service to which he was called was a '*desolate* service'. 'Domestic happiness not for me, or why taken away?' And again and again through thirty-four years as a widower, particularly on each anniversary of Emily's death, he told himself that she had been taken from him in order to teach him to pray more earnestly and to work less selfishly. It had come, as he had foreseen in his journal in 1838: 'I fear being scourged into devoutness.'

This was the bitter completion of his character. He naturally found it difficult to keep his vows to speak less to enthusiastic audiences and more to God, and to take no thought for the morrow. He never remarried, and found it impossible not to ache for Emily. Thus on 21 May 1867 his journal recorded that he went to church in London, to the French and British Institutions, to a debate in the House of Lords, for a ride with Bishop Ellicott, and to dinner at the Admiralty with the Prince of Wales and Disraeli; and the entry for the day includes these words: 'That unspeakable depression last night and to-day which sometimes visits me. A longing for satisfied affection, which is not satisfied. O Lord, let it bind me to THEE in whom is all my spirit longs for!' But to the end, there was a burning passion for the Church which was now his bride. Before Emily's death he had already formed the habit of many absences from home for preaching engagements. Now he was incurably restless and incurably communicative. It was his habit to write forty or more letters a day, and Tait justly spoke about his 'aptitude for business and a devotion to the details of business such as no man in this generation ever showed'. Perhaps the psychological key lay in Emily's grave.

A study ought to be made of the connexions between deaths and doctrines in Victorian England. One reason why Edward Bouverie Pusey became such an austere champion of the High Anglican kind of fundamentalism was the death of his wife Maria in 1839. Obviously it was not the only reason; his stern *Tracts for the Times* on Fasting and Baptism dated from before 1839. But as a rich young man he had been more at home in the world and a strong sportsman, and as a young Fellow of Oriel he had mastered Oriental languages in order to equip himself splendidly to be Professor of Hebrew. More, he had published a sympathetic account of German theology at a time when most English churchmen, if they knew anything about Germany, knew only about its decline into rationalism (one of Newman's stock themes). Pusey had been shaken by the English reaction to that publication, and had hastily turned back to the Fathers; but now the death of his wife plunged him into a deep and permanent melancholy. Sport, objective scholarship, and liberal sympathies were all laid aside. He imposed on himself such morbid mortifications that Keble, his spiritual director, had to beg him to take care. Among the attributes of a teacher he now lacked a free intelligence, and among the attributes of a saint he lacked joy, until death brought him to the grave beside Maria's in 1882.[10]

One reason why Henry Manning, Archdeacon of Chichester, ended up as the Cardinal Archbishop of Westminster was the death of his wife, Emily Wilberforce's sister, in all her beauty at the age of twenty-five, in 1837. He tried to console himself with Anglican work, writing his sermons by her grave, but his refusal of the invitation to follow Samuel Wilberforce as Sub-Almoner to the Queen (in charge of the Royal charities) in 1846 was an indication that Anglican honours would not heal his hurt. Wilberforce once shocked Prince Albert by remarking breezily that Manning would never have left the Church of England if they had made him a bishop; but it was not a perceptive remark.

Wilberforce himself stiffened in his churchmanship. As a young archdeacon he encouraged that obscure thinker, F. D. Maurice, and even when a bishop he tried to suggest a formula of concord to help Maurice out of his troubles at King's College, London; but later Maurice came to regard him as an enemy of serious theology. Maurice thought that this was because the bishop was drunk with the applause of churchmen. But there seems to have been another factor at work. Men around him often thought that his work was his consolation for his grief, but Wilberforce told himself over and over again that it must not be selfish work. To the Church as his bride he sacrificed his leisure: that was nothing. To her defence he sacrificed his career: that was a great deal. And to the faith of the Church as he understood it while a young man, he sacrificed also his intelligence.

3

Tait was among the many observers who agreed that Samuel Wilberforce's twenty-three years as Bishop of Oxford had changed the face of the Church of England. 'I cannot doubt that a new idea of a Bishop's work was set before the Church by your father's appointment', he wrote to Reginald Wilberforce in 1879. The tribute is the more remarkable because Tait, had he given way to his jealousy of Wilberforce, might have maintained that the remodeller of the episcopate was his own predecessor in the great see of London. Charles James Blomfield, the man who was accused by Sydney Smith of an 'ungovernable passion for business' because he wanted to reform St. Paul's Cathedral, was Bishop of London, 1828–56. Blomfield was, indeed, indefatigable in building churches and church schools, in raising money to pay for hard-working clergy, in promoting public health, and in

[10] See H. P. Liddon, *Life of Edward Bouverie Pusey*, 4 vols. (Longmans, Green, 1893–7).

sponsoring many public charities at a time when London's growth (doubling and more in the forty years from 1801) was creating the slums of Dickens and Mayhew. He had been a brilliant mathematician and classical scholar at Cambridge, and the razor-sharpness of his proud mind, contrasting with the flowers of Oxford scholarship studied in the last chapter, cut through administrative problems. More important still was his work for the Church of England as a whole. He was the ally and agent of Sir Robert Peel in the beginnings of the administrative reconstruction of the Church, and was the indispensable businessman among the Ecclesiastical Commissioners who had emerged as a permanent body in 1836. Why, then, did Tait, and public opinion, not put Blomfield first? Because there was about Blomfield a love of money or a lack of unction or a lack of theology (however one put it) which belonged to the eighteenth century. When he read in a tract from Oxford that he was a successor of the apostles, he did not quite know what to make of it. His spiritual or theological deficiences opened him to the satire of Disraeli in *Tancred*. 'There is a great spirit rising in the Church . . . a great and excellent spirit. The Church of 1845 is not the Church of 1745. We must remember that; we know not what may happen. We shall soon see a bishop at Manchester.' To which Tancred replied: 'But I want to see an angel at Manchester'.[11]

To a greater extent Samuel Wilberforce's style of pastoral zeal was anticipated by his own patron and second cousin, Bishop Charles Sumner of Winchester, and by Charles's elder brother John Bird Sumner, who was translated to Canterbury in 1848 after twenty years as Blomfield's successor at Chester. But the Sumners, although they set new standards of conscientious work as diocesan bishops and stirred up the parochial clergy, also had about them something of the eighteenth century.[12]

[11] His son Alfred wrote a *Memoir* of C. J. Blomfield in two volumes (John Murray, 1863). Olive J. Brose, *Church and Parliament: the Reshaping of the Church of England, 1828–1860* (Stanford University Press, 1959), and G. F. A. Best, *Temporal Pillars* (Cambridge University Press, 1964), are good modern studies of the origins and work of the Ecclesiastical Commissioners. A study of 'Blomfield and Peel' was contributed by P. J. Welch to the *Journal of Ecclesiastical History*, vol. xii, 1961, pp. 71ff. A fuller study was presented by the same author to London University for a doctorate.

[12] The son of a quiet country parson, John Bird Sumner fell under Charles Simeon's influence while at King's College, Cambridge, and set a new standard of decorum while in Lambeth Palace, walking to the House of Lords with an umbrella under his arm. He was the first bishop to condemn the Oxford tracts. Like his brother, Charles Sumner was promoted young: he became Bishop of Winchester at the age of thirty-seven, for forty-two years. He owed this (and earlier) promotion to the favour of Lord and Lady Conyngham; Lady Conyngham was the mistress of the Prince Regent. One of Charles Sumner's sons, George, wrote his father's biography, and inhabited a vast rectory in his diocese, at Old Alresford. It was in the drawing room of this rectory that George and

The truth was that neither Blomfield nor the Sumners possessed Wilberforce's infectious liking for people whether they were fashionable or poor. (In this, Samuel Wilberforce's predecessor was his father's friend, the saintly Henry Ryder, the first Evangelical to be a bishop—at Gloucester in 1815 and at Lichfield, 1824–36.) None of these bishops, however hard-working, combined as he did the talents of a manager with those of an orator. None knew so well what he wanted, or was so ruthless in getting it. None was responsible for Oxford, then the storm-centre of English religion; and while the Sumners and Ryder were ornaments of Evangelicalism, the Oxford Movement prevailed in the form in which Samuel Wilberforce accepted it.

Obviously many unwilberforcian bishops such as Edward Stanley at Norwich, or William Thomson at York, were among the instruments of the revival. This was the Gothic Revival, which all over England seemed to be restoring the zeal as well as the architecture of the Middle Ages.[13] But there was an angel at Oxford, magnifying his office, and because all the other bishops except Tait were in comparison rather dim, Wilberforce could be called (as he was by W. F. Hook, then Dean of Chichester) 'the great Lord Bishop of England'. He certainly knew how to make the best of his privileges as a pioneer. Compared with a modern bishop he would seem single-handed, for he had no professional secretary and (although he had himself been an active archdeacon) he took care that his diocesan officials were cyphers. He applied the personal touch to everything, and in the course of his paternalism spent far more money than a modern bishop would. He was so far from being the slave of any machine that he was for long periods away from his diocese, as an ecclesiastical statesman or social lion in London or as the squire of Lavington; such absences often accounted for nearly half the year. But everyone knew who was Bishop of Oxford.

When he was appointed at the age of forty, Prince Albert wrote him a long letter about his duties in the House of Lords. He was to abstain from party politics 'beyond giving a general support to the Queen's Government', but 'he should come forward whenever the

---

Mary Sumner founded the Mothers' Union in 1876, the idea being to unite 'lady mothers with cottage mothers' on a devotional basis. Samuel Wilberforce's son Ernest was the principal speaker at the meeting in Portsmouth nine years later which resulted in the growth of the Mothers' Union into a national and international body by the time of Mary Sumner's death at Winchester in 1921. See Joyce Coombes, *George and Mary Sumner* (Sumner Press, 1965).

[13] Some idea of the churches which stand as monuments to this revival may be gained from B. F. L. Clarke, *Church Builders of the Nineteenth Century* (SPCK, 1938). The architectural revival was initiated by the Cambridge Camden Society, for which see J. F. White, *The Cambridge Movement* (Cambridge University Press, 1962).

interests of Humanity are at stake'. 'As to religious affairs', wrote the Prince, 'a bishop cannot but take an active part in them; but let it always be the part of a *Christian*, not of a mere *Churchman*.' Albert clearly hoped that in Wilberforce he had found an eloquent ally in the causes of liberal uplift and social progress. But gradually Albert and Victoria came to understand that the young Bishop of Oxford had some High Church principles, with the result that Wilberforce noted in his journal in 1849 an 'evident withdrawal of Royal favour'. 'The Queen', she wrote to Gladstone on hearing of his death, 'admired and liked him *most before* he became a Bishop, and before he leant so much to those High Church views which did harm, and which are so great a misfortune to the Church.'[14] He could not even enjoy the nobility of martyrdom, for the Prince and his obedient wife concluded that they had been tricked into trusting Soapy Sam. 'He does everything for some object', said the Prince to Lord Aberdeen, whom Wilberforce tried to use as a peace-maker in 1855; and the Prince could not be persuaded by Lord Aberdeen that Wilberforce's object was good.

It was not that he alarmed the Court by developing much sympathy with any High Church extremes. A few days after his consecration, he wrote to Professor Pusey rebuking 'a subtle and therefore most dangerous form of self-will. . . . This seems to lead you to judge the Church which you ought to obey.' But he did seem too much the High Churchman in his handling of the crisis caused in Oxford by the Crown's (more accurately Lord John Russell's) nomination of Renn Dickson Hampden, Newman's rival and enemy, as Bishop of Hereford in 1847.[15]

Wilberforce joined with Charles Sumner, Blomfield, and ten other bishops in a Remonstrance against this appointment which, they claimed, would exite 'apprehension and alarm' in the minds of the clergy. Other bishops protested privately. Lord John Russell brushed all this aside, forcing Hampden's clerical opponents to institute proceedings for heresy against him in his capacity as Vicar of Ewelme in the diocese of Oxford. Under the Church Discipline Act of 1840 Wilberforce had to agree to this lawsuit, and he did so, hoping that Hampden would be so alarmed as to avow his orthodoxy and withdraw the writings which had been censored by the guardians of orthodoxy in Oxford. As Keble noted, with the cattiness to which that saint could yield, the new and young Bishop of Oxford had 'an earnest desire of peace joined to a fancy that he was the person to make it'. He wrote to Hampden urging all this, but Hampden in reply took the

---

[14] *Letters of Queen Victoria*, second series, vol. ii. p. 264

[15] His daughter Henrietta edited *Some Memorials of Renn Dickson Hampden, Bishop of Hereford* (Longmans, Green, 1871).

same line as the Prime Minister who had nominated him. Wilberforce's doctrinal questions were an insult; legally he was entitled to be Bishop of Hereford. At the same time Hampden pointed out (in a letter addressed to Provost Hawkins but passed to Wilberforce) that a pamphlet written by him in 1834, on which his accusers were relying, had not been reprinted and was not now being sold with his sanction, and that he was intending to revise the Bampton Lectures.

This skilful reply unnerved Wilberforce, who brooded over the Bampton Lectures more carefully than he had done before. As he read, he saw how difficult it would be to nail the learned but obscure lecturer down as a heretic. Only the pamphlet exposed Hampden to the law; and now Hampden had denied that it had been circulated according to his wish during the years to which the Church Discipline Act limited his responsibility to the Bishop of Oxford. Wilberforce therefore withdrew his consent to the case, and with his desertion the campaign against Hampden sputtered out. Pusey was left complaining that the Bishop of Oxford's conduct had caused a greater scandal than the original appointment. By opposing and yet allowing Hampden's consecration, Wilberforce had in fact got the worst of both worlds. The Court now regarded him as a traitor to Prince Albert's conception of liberal Christianity, while High Churchmen regarded him as unstable. Newman had long been calling him a humbug. Not many observers shared the insight of the charitable Arthur Stanley: '*He had nothing to gain by it*, any more than he had when he jumped out of the carriage to pick up geological specimens, so I cannot but think it is equally sincere; and any act of undoubted sincerity in him is worth ten times as much as it would have been in another person.' As he mulled over the situation, Wilberforce thanked the God who had removed the snare of ambition from him, and consoled himself with the thought that justice had been his aim throughout the negotiation. But obviously he was now in no position to dominate ecclesiastical politics, and he threw himself with all the more zest into diocesan work.

Berkshire had been added to the diocese of Oxford only in 1836, and Buckinghamshire only on his own appointment, so that Wilberforce's task was to unite as well as to renew the Church in the great area over which he now presided. His very first ordination gave the clue to his policy. Where before there had usually been only the academic examination, a brief interview, and the service, Wilberforce made the occasion intensely devotional, intensely personal, and, to the young men who knelt before him, intensely moving. He also transformed the service of confirmation, which had previously tended to be a formality conducted for large numbers in a few centres by a bishop with his mind in the House of Lords. Wilberforce would go to a village and confirm there, taking pains to make the occasion memorable for each candidate on whom he laid his hands. He seemed to be ubiquitous by means of horses or the new railways. He set himself to inspect the clergy, and to charm the leading laity; and visit by visit, year by year, in six hundred parishes he built up a triumph for himself and for his idea of the Church.[16]

The results were solid. Over a hundred new churches and seventy new parsonages were built in the diocese in his time, and over 250 churches were rebuilt or thoroughly restored. A theological college for ordinands was opened next to his palace at Cuddesdon, a village seven miles from Oxford, in 1854. It was intended to be primarily diocesan, although Cuddesdon College soon achieved a national status.[17] His control over his clergy was increased by the fact that he managed to become patron of over a hundred livings in the diocese, instead of thirteen when he arrived. He used his rural deans and his own energy to obtain and act on detailed reports about the preaching, visiting, and general life of the parish priests. The office of rural dean had been revised in the 1830s and 1840s (by Blomfield among others), but its was Samuel Wilberforce who taught them to gather their clergy regularly and who assembled the rural deans themselves annually at Cuddesdon. He led his clergy personally in spiritual retreats, and his lay people in missions. And at Culham he founded another college, this time for training schoolmasters for the church schools which were regarded as indispensable parts of the mission of the parish churches. The kind of advice which he gave may be illustrated from this letter to a priest who was sad because his parish seemed to be stagnant. Wilberforce reminded him that 'I know by eighteen years' experience as a parish priest so many of the parish priest's *difficulties*'; but he also pointed out that stagnation 'is a rare and exceptional thing in my diocese', and he frankly attributed it to the parish priest's idleness. 'Pray for the outpouring of the Spirit on your own soul and on your ministry, and then live in your parish, live for your parish, work in it as a man only can work who has come to his work from intercession for his people.'

Naturally a great challenge came from the need to fit the disciples of the Oxford Movement into the limits of the law and public opinion of England. He had to keep an eye on Cuddesdon College lest Romanizing ritual should destroy the confidence of Church of England people, and for this reason Henry Liddon, the first Vice-Principal, was

---

[16] Some of the background was sketched in D. McClatchey, *Oxfordshire Clergy, 1777–1869* (Clarendon Press, 1960). Wilberforce's 1854 Visitation Returns, ed. E. P. Baker, have been published by the Oxfordshire Record Society (1954).

[17] See Owen Chadwick, *The Founding of Cuddesdon* (Oxford, privately printed, 1954).

eased out. He had to keep an eye on the new sisterhoods, lest the revival of the religious life in the Church of England should be wrecked on Protestant suspicion. A later generation might think Wilberforce an over-fussy administrator, but it testified to his wisdom that he was able to hold in his diocese formidable Anglo-Catholic activists such as W. J. Butler the founder of the Wantage Sisters, T. T. Carter the founder of the women's community of St. John the Baptist at Clewer, and R. M. Benson the founder of the men's society of St. John the Evangelist in Cowley.[18]

Such an achievement cannot be appreciated without recalling the circumstances. Newman became a Roman Catholic a fortnight after Samuel Wilberforce became a bishop. Samuel's brothers Henry, Robert, and William, his sister-in-law Mary, his brother-in-law George Ryder, and his daughter Ella, all took the road to Rome, and his darkly tragic view of such moves did not arise solely from acute embarrassment. In 1853, after Robert's conversion, he thought of resigning the bishopric, 'in order that without the reproach of remaining in the English Communion for the sake of my preferments, I may testify with what little strength is given me for the rest of my life against the cursed abominations of the Papacy'. He did not resign, but he did testify.

He would argue that no healthy Englishmen of the nineteenth century would stand for the imitation of Rome. Any signs, however small, that the great Protestant decision of the sixteenth and seventeenth centuries was being undermined were condemned. Wilberforce hated any signs of affectation among clergy or ordinands, any crucifixes above the fireplace or sorrowful Madonnas on the walls, and above all any thought that a young person might discuss sex with a priest in confession. When the eccentric J. L. Lyne ('Father Ignatius') proposed to found a new monastic order wearing the old monastic dress, Wilberforce warned him: 'You are sacrificing everywhere the great reality for which you have sacrificed yourself to the puerile imitation of a past phase of service which it is just as impossible for you to revive in England as it would be for you to resuscitate an Egyptian mummy and set it upon the throne of the Pharaohs.'[19]

Tait, who sympathized with the religious earnestness and social usefulness of the revived sisterhoods, uttered similarly patriotic warnings. But Wilberforce added an argument which was not nearly

[18] For the revival of religious orders in the Church of England, see A. M. Allchin, *The Silent Rebellion* (SCM Press, 1958), and Peter Anson, *The Call of the Cloister* (rev. ed., SPCK, 1964). The first religious vows were those taken by Marian Hughes in Oxford in 1841, but the first community arose out of the work of the Sisters of Mercy in the disease-ridden slums of Devonport in 1848, for which see T. J. Williams, *Priscilla Lydia Sellon* (SPCK, 1965).

[19] A biography of J. L. Lyne has been written by Arthur Calder-Marshall, *The Enthusiast* (Faber & Faber, 1962).

so clear or so prominent in the teachings of Tait. It was the argument which replied to Newman and to all who had followed him: if you want to see a system which is no paper religion but manifestly holy, manifestly Catholic, manifestly apostolic, you can take a look at my diocese.

4

But how was the holy, Catholic, and apostolic character of the Church of England to be shown at the national level? In January 1852 Gladstone stayed with Wilberforce and immediately afterwards wrote a private memorandum recording their joint alarm about the ecclesiastical situation. The heart of the danger, as seen by these two churchmen, lay in the bishops' unwillingness to trust and defend traditional Christian doctrine authoritatively. Since 1833 the power to define the Church of England's doctrine had moved to the Judicial Committee of the Privy Council as the final court of appeal (previously there had been a special 'Court of Delegates'); on this body the Archbishops of Canterbury and York and the Bishop of London were outnumbered by the lay lawyers. The committee had recently ordered that Charles Gorham, an Evangelical who believed in conversion, should be instituted to a parish in Devon although the extremely conservative and extremely combative High Churchman who was Bishop of Exeter, Harry Phillpotts, had gone to all possible lengths in order to show that Gorham did not believe the Prayer Book's teaching that infants were regenerate (born again) in Holy Baptism.[20]

The bishops appeared indifferent to this danger, even those appointed before Lord John Russell's time; yet when in 1850 the Pope gave English titles to the bishops whom he sent to 'govern' the Roman Catholics in England, the bishops of the Church of England were prominent in the general outcry of Protestants against Papal Aggression. Romanizing stirred the bishops, but heresy—was not the Gorham Judgment heresy, when the Apostles' Creed included belief in Baptism 'for the remission of sins'?—left them unmoved. This stirred the Bishop of Oxford to the depths. The Gorham case was the reason given by his brother Robert, and by his brother-in-law Henry Manning for their renunciation of the Orders of a church under the control of laymen who flouted Catholic doctrine.

By the end of the year 1852, however, the situation had begun to

---

[20] The appointment of Phillpotts had been the Duke of Wellington's last act as Prime Minister in 1830. See J. C. S. Nias, *Gorham and the Bishop of Exeter* (SPCK, 1951), and G. C. B. Davies, *Henry Phillpotts, Bishop of Exeter* (SPCK, 1954).

brighten for Wilberforce and Gladstone. Lord John Russell's ministry fell, to be replaced for a few months by the Conservatives under Lord Derby; and Derby turned a blind eye to the Convocation elected by the clergy of the Province of Canterbury when it debated for three days instead of the usual one. Specially since the Gorham case, Wilberforce and other churchmen had grown convinced that the Convocation must be revived. It was older than Parliament, yet for 135 years it had been in virtual suspension because successive governments had not wanted the nuisance of clergymen arguing in public. In 1852 the Archbishop of Canterbury was very nervous about the whole affair, and the Archbishop of York refused to have a Convocation in his Province, so that York did not copy Canterbury until 1861. But the 'proctors' elected by the parochial clergy in the Southern Province—together with the deans, archdeacons, and some other dignitaries who greatly outnumbered them in the Convocation—did now meet for business. Although no layman was included, this step represented the beginning of the self-government of the Church of England. In 1861 'letters of business' enabling the Convocation to amend a canon (or ecclesiastical law) were issued by the Crown; and Tait, while he still regarded Parliament as the chief forum for debates and the chief instrument of legislation on ecclesiastical issues, made no attempt to undo the Convocations. Although a layman, Henry Hoare, had organized the Society for the Revival of Convocation, Wilberforce's indomitable advocacy of this revival gained, and deserved, the chief credit. The Church of England thus embarked on the slow journey which ended in the first meeting of its General Synod, jointly clerical and lay, on 4 November 1970.[21]

So the Gorham Judgment had led to the revival of the Convocation as the clerical forum. The next doctrinal crisis, because its chief figure was a bishop overseas, led to the creation of another feature in the modern Anglican scene: the Lambeth Conference of the bishops of the world-wide Anglican Communion.

The bishop concerned was Colenso of Natal, who had begun in the right road: he had decided to become a missionary as a result of one of Wilberforce's sermons, and Wilberforce had preached at his consecration as a bishop. The story of Bishop Colenso's alleged heresies, and of the volume of liberal *Essays and Reviews* which preceded that sensation, belongs to our study of Tait. Wilberforce was passionately

[21] The story was put in its historical context in Lecture 7 of the Bampton Lectures by E. W. Kemp, *Counsel and Consent* (SPCK, 1961), and in Chapter IV of K. A. Thompson, *Bureaucracy and Church Reform* (Clarendon Press, 1970). The Diocesan Church Conferences, of which the first was held at Ely in 1866, and unofficial national Church Congresses, of which the first was held at Oxford with Wilberforce in the chair in 1862, provided opportunities for some wider discussion.

convinced that Tait was wrong to defend Colenso's legal position, as he was wrong to defend the legal position of the contributors to *Essays and Reviews*. The arguments between the two men in these years were so heated that once, when Wilberforce threw a note across the table to him, Tait expected it to contain a debating point, only to find that Wilberforce was recommending a better make of boots for the sake of his health. Wilberforce was also convinced that his brother-bishops, not the English State, should decide whether or not Colenso was fit to be Bishop of Natal, and he threw his oratory and political skill behind the request which came from the Anglican bishops and clergy in Canada for a synod to uphold 'the truth of Religion' against critics of the Bible such as Colenso.

It was his own view, expressed to the House of Lords, that 'the Church of England in the colonies was a purely voluntary body, like the Wesleyans or any other body of religionists'; and he was keenly interested in the Protestant Episcopal Church in the United States. So he agreed with the Canadians, despite the suspicion of the more Establishment-minded divines in England such as Tait and Stanley. Archbishop Longley used him to negotiate with Colenso's principal accuser, Bishop Gray, and to write the message of the First Lambeth Conference which eventually met in September 1867. 'Keep whole and undefiled the faith once delivered to the saints', wrote Wilberforce to the faithful on behalf of the bishops. 'We beseech you to hold fast, as the sure word of God, all the canonical scriptures of the Old and New Testament.' Privately, Wilberforce reckoned that gathering 'a very great success. Its strongly anti-Erastian tone, rebuking the Bishop of London and strengthening those who hope to maintain the Establishment by maintaining, instead of by surrendering, the dogmatic character of the Church, was quite remarkable.'[22]

It is scarcely too much to say that Wilberforce discharged some of the most important of the duties of national leadership while Archbishops Sumner and Longley occupied Lambeth Palace. He did hope to go to York in 1862, and he received many letters of sympathy when William Thomson was appointed over his head; he accepted the pointed invitation of the Dean of York to preach in York Minster on the first public occasion after Thomson's enthronement. And it seems clear that he also hoped that Gladstone would reach power before Archbishop Longley reached heaven. From Disraeli he knew he could hope for little, for Disraeli no less than the Queen thought High Church views dangerous, and warned Wilberforce a month before Longley's death that 'it is all over with the Church of England, if she be disconnected with the State'. By September 1868, however, Gladstone was able to offer the see of Winchester, which old Charles Sumner had

[22] See Alan M. G. Stephenson, *The First Lambeth Conference* (SPCK, 1967).

at last resigned (while continuing to draw a pension from the revenues of the see and to live in Farnham Castle). The work would be harder, for the diocese then included South London with the whole of Surrey, Hampshire, the Isle of Wight, and the Channel Islands. But for Samuel Wilberforce it meant being enthroned in the city where Emily died and living at Lavington in her home, near her grave.

He plunged into all the work, but it brought severe heart attacks and he could no longer conceal his constant tiredness and depression. Then deliverance came. On 19 July 1873 he was far more cheerful as he went for a ride on Abinger Common. He was going to stay with his companion, Earl Granville. The summer's day was fine. The horse stumbled, he was killed instantly; and he was buried beside his wife.

What, then, was wrong with him? Within the terms of the religion which he acknowledged, not much was. Yet something was. 'The late Bishop of Winchester', wrote Matthew Arnold in his Preface to *God and the Bible*, 'was a man in high office and dignity, a man at the same time of great gifts; he spoke to the English public with authority and with responsibility proportionate to that authority; yet he freely permitted himself the use of clap trap.' Wilberforce showed that very clearly over *Essays and Reviews* and over Colenso, but an incident which later came to seem symbolic of the whole Victorian crisis of faith has not yet been recounted.[23]

At Oxford on a Saturday morning in June 1860 there was a meeting of one of the sections of the British Association for the Advancement of Science, to discuss some of the wider aspects of the new theory of the descent of man from the lower animals. The Bishop of Oxford spoke, with his genial charm and wit, with his eloquence about the dignity of man, with his stream of half-digested science. And as had happened before, one of his jokes was unfortunate. Surely it could not be on his grandmother's side that the evolutionist claimed descent from the apes? So a dedicated widower appealed to the Victorian sense of gallantry to the ladies; and so the proud son of the Wilberforces aroused the cheers and the laughter—now, as on innumerable other occasions. But in the audience (very reluctantly) was the scientist T. H. Huxley, the man who coined the word 'agnostic'. 'The Lord hath delivered him into my hands!' he whispered to his neighbour— for agnostic mid-Victorians were biblical. In a quiet, dignified reply, he annihilated the bishop, declaring that he would rather be descended from an ape than from 'a man highly endowed by nature and possessed of great means of influence and yet who employs these faculties and that influence for the mere purpose of introducing ridicule into a grave

[23] See Donald Fleming, *John William Draper and the Religion of Science* (University of Pennsylvania Press, 1950), pp. 66–73, and Owen Chadwick, *The Victorian Church*, Part II, pp. 9–12.

scientific discussion'. The undergraduates present led the applause for Huxley.

After that reply, even the laughing clergy, the ladies, and the fundamentalist admiral who had attacked man's evolution must have sensed they would have done better not to put around the story in advance that the Bishop of Oxford would 'smash Darwin'. And those among them who knew Archbishop Tait must have known that in such a debate he might have bored, but would not have exposed Christianity to a smash.[24]

<h1 style="text-align:center">5</h1>

Archibald Campbell Tait was born and educated in Edinburgh, the son of an eccentric and impoverished gentleman. Since his mother died when he was three years old, in 1814, he owed everything to his nurse, Betty Morton; and since he was born club-footed, he owed his ability to climb in life to the strange tin boots which a doctor made him wear in boyhood. The pale-faced, pathetically serious young scholar, knowing that scholarship was the only path upwards, entered Glasgow University and then (with a scholarship) Balliol College, Oxford.

He was called 'the little bishop' at home—a strange title, for the family was Presbyterian. Even more ominous was a conversation which took place during his first visit to London, in 1830, when on his way to Balliol at the age of nineteen. One evening he returned from a walk. 'Where have you been too, Archie?' he was asked. 'Walking through Lambeth', he replied. 'Through Lambeth!' was the astonished answer; 'why, what ever possessed you to walk through Lambeth?' 'Well, I wanted to see how I shall like the place when I get there.' When he reached Oxford he obtained one preliminary qualification. He was confirmed as a member of the Church of England.

His success in Anglican life began with a fellowship at Balliol in 1834. A year later he was appointed a tutor of this, one of the two foremost colleges in Oxford. Stanley and Jowett were among his first pupils; others included Frederick Temple and Matthew Arnold. In the course of his teaching he would urge his pupils to study the Bible with the honest care which they were expected to give to the Greek and Roman classics. (Later on, some of his former Balliol pupils embarrassed Tait by reminding him of this.) But he was very far from

[24] The best introductions to the Victorian debate between religion and science are in C. C. Gillispie, *Genesis and Geology* (Harvard University Press, 1951), and in R. M. Young's contribution to *The Victorian Crisis of Faith*, ed. A. Symondson (SPCK, 1970).

being too critical in religion. (When he delivered his 'charge' to the diocese of Canterbury in 1880, published under the title *The Church of the
Future*, he was still urging his hearers, as he had urged undergraduates
at Balliol, to turn to Bishop Butler.) It was in relation to slumbering
institutions that he would be a reformer. He published a pamphlet in
1839: *Hints on the Formation of a Plan for the Safe and Effectual
Revival of the Professorial System at Oxford*. This was based partly
on his first-hand knowledge of Germany. (Later on, Tait made use
of his knowledge of other universities with an effect momentous for
Oxford.) Soon he was ordained, and after the week's work in Balliol
would ride over to a neglected village, to sleep in a cottage before
taking the Sunday services.

This hard-headed Scot was never charmed by Newman. Evening by
evening he would argue in the Balliol Common Room with W. G.
Ward—a fat little man, in many ways like a character out of the
comic operas which he adored, who would kick off his shoes and settle
down over the port under the candles to enjoy his own brilliance as
the *enfant terrible* of the Oxford Movement. Ward, who used to say
that he was made a deacon as an Arnoldian and a priest as a New-
manite, was now a frequent contributor to the *British Critic*, which
Newman edited, and many of his articles were more or less anti-
Anglican.[25] One February morning in 1841 he handed to Tait Tract
Ninety, which he had challenged Newman to write. 'Here is something
worth reading.' Tait, already goaded by Ward, was shocked by Newman; and when a clergyman named Charles Golightly (an embittered
ex-disciple of Newman's) organized a protest, Tait's name was the
most weighty of the four college tutors who signed. And when Thomas
Arnold died, it seemed fitting that Tait should carry on the Doctor's
work, although other candidates for Rugby were his superiors in
scholarship, notably C. J. Vaughan, one of Arnold's favourites.[26]

[25] Ward's vast and shapeless book, *The Ideal of a Christian Church Considered in Comparison with Existing Practice* (1844), made clear enough his
feeling that Rome was nearer than Canterbury to the ideal. He was then strip-
ped of his Oxford degrees, married, and received into the Roman Catholic
Church, where he supported Manning against Newman. His son Wilfrid wrote
his life as well as Newman's, in two volumes (Macmillan, 1887–93).

[26] Vaughan became Headmaster of Harrow, where he raised the standards of
the boys, and their numbers from forty to 469. But in 1859 he was compelled to
resign when a letter arising from an infatuation with a boy in the school became
known, and four years later he had to refuse the Bishopric of Rochester when
threatened with exposure. See Phyllis Grosskurth, *John Addington Symonds*
(Longmans, Green, 1964), pp. 30–41. He became Vicar of Doncaster, Master
of the Temple in London, and Dean of Llandaff, and was specially notable as
a preacher to young men and as a trainer of some four hundred for Ordination:
see the extracts from his sermons, *The Word of Life*, edited by R. R. Williams
(SPCK, 1960). Bishop Westcott was on his staff at Harrow, and Archbishop

Stanley did some lobbying for Tait, but when the election was made his only reaction to the 'aweful' news was to beg his old Oxford tutor 'to lay aside every thought for the present except that of repairing your deficiencies'. As Headmaster of Rugby, Tait was never able to overcome the three sad facts that he was not a classical scholar of the first rank, that he had no previous acquaintance with an English school, and that he was not Thomas Arnold. He seemed dull, cold, and aloof. But Rugby in his time did not collapse, although a hundred extra boys came to the school as a result of the publication of Stanley's *Life*. The effort needed to maintain the Arnold tradition when all around knew that the glory had been buried beneath the chapel made the headmaster weary and drowsy. Eventually, in 1848, he was so ill with rheumatic fever that he was thought to be dying. His nurse was his wife Catharine, an archdeacon's daughter, Samuel Wilberforce's cousin, herself sweet, efficient (she supervised the Rugby School accounts), and High Church, all to Tait's advantage.[27]

What was to be done for Archie Tait, who clearly could not carry on as the sick and not entirely successful successor to Arnold? The answer seemed to be a cathedral, where in dignified retirement he could try to develop himself as a scholar. Accordingly in 1850 Lord John Russell sent him to the half-ruined cathedral of Carlisle and to a Deanery which Arthur Stanley had already refused as 'so remote'. On his first Sunday there, Tait found only ten communicants; there were only seventy-two on his last Sunday, more than he had ever seen before. Yet in the Lake District he recovered his health, although the action of his heart was always irregular. More, in Carlisle he fought his canons, cleaned up the cathedral's worst abuses, reorganized its grammar school, handed over its estates to the Ecclesiastical Commissioners (Carlisle was the first cathedral to do this), and emerged as a pastor and teacher of the poor—at that time an astonishing role for a dean. More yet, he accepted Lord John Russell's invitation to serve on the Royal Commission appointed to recommend reforms at Oxford.

He became the most active member of that Commission, which (with Stanley as secretary) was the instrument in sweeping away much of Newman's Oxford. The powers of the Heads of Houses were to be cut down; the status of the professors was to be raised; the insistence on ordination for fellows of colleges was to be relaxed; Gentlemen-Commoners were to be abolished (these were rich, and normally idle, undergraduates); scholarships were to be thrown open for a far wider

---

Davidson was among the 'Doves' whom he prepared for Orders. Dean Stanley, whose sister Catherine married him, frequently used to walk along the Embankment from Westminster Abbey to take tea with Dean Vaughan.

[27] Tait contributed long memoirs of his wife and son to *Catharine and Craufurd Tait*, edited at his request by William Benham (Macmillan, 1879).

competition; and undergraduates who could not afford to belong to a college were to be admitted to the university. This great Blue Book on Oxford, published 1852, caused there the greatest sensation to follow Newman's conversion. The iron Duke of Wellington took it to bed with him on the night of his death, and gradually the reforms proposed were effected. Tait added to the official report a boldly personal recommendation: that undergraduates should no longer be made to sign the Thirty-nine articles.[28]

He never wrote the scholarly book for which his friends hoped. Like Wilberforce, he was a man of action—but what action was there in Carlisle? He was in exile. 'At times', he wrote, 'I feel greatly depressed here by the uncongenial spirits amongst whom I am thrown.' But escape came through a bitter ordeal.

His consolation during the strain and illness at Rugby, and through the quarrels at Carlisle, was his family. Six daughters brought life and merriment to the Deanery. But between 10 March and 10 April 1856, five of them were laid in a single grave in Stanwix churchyard: first Charlotte ('Chatty'), then Susan, then Frances, then Catharine ('Catty') then Mary ('May'). It was scarlet fever. At the time, Tait wrote in the journal to which he had confided so many anxious prayers against depression or ambition: 'When last I wrote I had six daughters on earth; now I have one, an infant. O God, Thou hast dealt very mysteriously with us. . . .' Almost a quarter of a century later he arranged for the printing of his wife's detailed description of their piety, their innocence, their gaiety, their loveliness, and their deaths. In writing it, she had found some relief for the agony which remained with her and with him to their own deaths.[29]

With their one surviving child, the baby Lucy, they spent the summer in a borrowed house on Ullswater. They sought comfort in the hills and in the knowledge that their tragedy had aroused the sympathy of the whole English upper class including the Queen. But how could they return to the empty Deanery among the quarrelling canons? Then the royal sympathy combined with the Liberal government's gratitude for that report on Oxford, and with Lord Shaftesbury's gratitude for that moderation in theological liberalism. There was another entry in the journal.

Sept. 17th, 1856.—I have this morning received a letter from Lord Palmerston saying that he has the Queen's command to offer me the See of London. I am now (11 a.m.) about to take an hour of prayer. The subjects on which to pray are these—That I may not act rashly, seeing that I have no doubt

[28] The intrigues and battles in the university were chronicled and analysed by W. R. Ward, *Victorian Oxford* (Frank Cass, 1965).
[29] It forms the central portion of *Catharine and Craufurd Tait*.

about accepting the offer. . . . This is certainly not a post which I should ever have dreamed of for myself. The preparation which Thou hast given me for it has been deep affliction.

6

Tait wrote truly when he wrote that his agony as a father had been his main preparation as a Father-in-God. He certainly had little practical training to succeed Blomfield at the head of a thousand clergy in London. Neither Oxford, nor Rugby, nor Carlisle had familiarized him with ecclesiastical problems or personalities. Gladstone was indignant that he had been chosen instead of the tested Wilberforce, and so was Wilberforce. Twenty-six years after his first visit, Archie Tait of Glasgow returned to London with the equipment of a broken heart— which, added to his strong Scots mind, was enough.

'The only advice I should venture to offer is that you should do as little as possible', wrote Benjamin Jowett from Balliol.[30] But to Tait, as to Wilberforce, work was the great consolation in grief. He became as efficient as Blomfield had been, and in his eagerness for new churches launched an appeal for half a million pounds. But he was more earnest than Blomfield, for he knew that the Gospel had to match its strength against death. When people protested that this Bishop of London was not so dignified as his predecessors, his retort was that the Church of England might 'die of its dignity'. He preached in Covent Garden, from a railway train, and on the streets. He even encouraged Church of England services in theatres. Amid great excitement he persuaded Westminster Abbey and St. Paul's Cathedral to hold popular evening services. He gathered his clergy in St. Paul's and read them his 'charge'. It grew dark under the dome, but the bishop had some candles; through five hours Tait's voice went on, urging the clergy to efficiency and evangelism. The Evangelicals, although they still suspected him because of his associations with Balliol and Rugby, were compelled to acknowledge that he was a Christian.

The High Church ritualists of London—who in their desire to take the Oxford Movement into the imaginations of the poor were now indulging in practices which had held little interest for Newman, Keble, or Pusey—felt the lash of the ex-headmaster's pen as a disciplinarian.[31]

[30] It was a characteristic piece of worldly wisdom from one who as Master of Balliol, 1870–93, enjoyed nothing more than the successful careers of his pupils. Sir Geoffrey Faber's *Jowett* (Faber & Faber, 1957) is a first-class study of an educationist who calmly preserved a more or less Christian Platonism as his personal creed despite many bitter attacks from the orthodox.

[31] The very word 'ritualists' indicated the lack of understanding among educated Victorians, for the new enthusiasts almost completely adhered to the

'I must, therefore, lay my commands upon you to discontinue the practice you have introduced without my authority . . . of lighting the candles on the Communion Table in broad daylight.' 'As to the green vestments, stoles, or whatever they may have been . . . I very deeply regret that you should think it right to assume the unusual garments you described to me. . . . If you continue with this, it is against my express order.' Most conservative High Churchmen (for example, Pusey) applauded such commands—especially when the alternative might be the riots seen Sunday after Sunday in the dockland parish of St. George-in-the-East, when these illegal Roman ornaments were seen in church.

Was he overtaxing his strength? Lord Palmerston thought so, and in 1862 offered him the lighter work of York, intending to move Wilberforce to London. But Tait was enjoying London too much; he stayed on, despite a severe heart attack, for some of the most stormy years of Victorian religion.

Because he was Bishop of London, and because he was the canny Archie Tait, he could not do everything which Stanley, for example, wanted done to bring in a new era. In 1860 Benjamin Jowett and six other Broad Churchmen, including H. B. Wilson who had been one of the tutors against Tract Ninety and Frederick Temple who was now Headmaster of Rugby, published a volume of *Essays and Reviews*. For a time there was a lull. Then Wilberforce fiercely denounced the volume, called for replies to it, and increased its circulation amid the excitement. Tait did not leap to the defence of these 'seven against Christ'. Indeed, he signed his name to the reply made by the Archbishops of Canterbury and York and twenty-four diocesan bishops to a very agitated protest from some country parsons in Dorsetshire. The bishops expressed 'the pain it has given them that any clergyman of our Church should have published such opinions as those concerning which you have addressed us. We cannot understand how these opinions can be held consistently with an honest subscription to the formularies of our Church, with many of the fundamental doctrines of which they appear to us essentially at variance.' This statement was drafted by Wilberforce. Connop Thirlwall, whom Tait called 'the most learned man of the century', was among the twenty-three bishops (out of twenty-six) who supported its condemnation of *Essays and Reviews*.[32]

---

authorized *rite*, the words of the Book of Common Prayer, and ought to have been called 'ceremonialists' on account of their desire to add colour and movement to this rite.

[32] Connop Thirlwall, who is said to have been fluent in Latin and Greek at the age of four, was dismissed as a tutor at Trinity College, Cambridge, for advocating that Dissenters should be allowed university degrees, but wrote a history of Greece in a Yorkshire rectory. Ecclesiastical life so absorbed him

So was the now comfortable Bishop Hampden; and Charles Kingsley was among the vicars who advised their curates not to trouble themselves with the book but to concentrate on parish work.

Tait's feebleness in signing Wilberforce's condemnation of *Essays and Reviews* brought wounding letters from his Broad Church friends. Stanley reminded him that he had already declared his own opinion that the essays by Jowett and Temple, if not the others, had nothing seriously wrong with them; 'what can I say in your defence?' Temple was so deeply embittered that he never entirely forgave Tait. He, too, recalled that in private Tait had raised no great objection to his own contribution. Yet now Tait had condemned the whole book, and had virtually demanded that its authors should recant or resign.

'If you do not wish to alienate your friends, do not treat them as you have treated me', Temple wrote in his fury. 'What you did had not the intention, but it had all the effect, of treachery. You will not keep friends if you compel them to feel that in every crisis of life they must be on their guard against trusting you.' In his next letter Temple poured salt into the wound. 'You ought not to make it impossible for a friend to calculate on what you will do. I do not care for your severity. I do care for being cheated.' In a third letter Temple added vinegar, by referring to Tait's wish to appease the Evangelicals. 'Your friends complain that they cannot count on you: your enemies say that they can, and that you will always do what is popular with the Low Church party.' Thirty years later, when he was himself Bishop of London, Temple allowed Tait's biographer, Randall Davidson, to print these letters in full. But Davidson in his own life suffered from Temple's unalterable suspicion of Tait and his men, as traitors to the cause of intellectual honesty.

In his replies to his wounded friends Tait insisted that the volume as a whole was dangerous, and that any of its contributors who did not wish to be associated with its tendency and fate should withdraw their contributions. Jowett and Temple refused to desert their colleagues in this way, although they let it be known that they had had no idea about what was in the other essays until the printed book had reached them. Tait's second line of defence was to plead his responsibility as a bishop. Despite that, could he not keep his friends? 'It is the misery of an official position', he wrote to Temple, 'that if a man is determined that his private friendships and public acts shall never appear to come into collision, he must give up his friendships.' Jowett and Temple were little moved by the pathos here. But thirdly, Tait argued that what was really needed was a doctrinal restatement,

that this was his only substantial book, and he grew theologically timid, but he kept up a running commentary on religious developments as Bishop of St. David's, 1840–74. See J. C. Thirlwall, *Connop Thirlwall* (SPCK, 1936).

instead of the critical and negative tone of *Essays and Reviews*. 'It is a poor thing to be pulling down; let them build up.' This was the one argument which eventually convinced Temple (not the more academic Jowett, although Jowett was reconciled with Tait as the latter lay dying).

Tait, who seems to have been as embarrassed by the affair as Wilberforce had been by Hampden in 1847, soon seized the opportunity to vindicate himself as a friend of honest thinkers. Two of the contributors were brought before the Judicial Committee of the Privy Council, on which Tait sat with the two archbishops and four lay judges. They were accused of publishing views on the inspiration of the Bible, and on the everlasting punishment of the wicked, which were too liberal to be compatible with the doctrines of the Church of England. The two archbishops agreed with this accusation. The laymen thought the charges 'not proved'. Tait voted with the laymen.

Another storm of abuse now fell on his head. 137,000 laymen congratulated the archbishops. Eleven thousand clergymen signed a declaration that the Bible was to be regarded as divinely inspired 'without reserve or qualification', and that punishment in hell would be 'everlasting'. And it was not merely an outcry from the mob. Gladstone, while thanking Tait for sending him some sermons and while expressing 'cordial respect for your pastoral zeal and labours', made it clear that he agreed with the archbishops in dissenting from the judgment in favour of *Essays and Reviews*. 'It appears to me that the spirit of this judgment has but to be consistently and cautiously followed up in order to establish, so far as the Court can establish it, a complete indifference between the Christian Faith and the denial of it.' Tait's only ally among the bishops was Connop Thirlwall. But his vote had made it possible for Broad Churchmen to remain parsons of the Church of England. By so voting in defiance of clerical opinion Tait had recovered his integrity, and had discovered his vocation. He wrote privately at this time: 'I feel my own vocation clear, greatly as I sympathize with the Evangelicals, not to allow them to tyrannize over the Broad Churchmen'—despite their alliance with the High Churchmen for this purpose. He would protect the ewe lamb of theological liberalism against the beasts once described as 'the High Church rhinoceros and the Evangelical hyaena'.[33] But Tait, who still felt that the publication of *Essays and Reviews* had been foolish, and some of its contents dangerous, added: 'What is wanted is a deeply religious liberal party, and almost all who might have formed it have, in the alarm, deserted. . . . The great evil is that the liberals are deficient in religion, and the religious are deficient in liberality.'

Next year Tait further angered many clergymen by supporting

[33] Matthew Arnold, *Essays in Criticism* (Macmillan, 1865), p. 29.

Stanley's plea for a relaxation of the terms on which the clergy accepted the Thirty-nine Articles; and when Archbishop William Thomson gave his patronage to a grand *Speaker's Commentary*, designed to inform but also to reassure the faithful about modern study of the Bible, he refused to have Tait as a contributor. He feared that Tait would bring Stanley into the project.[34] It did not escape notice that Tait, whose protest had been the instrument to break Newman's Anglican career because Newman had placed a dishonest interpretation on the Articles, was now the patron of Article-evading liberals. When the Clerical Subscription Act of 1865 was passed to satisfy the consciences of the mid-Victorian liberals, and to decide the terms of assent to the Articles by clergymen of the Church of England for more than a century, the complaint seemed justified that Broad Churchmen were being treated more leniently than Anglo-Catholics; for while they were prepared to assent to the Articles as 'agreeable to the Word of God', in accordance with the new Act, these liberals made no secret of their own disagreement with many of the Articles' doctrines. Tait was blamed, and became no more popular in the next doctrinal crisis.

John William Colenso was a Cambridge mathematician (*Colenso's Arithmetic* was known to countless schoolboys), and a tough-minded man who battled with poverty. Having been a Norfolk vicar and a disciple of F. D. Maurice, he sailed out in 1853 to become the first Bishop of Natal. This was at the invitation of Robert Gray, Bishop of Cape Town and a disciple of Samuel Wilberforce.[35] All seemed to be going well and quietly until in 1861 there appeared *St. Paul's Epistle to the Romans: Newly Translated, and Explained from a Missionary Point of View*. This small commentary, printed by African converts, expounded Pauline theology in the light of the Maurician doctrine that all men were united to Christ from birth. To be a missionary in Natal, Colenso was saying, was to place before the Zulu the fact that he was already redeemed. This book profoundly shocked Robert Gray; it shook Maurice himself. For when Maurice's message was clarified like this, what became of the contrast between the heathen's blindness and the Church's sacraments? And what became of the contrast between heaven and hell? Gray wanted the Church of England to dissociate itself from the heresy, and Wilberforce wrote to Colenso ('one very dear to my heart') that surely the loneliness and autocracy of a colonial bishop's position 'cannot be the most favourable position

[34] Thomson in his reforming Oxford days had agreed to contribute to *Essays and Reviews*, but with his usual luck had sent in his essay too late for the printer.
[35] The relationship between these two men, which acted out the Tait-Wilberforce tension on South African soil, may be studied in two modern biographies: Peter Hinchliff, *John William Colenso* (Nelson, 1964), and Audrey Brooke, *Robert Gray* (Oxford University Press, 1947).

for the discovery of religious truth'; but Tait shrewdly refrained from reading the book, explaining that when he had time to read, the book must be a good one. 'London was strong against action as action', wrote an indignant Wilberforce to Gray. '"Was not prepared to say," etc. The old story, "Did not know that it went beyond the teaching of Mr. Maurice. . . ."'

Colenso now added to his offence by publishing a discussion of the first books of the Bible. Zulu converts had asked him whether the Old Testament was truer or more moral than their own ancestral fables. Colenso, who had already shown his capacity for quick work by becoming the leading authority on the language and literature of the Zulus, set himself to work through the sacred scriptures in the light of such German commentaries as he was able to acquire and with the mathematical equipment which he already possessed. His labours in his study at Bishopstowe near Pietermaritzburg now drove Colenso to declare that the writings traditionally attributed to Moses and the Book of Joshua were not free of mathematical, historical, or moral error. Urged on by Wilberforce, Gray now determined to depose him from his bishopric. For Robert Gray nursed solemn ideas about his responsibilities as the Metropolitan of South Africa. He was building a new part of the Catholic Church, but at the same time he was studying the Fathers and wishing to revive their orthodoxy and discipline. He would contend for the Faith once delivered to the saints, whatever the cost. His aged father's episcopal palace had been burned down by the mob in Bristol, in 1831; old Bishop Gray had nevertheless insisted on appearing in his cathedral. Robert Gray in Cape Town was not the lesser man.

This move, however, drove Tait to take a firm stand, for he shared the conviction of most Victorian churchmen—Lord Shaftesbury, for example—that Gray had no legal power to take such a step against Colenso, who had been appointed by the English Crown through Letters Patent. Already in 1858 Tait had opposed Wilberforce's plea that Gray should be encouraged to consecrate more bishops to work with him and Colenso (then his ally). Wilberforce and Gray had wanted these bishops 'to head aggressive missions in the parts of South Africa which are exterior to the Queen's dominions', but Tait had conveyed to Wilberforce a belief that 'bishops in Roman Catholic countries should be sent by the Pope; in our country the Bishops should be sent by the Queen, who stood in the same place as the Pope'.

Tait's attitude to the problem of Colenso was, therefore, complicated, but it is interesting to note that it virtually coincided with Maurice's. (When the excessively conscientious Maurice announced that he would resign his income as an incumbent in London in order to be free to criticize Colenso without seeming to be defending the *status quo,* Tait patiently dissuaded him.) On the one hand, Tait believed that Colenso's thoughts about the Old Testament were 'rash and arrogant' and that his teachings about the person of Christ were heretical, so that if Gray had prosecuted Colenso in an English law court, and if the doctrinal issue had come to the Judicial Committee of the Privy Council, Tait would almost certainly have voted against Colenso. Accordingly, Tait was the author of an appeal from the English bishops to Colenso to resign if he could not share the Church's acceptance of the whole Bible as the Word of God; among the bishops, only Thirlwall refused to endorse this appeal. On the other hand, since Gray was reluctant to have the doctrinal issue decided by English lawyers, since the Privy Council ruled that Gray had no right to depose him, and since Colenso refused to go quietly, Tait was unwilling to take actions which would acknowledge the authority of Gray (or of Gray's ally Wilberforce) to decide who was to be Bishop of Natal. Tait did not inhibit Colenso from preaching in London, although much pressure was brought on him to make this gesture, and he led the majority of the English bishops in refusing to arrange for a new bishop to be consecrated for Natal. When the timid Archbishop Longley refused to ask the overseas bishops what they thought about the problems of maintaining doctrinal unity and the royal supremacy in the colonial churches, Tait issued a questionnaire on his own responsibility, and armed himself with many replies which were gratifyingly hostile to the Gray–Wilberforce solution of these problems.

When the first Lambeth Conference was convened, Tait was expected to join the bishops who boycotted it as a Gray–Wilberforce plot. Instead, he and Thirlwall agreed to be present. By their attendance they hoped to make sure that Archbishop Longley fulfilled his promise to keep the Colenso affair off the Lambeth agenda. When Longley failed in this, Tait resisted the plan of Gray and Wilberforce to get the bishops' conference to approve the consecration of a new bishop for Natal, and won. Gray 'made my blood boil', he wrote in his journal. Tait spoke in 'severe rebukes' to Bishop Selwyn of New Zealand who attacked the establishment of the Church of England. When other bishops urged him to be a disciplinarian against the Colenso type of Broad Churchmanship as he was against the Anglo-Catholic ritualists, he 'let it be distinctly understood that I thought the Romeward tendency more dangerous for our clergy than the tendency towards free-thought'.

In the short run, nothing much came out of the Colenso affair. It was not the Bishop of Natal who laid down the lines for Anglican advance in theology or biblical criticism; nor was Tait's stand on legality enough in the mounting doctrinal crisis. It was not Colenso or Tait, with their insistence on the royal supremacy over the colonial

churches, who saw the pattern of the future for the Anglican Communion. On the other hand, Colenso did remain Bishop of Natal in
the eyes of the law of England, and that checked the Wilberforce–
Gray tendency to make the bishops the custodians of the old-style
Catholic Faith; and the Lambeth Conference never got off the ground
of ecclesiastical diplomacy and compromise, to float in the air of the
great Catholic tradition as a 'synod' with power to discipline heretics.

From 1865 until his death in 1883, apart from one visit to England,
Colenso remained in Natal. For a time he was compelled to share
the cathedral in Pietermaritzburg with a dean who had supported
Gray in deposing and excommunicating him. When he recovered sole
possession of the cathedral from Gray's supporters by another legal
action, he was still short of clergy and money. From 1869 onwards the
more effective Anglican bishop in the area was Gray's nominee, W. K.
Macrorie, and Colenso recovered the initiative only in the political
sphere, for in the last ten years of his life he emerged as a courageously outspoken supporter of the rights of the African people in Natal.
Stanley invited him to plead for the Zulus in Westminster Abbey
(knowing what a storm would follow, Colenso refused), and defended
him amid shouts at a meeting of the Society for the Propagation of
the Gospel in 1881.

The Bishop of Natal [he said] is the one colonial bishop who has translated
the Bible into the language of the natives of his diocese. He is the one colonial
bishop who, when he believed a native to be wronged, left his diocese, jour-
neyed to London, and never rested till he had procured the reversal of that
wrong. . . . For these deeds he will be remembered when you who censure
him are dead, buried, and forgotten.

On Colenso's death in 1883, Tait's successor refused to consecrate
another bishop for the 'Church of England in Natal', and the schism
was very gradually healed. Gray had died eleven years before. The
principal legacy of his dispute with Colenso was the hymn 'The
Church's One Foundation', written by an admiring curate in Windsor,
S. J. Stone.[36]

Yet the cause of truth was involved amid the compromises of Lambeth and amid the schisms and heresies which distressed the South
African Anglicans. In England, Stanley and Maurice were only two
among the forward-looking clergy who congratulated Tait on this
stand for the rights of the Crown, which was incidentally also a stand
for theological liberty; and there can be little doubt that Tait's attitude

[36] The Church of the Province of South Africa has won distinction among
the provinces of the Anglican Communion for the courage with which some of
its leaders have applied Gray's Catholic spirituality to Colenso's defence of the
Africans. An outline of its history was supplied by Peter Hinchliff, *The Church
in South Africa* (SPCK, 1968).

to Colenso effectively represented the wishes of many thoughtful laymen in the Church of England in the 1860s. There was a widespread sense that the old Christian system was being broken up. There was a widespread alarm because a few clergymen seemed to be substituting a vague new religion or 'rationalism' for Christianity; Colenso might be one of these. There was widespread contempt for the more common clerical reaction of looking back to the Middle Ages or to Rome for escape. And there was a widespread desire to use the State's control over the Church of England at home and overseas in order to penalize 'Rats and Rits' (rationalists and ritualists)—and in order to protect the liberty of those who, like Stanley or Maurice or Frederick Temple, were trying to find an honest way of remaining Christians in the age of science and democracy. Tait, although unpopular with many of the clergy, embodied these trends in mid-Victorian thought, and was well qualified to become in 1868 the Layman's Archbishop.[37]

7

As Primate Tait established an ascendency over the Victorian mind, and when he died Queen Victoria asked for a lock of his hair. It was an honour that she did not bestow upon Disraeli. Men and women in many different walks of life, belonging to many different schools of thought, trusted him, and they knew that his devotion to duty as he saw it made Lambeth Palace resemble a government office. No Archbishop of Canterbury had exercised such influence since the Middle Ages. For the nearest equivalents men had to go back to William Laud and John Tillotson in the seventeenth century—but Laud the High Churchman owed his execution to his unpopularity, while Tillotson the Broad Churchman (Tait's hero) had to see most of his ideas frustrated by the clergy.[38]

Unfortunately much of Tait's Primacy was consumed by the battle against the ritualists, with the Public Worship Regulation Act of 1874 as the weapon. Tait knew that when appointing him Archbishop of Canterbury the Queen and Disraeli intended that he should enforce

[37] An assessment of the doctrinal crisis of the 1860s has been provided by A. O. J. Cockshut, *Anglican Attitudes* (Collins, 1959).

[38] An anonymous 'churchman of the diocese of Canterbury' published a pamphlet comparing *Laud and Tait* (1885) in order to qualify the chorus of praise for Tait at his death. Tait had neglected the spiritual life of his diocese, had promoted the wrong men, and had been a boring speaker ('thud, thud, thud'). The point about the title was that Wilberforce's policy was often said to resemble Laud's, and of course the clear implication was that the wrong man had gone to Canterbury in 1868.

the law against the small number of Anglican priests who were imitating Roman Catholic practices. When the Pope was declared infallible in 1870, anti-Catholic prejudice in England found a fresh cause for alarm; even Gladstone, who deplored the attempt to regulate religious life by Act of Parliament, was stirred to write at length against the menace of 'Vaticanism'. In 1871 the Judicial Committee of the Privy Council clearly condemned an Anglo-Catholic priest in Brighton, Father Purchas, for wearing the medieval priest's vestments, for adopting the eastward position to face the altar not the people, for using wafers instead of ordinary bread, and for mixing water with the wine ceremonially. Lord Shaftesbury was bent on legislation to enforce such a prohibition of ritualism, and 60,000 people signed a 'memorial' to the Archbishops organized in 1873 by the Church Association. Above all the Queen insisted, and talked of abdicating if she did not get her way. It became inevitable that voices such as Maurice's, appalled by the prospect of a religious persecution, should be drowned, and that Tait should sponsor legislation. If he had not been willing to do so, more extreme laymen would certainly have pushed legislation through, either out of a passionate Protestantism, as in the case of Lord Shaftesbury, or out of a sense of the electoral advantages to be gained by appeasing the popular clamour, as in the case of Disraeli.

Tait's first idea was that the diocesan bishops should be strengthened as judges in liturgical matters, with diocesan councils to advise them. He optimistically believed that the few mule-like Anglo-Catholic priests would soon be brought to their senses by a combination of the stick of this new legal discipline with the carrot of pastoral kindness. However, such episcopal action was unlikely to be stern enough to satisfy the Protestants under Lord Shaftesbury, who amended Tait's Bill so that there should be only one judge, and he a layman. Tait spoke against this amendment but, sensing the power of the anticlerical suspicion, voted for it. The one point on which he would not give way was his insistence that the diocesan bishop should have the power to veto any proceedings. This combination of Shaftesbury's zeal with Tait's caution was presented to a cheering House of Commons by Disraeli as a 'Bill to put down ritualism'. But Shaftesbury's amendments resulted in more problems for the Archbishop than he realized at the time. They created a further impression that the English State was attempting to override the theological convictions of Anglo-Catholic churchmen, as in the Gorham and Colenso affairs; but more: since the new lay judge turned out to possess, and to be willing to exercise, the power of imprisoning for contempt of court, Shaftesbury's amendments gave to Anglo-Catholic churchmen the fertile boon of martyrdom.

The greatest error of Tait's life was his failure to foresee these dangers in 1874. His experience as Bishop of London had taught him to respect the pastoral earnestness of some of the ritualists, and to hate the Protestant bigotry and violence of some of their opponents (usually from outside their parishes), which was why he insisted on the right to veto prosecutions. But Anglo-Catholicism to him still meant the logic-chopping of Tract Ninety or the sentimentally medieval antics of the first London ritualists. He completely underestimated the spiritual power of the movement.

For example, he did not see that a man such as Richard Church, whom Gladstone brought from a Somerset village to be Dean of St. Paul's in 1871, typified the High Church priest who was respected because of his human quality. Church, one of the greatest of all scholar-journalists and pastor-preachers, with a mind stocked with the culture of Europe, had been the proctor who had exercised his right to veto the condemnation of Tract Ninety by the University of Oxford in 1845. He had become Newman's closest colleague at Oriel, but had remained an ornament of the Anglican tradition. Now he became Gladstone's chief ecclesiastical counsellor. Diffident as he was, he insisted on taking the eastward position at the altar; and he fought Tait's policy. When in 1865 Tait supplied a Preface for *A Collection of Judgements of the Judicial Committee of the Privy Council in Ecclesiastical Cases relating to Doctrine and Discipline*, Church wrote a review which ridiculed the idea that English lawyers could pronounce on the doctrine and worship of Christendom, and which rebuked Tait for lending a bishop's authority to such secular aggression. When the Archbishop of Canterbury led the attack on High Church ritual, the Dean of St. Paul's let it be known that he was contemplating resignation and he lent the authority of his name to those who deplored the use of the secular arm.[39]

Such a movement was not going to be blackmailed or bludgeoned into conformity with the Protestant Establishment. Instead, it was a movement which operated with a Victorian energy and self-righteousness like Tait's own, and which was looking for martyrs as mascots; and in this atmosphere the Public Worship Regulation Act was a very foolish measure. Its new lay judge was Lord Penzance, an eager Protestant who had previously specialized in divorce cases. Tait was genuinely distressed when there were five cases of imprisonment

[39] B. A. Smith, *Dean Church* (Oxford University Press, 1958), supplements the *Life and Letters of Dean Church* which his daughter Mary compiled (Macmillan, 1895). Dean Church considered Samuel Wilberforce the Church of England's greatest bishop for a century and a half (*Occasional Papers*, Macmillan, 1897, ii, 336).

at Penzance's orders under the Act (Tooth in 1877, Dale and Enraght in 1880, Green in 1881–2, and Cox in 1887). And he had every reason to be distressed. Quite apart from a bishop's embarrassment at the spectacle of priests in prison for obeying their consciences, and quite apart from the agitation among the clergy whose organs were the newly founded English Church Union and the *Church Times,* these punishments turned public opinion away from the witch-hunt against the ritualists. By the end of Tait's Primacy the Public Worship Regulation Act was doomed, and he knew it. He changed his mind to a greater extent than either he or his admirers cared to admit. Gladstone, for example, told Pusey that in the Tait of 1881 he could scarcely recognize the man who had allied himself with Disraeli against the ritualists in 1874.

Was this futile battle such a blot on Tait's government of the Church that it ought to overshadow everything else? Certainly the details of Anglo-Catholic ritualism in conflict with mid-Victorian law make tedious reading today, and there is a natural tendency to conclude that the archbishop who presided over such petty excitements was a man so entirely Victorian as to be of no permanent interest. But at the time Tait, for all his mastery of the historical and legal precedents in England, was not excited himself. This came out when a consecrated wafer was produced in Lord Penzance's court and retained as a piece of evidence. Protests against this blasphemy poured into Lambeth Palace, to Tait's dry amusement. He quietly asked for the wafer to be brought to him, and ate it. Thanks now poured in, but Tait was still contemptuous.

A man with such a low estimate of the controversies which fascinated the average clergyman or the devout churchgoer may easily be reckoned a bad appointment as a Father-in-God, and it is probable that had Tait been born a century later he would have ended up in university life as a Vice-Chancellor; certainly no system of electing bishops would have produced Bishop Tait. Yet his inner remoteness from the battles did have its compensation. He shared both the layman's dislike of parsons in strange clothes and the layman's dislike of priests in prison. It became his ambition to leave the Church of England in peace. He secured the appointment of a Royal Commission on Ecclesiastical Courts in 1881, and chaired its laborious and largely fruitless investigations. One practical step he could take. In 1882 he knew that he was dying, and he deliberately used this status in order to persuade one of the most publicized and most prosecuted of the ritualists, Arthur Hugh Mackonochie, to leave his church, St. Alban's, Holborn. Father Mackonochie clung to his church when Tait first suggested an exchange with another Anglo-Catholic priest, Father Suckling of St. Peter's, London Docks; but he could face anything except a dying bishop who was a fellow-Scot, and eventually agreed.[40]

Tait concentrated his attention on what, writing to Mackonochie in his last month of his life, he called 'the prevailing sin and unbelief'. The only aspect of Anglo-Catholicism that impressed him was its hold on the loyalty of certain congregations including working-class folk. Because of that, even ritualists might eventually be considered on the right side in the real battle. But in the main, Tait pursued these great issues whatever might be the reactions of the clerical mind. Thus, while opposing secular funerals, he was convinced that it was both charity and justice to allow fellow-Christians to be buried in the parish churchyards with the benefit of a Nonconformist service if that was their wish. He supported the Liberal government's legislation to this effect in 1880. The greatest clerical outcry in Tait's whole life followed. Three-quarters of the clergy petitioned against the concession. Bishop Wordsworth of Lincoln called it an 'Act for the martyrdom of the National Church', and Bishop Ellicott announced that he would not consecrate any new churchyards. The Archbishop most courteously dismissed all that as hysteria; and within a few years, when the parish churches were seen to be standing although a few Nonconformist funerals had approached their hallowed walls, even clergymen acknowledged that he had been right.

In some other reforms which he advocated, Tait was defeated. An example was his wish to see a relaxation in the public use of the fifth-century Athanasian Creed.

The Prayer Book ordered that on each of the main Christian festivals, including Christmas Day, Easter Day and Whitsunday, parson and people at Mattins should together profess:

> Whosoever will be saved: before all things it is necessary
>   that he hold the Catholick Faith.
> Which Faith except every one do keep whole and undefiled:
>   without doubt he shall perish everlastingly.
> And the Catholick Faith is this. . . .

A comprehensive summary of Trinitarian and Christological doctrine followed. Various churchmen, including Archbishop Tillotson, would have been glad to see a creed so detailed and so damnatory removed into obscurity, but the Oxford Movement had encouraged obedience to the Prayer Book's directions and the later ritualists were enthusiastic about *this* part of the Book. By the 1870s, few thoughtful members of

[40] The move broke his heart. He perished five years later in a Highland storm one December night, and the circumstances suggested that he had courted death. See Michael Reynolds, *Martyr of Ritualism* (Faber & Faber, 1965). Joyce Coombs, *Judgment on Hatcham* (Faith Press, 1969), was a biography of another ritualist of the time, Arthur Tooth, who survived until 1931.

the Church of England were willing to re-open the Trinitarian and Christological questions in theology, but equally few shared Newman's enthusiasm (in the *Grammar of Assent*) for the Athanasian Creed as 'the most simple and sublime, the most devotional formulary to which Christianity has given rise'. More practically few wished all churchgoers on all the festivals to hear the Church teaching the everlasting damnation of all who did not answer the mysterious questions with a complete correctness. Lord Shaftesbury, that pillar of orthodoxy, organized a petition of 6,000 leading laymen against the compulsory use of the creed.

In 1870 a Royal Commission accordingly recommended that in the Prayer Book a new rubric should be printed, explaining 'that the condemnations in this Confession of Faith are to be not otherwise understood than as a solemn warning of the peril of those who wilfully reject the Catholic Faith'. Tait believed this explanation to be inadequate, and announced his view that the creed 'should not retain its place in the Public Service of the Church'. But then the most respected Anglo-Catholic spokesman, Henry Liddon, let it be known that he would retire from the ministry of the Church of England if any damage were done 'to this most precious creed', and Dr. Pusey sent in a similar threat from Oxford. Liddon never forgave Tait; he would always absent himself from any service or meeting where Tait was to be prominent.[41] But in the end all that happened was that the Convocation of Canterbury passed a resolution containing the words suggested in 1870 and adding (without producing evidence) that the creed 'doth not make any addition to the faith as contained in Holy Scripture'. So the Athanasian Creed was saved. 'And there,' commented Arthur Stanley, 'it will go on standing until it carries off the other two creeds on its back, but Stanley was too gloomy, for the creed gradually fell into disuse while the Apostles' and Nicene Creeds continued in daily or weekly use.

Tait, while lacking the theological courage of a Colenso, possessed some understanding of the challenges to belief. 'When I was young', he said in his charge at Canterbury in 1876, 'we were told there was no such thing as an atheist in the world, but all that is changed.' Yet his own religion was not primarily intellectual. It was a defiance of the grave—of five small graves. He said about sceptics in 1876: 'We must reach their hearts in hours of sickness and approaching death

[41] Henry Liddon, the disciple and biographer of Pusey, was a canon of St. Paul's, 1870–90, and also a professor at Oxford, 1870–82. He refused to be made a bishop, and there is much truth in the comment by G. W. E. Russell: 'Providence had placed him exactly where his singular gifts could be used to the best advantage; he was untrammelled by executive office, and he remained until the end of his life the chief teacher of the English Church.' See J. O. Johnston, *Life and Letters of Henry Parry Liddon* (Longmans, Green, 1904).

and when friends are taken from them; then we may find their consciences awake and their hearts open, ready to return to the faith of their childhood, and to believe in the great Redeemer.' Four years later, in an outspoken review of Mozley's *Reminiscences of the Oxford Movement*, he was still insisting that Newman's influence had been disastrous in trying to stiffen the great National Church 'after an alien and antiquated model', whereas Arnold's influence had appealed to the consciences 'of the vast majority of intelligent persons throughout the Kingdom'. What he really cared for was that the Church of England should remain established as the national recognition that the Christian promise of eternal life was true.

The defence of the Establishment was for Tait no light matter. No sooner had he reached Lambeth than Gladstone became Prime Minister with a mandate for Irish disestablishment. Tait and his ally Queen Victoria had to content themselves with securing some financial concessions to the Anglican clergy in Ireland, and with some pacifying tactics which slightly lessened the bitterness of the Parliamentary debate. But it did not amount to much, and the anxiety of that first year's negotiations brought Tait once more face to face with death. Another heart attack left him partially paralysed in November 1869, and his left arm never truly recovered. His resignation or death was expected, but he convalesced through 1870, and spent the next winter on the Riviera. His illness alarmed the Government into allowing the consecration of a Bishop of Dover, to carry the main burden of the episcopal work in the Canterbury diocese. (It was part of a move to increase the number of bishops: in 1874 Parliament allowed the creation of new dioceses of Truro, St. Albans, Liverpool, Southwell, and Wakefield—provided that the money could be raised for the new bishops, which caused some delay.) Tait then devoted himself to the central administration of the National Church, for which, as he believed, his life had been spared.

He defended the National Church both by the shrewdness of his leadership during successive crises, voicing the instincts of thoughtful laity but never driving the clergy too much, and by the zeal with which he did his duty as a spiritual peer. When newspapers arrived, he always had the foreign and domestic political news read to him first; ecclesiastical controversies, which in those days could fill many newspaper columns, could wait. He treated the House of Lords with great seriousness (he was scandalized by Disraeli's *Endymion*, which viewed politics as a game), and the compliment was repaid. Distinguished lawyers used to reckon him a first-class judge, and there were those who believed that he would have made a powerful Prime Minister. In 1879 he even impressed a delegation from the Trades Union Congress with the breadth of his political insight. In a role which was less dignified, he was an indefatigable, cunning, and remarkably successful lobbyist for ecclesiastical legislation. Like every other politician, he often had to compromise or to admit defeat; he could not preserve the compulsory collection of the 'church rate' to repair the parish churches (this was made illegal in 1868), and he could not preserve the full position of the Church of England in the nation's universities or schools. But partly because Tait was now so often crossing the river from Lambeth to Westminster, the complete severance of Church and State seemed an idea more improbable in the 1870s than in the 1860s.

This achievement had international repercussions, for Tait used his prestige at home to build up the position of Canterbury in the whole Anglican Communion. He did this without ever echoing the Wilberforce–Gray line about Anglicanism overseas as an exciting adventure in English Catholicism free from the shackles of the Establishment; his approach was pragmatic. When Bishop George Selwyn persuaded the American bishops to ask for another Lambeth Conference, Tait replied that he was willing to convene such a gathering provided that the bishops thought that they had enough subjects to discuss. In the end a hundred bishops assembled in 1878. He dominated the meeting, not by holding up any new vision of the Church, but by his mastery of the problems of the existing mixture of constitutions and theologies within Anglicanism. 'I believe', he told his brethren, 'that there are not more than three persons in England who can give you a definite idea of what the constitution of a Colonial Church is. I rather pride myself on being one of the three. . . .'

That second Lambeth Conference took place little over a month after the death of Tait's only son, Craufurd. Before the year was out, he had buried his wife. Now that death had touched him once more, all around him noticed that the Archbishop had been purged of most of the lingering traces of arrogant impatience. His chief domestic happiness in the years which remained to him was watching his chaplain, Randall Davidson. This young man, a rising Scot, who reminded him of his own youth, married his daughter Edith and handled most of his letters and many of his interviews under his general instruction. Craufurd Tait had been ordained amid his proud father's hopes. After the son's death, the son-in-law became the heir of the whole legacy of Tait's life and work.

Archibald Tait from Glasgow was buried in the churchyard of Addington Park, the country house of the archbishops, four miles from Croydon. If religion be defined as an excitement over the glamour of the Church, or as a facility in devout emotions, it is true to say, as the *Church Times* said in 1877: 'What music is to a man with no ear, that religion is to Archbishop Tait.' And Gladstone said: 'Tait was a very considerable person; but I doubt if he ever read a theological book in his life.'[42] But C. J. Vaughan, whom he had defeated for the headmastership of Rugby forty years before, wrote the inscription on his monument in Canterbury Cathedral.

A GREAT ARCHBISHOP,

JUST, DISCERNING, DIGNIFIED, STATESMANLIKE,

WISE TO KNOW THE TIME AND RESOLUTE TO REDEEM IT,

HE HAD ONE AIM:

TO MAKE THE CHURCH OF ENGLAND MORE AND MORE

THE CHURCH OF THE PEOPLE:

DRAWING TOWARDS IT BOTH BY WORD AND GOOD EXAMPLE

ALL WHO LOVE THINGS TRUE AND PURE,

BEAUTIFUL AND OF GOOD REPORT.

FOR FURTHER READING

The Life of the Right Reverend Samuel Wilberforce, D.D., Lord Bishop of Oxford and afterwards of Winchester, with Selections from his Diaries and Correspondence, was published in three volumes (John Murray). The first (1880) was by Canon A. R. Ashwell of Chichester, who died two days after correcting the proofs. Reginald Wilberforce, the eldest son, was responsible for the second and third volumes (1881–3). These volumes were compiled hastily and untidily, but they incorporated many passages from Wilberforce's diaries (which do not appear to have been preserved) and correspondence. For a sneering modern sketch, see J. C. Hardwick, *Lawn Sleeves* (Basil Blackwell, 1933). For a study of the Wilberforces and Henry Manning up to 1854, based partly on manuscript sources (listed with a bibliography of published works), see David Newsome, *The Parting of Friends* (John Murray, 1966). For a modern biography also incorporating research, see Standish Meacham, *Lord Bishop* (Harvard University Press, 1970). *The Letter-books of Samuel Wilberforce, 1843–68*, ed. R. K. Pugh, were published by the Buckinghamshire and Oxfordshire Record Societies (1970).

The Life of Archibald Campbell Tait, Archbishop of Canterbury, in two volumes (Macmillan, 1891) was, appropriately enough, better organized and more discreet than the volumes about Wilberforce, thanks to the devoted labours of Randall Davidson and William Benham, Vicar of Margate. In places these compilers were too devoted. For a modern historian's study filling in some details gleaned from the Tait papers at Lambeth Palace and from other sources, and giving a cooler verdict on the achievement, see P. T. Marsh, *The Victorian Church in Decline* (Routledge & Kegan Paul, 1968)—a book which, however, does not justify its title.

M. A. Crowther, *Church Embattled* (David & Charles, 1970), is a well-researched study of religious controversies in the age of Tait and Wilberforce.

[42] G. W. E. Russell, *Portraits of the Seventies* (Fisher Unwin, 1916), pp. 341–353.

1801·85 *1805- 72,*

Shaftesbury and Maurice

1

'Revolutions', he wrote in his journal for 25 March 1848, 'go off like pop-guns!' Yet Lord Ashley, who three years later was to become the seventh Earl of Shaftesbury, did not believe that the explosions rocking the Continent must be followed by a violent class struggle in England. On 13 April, rejoicing over the collapse of the Chartist demonstration in London, he wrote: 'The middle classes are content, and so are nineteen-twentieths of the working people; but this will be of no avail against indistinct terrors, ignorant uneasiness, and speculative, not social, policies.'

His basic confidence in the social order is the more interesting because his knowledge of the defects of capitalism was far from indistinct. As he inspected the mills in Yorkshire where the 'hands' were slave-armies of women, children, and labourers bewildered by their uprooting from the soil, or as he visited the hovels which provided some kind of shelter to the new London poor, or as he poked into the places (one was inside the lawn-roller in Regent's Park) where filthy, verminous, and illiterate children huddled, Shaftesbury was walking where all too many of his fellow-Englishman lived. Consequently he saw legislation as sacred; he saw inexhaustible agitation and negotiation to secure reforms as necessary; and he saw the inspection of the enforcement of laws as a daily task worthy of all the energy of a Christian gentleman.

But it was a condescending compassion. It was the vision of Tory Democracy, with 'social' aristocrats leading the 'ignorant' people against the 'speculative' merchants; the heady vision of the Young England of noble scions around the climbing Disraeli. The theory was summed up when in 1848 Lord Ashley produced his answer to the Chartists. He persuaded Prince Albert to inspect some working-class dwellings and then to take the chair at a meeting of the Labourer's Friend Society, despite the hesitations of the politicians. This man whose indignation swept through so many factories always disliked trade unions. He also disliked the idea of life peerages as a blow to the aristocracy; he publicly opposed Disraeli's notion of adding to the Queen the title 'Empress of India'; and he attacked the Salvation Army as another vulgar innovation.

Later generations have forgiven his prejudices as an aristocrat born in 1801, but his fame has seemed more badly tarnished by the bigotry of his fundamentalism. The causes which he led to the incalculable benefit of his age were upheld by him on the basis of a religious faith opposed to that age's whole intellectual life. He was a man of God, but he never wearied of arguing that to be a man of God meant to be a man of the infallible Bible. ('The blessed old book is "God's Word written", from the very first syllable down to the very last.') He was a Christian who had compassion on the crowds—and who believed that the essence of Christianity was a narrow and unhappy creed.

Again and again in his journal Shaftesbury complained that he was virtually alone in his struggles. It became his habit (in and after 1838) to sacrifice leisure to these secret moans, the egoism of an exhausted man, and although he nearly destroyed the journal he decided in the end to let his biographer use it. The real tragedy of these passages is that, while his fellow Evangelicals were often open to Shaftesbury's condemnation, there were others in England who had a social conscience, but who were not rigidly Evangelical. The Chaplain of Guy's Hospital, Frederick Maurice, warned him in a pamphlet of 1843 of the dangers of admitting only fellow-Evangelicals into his crusades. But the pamphlet breathed sympathy. 'The intercourse into which your Lordship's benevolent labours have brought you, with the middle class of our countrymen, must have made you sensible of the very strong Protestant feelings which pervade it. Take away its Protestantism and it becomes a trading class indeed; that and nothing else.'[1] Such pacifying words were wasted. Shaftesbury had taken the chair at a meeting to demand that Pusey—who was his cousin—and other Tractarians should be more firmly disciplined by their university; and Maurice, who disagreed with Pusey's views, had been stirred to defend Pusey's freedom. But now Maurice's sympathy was repulsed, and Shaftesbury united with Pusey only once, when the two orthodox patriarchs denounced Frederick Temple for liberalism. It was a tragedy, because, although Evangelicalism and liberalism were doubtless destined to collide, in its early stages Tractarianism had not been anti-Evangelical. Shaftesbury's personality on the one side seems to have been as significant as Hurrell Froude's on the other in widening the breach and increasing the bitterness.

Yet this sour man was in some ways the embodiment of Christian mercy. He was so overwhelmed by the problems and pains of his contemporaries that he believed the only solution to be the Second Coming of Jesus. He printed a prayer in Greek, 'Even so, come Lord Jesus!', on his envelopes, and he declared that he advocated the

[1] F. D. Maurice, *On Right and Wrong Methods of Supporting Protestantism* (Parker, Oxford, 1843), pp. 4–5.

Anglican–Lutheran bishopric in Jerusalem, which to Newman was the 'ultimate condemnation' of Anglicanism, in order to hasten the Coming. When he died, they erected as a monument to him the statue of Eros in Piccadilly Circus, so that the Greek god of desire might shoot his arrows into the idlers, the shoppers, and the pleasure-seekers. It would be hard to think of a more inappropriate memorial. Had he not been such a stalwart Evangelical, they could have put in the heart of London a sign of the love which he did practise: a crucifix.

2

The centre of the old Evangelical scheme of salvation was the experience of alienation from God the Father, without virtue or hope until one accepted the good news of the perfect sacrifice offered on Calvary to appease the just wrath of the Father and to reconcile the Father to sinners. Inevitably many who accepted the Evangelical doctrine had not gone through this experience with much intensity. They had taken the doctrine from parents or teachers with whom they were on good terms. Samuel Wilberforce, for example, was a young Evangelical because his father was William Wilberforce. Sometimes people experienced something like the Evangelical conversion in connection with a shock to their position on earth, as John Henry Newman did in 1816, without having been thoroughly miserable. It was relatively easy for such people to drift away from a strict Evangelicalism.

But for some this Evangelical doctrine expressed, as no other available theology could, escape from the mire. When John Wesley felt his heart 'strangely warmed', it was after a long failure to reach holiness as an Oxford don or effectiveness as a clergyman. Thomas Scott, to whose writing Newman owed so much, was a dim curate of Unitarian views until he was converted by John Newton, the preacher and hymn-writer who had formerly lived in sin as 'white trash' in West Africa and as the captain of a slave-ship. Such men knew that they had been ransomed. And for some, deliverance had come in childhood through a Christian whose love did something to compensate for the absence, indifference, or hostility of parents. We have just seen how the orphaned Archie Tait got his faith from his nurse, Betty Morton. The seventh Earl of Shaftesbury was a Christian because of his nurse, Maria Millis, whose love was more or less the only comfort he knew as a child. He always carried Maria Millis's watch about with him, but also something timeless. To a man who had been miserable because his earthly father and mother had showed no love, the Evangelical doctrine about the angry God, the doomed race, and the propitiating Saviour might be more than theology out of books. Such a man felt himself to be an actor in the drama of Redemption; and anything that touched this Gospel touched such a man's heart. Broad as he was, Tait accordingly thought *Essays and Reviews* not religious enough, while Shaftesbury, with his narrower mind, campaigned against that volume vehemently. Shaftesbury also denounced Seeley's prosaically and moralistically liberal portrait of Jesus, *Ecce Homo* (1866), as 'the most pestilential book ever vomited from the jaws of Hell'.

Such experience of a personal salvation in manhood or childhood lay behind the doctrinal inflexibilities of many Evangelicals, and it was natural that the young Lord Ashley should identify himself with the Evangelical party, as he gradually did while he was learning his own mind in the 1830s, without, so far as we know, any great crisis of conversion. Those who had not shared Shaftesbury's bitter youth now tended to notice only his rigidity and gloom (but great Evangelicals such as John Newton and William Wilberforce had not been gloomy); just as those who did not find churchgoing irresistible, and who were not particularly anxious that everyone should have the opportunity to go to church and to be quiet before and after, were depressed by the Victorian Sunday, which owed much to Shaftesbury. Shaftesbury's own eldest son, Anthony, was a rebel who reduced him to despair and who shot himself in a London cab less than a year after inheriting the title.

In an age when many holy men such as Newman felt little obligation in the social field, and when many devout Evangelicals insisted that the poor whom they helped should be the 'deserving' poor, Shaftesbury helped those who were powerless to earn or reward help. As an ambitious young Westminster politician he did not acquaint himself with factories or slums, but not much pressure on his conscience was needed to send him there. He would in this connection recall another experience as a boy. After a terrible school at Chiswick—which he afterwards compared with Dotheboys Hall in the no less bitter mind of Dickens—he enjoyed a happier four years at Harrow. While there he saw a pauper's funeral; those who carried the coffin were all drunk. An Indian prince, Gautama the Buddha, when he had a similar shock as a young man resolved to find the path of liberation from a world of suffering, but the English boy who had heard the Gospel of Christ from Maria Millis formed a resolve (dormant, admittedly, for years) to relieve suffering. This eventually meant being prepared to take endless trouble to bring practical help to those in physical or mental distress. Having been miserable himself—lonely, insulted, hungry, and cold although heir to the earldom, for his parents left him to contemptuous servants—he came to identify himself with the broken-hearted and the captives. When he had come into the family honours, he still could not banish a boy's nightmares or a man's memories from his mind, and each summer, while he took his own family to country houses or to fashionable spas on the Continent, he would cut cruelly into his own relaxation by remembering those in the slums for whom sunshine meant heat and stench.

His parents gave him the means, as well as unintentionally the impetus, to live this life of piety and service. His feckless mother, who was dedicated to the pursuit of fashion, was a daughter of the Duke of Marlborough, but at least she provided Maria Millis, who had been a maid in Blenheim Palace. His brutal father—from whom he was estranged for ten years until formally reconciled in 1839, only to be estranged again—was prominent in the House of Lords; he was the chairman of its committee work for forty years. The young man marked his independence by gaining a First at Oxford, yet when he was elected to Parliament at the age of twenty-five it was as member for the Duke of Marlborough's pocket borough, Woodstock. When he was noticed by both Canning and Peel, and appointed to a junior office in Wellington's government, it was because he was a promising Tory. When he was elected for his father's county town of Dorchester in 1830, the election was expensive. When he married, it was to the gay daughter of the fifth Earl Cowper. Only the deep misery of his childhood could have scarred him enough to make him more than an ornament of this Tory world. In these early days he grew passionately interested in astronomy, and might have become an amateur of science, as his ancestor, the third earl, had been a philosopher and man of letters; but he turned away from the stars, and his first important speech to the Commons was on the treatment of lunatics. Once he had decided what battle to enter, he hit out to the end with an obstinacy recalling the death of his younger brother in a schoolboys' fight at Eton.

His life was determined when in 1833 he took over the Parliamentary sponsorship of the Ten Hours Bill from Michael Sadler, who had lost his seat in the election. At this stage Lord Ashley was the handsome, sensitive, and religious heir to an earldom. A committee went to Westminster to seek a new advocate for the restriction of the daily working hours in the factories, initially in the interests of the women and children employed as cheap labour (but everyone knew that working men would benefit); this committee was recommended to try him, but he had almost no knowledge of industrial conditions apart from what he had picked up by reading *The Times*. It says much for his developing strength of character that his wife, the beautiful Minny, was already converted to an Evangelical seriousness and was foremost among those who now urged him to take up the cause.

He paid for his courage. He could still boast to Peel, 'I know that I have conciliated thousands of hearts to our blessed Constitution'. And he still wanted office, for despite his growing family his father refused him a proper allowance and he hated living in debt to money-lenders who lent at a high interest rate on his expectations; 'my finances are very, very low'. But he was marked as radical, or at least as unreliable. Although Peel at one stage thought of putting him in charge of the Irish problem, all that was offered to him was a seat on the Admiralty Board, and then a post at court. It was clear that he would never now be entrusted with power by Peel: 'he wanted my name, and *nothing* but my name. Had he desired anything else he would never have pressed on me a department in which I could exhibit nothing good but my legs in white shorts. . . .' Being very human, he often felt the contrast with his youthful visions of political glory. One journal entry reads: 'I have laboured almost incessantly for four-and-twenty years, and I have never received an honour, or notice of any sort or kind, great or small, from the Crown, the Minister, or the public, except the citizenship of the small borough of Tain, in Scotland.' But he made it a point of honour to refuse the offer of the Garter in 1854 and the possibility of becoming Home Secretary in 1866.

He paid another penalty in his fight with the factory owners over the Ten Hours Bill. He represented an agricultural constituency and would inherit a large estate. These facts were embarrassments when the industrialists made legitimate propaganda out of low wages and insanitary housing in Dorset. Why did not Lord Ashley do something for farm labourers doomed to bring up families on ten or eight shillings a week in filthy cottages, instead of interfering in the far better paid work of Lancashire or Yorkshire mill-hands? All that Ashley could do was to utter a guarded warning against the neglect of the labourers when addressing the Sturminster Agricultural Society in 1843; and that speech was enough to end his reconciliation with his father, one of the worst employers in Dorset, itself one of the most backward counties. Finally, when Peel deserted the protection of the landowners by proposing the repeal of the Corn Laws (which had kept the price of bread high), the industrial employers of labour rejoiced and Ashley, although their enemy, found himself converted to their side and compelled to resign as M.P. for Dorset. So it was that when prolonged agitation behind the Ten Hours Bill at last secured an Act of Parliament, in 1847, Lord Ashley had no seat in Westminster and the honour of sponsoring the Act fell to John Fielden, himself one of the largest cotton-spinners.

There was also an epilogue which emphasized Lord Ashley's ambiguous position. It was found that the limitation of working hours by the 1847 Act was not tight enough, because the factory-owners now worked 'relays' or a shift system. Parliament must brace itself to legislate again. At this stage, in 1850, Ashley suggested a compromise to the working men's committees whose battles he had fought so faithfully: a sixty-hour week. He was rewarded by their fury. 'I won for them *almost* everything; but for the loss of that very little, they regard me as an enemy!' In fact it was a Conservative government that finally accepted the full Ten Hours demands in 1874. Many historians—for example, the Hammonds in their *Lord Shaftesbury*—have criticized him for not being thorough in his attention to the problems of industrial workers; but that is to misunderstand the man. He had entered the campaign not because he was a man of the Left, but because he was a Christian aristocrat who took pity on women and children. As such he lived down the controversy of 1850, becoming known universally as the Working Man's Friend.[2]

His exclusion from office did not deter him from the work which now commanded his conscience. He had found his vocation in the Parliamentary advocacy of social reform, in tours to gather evidence for it on the spot, in endless duties to inspect its enforcement, and in personal philanthropy to supplement it. One by one he took up the causes of the oppressed. As early as 1828 he had been made a Commissioner in Lunacy; six years later he became Chairman of the Commission. He was the chief architect of the Lunacy Act of 1845, and at the time of his last sickness in 1885 was still active in detailed labours in the oversight of the treatment of lunatics. This cause alone would have secured him a true glory, but he also shouldered heroic burdens of work on the Public Health Commission formed in 1848 to force sanitation into one town after another. He did more than any other man to regulate the lodging houses where so many working-class people had to live. He befriended the blind, the cripples, the destitute incurables; the women and children wearing their bodies out in the factories or underground in the mines or as 'gangs' at work on the farms; the boys made to climb chimneys as sweeps; the children beaten into being acrobats; the vagrant boys or the adult thieves whose only hope of escape from a life of crime was the scarcely believable luxury of emigration or training; even the cabmen who needed cheap and respectable clubs. He was not interested in the sufferings of Englishmen only. He insisted on denouncing the British profit from the opium trade imposed on China; he probed into the conditions of factory labour in India; he defended the liberties of Italians and Poles; he fought to restrict the vivisection of animals in laboratories. The older school of politicians was very slow to accept the possibility of action by the State in such fields, and slower still to accept its desirability. 'Is the House prepared to legislate for all these people?' asked Peel in a debate about the factories in 1844. 'Yes!' was the answer shouted back, but Peel threatened to resign if it did.

[2] A comprehensive study has been provided by J. T. Ward, *The Factory Movement, 1830–1855* (Macmillan, 1962).

Until he was fifty years old this courageous reformer was hindered financially by his father's survival and emotionally by his father's hatred. When eventually he became Earl of Shaftesbury his work increased, for his creditors demanded the repayment of his own debts and the estate's, and his conscience drove him to improve the disgraceful conditions of his labourers and tenants. The confusion in the estate's affairs plunged him into piles of paper; he then turned back to philanthropy in London. only to find that his agent in Dorset swindled him and had to be sued in protracted and expensive legal actions. At no stage did he have a competent secretary or assistant, yet as his fame and involvements increased his hand-written correspondence exhausted him: 'My mind is as dry as a gravel road, and my nerves are sensitive and harsh as wires', he was writing in 1857. His chief pleasure became not his estate but the Ragged Schools, small charitable institutions for very poor boys and girls. He could ask for the prayers of the children, boast of their successes, and treasure their letters. He also found consolation in the work of the Young Men's Christian Associations, then on a strong Evangelical foundation.

Another form of public service which would have brought some pleasure to many other men seems to have been regarded by him as a burden: he was chairman of innumerable missionary and charitable meetings. Although some of the most active of the Evangelicals or their sons concentrated on the labours of the parish or diocese, their favourite societies also still flourished, as in William Wilberforce's day. The most influential of them on the home front was the Church Pastoral Aid Society, founded with the young Lord Ashley as President in 1836 in order to supply Evangelical curates and 'lay agents' in 'popular' districts. The most scholarly was the Parker Society founded with the same President in 1840 in order to reprint the divines of the English Reformation. But there were many others—too many. In addition there were many rallies in defence of the Bible, or special services in theatres or in Exeter Hall in London (the scene of much of this oratory, built in 1831). He was expected to dignify the proceedings, to read a lesson, to speak. He was always applauded, yet he allowed himself so little time for rest or preparation that he knew that his speeches were usually stale and often they bored him.

'Is he thinking more of the clubs of St. James's Street than the audience of the Heavenly host?' he asked about Lord Raglan's conduct in the Crimea. The question never arose about him; and he was as indifferent to the universities as to the London clubs. He had not endured the abuse of the factory-owners, or the learned arguments of eminent doctors produced to testify to the beneficial effects of machine-minding on the health of women and children, in order to capitulate to scholarly critics of the Bible. He had not spent so many hours unravelling the case histories of people thought justly or unjustly to be lunatics, in order to have others hint that his religion had damaged his mind. Once a lady appeared before him while he was acting as a Lunacy Commissioner. 'Are you aware, my Lord, that she subscribes to the Society for the Conversion of the Jews?' 'Indeed! And are you aware that I am President of that society?'

He was the most prominent Evangelical statesman at a time when there was no major Evangelical thinker, with the result that the leadership of that party's many organizations largely devolved on him while the leadership of the party's intellectual life went by default.[3] Yet when he compared his position with that of William Wilberforce he admitted that he was not consulted by many near-equals about personal matters, as had continually happened to his great predecessor. He gave the explanation that many Evangelical pastors had been raised up in the parishes, which was true enough; but he might have added that, in comparison with William Wilberforce, he repelled intimate confidences because he was habitually wrapped up in his own melancholy. He also lacked the vision of the progress of the people as a great co-operative enterprise, for he was too fond of presiding over a private society or voluntary school which distributed benefits paternally. The world of the charities had become such a jungle in his lifetime that the Charity Organization Society (later renamed the Family Welfare Association) had to be founded, but he was far from enthusiastic about its work. He regarded education by the State as 'a water rate to extinguish religious fire among young people' and in 1870 he maintained that compulsory education up to the age of ten would be adequate. The large-scale movement of Evangelically minded Christians into the wider world of social reform and popular education, digging to the roots of poverty, had to wait until after his death—when the leaders were mostly Free Churchmen.[4]

He knew little of the joy of the saints, but he did receive a more

---

[3] The most prominent dynasty among the Evangelicals produced Henry Venn, Vicar of Huddersfield, his son John, Rector of Clapham, and spiritual leader of the 'Clapham Sect', and his grandson Henry, Secretary of the Church Missionary Society, 1841–72. There were some formidable Evangelical preachers in the middle of the century, and many good pastors, but no commanding bishops until the two who founded the Anglican diocese of Liverpool, beginning in 1880, J. C. Ryle and F. J. Chavasse. See G. R. Balleine, *A History of the Evangelical Party in the Church of England*, 3rd ed. (Church Book Room Press, 1951), and Marcus Loane, *Makers of our Heritage* (Hodder & Stoughton, 1967). Canon Michael Hennell's forthcoming history of the Victorian Evangelicals will fill a gap.

[4] An appraisal of their social work in the Victorian era was provided by Kathleen Heasman, *Evangelicals in Action* (Bles, 1962). For the context, see David Roberts, *Victorian Origins of the Welfare State* (Yale University Press, 1960).

mundane reward: some taste of power in making ecclesiastical appointments. This came about because his mother-in-law took Lord Palmerston as her second husband. Palmerston knew almost nothing of theology or clergymen, but respected Shaftesbury. Shaftesbury on his side approved of 'Pam', who had supported factory legislation when Gladstone, for example, had fumbled, and who had raised high the reputation of Britain for a moralizing interference in the affairs of European nations. While Palmerston was Prime Minister (1855–65, with one year's interruption) Shaftesbury therefore became the bishop-maker behind the scenes. Despite the lamentations of Samuel Wilberforce and others, he used his power well on the whole. The Prime Minister's only instruction was that the bishops should be men who got on with the Nonconformists, and Shaftesbury, although he naturally preferred to produce an Evangelical for promotion, did not exclude all Broad Churchmen. For example, he recalled: 'I suggested to him Dr. Tait for London . . . believing that the Broad Church ought to be represented . . . and selected Dr. Tait as the mildest among them.' He often gave vent to impatience with the dignitaries of the Church, mainly because they did not support him enough in social reforms, and as an anti-Tractarian he declared that 'nothing would more tend to induce great numbers of people to join our Church than the putting an end to a state of things under which Ordination is left in the hands of a single individual'. But, being an aristocrat, he did believe very firmly in the usefulness of strong leadership. Palmerston persuaded Shaftesbury to accept the Garter as a reward for his labours, and was persuaded by him to make a Christian deathbed.

3

To Frederick Denison Maurice, the revolutionary dramas of 1848 went beyond any sphere to be covered by Prince Albert's benevolence. When he preached on Advent Sunday that year his excitement was still intense.

The flourishes and exaggerations of rhetoric, puerile always, become absolutely ridiculous when they are set side by side with the experiences through which Europe has been passing and is passing. Do you really think the invasion of Palestine by Sennacherib was a more wonderful event than the overthrowing of nearly all the greatest powers, civil and ecclesiastical, in Christendom?

The year seemed to Maurice a veritable Apocalypse. When, later on, he came to lecture on the last book in the Bible, he was to compare the Babylon of St. John the Divine's vision with Victorian London; and now in 1848 he heard the thunder of destiny.

He was also stirred, more than Lord Ashley was, to do something for—and with—healthy, male workers. One practical result of the agitation was that he became President of the Society for Promoting Working Men's Associations, and one great achievement of this society was to promote legislation which made it far easier for such 'associations' to register themselves, to protect themselves against fraud, and in general to establish themselves as legal entities. With the backing of John Stuart Mill and lesser economists, with the blessing of a Conservative (Derby–Disraeli) government which wished to court the workers, and with remarkably little opposition, an Act to protect 'Industrial and Provident Societies' was passed by Parliament in 1852. It was the charter of all modern co-operatives. Although its terms were modest enough (it did not grant limited liability), Shaftesbury refused to sponsor it, and the M.P. whose name was associated with this measure was the otherwise obscure Robert Slaney.

The only occasion when Maurice and Shaftesbury collaborated seems to have been the launching of one of the associations—a short-lived experiment to help women skilled at needlework. Maurice sent £25 with a letter saying that his name as one of the sponsors was 'likely to disgust Lord Shaftesbury and his friends'. It was just as well that he was not present at the inaugural meeting in Shaftesbury's home, for the proceedings included a proposal from Thomas Carlyle that the problems of distressed needlewomen should be solved by shipping them to California, where they would find husbands. It was also just as well for the needlewomen that Shaftesbury was not made more aware of the philosophical implication of their 'association' in the minds of the Christian Socialists who looked to Maurice as their prophet. One of these, John Malcolm Ludlow, who was present at the meeting, was still smarting under the peer's patronage when he wrote retrospectively in 1868: 'Lord Shaftesbury's ideal was one of dumb instinctive obedience, not of self mastery in the harmonious fellowship of work. Substantially he had to work *de haut en bas*. He delighted in raising the humble, and the humbler the better. . . .'[5]

It was in Maurice's house that Charles Kingsley composed his placard during the evening of 10 April 1848, after the failure of the Chartist demonstration: 'The Almighty God, and Jesus Christ, the poor Man who died for poor men, will bring freedom for you, though all the Mammonites on earth were against you. . . . Workers of England, be wise, and then you *must* be free, for you will be *fit* to be free.' To be sure, the courage of this manifesto has been exaggerated by later writers who have pretended that the whole religious world of the day was hostile. In fact preachers and religious journalists seem to

[5] N. C. Masterman, *John Malcolm Ludlow* (Cambridge University Press, 1963), pp. 98–9.

have sympathized on the whole with the early attempts of Maurice and his friends to get alongside the workers, just as the reaction of Chartists to such support seems to have been favourable on the whole, although no great notice was taken in any quarter. But those few who like Kingsley could stammer out at a meeting 'I am a Church of England clergyman . . . *and* a Chartist' were doing more than sympathizing. Telling the workers to be wise was no novelty. The courageous innovation lay in working alongside them so that they might raise themselves; and it was this that in the 1850s brought on Kingsley, and on Maurice, the wrath of the religious Tories of the *Record* and the *Quarterly Review*—and of secularists such as Karl Marx who feared competition from the Christian Socialists' 'holy water'.

Interference in the workings of the new industrial society was, indeed, so daring for a Church of England man that, just as Lord Ashley did not identify himself with factory reform until 1833, so Maurice did not become a Christian Socialist until 1848. Of course neither man had been totally oblivious before his conversion to reform. The young aristocrat had already undertaken his work for lunatics; the young clergyman had ministered to the sick of London as Chaplain of Guy's Hospital, and had welcomed Carlyle's *Chartism*. And of course there were other examples of practical sympathy with the workers in the Church of England (specially in the North) before 1848, and before 1833.[6] But it is significant that Ashley could feel so isolated in his social crusading. The Tractarians were more worried about the suppression of bishops in Ireland than about the deaths of babies in the slums which Oxford colleges owned. Samuel Wilberforce was advised by his father that a Northern industrial parish was no place for a young clergyman to cultivate his devotional life. Many churchmen were worried by the fear of revolution which had contributed to the appeal of William Wilberforce; some were worried into urgent words, such as the semi-radical Arnolds (or the romantically Tory Poet Laureate, Robert Southey, whose hatred of the barbarism in the new manufacturing towns impressed both Shaftesbury and Maurice).[7] But fewer were worried into effective sympathy.

Therefore when a movement called itself 'Christian Socialist', it was combining the two words in a startling paradox. By the end of the century, in the days of Westcott and Gore, the Christian Social Union was to be a nursery of bishops, and the rise of the Labour Party was to owe much to the work of the local churches and chapels

---

[6] Among parish priests moved to action by the distress of their people the name of George Bull, whose indomitable eloquence prepared the Ten Hours Movement before and after Ashley's involvement, deserves special honour. See J. C. Gill, *The Ten Hours Parson* and *Parson Bull of Byerley* (SPCK, 1959–63).   [7] See Jack Simmons, *Southey* (Collins, 1945).

in training men to concentrate, to combine and to speak up for idealistic purposes.[8] Ludlow lived to speak at the Pan-Anglican Congress of 1908, rejoicing in that scene of social idealism at the age of eighty-eight. But in the 1840s not only were most Christians unsocial: all Socialists were thought by respectable property-owners to be atheistic and violent. Maurice joined the two words with his usual educational purpose, for the paradox would make men think. To encourage men further, he edited the penny tracts, *Politics for the People*, and Ludlow edited the journal, the *Christian Socialist*. The idea of tracts had been in Maurice's mind for years, and he had also had the idea of calling them Cambridge Tracts. However, neither the tracts nor the journal reached a large audience, or lasted long. As a journalist Maurice was no Newman, and Christian Socialism never possessed the intellectual coherence of Oxford Tractarianism.

Much of the material which it sponsored was diffuse, aimed at making churchmen sympathetic and workers wise. Kingsley emerged as the movement's only vigorous popular publicist, with his novels about farm labourers and tailors (*Yeast* and *Alton Locke*) and his shorter writings as 'Parson Lot'. The political thrust, when this emerged, was towards 'associations'—co-operative workshops where the capital would be provided initially by well-wishers and subsequently by ploughing back profits. The idea was in the air of early English Socialism, but Maurice himself owed it to a letter from Ludlow (now lost) which passed on some of the excitements of the French experiments and some of the warnings of the French disturbances. Ludlow's own strong personality reinforced this dramatic message from Paris. He had been left fatherless and had been taken by his mother for a first-rate education in France. He had become a conveyancer (solicitor) in London because his mother had told him that his father would have wished him to be an Englishman, but had felt lonely and near suicide in a strange land. He had met Maurice because he wanted advice about how to do social work in his spare time; Maurice had referred him to the nearby parish priest, but had kept in touch with Ludlow because he gave to this work some of the collections in Lincoln's Inn Chapel, where he was Chaplain. Now in 1848 Ludlow virtually appointed Maurice his spiritual father, and summoned him to lead a crusade. When the crisis was over, it was Ludlow who kept up the pressure on the London group to produce something like the newspaper he had envisaged for France (it was to have been called *La Fraternité Chrétienne*) and something like the working communities he had glimpsed there, notably Fourier's scheme for college-like *phalanges*.

[8] Stephen Mayor, *The Churches and the Labour Movement* (Independent Press, 1967), is a study based mainly on newspapers since 1850.

Many small producers' co-operatives were founded in England during and after 1850, and conferences of their representatives were gathered. Ludlow believed passionately that they pointed to the salvation of society, and was never completely disillusioned. In the twentieth century the banner was handed on to the Guild Socialists such as G. D. H. Cole, and to many later advocates of 'partnership', 'co-ownership', or 'profit-sharing' schemes for industry. But the main emphasis in the powerful Co-operative Movement derived from the Toad Lane Store in Rochdale, not from the idealists of the London workshops. Producers' co-operatives ran into many difficulties. Some of their members were fraudulent, and others inefficient. Wages were a problem, once it was agreed that it was unrealistic to make these equal, and prices too, until consumers were regenerate. All the time it was difficult to secure the orders and to market the goods. Not surprisingly, most workmen preferred to get regular wages from capitalists. On the other hand, consumers' co-operatives found competition with the capitalist system easier, for they paid dividends to purchasers and could with relative ease manufacture their own goods for sale to their own members. Consumers' co-operatives never enjoyed the sacred ideology which Maurice and Ludlow bestowed on the workers whose associations they promoted, yet few could deny their economic benefits, nor the advantage to them of the 1852 Act.[9] Even they, however, did not lay down the high road of Socialism. That road was provided by state interference, growing in England almost continuously during and after the 1870s. Ludlow, who was appointed Chief Registrar of Friendly Societies in 1875 and who encouraged many steps towards social security either as a civil servant or as a writer, would say to the end of his long life that to him Socialism was a faith, not a business. He often struck men of the world as being doctrinaire, perhaps because his mind was French. He thought it vitally important that Maurice, the only major prophet he knew, should guide the advance, and should be supported by 'a true and holy Jesuitry'. When Maurice abandoned the leadership of Christian Socialism Ludlow did not attempt to take it up, although he often looked back and asked himself whether he should have done more.

The immediate cause of Maurice's withdrawal from 'politics for the people' was his concentration on his Principalship of the Working Men's College, first housed in the premises of the defunct Needlewomen's Association, but many tensions had arisen before 1854 among the Christian Socialists. They were tensions between those who re-

[9] G. D. H. Cole, *A Century of Co-operation* (Co-operative Union, Manchester, 1944), p. 113, concluded that 'the Christian Socialist incursion . . . was, indeed, a curious episode exceedingly unpractical in its methods. But it had lastingly beneficent results'.

garded the work as primarily political or economic, and those who regarded it as educational. Maurice was in the latter group, Ludlow in the former, although he loyally became Maurice's chief lieutenant in the college. More typical of the future than either was Vansittart Neale, a barrister with no clear theological views but with a grasp of the practical problems of co-operatives and trade unions—and with a personal fortune which he spent on the work. Maurice distrusted his own abilities as an administrator (wisely), and dreaded the formation of a party bearing his name; to the dismay of the jealous Ludlow, he therefore welcomed Neale's dominance. The political and economic movement moved out of its heroic days, and all that seemed to be left of the spirit of 1848 was an educational ideal. Between the prophetic Maurice and the efficient Neale, Ludlow was left suspended— or, to be more accurate, stranded in a house made by the builders' co-operative at Wimbledon. He and the author of *Tom Brown's Schooldays*, who lived next door, had a common library and on Sundays would hold services there, reading aloud the sermons of Thomas Arnold and Frederick Denison Maurice.

For as long as possible Ludlow clung to the belief that he could make Maurice into a practical man. He wrote to him: 'It does seem to me that you are liable to be carried away by Platonistic dreams about an Order, and a Kingdom, and a Beauty, self-realized in their own eternity, and which so put to shame all earthly counterparts that it becomes labour lost to attempt anything like an earthly realization of them. I do not think this is Christianity.' That outburst came because Maurice had just prohibited the publication of a pamphlet by a future Viceroy of India (Lord Goderich, later the Marquis of Ripon) on *The Duty of the Age*. This pamphlet, which had been set in type as a Christian Socialist tract after Ludlow's warm approval, had shocked Maurice by its stress on democracy as the trend of the future and—what worried a theologian more—as the will of God. Maurice always believed in monarchy, for Christ was King, and in aristocracy, for men were governed by their best parts and not by their animal instincts, but he could find no support in theology for government by the people. He ran the Working Men's College on paternalist lines, and disapproved of the extension of the Parliamentary franchise in 1867.[10] And the intellectual remoteness from an increasingly democratic age made Ludlow protest: 'you go and sport yourself in a quiet pool of your own.'

[10] See J. F. C. Harrison, *A History of the Working Men's College, 1854–1954* (Routledge & Kegan Paul, 1954). Maurice remained Principal until his death, which brought to a head demands for a new constitution giving more of a say to the teachers and students. Yet Harrison agrees that Maurice's personal attractiveness and humility, and his wish to have discussion honest and free, held the experiment together through its early years.

Ludlow later confessed that 'the Maurice I had devoted myself to was the Maurice of my own imagination'. Perhaps enthusiasts ought to have been warned on the very day of the Chartists' demonstration, when Maurice, who had previously enrolled as a Special Constable in order to protect property, stayed at home because he had a cold and wished to preserve his voice for his Sunday sermon. Certainly in 1852, while he was wrecking the Christian Socialist movement as Ludlow conceived it, he gave a convincing apologia. He did not merely say that he was more interested in education than in politics, although his work for King's College, for the Queen's College for women, and (in the near future) for the Working Men's College might have provided a sufficient alibi. Nor did he merely disclaim the aptitude for oratory and business of, say, Shaftesbury. (He had a habit of lecturing with his eyes closed which, we are told, encouraged disorder when his audiences were present under compulsion, and we may gather that when his audiences were voluntary they might be small.) It could not be said of him, as it could be said of Shaftesbury, that he avoided some controversies because he had a large vested interest in the economic order; nor was personal ambition involved, for like the Oxford Tractarians he had pledged himself to avoid ecclesiastical preferment and the favour of politicians. In 1849 he had written, and had meant it: 'My vocation is with the discontented, weary, hopeless, with all that are in debt and disgrace, with outcasts and ragamuffins in the different bodies.' But Maurice knew that his vocation was not limitless. His integrity as a spiritual teacher seemed to demand refusal to get involved in arguments over the division of the political and economic inheritance among the discontented.

That letter of 1849 had hinted at the foundations. 'I have no notion that things can be kept going upon our present ground of mutual hatred and suspicion. The end of that rotten system must be at hand, and the only work I desire is that of preparing people for it, by showing them that there is a Rock to stand upon when the rains descend and the winds blow.' Now in 1852 he wrote to Ludlow:

My business, because I am a theologian, and have no vocation except for theology, is not to build, but to dig, to show that economy and politics (I leave physics to dear Kingsley . . .) must have a ground beneath themselves, that society is not to be made anew by arrangements of ours, but is to be regenerated by finding the law and ground of its order and harmony, the only secret of its existence, in God.

Both Ludlow and Maurice agreed in the aim of the Society for Promoting Working Men's Associations: 'to diffuse the principle of Co-operation as the practical application of Christianity to the progress of trade and industry.' To Ludlow, however, the associations were the first steps in a political programme, putting capital into the

hands of the workers. To Maurice these small experiments were prophetic signs, declaring against every economist's emphasis on general
or corporate or class selfishness that men were brothers, tied by blood
not money in a Divine Order which already existed. The profits of the
co-operatives interested him less than their brotherhood; their value
as pointers to the future less than their value as revelations of present
facts. He was a little more practical over the management of colleges,
but when he came to expound his philosophy of adult education, in
his lectures on *Learning and Working* (1855), he showed a similar
contempt for commercial considerations. We cannot wonder that some
of the Christian Socialists who referred to him as 'the Prophet'
privately found him maddening. On the other hand, Maurice the
visionary has held a more permanent interest than Ludlow the reformer. The hard times of the Hungry Forties passed, thanks in part
to reforms but mainly to the unregulated expansion of the economy,
although much distress remained in the shadows of Victorian life.
But Maurice's reforms in the kingdom of faith and the imagination
have continued to command attention.[11]

John Stuart Mill himself witnessed to the primacy of the theological
debate. In the last chapter of his *Autobiography* he noted that the
reforms after 1848 'had been attended with much less benefit to human
well-being than I should formerly have anticipated' because they had
not altered the average Englishman's confused habits of mind. Mill,
writing about 1861, added:

When the philosophic minds of the world can no longer believe its religion,
or can only believe it with modifications amounting to an eventual change of
its character, a transitional period commences, of weak convictions, paralysed intellects, and growing laxity of principle, which cannot terminate until
a renovation has been effected in the basis of their belief, leading to the evolution of some faith, whether religious or merely human, which they can really
believe: and when things are in this state, all thinking or writing which does
not tend to promote such a renovation, is of very little value beyond the
moment.

4

'The world', wrote Tom Hughes, 'has only had three great theologians, Augustine, Luther and Maurice, and the greatest of these is

[11] The number of modern editions of Maurice's works illustrates his continuing appeal: *Theological Essays* (1957), *The Kingdom of Christ* (1958), *The
Prayer Book* (1966), *Learning and Working* (1968). M. B. Reckitt, *Maurice to
Temple* (Faber & Faber, 1947), was an account of a century of Anglican social
teaching by one who believed that the theory of 'Christian sociology', where
Maurice had laid down guiding lines, was more important than any pragmatic
reform in 'the reconstruction of society on Christian principles'.

Maurice.'[12] Since the second world war several books have offered
enthusiastic introductions to the thought of Maurice, whose published
writings may be said to need summary, for another commentator,
Claude Jenkins, reckoned that they contained nearly five million
words.[13] Yet in his own lifetime Maurice knew that he was often
regarded as a 'muddy mystic', and after his death Leslie Stephen's
memoir in the *Dictionary of National Biography*, while describing his
character as 'very fascinating', left the impression that the only interest
of his mind lay in its confusion. Matthew Arnold observed that Maurice
passed his life 'beating the bush with deep emotion and never starting
the hare', while John Stuart Mill paid the wry tribute that 'there
was more intellectual power wasted in Maurice than in any other of
my contemporaries'. Part of the blame attaches to Maurice's habit of
dictating some of his books, walking up and down, hugging a pillow,
and furiously poking the fire. But, even when he did not dictate, the
style was the man: his manuscripts show the haste with which he
wrote. He was essentially a preacher out to warn or comfort, who
did not mind if the fire was scattered or if the pillow induced mental
sleep. In this he was like Augustine and Luther, but although Maurice
was the greatest English theologian of the nineteenth century he did
not attain their greatness, for he did not have their ruthless clarity
or the world-transforming courage of their radicalism.

Like Shaftesbury, he had an experience as a boy which eventually shaped his life. He owed much to Plato and to Coleridge, because
he found in their philosophies echoes of his own experience, but he
gained few of his theological insights from the Cambridge tutor who
took him through Plato (Julius Hare, who became his brother-in-law),
and he was too shy to meet Coleridge. He was, like Shaftesbury, a
man of the Bible—and was more truly biblical, for he objected to the
Evangelical (or Tractarian) 'system' of 'notions' which tended to
prevent the Bible from speaking for itself; yet his exposition of the
Bible was full of pet ideas and reiterated jargon. We are told that he
borrowed many of these special meanings for common theological
terms from his mother. It is certainly clear that essentially his thought

[12] *Memoirs of Daniel Macmillan* (Macmillan, 1882), p. 284. While still a
poor clerk, Macmillan urged Maurice to give a lead in improving the conditions
of the poor. Later he became his publisher; he was devoted, although he complained that the Prophet wrote too much, and his friendship with Maurice and
other religious pundits of the Victorian age laid the foundations of his firm's
success, first in Cambridge and then in London.

[13] I am also indebted to Dr. Frank McClain, one of the American scholars
interested in this field. Dr. McClain's use of unpublished material has been
more thorough than any previous scholar's, and the publication of his study as
Maurice the Man and the Moralist (SPCK) is awaited to commemorate the
centenary of Maurice's death.

was home-made. His was a home intensely pious and intensely intellectual, and at first it seemed that on leaving it he would concentrate on the enthusiasm for current affairs which he inherited from his father. After leaving Cambridge he tried his hand as a London journalist and as a novelist (his *Eustace Conway* was published in 1834). But the novel showed that what really stirred him was the drama of a conflict of religious opinions in a family, and it hinted at a deeply theological solution.

His father was a Unitarian minister, insisting on the reality and unity of God but teaching mainly about morals and politics. With his tolerant liberalism, Michael Maurice baptized in the name of the Father, and of the Son, and of the Holy Ghost; 'in the name of an abstraction, a man, and a metaphor' as a friend remarked pleasantly. (Who would have ventured on such a pleasantry with any other member of the family?) Such a religion was not enough for his three eldest daughters, who had themselves baptized again and who wrote to him in 1816: 'We do not think it consistent with the duty we owe to God to attend a Unitarian place of worship.' One of these girls became a Baptist, although the others were Anglicans. Nor was it enough for his wife; she soon became an earnest Calvinist in the Church of England, sending letters of religious advice to her husband but believing that she was not herself numbered among the elect of God.

Nor was it enough for Frederick. But the boy was loyal to his father's example which combined integrity with broad mindedness, and probably he also noticed the patience with which his father received letters about theology from the women living under his roof. He therefore refused to undergo a thoroughly Evangelical conversion in his boyhood, or to sign the Church of England's Articles in order to proceed to a Cambridge degree and a career. What crisis there was came to its climax when he was aged twenty-six, in 1831, feeling the need of a 'personal deliverer'. He was baptized in Oxford as a member of the Church of England, and spent almost the whole of the next three months at the deathbed of his sister Emma, conversing mainly on Evangelical themes. That winter he was able to inform his father that he had found the satisfying answer to 'the one great cry of human nature in all ages'. 'If the Infinite, Incomprehensible Jehovah is manifested in the person of a Man, a Man conversing with us, living among us, entering into all our infirmities and temptations, and passing into all our conditions, it is satisfied; if not, it remains unsatisfied.' By moving beyond his father's position he had found his own faith to proclaim, and he spoke the Trinitarian blessing as his last words early on Easter Monday, 1872. But he could never say that he had passed from secular darkness into Evangelical light, for the Christ whom he had found as the one Redeemer was a Christ who preached a message not utterly remote from Michael Maurice's.

This discovery of Christ as the shining centre of the universe, and this refusal to banish anyone to outer darkness, provided the message, reached after countless hours of theological argument in his family, and after years spent like Jonah trying to escape his destiny to be a preacher. No attack by agnostics or Evangelicals could ever move him. Yet he was so assured as to be tolerant. The whole of a personality deeply Christian lay behind his refusal to place the Socialists, or his pragmatic collaborator Vansittart Neale, beyond the pale of Christianity. His greatest scholarly work was a history of *Moral and Metaphysical Philosophy* (1861), designed to show how a Christian might learn from the intellectual life of mankind. He went far towards saying that each nation's history was its own Old Testament; not only England's or Germany's, but also the Eastern nations' (about which he, naturally, knew far less). When in 1845–6 he delivered the Boyle Lectures on *The Religions of the World*, he was clear both that Christ was the Revelation of God and that Muslims or Buddhists were seeking God in sincerity and with some success. Maurice dared to express this wide vision at a time when Reginald Heber was hymning the religion of Buddhist Ceylon in these terms:

> The heathen in his blindness
> Bows down to wood and stone.[14]

The nature of Maurice's own spiritual pilgrimage also determined the nature of his vision of the Church. Unlike Newman, he did not see the Church as the substitute for, and therefore effectively the enemy of, the natural family and the normal life. On the contrary, Maurice proclaimed—like Keble, but with a passionate conviction which never lost its urgency however often he repeated himself—that men entered the Church through the family. If they were faithful to the duties of family life, they would be faithful also to the duties of national citizenship, and if they understood themselves properly as members of families and nations, they would enter into their heritage as members of the Church, the universal family.

Maurice expounded his vision of the Church to a Scotsman, Thomas Erskine, whose own generous views had provided a large influence and encouragement.

The Church—it seems to me—is a part, the highest part, of that spiritual constitution of which the nation and the family are lower and subordinate parts; implied in the acts we do and the words we speak, established before all worlds, manifested as the true and everlasting kingdom when the Son of

[14] 'Ceylon' was later changed to 'Java'.

God died, rose, and ascended on high, testified as the common property and inheritance of men by certain forms and ordinances which convert it from an idea for the mind into an actual reality for all who will enter into it and enjoy it, and which prove God to be true though all men be liars.

Maurice went so far as to deny that Christianity was 'a religion'. To call it a religion was to limit or corrupt its message about God the Father of all. 'We have been dosing our people with religion, when what they want is not this but the living God.' And the living God, the God of Jesus Christ, was not remote. 'The revelation of Christ', he wrote to his sister Esther (Mrs. Julius Hare), 'must be the revelation, however gradually, of all these hidden principles and secret powers, and directing laws, which men in all directions have been seeking after; must be the revelation of all the relations in which they stand to each other and to God's universe.' In the same letter he envisaged 'the Son of God vindicating the name of the carpenter's son which He bore upon earth by asserting every energy of man's bodily frame, every natural machine as His'.

This vision of Christ as 'the Ruler over the universe now' arose from a boy's protest against the theological quarrels which were tearing his father apart from his mother and which were dividing his seven sisters. The vision was strengthened by his early experience as a clergyman. He served as a curate under an incumbent who had a theory about the Revelation of St. John the Divine. There was nothing extraordinary about that; stranger, however, was the nature of Mr. Stephenson's theory, as recalled by his curate. At an early stage

he maintained that the hills and valleys of this earth, redeemed, purified, and regenerated, were to be the scene of the felicity of the ransomed children of God. . . . This opinion he never changed, but deeper study and meditation . . . led him to conclusions very different from those which are adopted by modern readers of prophecy generally. . . . He became convinced that the greater part of those Scriptures which are usually referred to a far distant period, were actually accomplished when the Jewish polity passed away and the universal Church rose out of its ruins . . ., that these events were nothing less than the actual manifestation of Christ's Kingdom, the actual establishment of a communion between the two worlds, the creation of a new heaven and a new earth.

It was a version of the old millenarian belief that Christ and his saints would reign on the earth for a thousand years; but it added that they were *already* reigning. In the midst of such speculation Mr. Stephenson's curate heard the one message he needed. When Maurice, still suffering from shyness and a 'great depression of spirits', moved to London and Guy's Hospital, he remembered the message and lived by it. He found courage to approach the sick, or to lecture to the medical students, only because he now believed that the goodness which he found in them (among much else) pointed to the fact that they, too, were already citizens in Christ's Kingdom, for they had been baptized. 'It seemed to me that except I could address all kinds of people as members of Christ and children of God, I could not address them at all.'

He therefore shared the Tractarians' insistence that the Church was constituted not by feelings or 'notions', but by objective realities. What, however, were the sacraments? In 1837 he was crossing Clapham Common on his way to an Evangelical meeting and reading Dr. Pusey's immense Tract Sixty-seven on Baptism. 'The baptized child was holy for a moment after its baptism, by committing sin it lost its purity. That could be recovered by acts of repentance and a system of ascetical discipline.' So he understood as he read, and the apparent denial of the sure status of all the baptized horrified him. He now publicly broke with the Tractarians, who had previously been hoping that he would join them in Oxford as Professor of Political Economy, and in 1841 he published an open letter to Archdeacon Samuel Wilberforce, entitled *Reasons for Not Joining a Party in the Church*. But he did not prefer the Evangelical view of Baptism, which tended to imply that the service mattered little in comparison with the emotions of the 'second birth'; and he was soon to incur the wrath of that party by his open letter to Lord Ashley against the persecution of Pusey. What he did believe he poured out in a book which was published in 1838 as a series of Anglican tracts for Quakers. He revised these chapters in 1841, to form his most important work, *The Kingdom of Christ*.

He chose to address the Quakers because he believed that the Society of Friends was 'likely to perish by a slow decay' unless its members would move beyond the spirituality of its founder in the seventeenth century, George Fox. The decay had come because the Quakers had fallen victims to the disease of the age, 'money-getting', but this itself could be traced to Fox's trust in an 'inward light' when he ought to have been humble enough to receive the only light and power greater than the appeal of 'money-getting'.

For a description of this light and power Maurice turned to Luther, who 'told men that union with Christ was deliverance from sin and condemnation; that that union was claimed and maintained by faith; that faith was therefore justification'. Maurice understood the heart of Lutheranism as very few other Englishmen did; yet he rejected the 'mysteries' which had corrupted the 'principles' of the Reformation. What he offered in the place of Lutheran orthodoxy was a series of 'hints' about the nature of the Catholic Church with this experience of faith at its heart. To him as much as to the Tractarians, the Church was 'built upon the very nature of God himself, and upon the union which He has formed with His creatures'; yet, true to the way in which he had experienced faith, he preferred to begin with the natural family, 'the true order of the world'. In the Church there were certain 'signs' which pointed to Christ as King and God as Father. These were Baptism itself, the sacrament which asserted the 'constant union' between God and his children; the creeds which were confessions of 'the Name' of our salvation; liturgical forms of public worship, the family's praise of the Father; the Eucharist, the family's communion, nourishing body and spirit with its witness to the finished work of Christ; the orders of ministry including episcopacy, signs of the universality of Christ's Church; and the Scriptures. So the Church George Fox had dismissed as 'steeple-houses' was idealized by Maurice, but also identified with the world as it 'really' was.

When you go into the town to market, look up at the churches and say, — 'This, too, is my Father's dwelling place; these are witnesses that I am a citizen of the New Jerusalem, that I belong to an innumerable company of saints and angels, and that all these men who are about me, are of the same family. The city and the men in it are holy.'

It is not difficult to see how the experience reflected in *The Kingdom of Christ* enabled Maurice to prophesy with a vision of the City of God in 1848, and to persevere with his message. 'The desire for unity, and the search after unity both in the nation and in the Church, has haunted me all my days', he told his son Frederick when he was near the end, after confessing that 'I have laid a great many addled eggs in my time'. He ascribed parties in the Church to the devilish spirit of sectarianism and refused to be the leader of a Broad Church party, as he had refused to organize the Christian Socialists. 'I am sure the Liturgy will torment us so long as we continue selfish and divided, therefore I would cling to it': that was one of his ways of extolling the Prayer Book. He defended the Thirty-nine Articles on the ground that they preserved the Church from the 'superstitions' of the nineteenth century. He was reluctant to abandon the use of the Athanasian Creed, claiming that it had never made him feel uncharitable. And he magnified his clerical office, writing: 'If we called the four Gospels "The Institution of a Christian Ministry," we might not go very far wrong.' But the desire for unity which made him for practical purposes a conservative in ecclesiastical politics also made him a preacher of social reconciliation and joint progress, and a High Statesman. 'The State is as much God's creation as the Church, even as the body is just as much his creation as the spirit.' On this basis he struggled to reassert Richard Hooker's theme of the unity of Church and State. To him, this seemed as appropriate in Victorian as in Elizabethan England; but he also looked forward to the time when the

Episcopal Church in the United States would have earned establishment as the National Church. (Until then, were the United States a true nation?) He was not greatly interested in those privileges for the Church of England's bishops and clergy which might be affected by Parliamentary pressures, but he declared: 'The duty which the State owes to the Church . . . is simply this: to give the Church free scope to educate the people.'[15]

Maurice had little sympathy with the Dissenters' protests against an Anglican monopoly in state-supported schools: 'you, not we, are the exclusionists.' His failure of imagination here was one of the indications that his zeal for Anglicanism was the zeal of a convert from Unitarianism.[16] It was his experience that the Church of England meant liberty of spirit, and he could not understand those for whom it would be a prison. After his restless years in Cambridge and London he had enrolled at Oxford, again as an undergraduate, in order to prepare for Anglican ordination; and even Oxford's insistence on the signing of the Thirty-nine Articles on entry (Cambridge required it only on graduation) had seemed glorious to him, as he declared while a curate in his pamphlet *Subscription No Bondage*. Thomas Erskine once observed that his friend could find a good reason for *anything*, and Maurice came to admit that it had been a mistake to require undergraduates to subscribe to the Articles. We must confess that his detailed arguments often amount to 'vague generalities' or 'declamations', the very things which the Utilitarians sought to expose. But no Christocentric vision could be, in principle, more inclusive.

5

Maurice's experience led him to correct the Evangelicalism of his day. He rebuked its whole atmosphere as shown in Shaftesbury's life: both the emotionalism of its introspection and the bitterness of its polemics. He rebuked it with a wider vision of the People of God, and in the fifteenth of his *Theological Essays* he poured forth his vision in tumbling paradoxes: 'The world contains the elements of which the Church is composed. In the Church, those elements are penetrated by a uniting, reconciling power. The Church is, therefore, human society in its normal state; the world, that same society irregular and abnormal.

---

[15] C. K. Gloyn, *The Church in the Social Order: A Study of Anglican Social Theory from Coleridge to Maurice* (Pacific University Press, Forest Grove, Oregon, 1942), is a good study, although almost inaccessible in England.

[16] Another indication was the failure of the author of *The Kingdom of Christ* to understand the Society of Friends. See Elizabeth Isichei, *Victorian Quakers* (Clarendon Press, 1970).

The world is the Church without God; the Church is the world restored to its relation with God, taken back by Him into the state for which he created it. Deprive the Church of its Centre, and you make it into a world.' And he is generally held to have won his case against the Evangelicals' customary theology at four vital points.

The first point was the Evangelical obsession with the depravity of mankind. Maurice's own mother believed that she had no hope of salvation, and a letter to her in 1833 was typical of his efforts to lift her out of her gloom.

My text is this, 'Know ye not that Jesus Christ is in you?'... The truth is that every man is in Christ; the condemnation of every man is, that he will not own the truth; he will not *act* as if this were *true*, he will not believe that which is the truth that, except he were joined to Christ, he could not think, breathe, live a single hour. This is the monstrous lie which the devil palms upon poor sinners. 'You are something apart from Christ. You have a separate, independent existence.'

The Evangelicals started from the sin of Adam, and some of them like poor Priscilla Maurice fixed themselves there. Priscilla's son knew why, and as late as 1854 he wrote to his sister Esther: 'How thoroughly one knows that the Devil is the spirit of despair!' But he was convinced that Christian theology should start with the original righteousness, with the Lordship of Christ, and when he wished to arouse a sense of sin he said: 'You are under a law of love; you know you are, and you are fighting with it.'

The second point where Maurice corrected Evangelical theology was its interpretation of the Atonement. It was fatally easy to present the Evangelical scheme of salvation in such a way as to suggest that the Father's justice demanded the Son's sacrifice as a transaction to be completed before the Father's love could be shown. Indeed, the second of the Thirty-nine Articles which Maurice extolled declared that Christ died 'to reconcile his Father to us'. Maurice believed in the sacrifice offered by Christ, but he preferred to speak of Christ as men's representative—as 'the Head and King of our Race' into whom we are incorporated as one Body—rather than of Christ as the substitute for men's sins. He saw Calvary as the supreme manifestation of the love of the Father: 'Christ satisfied the Father by presenting the image of His own holiness of love'. And he saw the sacrifice of Christ as a sign of the eternal relation of love between the Persons of the Trinity: 'we must not dare to speak of Christ as changing that Will which he took flesh and died to fulfil'. Indeed, he saw all human life as founded on love, and love as founded on self-sacrifice; sacrifice is 'the law of our being'. He repeated such phrases often, bringing together the Trinity, the nation, and the family; and he repeated them sincerely.

He poured himself out for others in a life which reflected his doctrine of the Trinity. In particular his second wife Georgina, whom he married in 1849 four years after Annie's death, was a Victorian invalid who needed, or seemed to need, his constant self-sacrifice.

The third point of Evangelicalism where Maurice prevailed was its doctrine of hell. When consigning obstinate sinners to everlasting punishment Evangelical preachers were only echoing the belief of Christendom, but they seemed to sentence more people to this fate, since many concluded that the only members of the human race with a hope of escaping it were those few who before their death had put their trust in Christ's sacrifice as the substitute to appease the wrath of God. Calvinists limited the numbers escaping hell to those predestined by God. In the last of his *Theological Essays* (1853), Maurice repeated an argument which he had made public in his earlier writings, to the effect that the Greek word *aionios* in the biblical description of hell meant not 'endless' but 'eternal'. His conservative instincts battled with his human sympathies here as in Christian Socialism, and he denied that he was a universalist who believed that all men were bound to be saved. But he also denied that sinners would experience everlasting tortures, and as he lay dying he thought about the mysterious passage in the First Epistle of Peter on the harrowing of hell. 'As the ark saved the eight souls as a promise that *all* should be saved', he mused, 'so baptism saved those who were baptized, thus figuring God's salvation of all.' When he wrote on everlasting punishment in his *Theological Essays* he knew, as he said, that he was writing his own death-sentence as a professor at King's College. But he could do no other. 'I am obliged to believe in an abyss of love which is deeper than the abyss of death: I dare not lose faith in that love. I sink into death, eternal death, if I do.' Modern theologians have tended to comment that Maurice's conviction that the Kingdom of Christ was already present on earth, and his conception of eternity, both reflected Platonist idealism rather than biblical eschatology, but that has not prevented the very widespread acceptance of his protest against the old pictures of hell.

Temporal punishment came soon. King's College, London, had been founded as an Anglican reply to the 'godless' University College; power over it was vested in trustees who were mostly devout peers, and in the Principal, who was then the unimaginative Dr. Jelf (Maurice had refused to be a candidate for the post). Maurice's supporters rightly believed that the peers were not deeply involved in the metaphysical foundations of the intellectual problem of conceiving eternity. But during the first three months of 1852 there had been a major industrial dispute in the shape of a national lock-out, marking the rise of the first of the modern trade unions, the Amalgamated Society of

Engineers, to whom Ludlow gave legal advice. The trustees of King's College, as they turned over publications such as Charles Kingsley's exposure of the conditions of tailors in *Cheap Clothes and Nasty*, saw what might be the consequences of a decline in the lower orders of belief that strikes and other rebellions against authority would bring everlasting punishment. Professor Maurice at that stage occupied two chairs in King's College, one of English Literature and Modern History, the other of Theology. The majority on the trustees' council refused the suggestion of Bishop Blomfield that competent theologians should examine the professor's writings. Instead the trustees felt 'it to be their painful duty to declare that the continuance of Professor Maurice's connection with the college as one of its professors would be seriously detrimental to its usefulness'. They also felt competent to declare the two chairs vacant; but in so doing they made the ex-professor an underdog, and dramatized for the British public the moral iniquity of the old belief. (Tennyson wrote a poem about it all.) When Maurice was elected Knightsbridge Professor of Casuistry and Moral Philosophy at Cambridge in 1866, his name seemed to have been cleared at the expense of the everlasting punishment of the wicked.

The fourth point where Maurice gained the victory over Evangelicalism such as Shaftesbury's was its belief in the verbal infallibility of the Bible. Maurice in the pulpit, in the Bible classes which he loved to conduct, and in private conversation breathed an intense reverence for Holy Scripture. 'I am conscious of just as much unbelief about the books of the Bible, as I am about the facts of nature and my own existence,' he boasted when writing 'On Inspiration' in his *Theological Essays*. When he said that 'the Bible itself forces us to ask a multitude of questions', he had in mind not so much questions arising out of science as moral questions; this remark was made in connection with Elisha's cursing of the impertinent children.[17] When Colenso applied criticism to some of these books he took fright, telling him that 'Samuel must have been a horrid scoundrel if he forged the story about the I AM speaking to Moses'. Later he refused to meet the heretical bishop. His own references to the problem of the authority of the Bible have not retained much value, because he understood so little of the problem. But while Shaftesbury (or Pusey) believed that Christianity depended on questions about the authorship and authenticity of the books of the Bible, Maurice's orthodoxy (somewhat like Newman's) had a certain flexibility. Newman depended on the Church for his religion, and Maurice, the Christian Platonist, depended on a direct insight into the transcendent meaning of the life recorded in the Bible and in every family's and nation's history as well as in the Church. Their hearts were not where Shaftesbury's was; and while neither

[17] *The Prophets and Kings of the Old Testament* (Macmillan, 1853), p. 147.

was much interested in scientific or historical criticisms of the biblical text, each shared Coleridge's conviction that Christianity could, and should, survive without the 'Bibliolatry' which pretended that all the Bible's facts must be accurate and all its opinions divine. 'I leave critics to discourse about documents, what their value is, or whence they came. I merely take what I find.' So Maurice declared in one of his last books, *Social Morality*. At least such an attitude was better than Shaftesbury's (or Pusey's) hysteria against the critics.

In comparison with the academic negatives of the theological liberals, Maurice could claim that the Bible had 'found' him (to use Coleridge's phrase) as profoundly as it had found Shaftesbury. At one discussion in London after *Essays and Reviews* and Colenso, a Member of Parliament raised an easy laugh by remarking: 'Sometimes one would like to know what the clergy *do* believe nowadays!' Maurice arose and seemed to be on fire as he recited the Apostles' Creed. He added that he was bound to protest against all attempts to set up money or other idols in place of the teaching of the living God. The discussion abruptly ended. Such a display of prophetic emotion made it easier for later theologians to work quietly, thus bringing nearer the day which he had seen from afar in a letter of 1849: 'I cannot but think that the Reformation in our day, which I expect to be more deep and searching than that of the sixteenth century, will turn upon the Spirit's presence and life. . . .'

Maurice had one other major controversy, and he looked back on it with the conviction that it had been the most important of his life, although also with the knowledge that in his 'great heat and vehemence of spirit' he had mismanaged it. One Sunday in 1858 William Thomson, who was soon to grace the throne of York, earned his Sunday dinner with Maurice after the Lincoln's Inn service by a horrifying account of the current series of Bampton Lectures in Oxford. In essence, he declared, they were atheism. Actually they were some very shrewd remarks by Henry Mansel on *The Limits of Religious Thought*, anticipating many modern objections to 'natural religion' or 'metaphysics' on the convincing ground that the human mind cannot understand the eternal or divine. To Mansel the Unconditioned was inconceivable, and the German philosophical tradition as echoed by Thomas Carlyle, speaking so volubly about the Infinite or the Absolute, was so much confusion or humbug. Theology was concerned not with God in himself, but with our symbols of him, for 'the primary and proper object of criticism is not Religion, natural or revealed, but the human mind in its relation to Religion'. Mansel accepted orthodox Christianity, to him a religion of revelation and miracle. 'For the infinite, as inconceivable, is necessarily shewn to be non-existent; unless we renounce the claim of reason to supreme authority in matters of faith, by admitting that it is our duty to believe what we are altogether unable to comprehend.' But he added disconcerting warnings that his arguments in support of 'God manifest in the flesh' were not demonstrations and that the contents of the revelation were 'regulative', not simply descriptive. What was revealed was what God had chosen to reveal, so that man might think about him in that way 'for the sake of action'.

These Oxford lectures seemed designed to appeal both to infidels and to the irrational 'orthodox', but they did not appeal to Maurice. In an elaborate onslaught through sermons and open letters published as *What is Revelation?* (1859), he attempted to undo the damage. He tried to vindicate reason as leading to revelation, and the revelation in Christ as unveiling the mysteries of God. He thundered against those 'who make orthodoxy an excuse for denying the Union of the Father with the Son, the perfect Manifestation of the Father in the Son, the desire of the Father and the Son by the Spirit to bring all men into the obedience of the Truth'. He proclaimed that God's self-revelation communicated God's reality authentically; it was not merely 'regulative'. He did not possess the training or the temper to deal satisfactorily with the philosophical problems involved—cognition, analogy, and so forth—any more than he could write authoritatively about biblical criticism. 'The controversy,' as a Dean of St. Paul's has observed, 'resembles what one might imagine to have taken place had a discussion ever happened between Aristotle and one of the Minor Prophets, except that Mansel wrote much better than Aristotle and Maurice more copiously than any Minor Prophet.'[18] But Maurice said enough to help later theologians such as William Temple who, while distinguishing the event (of the personal revelation of God in action) from human speculations, were to argue that truth was thus surely apprehended—and was compatible with other truth reached in other ways.[19]

Maurice was at one with Newman in finding the cold, clear tone of Mansel, or before him Butler, religiously unsatisfactory. More than this was needed if there was to be a barrier against unbelief. In the tenth of his *Theological Essays*, he suggested that perhaps Butler's talk about probability had been due to the wish of that 'great and good man' to talk in their own language with fashionable gamblers.

[18] W. R. Matthews, *The Religious Philosophy of Dean Mansel* (Oxford University Press, 1956), p. 18. Mansel was appointed Dean of St. Paul's by Disraeli in 1868, but did not live long enough to make much of a mark on the cathedral.
[19] Ian T. Ramsey, *On Being Sure in Religion* (Athlone Press. 1963), considered some of these issues in a series of Maurice Lectures at King's College, London.

But Butler's basic appeal to the moral sense also dissatisfied him. His Cambridge lectures on *The Conscience* (1868) showed him as the honoured veteran who was still aware that 'the more there is of conscience in me—the more I confess a higher law—the greater will be my degradation and the sense of it'. It seems clear that his shyness and depression as a young man, morbidly interpreted by him as degradation, resulting in part from the theological tempests which had wrecked his home, made him turn for shelter to the Church of England with a rather extravagant loyalty, combined with a rather extravagant hatred of all religious parties and sects. John Stuart Mill wrote that Maurice's 'great powers of generalization, rare ingenuity and subtlety, and a wide perception of important and unobvious truths' had led him to the conclusion that 'the Church of England had known everything from the first, and that all the truths on the ground of which the Church and orthodoxy have been attacked (many of which he saw as clearly as any one) are not only consistent with the Thirty-nine Articles, but are better exposed in those Articles than by any one who rejects them'; and Mill attributed this waste of a mind to 'that timidity of conscience, combined with original sensitiveness of temperament, which has so often driven highly gifted men into Romanism'. Mill's verdict was only slightly unfair. It is therefore worth seeing what separated Maurice from Newman.

Revelation was not for him, as it was for Newman, 'the substitution of the voice of the Lawgiver for the voice of conscience'; for his Christ came to strengthen, not condemn. Revelation was, indeed, no system, moral or dogmatic, to which 'assent' must be given; it was the Father shown by the coming of Christ even when Christ was not named, and the right response could only be the obedient love of a son. Of course Maurice lived in awe of the Holy One, but his most characteristic reaction was one of a confident, if humble, familiarity. Characteristically, he replied to Newman's *Essay on Development* in an enormous Preface to a book of sermons on the Christ, the eternally sympathetic high priest of men, as pictured in the Epistle to the Hebrews; and privately he wrote about the *Essay* that 'of all books I ever read it seems to me the most sceptical' (but this was before he read Mansel). Maurice's essential answer to Newman was to invite men to turn again to the Christ of the Scriptures. They would find there the manifestation of the loving power of God as the crown of their daily experience; and they would receive the Spirit of God in their own hearts, to cry *Abba*, Father. Maurice did not have anything like Newman's *Grammar of Assent* in mind when he told a correspondent in 1865:

I go great lengths with you in your bold saying that Butler's 'Analogy' should be written over again in our time. . . . Revelation must be the discovery of God to a creature formed to know him and to be like him. . . . I own that I never have been, and never will be, content with probable evidence when it is opposed to demonstration. I ask for a demonstration of the Spirit with power to my spirit.

The 'demonstration of the Spirit' was no bad description of Maurice's own theological aim, in the context of the movement of 1833. For certainly the effects of the Oxford Movement went far beyond anything in the mind of Newman or Keble. Seeing something of the Church's crisis, they tried to revive its past. They appealed to the writings of the Fathers, hoping that (suitably edited) these might be imposed on those modern questioners who were not too wicked. What they did was to begin the revival of theology itself as the articulation of a faith under challenge; theologians now studied more laboriously and thought more profoundly. They tried to bring back some Roman Catholic, or seventeenth-century, or medieval, or earlier forms of devotion, hoping that the spirituality of Christendom (suitably selected) might overawe modern materialism. What they did was to make men worship with a more penitent sense of the holy God to whom they prayed, and with more encouragement from the saints of Christian history. They tried to exalt bishops and priests as mystagogues. What happened was that in the everyday scenes of English clerical or church-going life a change was noticeable. 'The vibration of an intellectual movement', as George Eliot wrote in her chronicle of Amos Barton and his parish of Shepperton, 'was felt from the golden head to the miry toes of the Establishment.' But what was to be fundamental belief of the revival, when Evangelicalism had failed to convince the intelligence of the age? It was Maurice's task to answer this challenge; and much of his answer, as this was perceived through his own jargon and emotionalism, did persuade many people in Victorian England, as the circulation of his writings showed. It was foolish of Newman to dismiss it: 'to use general terms and glowing words is to Mauricize'.[20]

In 1837 Maurice hinted what such a demonstration of the Holy Spirit might mean to the nineteenth century.

The Oxford Tracts [he told a friend] are, for the most part, more unpleasant than I quite like to acknowledge to myself or to others. Their error, I think, consists in opposing to 'the spirit of the present age'[21] the spirit of the former age, instead of the ever-living and acting Spirit of God, of whom the spirit of each age (as it presents itself to those living in it) is at once the adversary and the parody. The childlike spirit of the fathers, say they, must be brought in to counteract the intellectual spirit of these times—the spirit of submission to Church authority against the spirit of voluntary association. Nay, I contend, but the spirit of earnest and deep reflection is that which God would cultivate in us to oppose the superficial intelligence of the day, the spirit of Christian

20 *Letters and Diaries*, xiv, 181.
21 Maurice used the original Greek.

or Church liberty (the service which is freedom) to counteract the lust for independence, the spirit of unity to overthrow the spirit of combination. Thus I am entirely opposed to them, while yet our lines of thought will often coincide. . . .

Changing a few words, he could have written the same about Lord Shaftesbury and the other Evangelicals.

FOR FURTHER READING

Edwin Hodder compiled *The Life and Work of the Seventh Earl of Shaftesbury, K.G.*, in three volumes (Cassell, 1886). G. F. A. Best, *Shaftesbury* (Batsford, 1964), made some corrections and additions. Other studies of Shaftesbury's work have been contributed by J. L. and Barbara Hammond (Constable, 1923), J. Wesley Brady (Allen & Unwin, 1926) and Barbara Blackburn (*Noble Lord*, Home & Van Thal, 1949).

The Life of Frederick Denison Maurice, Chiefly Told in His Own Letters, was edited by his son Frederick in two volumes (Macmillan, 1884) and greatly enhanced his reputation. A selection of these letters was made by J. F. Porter and W. J. Wolf under the title *Toward the Recovery of Unity* (Seabury Press, New York, 1964). The best introduction to his thought, and to some influences on him, is *F. D. Maurice and Company* by A. R. Vidler (SCM Press, 1966). Perceptive essays on *F. D. Maurice* have been provided by a Quaker theologian, H. G. Wood, and an Anglican archbishop, A. M. Ramsey (Cambridge University Press, 1950, 1951). Part of the interest of another *Introduction to F. D. Maurice's Theology* is that it came from a parish priest in New Zealand, W. Merlin Davies (SPCK, 1964). See also Charles E. Raven, *Christian Socialism, 1848–1854* (Macmillan, 1920), corrected and supplemented by Torben Christiansen, *Origin and History of Christian Socialism, 1848–1854* (Aarhus University Press, 1962).

5

Stanley and Gladstone

1

In the autumn of 1866 Gladstone took refuge from English politics, which were then in a most unsatisfactory condition.[1] The Conservatives were in power, the Liberals were in confusion, and Parliament was in recess. Disraeli was so diabolically clever that some new trick was sure to be produced in the next Parliamentary session. (It was. Disraeli's Reform Bill of 1867 more than doubled the increase of the electorate originally proposed by Gladstone, and enough members of a bemused Conservative Party supported it.)

Gladstone himself, despite innumerable requests for his advice and invitations from the constituencies, had temporarily exhausted his eloquence. At the end of September he therefore took his wife and daughters to live in Rome. He complained about the rain, and developed influenza. Two outbreaks of fire damaged his hired apartments. But he survived, and was a keen listener to many Italian sermons. Such relaxation set him up for another year of debates in Westminster. When that year was over, a triumph was to come. He would be Prime Minister, a prophet with a majority of 112. He was also to publish *A Chapter of Autobiography*, informing the public why his attitudes to Church and State had undergone a revolution over thirty years.

During those weeks of the Gladstones' stay in Rome, the Dean of Westminster and his wife occupied the floor above. The Gladstones and the Stanleys dined together each evening. The two men enjoyed Rome in different ways. Both were, of course, given audiences by Pope Pius IX, and both were, of course, shocked by the papal ignorance of Anglican personalities. ('Ah! Wilberforce! He is one of the Oxford professors!') Stanley told his friends afterwards that he wished he had the courage to ask His Holiness what it was like to feel infallible. But Gladstone was seriously interested in Italian politics. He had once translated from the Italian a four-volume history of the

---

[1] For the political background, see M. J. Cowling, *Disraeli, Gladstone and Revolution* (Cambridge University Press, 1967), and John Vincent, *The Formation of the Liberal Party, 1857–68* (Constable, 1966).

territory still under the political control of the popes, covering 1815–50, in order to expose that iniquity. In 1852 he had described the temporal power of the Papacy:

A monarchy sustained by foreign armies, smitten with the curse of social barrenness, unable to strike root downward or bear fruit upward, the sun, the air, the rain soliciting in vain its sapless and rotten boughs—such a monarchy, even if it were not a monarchy of priests, and tenfold more because it is one, stands out a foul blot upon the face of creation, an offence to Christendom and to mankind.

Stanley, on the other hand, was attracted by the ramshackle glamour of the Papal States, for Rome in 1866 somehow survived as a visible reminder of the history of the vicar of Christ as the heir of the Caesars. For Stanley, all Christendom was conjured up from the past by the sight which Newman had sketched in his *Apologia*: 'a few old men, with red hats and stockings, or a hundred pale students with eyes on the ground, and beads in their girdles.'

Dean Stanley was an establishmentarian. When Gladstone was to raise the Irish religious question, Stanley was to have his answer. Why could not the Roman Catholics and the Presbyterians join the Anglicans, as three State Churches? This was because Dean Stanley's imagination dwelt in the past. While in Rome he dreamed that he had been elected Pope, and had hastened to consult fellow-members of his London club, the Athenaeum. What papal name would be most suitable for an Englishman? Stanley fancied the legend that St. Paul had once preached in Britain, but the name would have to be Pope Paul VI and there was a Latin poem warning against six as an unlucky number. So Stanley, whose mind was then full of the commemoration of the Conqueror's coronation in the Abbey, decided to be Pope William I. In the Rome of 1866 he refreshed himself for his own battles of 1867, which were to include a refusal to allow the first Lambeth Conference to hold its concluding service in Westminster Abbey.

2

The Abbey provided an almost ideal platform for Arthur Penrhyn Stanley, who became its Dean in 1863 and was buried within it in 1881. He made its past live at a time when there was a public appetite for history. Within five years of his arrival he published a large and deservedly popular volume of *Historical Memorials of Westminster Abbey*, and it was his delight to uncover the coffins of monarchs whose last resting places had been forgotten. (Tait was summoned when the coffin of James I was found. 'Stand back! Stand back! And let the

first Scottish archbishop look upon the first Scottish King of England!')
He caused new monuments or windows to be erected to Chaucer and
Keble, to George Herbert and John Wesley; and he loved to preach
in tribute when an eminent Victorian died. He would have approved
when, not long after his own funeral, they buried Charles Darwin in
the Abbey.

He was not the perfect dean. The simplest arithmetic perplexed him
and he got the worst of the bargain with the Ecclesiastical Commissioners when they took over most of the Abbey's estates. The annual
income which the Commissioners allowed the Dean and Chapter was
so low that a fresh arrangement had to be made by Parliament after
Stanley's death, when 'he had left both the fabric and the finances of
the Abbey in a deplorable state'.[2] Much of the business of the Dean
and Chapter bored him. 'As far as the actual work of the Dean is concerned,' he wrote on moving to Westminster, 'it is far more unsuited
to me than that of a bishop. To lose one's time in Confirmations is
bad, but to lose it in leases and warming plans is worse.' He was almost
completely tone-deaf and colour-blind; he had no sense of taste or
smell; his eyesight was very short; his collar and tie had a habit of
separating; his buttons were usually done up in the wrong buttonholes,
and he never wore a dean's gaiters because of the buttons. He was also
no preacher for regular, pastoral courses; his voice would betray his
boredom as he read out an old sermon. Yet it is fair to say that 'he
more than any other single individual was responsible for making
Westminster Abbey what it is today in the eyes of the multitudes who
visit it.'[3] On his deathbed he dictated the words: 'As far as I understood what the duties of my office were supposed to be, in spite of
every incompetence, I am yet humbly trustful that I have sustained
before the mind of the nation the extraordinary value of the Abbey
as a religious, national, and liberal institution.'

He loved to include the living as well as the dead in that 'great
Temple of silence and reconciliation'. The Stanleys were popular
figures and could afford to be hospitable at the Deanery, where they
specially delighted to bring estranged churchmen together. The Dean
was, indeed, so interested in his contemporaries that *The Times* had
to be read to him over breakfast; had he read it himself, he would have
forgotten the meal. In the Abbey he made Bach's Passion music part
of an Anglican service for the first time, but took a more personal
pleasure in his annual children's service on Holy Innocents' Day. He
invited Pusey and Keble to preach; they refused, but he secured Liddon

---

[2] Lawrence Tanner, *Recollections of a Westminster Antiquary* (John Baker,
1969), p. 23.
[3] Michael Stancliffe has discussed 'The Reign of Dean Stanley' in *A House of
Kings*, ed. E. F. Carpenter (John Baker, 1966), pp. 300-26.

and Jowett. He even produced non-Anglicans as lecturers, ignoring many protests; and he included a Unitarian minister in a Holy Communion which he celebrated for the scholars beginning work on the revision of the English Bible, to widespread fury.

It was a comprehensiveness in the spirit of Thomas Arnold. It could not fail to be, for his years in the Sixth at Rugby determined his course until the day when Matthew Arnold and Frederick Temple, along with ten other representatives of the Victorian achievement, bore his coffin to King Henry VII's Chapel. Those who on the whole approved of Arnold approved of his biographer. Tait, for example, believed that Stanley's influence 'confirmed in the faith of the Lord Jesus Christ vast numbers of persons who would otherwise have wandered from it'. Those who opposed Arnoldianism as heretical, or who had come to distrust its religiosity, regretted that Stanley exercised such charm in his propaganda. When Stanley was appointed Professor of Ecclesiastical History at Oxford in 1856, Jowett was the only resident in Oxford who wrote to congratulate him. When he moved to Westminster, his Oxford colleague Pusey wrote: 'I believe the present to be a struggle for the life or death of the English Church, and what you believe to be for life I believe to be for death; and you think the same reciprocally of me.' But both admirers and opponents had to concede that Stanley possessed more charm than the headmaster who was his hero.

One reason why he was more charming was that his life was easier. Thomas Arnold had to fight, like Tom Brown in his school. His father died when he was aged five; in order to support his own family, he had to struggle in competition for the favours of other boys' parents at Laleham and Rugby. He had to fight to tame Rugby School, to subdue local citizens wanting their sons to be educated on the cheap, and to outwit local gentlemen wanting to muzzle his prophetic politics. It is characteristic of Stanley that his *Life* makes clear neither the emotional origins nor the full tribulations of his hero's warlike temperament. For Stanley's own life was favoured, from his birth in the year of Waterloo. His childhood was spent in Alderley Rectory; his uncle was Lord Stanley of Alderley. He was excused from fagging and apparently even from teasing at Rugby, although he had the delicacy of a girl. Long afterwards Rugbeians remembered that his watch was attached to his person by a pink cord. One may suspect that as he grew up he found his father not entirely fascinating. The father was a parish priest whose theology was liberal and whose hobby was science, and he became a reforming and popular Bishop of Norwich. Arthur Stanley dutifully wrote a memoir, but there are reports that he tended to be silent when home for the holidays. However, Thomas Arnold came into Stanley's life as a second father. One may suspect that he had little natural inclination to love women apart from his mother. However, his friendships with men were pleasant, no one ever dared to mention any coarseness in his presence, and when he needed a wife he married one to whom he grew devoted. When she died he knew loneliness and depression for the first time in his life, and he was glad to join her; their monuments in the Abbey are adjacent, among the kings and queens.[4]

A period of comparatively slight unease came when on graduation he thought that the Fellows of Balliol (apart from Tait) distrusted him because he was a disciple of Arnold; so he became a Fellow of University College instead. He was a great success there; his *Life of Arnold* established him as a man of letters in his twenties. When his father died, he was able to provide a home for his mother in the shadow of Canterbury Cathedral, where he became a canon enchanted by the cathedral's memories. At no stage did he lack a substantial stipend, supplemented by inherited wealth, which enabled him to indulge without stint his love of travel. His mother died while he was travelling with the Prince of Wales in the East, but his engagement to Lady Augusta Bruce, Queen Victoria's favourite Lady-in-Waiting, was announced on the same day as his acceptance of the Westminster Deanery. He thought well of everyone, including both the Queen and the Prince of Wales. (He had been sent to the East with the Prince by a Queen who wanted the Prince to be made more ethical, and more intellectual; yet he became great friends with the young man.) It is not surprising that, flourishing in a period which was in any case happier than the 1830s, he radiated optimism and benevolence, and disarmed many of those who criticized his theology by refusing to quarrel with them.

But what was his theology? Although he spoke or wrote so often about Christ and Christianity, he deliberately avoided the discussion of doctrine, so that it was hard to tell whether his personal opinions were closer to Thomas Arnold's or to Matthew's. Men knew that he had been deeply impressed by the beauty of the lake of Nicaea, but they were not so sure what he thought of its creed. In 1847 he published *Sermons and Addresses on the Apostolical Age*; he presented the apostles as human beings, and no one took much notice. In 1881 he published a volume of essays on Baptism, the Eucharist, and other ecclesiastical subjects (*Christian Institutions*). His admiring biographer has stated the trend of this, the Dean's last effort at theology.

The ceremony of Baptism survives because of the passage from darkness to light, from uncleanness to purity, which it typifies, and because of the natural reverence for a tender conscience, which softens the most hardened in the

[4] The story of his marriage may be traced in *Later Letters of Lady Augusta Stanley, 1864–1876*, ed. A. V. Baillie and H. Bolitho (Jonathan Cape, 1929).

presence of an innocent, trusting infant. In the Eucharist, the permanent elements, which have withstood the shock of centuries of change, are the moral effort to dwell in the love of God, and the spiritual unison and harmony with the Divine Spirit.

Stanley himself summed it all up in his closing pages on the 'eleventh commandment': love.

He announced, but in private, that he was too familiar with the legendary miracles of the Middle Ages to be confident about the miracles of the Bible. He wrote extensively about the Old Testament without making it clear what exactly had happened; he was perhaps wiser in his time than Colenso. ('Mr. Dean,' Disraeli once remarked to him, 'no dogmas, no deans.') He concluded his *History of the Jewish Church* in three volumes before the birth of Christ; again, this was a wise decision, for he probably agreed with the possibility at which Newman hinted in conversation with him during 1864—that the gospels were 'not a regular history, but biographical anecdotes strung together'. At any rate, Matthew Arnold found Dean Stanley far more edifying than Bishop Colenso, and said so in an enthusiastic review. Stanley did publish a commentary, on the Epistles to the Corinthians in 1855; but young Mr. Lightfoot of Cambridge politely tore it apart in a review. 'He says, and I think he is right,' wrote Stanley to a friend, 'that in undertaking to write critical notes I have completely mistaken my vocation.' He would also have courted disaster had he been ambitious to research scientifically into biblical or later history. He wrote much and well, and he knew more history than Professor Charles Kingsley of Cambridge; but it was his ambition to string biographical anecdotes together in order to adorn a moral, for he was an evangelist, although without dogma.

A central theme in his message was a hatred of intolerance. Having as a boy and biographer dedicated all his skill to the defence of Arnold, he never lacked the chivalry needed to speak up for those whom he regarded as the victims of orthodox persecutions. He spent much time on getting Jowett's salary as Professor of Greek increased from £40 a year, against the bitter hostility of Pusey and his allies, but he also defended W. G. Ward's right to express his Catholic ideal and remain a Master of Arts. While Dean of Westminster he involved himself in the controversies about the Athanasian Creed and the Thirty-nine Articles because he viewed with dismay the decline in the ordinations of clever young men such as he had been himself. He was no modernist: he made himself a nuisance to the revisers of the English Bible by pleading that archaisms should be kept. But he wanted to encourage churchmen to accept the Church of England's formularies in his own imprecise spirit, in order that more and more Victorians might enjoy the Anglican heritage as he did.

He valued ecclesiastical history because it showed the really super-natural fact about Christianity: its moral influence. But he did not share Thomas Arnold's moralizing contempt for large tracts of the past. Almost everything was sacred. In the Abbey he was glad to find that the coffin of Elizabeth I rested on top of that of his sister, 'Bloody' Mary, and wherever he went on his travels he was thrilled by any scene which could be associated with any form of spiritual nobility. As a boy he joined 'the religion of Walter Scott'; his lectures in Edinburgh on the history of the Church of Scotland caused pleasure there and alarm in Oxford. Towards the end of his life he found American history fascinating and the American climate 'transplendent, trans-lucent, transcendent'. But stranger still for a liberal Anglican was his enthusiasm for the Middle Ages. In his *Historical Memorials of Canter-bury* (1855) his reconstruction of the murder of Thomas Becket made one of the most vivid pieces in all English historical writing. His *Lectures on the History of the Eastern Church* (1861) showed how alert he was to a Russia light-years away from the Victorian Church of England. All history was to him like Bunyan's 'House Beautiful'.

He believed that the Church had nothing to lose from fellowship with any good (or colourful) man or woman. The gathering of scientists, journalists, and other members of the Victorian élite (including Glad-stone) to mull over theological and philosophical problems in the Metaphysical Society was essentially his idea. In the Preface to the last volume of his *History of the Jewish Church*, he offered a curious but characteristic explanation of Ancient Israel's decline: it was not Broad Church enough.

It is a striking example of that degradation which, by an almost universal law, overtakes Religion when, even while attaining a purer form, it loses the vivifying and elevating spirit breathed into it by close contact with the great historic and secular influences which act like fresh air on a contracted atmos-phere, and are thus the Divine antiseptics against the spiritual corruption of merely ecclesiastical communities.

How much Caiaphas would have learned from the Metaphysical Society!

On the other hand, the story of Israel before its decline into ecclesi-asticism seemed to Stanley delightfully elevated. His book of 1856 on *Sinai and Palestine* was the most successful of his publications, and his first lecture as Professor of Ecclesiastical History at Oxford began with Abraham. Part of the appeal was visual, for the Middle East in the 1850s was romantically exotic to Englishmen although its place names were familiar to every reader of the Bible, and Stanley was an excellent scene-painter; as he wrote at the time to his headmaster's widow, 'the framework of the book is the result of that connection of history and geography which I have never ceased to enjoy since it was first imparted at Rugby'. But part of the appeal lay in the historian's determination to write about the best in people. So the world of Oriental glamour could be visited like a sweet country parish, and brave Abraham could be treated as an ancestor of Thomas Arnold.

Perhaps Stanley was too generous to other men to be accurate either as an historian or as a theologian, and perhaps that other dean of high Victorian London, Richard Church at St. Paul's, was right to say tartly that 'Stanley had intellectual defects, like his physical defects as to music, or smell, or colour, or capacity for mathematical ideas, which crippled his capacity for the sympathy he wished to spread all round him'. But Lord Bryce observed: 'In the England of his time there was no personality more attractive, nor any more characteristic of the country than Arthur Penrhyn Stanley.'[5] Matthew Arnold wrote his last poem (*Westminster Abbey*, 1882) as a tribute to the light which had shone. Gladstone summed up the truth when he wrote to Queen Victoria after the death: 'there may be, and must be, much diversity as to parts of the opinions of Dean Stanley, but he will be long remembered as one who was capable of the deepest and widest love, and who received it in return.'

3

In May 1898 the body of William Ewart Gladstone lay in state in Westminster Hall, and was then buried in the Abbey. He had died in his eighty-ninth year. Almost as much as the funeral of Queen Victoria three years later, those obsequies stirred reflections about the nineteenth century; and much more than the Supreme Governor of the Church of England (who really preferred Prince Albert's fellow-Lutherans or the Presbyterians around Balmoral), Mr. Gladstone was correctly identified as an Anglican.

He seemed to many to have betrayed the Church's cause by disestablishing Anglicanism in Ireland and by allying himself—with whatever hesitations and obscurities—with those who wished to see it disestablished in England. During the last thirty years of his life he was, indeed, thought by many to be the enemy of all English institutions. The Queen grew to hate him. In 1880 she told her private secretary that 'she will sooner *abdicate* than send for or have anything to do with that *half-mad firebrand* who would soon ruin everything, and be a *Dictator*'. It was not merely that his speechifying irritated her (while Disraeli had the tact to address her as the stupidly conservative and obstinately lonely widow, susceptible to flattery, that she

[5] See the sketch in his *Studies in Contemporary Biography* (Macmillan, 1903), pp. 69–84.

was); nor was it merely that she was alarmed by the politics of 'the People's William'. She also seems to have thought that his eloquence about the moral imperatives of democracy was so much humbug. Gladstone himself attributed her attitude to her acceptance of the rumours that, after a day's administration of oratory at a very exalted level of ethics, he would take his pleasure with prostitutes met in the London streets.

However, neither the guarded support which he gave to disestablishmentarians nor the lavish friendship which he gave to prostitutes really justified the Queen's hatred of him. While they were undergraduates at Oxford, he and some friends resolved to undertake a definite work on behalf of the outcasts, and they drew lots to decide which particular category of outcasts would fall to each member of this group. Gladstone's efforts which were begun as a result of this lottery continued when he became the most eminently respectable statesman in the world. No aspect of his life was more extraordinary. While in the cabinet, loaded with work and worry, even while Prime Minister, he would give hours in the late evening to this task. Armed only with a stick, he would enter alleys where the police feared to go, knowing that the brothel-keepers maintained a small army of thugs for the protection of this thriving and lucrative trade. He would speak to prostitutes with a courtesy which constantly exposed him to blackmail or suspicion; the wonder is that there were not more incidents of blackmail, and that the rumours about his intentions were not used more freely by his potential rivals. He would invite the prostitutes back to his home, and take endless trouble with those who were willing to be reclaimed. He spent £83,500 of his own money on them. In his eighties he still gave detailed attention to this work, although he thought that it had cost him the Queen's confidence and although some of his closest associates had been courageous enough to warn him of its other dangers.

Why did he do it? Whatever may have been the truth about the undergraduates' lottery, his persistence in this particular form of charitable activity, when almost anyone else in his position would have excused himself on the grounds of official duty and dignity, is the most dramatic possible illustration of his energy. Just as he walked mountains or felled trees during his holidays, so during Parliamentary sessions he was out on the streets of London while his colleagues dined or intrigued or slept. Just as he addressed Members of Parliament with a unique blend of copious emotion and exactly mastered and massed detail over a period of sixty-one years (until the day of his last speech came in 1894, and that speech was a passionate attack on the House of Lords), so he took infinite pains in innumerable conversations with brainless women. If only he had treated the Queen like a prostitute!

A later generation, accustomed to Freudian analysis, will point to the charms of the sinners who attracted Gladstone's zeal. It is clear that Gladstone was highly sexed. Perhaps this contributed to his lack of censoriousness, astonishing in one who habitually spoke like an Old Testament prophet. He got on well with that frank hedonist the Prince of Wales, and even smoked cigarettes at his table. While he did good to them, he seems to have enjoyed the company of two ladies whose virtue was far less secure than his own: Lillie Langtry who was the friend of the Prince of Wales, and Skittles Walters who was the toast of Englishmen in Paris. Although he insisted on his Irish ally Parnell resigning when he was cited in a divorce case, he had previously corresponded with Parnell's mistress, Kitty O'Shea, in attempts to drive a political bargain. He knew perfectly well that Lord Hartington, who succeeded him as Liberal leader in 1875 (but made way for his return to power in 1880), was more intimate with the Duchess of Manchester than with Lady Hartington. He was a man of the world. What made him break Parnell, and therefore end his own hope of solving the Irish question, was not Parnell's immorality but Parnell's refusal to see that he must bow, at least for a period, before the public indignation which had been aroused by the public scandal.

Gladstone was eager to marry Caroline Farquhar, and when that young lady refused him (protesting that 'the terrifying intensity of his eyes makes one go cold'), Lady Frances Douglas. We can gather what Caroline Farquhar suspected from her action when, many years later as a married lady, she found herself kneeling near him at the rail to receive Holy Communion. She immediately got up and left the church. But she was wickedly wrong. This man with such a rare energy was never suspected by anyone who knew him of being unfaithful for a second to Caroline Glynne, with whom in the end he made a perfect marriage.[6] Nor did he ever think of betraying his Lord, with whom he spoke in daily prayer, and for whose sake he kept a daily journal to account for his expenditure of time.[7] 'We should deal with our time', he advised his eldest son in 1855, 'as we see in a shop a grocer deal with tea and sugar, or a haberdasher with stuffs and ribands: weighing or measuring it out in proportions adjusted to that which we are to get for and by it.'

While an undergraduate he thought very seriously that he should, and would, consecrate the extraordinary energy of which he was already aware to work as a priest. He wrote long and solemn letters to his father in 1830, with this theme: 'I do not see how I am to persuade myself that any powers, be they the meanest or the greatest, can

[6] See Georgina Battiscombe, *Mrs. Gladstone* (Constable, 1956).
[7] Publication of *The Gladstone Diaries*, ed. M. R. D. Foot, was begun by the Clarendon Press in 1968.

be *so* profitably or *so* nobly employed as in the performance of this sublime duty.' His father persuaded him to aim at public life rather than the narrower sphere of a parochial clergyman. 'You will allow me to doubt whether the picture your perhaps too sanguine mind has drawn in your letter before me, would ever be practically realized.'

William Ewart Gladstone seems always to have believed that his father was right, and that it was also God's will that he should be a statesman. However, he was delighted when his second son, Stephen, became a clergyman and when his daughter Mary married a penniless curate. In 1850, in a letter to the future Cardinal Manning, he was still able to speculate about what his task might have been, had he been ordained himself. 'My course would be set to work upon the holy task of clearing, opening and establishing positive truth in the Church of England, which is an office doubly blessed, inasmuch as it is both the business of truth, and the laying of firm foundations for future union in Christendom.' These were not empty words. In his earlier years he enjoyed reading his own sermons to a congregation composed of his own servants. He read more theology, and wrote more, than most clergymen. His appetite for ecclesiastical facts and his sympathy with Christian believers were truly ecumenical. And the courageous tenderness of his work for prostitutes showed that he not only might have been, but actually was, a great pastor.[8]

Inevitably such a Prime Minister regarded the responsibility for the key ecclesiastical appointments as one of the most important of the duties attached to the supreme political office. He took great pains over his own nominations to bishoprics, deaneries, and canonries, and he was interested enough to care what other patrons did. He was far too acutely aware of his responsibilities to confine his patronage to High Churchmen or to supporters of the Liberal Party; anyway, there were not many leading churchmen available who combined the roles as he did. Two of his most successful episcopal appointments were of men who were not quite gentlemen, but who attracted him because they were Liberals, and above all honest thinkers and hard workers: Frederick Temple, and James Fraser the second Bishop of Manchester.[9]

Gladstone made St. Paul's Cathedral what it was to mid-Victorian London. When the Deanery fell vacant through the death of Mansel

[8] See Richard Deacon, *The Private Life of Mr. Gladstone* (Muller, 1956); and for another great Christian's onslaught on the problem of prostitution, E. M. Bell, *Josephine Butler* (Constable, 1962).

[9] Fraser began by clearing up the mess which James Prince Lee had left behind, and built up the Church in the centre of England's industrial life, in labours heartily approved by the author of *Tom Brown's School-days*. See Thomas Hughes, *James Fraser* (Macmillan, 1887). Dean Wellesley correctly told the Queen that Fraser 'will get on with those sort of people'.

in 1871, he offered it first to W. F. Hook, and then, when Hook refused, to Richard Church, who was then the 'High' and scholarly pastor of a village of two hundred souls. Had Church shown any taste for ecclesiastical politics and administration, the Primacy might have been his on Tait's death, for although acknowledging that he was a recluse in poor health Gladstone revered Church. Gladstone also appointed Henry Scott Holland, then a don under forty years of age, to a canonry of St. Paul's in 1884. He thus gave Scott Holland a pulpit from which he fascinated vast congregations until another Liberal Prime Minister, Asquith, moved him back to Oxford in 1910. Scott Holland combined a magician's flow of rhetoric with a Catholic sense of the sacramental life of the Church and a Socialist sense that the life of society ought to be a sacrament of the reign of Christ.[10] Through such appointments, Gladstone preached by proxy.[11]

During his first period as Prime Minister, 1868–74, he filled no fewer than twelve bishoprics and eight deaneries. At the time he jotted down what qualities he looked for in bishops.

Piety. Learning (sacred). Eloquence. Administrative power. Faithful allegiance to the Church and to the Church of England. Activity. Tact and courtesy in dealings with men. Knowledge of the world. Accomplishments and literature. An equitable spirit. Faculty of working with his brother bishops. Some legal habit of mind. Circumspection. Courage. Maturity of age and character. Corporal vigour. Liberal sentiments in public affairs. A representative character with reference to shades of opinion fairly allowable in the Church.

'Who is sufficient for these things?' may well be the reaction of a later generation; yet Gladstone and his successors at Downing Street did find Victorian churchmen who passed most, if not all, of these tests for the episcopate. There can be no doubt that Gladstone would have passed all of them himself, and would have filled the throne of St. Augustine with high distinction, had it been possible for Queen Victoria and Disraeli to combine to appoint him Archbishop of Canterbury in 1868. A twentieth-century scholar has permitted himself to speculate along that fascinating line. 'After all, would not Gladstone's political achievements have been carried out, in one way or another, even if he had not been at the political helm? Whereas, if the Church had been under his leadership, history might have pursued a very different course, and it might be in a very different condition to-day.'[12]

[10] A selection of writings by *Henry Scott Holland* was edited by B. M. G. Reardon (SPCK, 1962). Scott Holland's *A Bundle of Memories* (Wells Gardner, Darton, 1915) included many exuberant tributes to his companions in these happy crusades.

[11] G. L. Prestige, *St. Paul's in its Glory* (SPCK, 1955), is an account of the life of the cathedral from 1851 to Dean Inge's appointment in 1911.

[12] A. R. Vidler, *The Orb and the Cross* (SPCK, 1945), p. 157.

4

The story of the connections between Christianity and democracy in his mind cannot be other than tangled, until that story issues in the supremely Gladstonian idea of the politics of democracy as the politics of morality.

In his last speech to the Commons, Gladstone boasted that the electorate was now six millions, of which two millions had been added by his own Reform Act in 1884. But the numbers of the new electors were not the key fact in the politics of the end of the nineteenth century. What mattered even more was the 1884 extension to the electorate in the county constituencies of the principle on which Disraeli had based the electorate for the borough seats; and that mattered not only because the counties had tended to vote Conservative in the period 1867–84. The crucial change made when workers in the villages were included in the electorate under Gladstone in 1884 was the acknowledgement of the principle which he had suddenly laid down during a Commons debate twenty years before (to the dismay of Lord Palmerston, who was then Prime Minister). Gladstone declared in 1864: 'I venture to say that every man who is not permanently incapacitated by some consideration of personal unfitness or political danger is morally entitled to come within the pale of the Constitution.'

That proclamation of the democratic principle shocked Palmerston; and it had to be explained away by Gladstone at the time, because he was in so many ways a conservative Chancellor of the Exchequer. Palmerston then, and the Queen later, could regard him as a traitor to the governing class. Indeed, Gladstone often surprised himself by his radicalism. In his heart he was a conservative to the end of his days. This came out when he spent a week among the Fellows of All Souls in Oxford in 1890, reading the lessons and lamenting innovations. As he lay dying in great pain from cancer, he would recite the first verse of Newman's 'Praise to the Holiest in the height', and dictated a reply to one message which reached him. 'There is no expression of Christian sympathy which I value more than that of the ancient university of Oxford, the God-fearing and God-sustaining university of Oxford. I served her, perhaps mistakenly, but to the best of my ability. My most earnest prayers are hers to the uttermost and to the last.'

That might be assessed as an old man's nostalgia for the scenes of his youth, or his youthful Toryism might be pardoned as immature; but even at the height of his powers Gladstone lived by the old values. He is so securely fixed in English history as an architect of democracy that it is important for us to remember that as late at 1858 Gladstone was begged to take charge of India or the other colonies in the Conservative administration. On that occasion Disraeli wrote to Gladstone, assuring him that if he joined Lord Derby's cabinet he would find that 'all its members are your admirers' and some of them 'warm friends'. Disraeli acknowledged that 'our mutual relations have formed the great difficulty', but he appealed to Gladstone to accept his own leadership of the Commons for the time being, on four grounds.

Don't you think the time has come when you might deign to be magnanimous? . . . I may be removed from the scene, or I may wish to be removed from the scene. Every man performs his office, and there is a Power, greater than ourselves, that disposes of all this. . . . Whatever office you filled, your shining qualities would always render you supreme. . . .

Gladstone replied to this flattery with the warmth of ice, but it was then possible for men to think that his hatred of Disraeli, rather than any political priciple, was the main reason why he did not announce himself as a Conservative. (His attitude to Dizzy resembled the Queen's attitude to him: this rhetorician had debased the currency of public life.) At the age of forty-nine he could not be classed as an ardent reformer, except in the dismally technical fields of taxation and tariffs. The one master whom he owned in politics was the Conservative Prime Minister who had given him his chance to develop and display his outstanding skill for finance, Sir Robert Peel; and if we ask why Peel gave Gladstone such a great chance at such an early age, when he fought shy of Shaftesbury, we get the answers that Gladstone's administrative capacity was reckoned stronger than Shaftesbury's—and his conscience less dangerous. Hounded from office by Disraeli's unscrupulous rebellion, Peel had died in 1850, but eight years later Gladstone still needed to be warned by his closest political ally, old Sir James Graham, that 'the reconstruction of the fossil remains of the old Peel party is a hopeless task'. And as it was, Gladstone did accept a colonial assignment from the Derby–Disraeli administration. He went out to the Ionian Islands, which were then under British rule, as Lord High Commissioner.

One main reason why he obeyed that temporary call to the isles of Greece was that they reminded him of Homer; and one main reason why he gave a lifetime's devotion to the poetry of Homer was that the ancient Greek bard (in this so unlike Disraeli) constantly pictured human nature in heroic proportions. In the words of Gladstone with which Morley concluded his biography: 'Be inspired with the belief that life is a great and noble calling; not a mean and grovelling thing that we are to shuffle through as we can, but an elevated and lofty destiny.' Gladstone often added that Homer *was* Homer, and not a committee—and how relevant that seemed, as an answer to the German critics who were trying to abolish Moses! He would insist, too, that the noble glories of Homeric Greece had been a preparation for the Gospel—as surely as the glories of Israel, or, as he would sometimes bring himself to confess, even more surely.[13] He did not remain a Conservative statesman after the fall of Peel, but in politics or in Homeric studies as much as in his more directly theological work, he was always a conservative preacher.

Like many other preachers, he was able to cast a prophetic mantle over causes which history has judged more cynically. He entered politics in 1832 as M.P. for Newark; this borough was then in the pocket of the Duke of Newcastle. Before casting their votes in his favour 887 electors had consumed more than two thousand pounds' worth of encouragement, half contributed by the Duke and half by Gladstone's father, who was a millionaire slave-owner.[14] The M.P., then aged twenty-three, was properly expected to defend both the aristocracy and the slave-owning on which his whole position depended. This he did with such eloquence that in 1834 Peel gave him a junior ministerial post, and next year made him Under-Secretary for the Colonies. When Gladstone followed Peel in the repeal of the Protectionist corn laws, the Duke of Newcastle was so incensed that another seat had to be found; and so Gladstone came to represent in Parliament the Oxford University which Newman had just abandoned. It was now his duty to resist proposals to change Oxford, and this he did until the report of the commission including Tait and Stanley persuaded him that some changes were inevitable. He preserved copies of 350 letters written in his own hand as the pilot of the 1854 Act which reformed the university; but the admission of Dissenters to degree courses was not included in the Bill as first presented to the Crown, and even after the Act the Anglican monopoly of the teaching posts was protected. This conservatism coincided with Gladstone's own idea of a university as well as with the interests of his constituents, and it was not until 1871 that he sponsored an Act to abolish all religious tests at Oxford. He was proud to represent Oxford; he worried about the effect on the dons of the reforms which, after initial horror, he gradually came to support; and when he was defeated in the university's Parliamentary election in 1865, he wrote in his journal: 'A dear dream is dispelled. God's will be done.' It is also worth remembering that he fought with great passion against the passing of the 1857 Divorce Act, the first clear departure of the laws of England from

[13] J. L. Myres included a chapter on Gladstone in his *Homer and his Critics* (Routledge & Kegan Paul, 1958), and remarked: 'A man like Gladstone stood for a personal Homer because, so far as ability went, he could have written an *Iliad* himself.'

[14] Sir John Gladstone (originally Gladstones), who rose from humble origins in Edinburgh, left about £600,000 on his death in 1851 at the age of eighty-seven. But he had transferred very large assets to his sons during his lifetime.

the laws of the Church. Although divorces were already obtainable by the rich who could procure special Acts of Parliament, Gladstone argued that the general provision of such facilities by the State threatened public morality; and he was specially indignant that clergymen were to be compelled to lend their churches for remarriages.

He had to appeal to morality in his defence of privileges, imparting a sacred air to those who owned land, or slaves, or an educational monopoly. To the end he maintained that a landowner's influence could be greatly beneficial, and perhaps the proudest achievement of his life was to rescue the Hawarden estate in North Wales for his family after a financial disaster in 1848 for which he was in no way responsible. He shared Disraeli's own liking for dukes in politics, and like Disraeli at Hughenden (but more convincingly) he believed that an M.P., even a Prime Minister, ought to spend as much of his time as possible as a country gentleman. Accordingly he spent about half the year at Hawarden through half a century. In this rural retreat he built a 'Temple of Peace' where he toiled at his books and papers, and he and his family did much good in the district. From the way in which he spoke about landowners over many years, a visitor unfamiliar with England might have supposed that such a use of landed privilege was normal.[15]

Lord Macaulay's description of him as the 'rising hope of those stern and unbending Tories' came in a famous review of Gladstone's book on *The State in its Relations with the Church* (1838). The book was, indeed, too unbending for the Tories: its naïvety embarrassed the young Gladstone's political associates, including Peel. By way of explanation Gladstone doubled its length for a later edition, but he grew to be embarrassed by it himself. As the author of this fervent plea for state support for the Church of England, he felt it his duty to resign from Peel's government in 1845 because Peel proposed to increase a government subsidy to Maynooth College, which trained Roman Catholic clergy. He acted on his conviction although he was greatly enjoying his magnificent work as President of the Board of Trade, and although he supported the proposal about Maynooth a few months later, this resignation baffled Peel even more than the book had done. However, the book can be defended, precisely as an attempt to find a moral ground on which Anglican privilege could be sustained.

Gladstone first reviewed the theories used previously in defence of the Establishment. He rejected as outmoded Hooker's theory in the sixteenth century that Church and State were two aspects of the one

[15] Hawarden Castle belonged to his wife's family, the Glynnes. Gladstone observed that the immense labour which he expended on the estate's problems was sent by God to train him as Chancellor of the Exchequer. He reckoned that he had also spent £267,500 of his own money on Hawarden.

nation, and Warburton's theory in the eighteenth century that Church and State should be allies for the sake of utility. On the one hand, England in the 1830s had to acknowledge the existence of a plurality of churches; on the other hand, the State should not regard its moral responsibility as discharged by a mere alliance with a convenient denomination. No, what was at stake was religious truth. Gladstone's own theory was that the State, while not identical with the Church, constituted a 'moral personality' and as such had a duty to establish and endow the teaching of the truth which the Church of England taught. The nation as a corporate 'person' with a conscience must profess and propagate a religion. Anglicanism in Ireland, for example, might be in the minority, but if its bishops were in fact the successors of the apostles, and if the apostolic Gospel was in fact the most important truth which the people needed to learn, the State must confine its encouragement to Anglicanism. Having in this way established the State's duty, Gladstone felt obliged to consider the possible deterioration of personal religion under the burden of wealth, but he felt able to come down in favour of accepting the State's support. When he estimated the damage to the Catholic faith in the Church of England which might come through state control, he managed to reach a similarly comforting conclusion. Of the two remaining chapters, one was a detailed survey of the relations of Church and State in the various territories over which Queen Victoria had begun to reign, and the other was a warning that the movement towards the dissolution of the connection between Church and State, by encouraging 'social atheism', would end in the destruction of social morality.

It was easy for Macaulay, and for Gladstone himself, to see the weakness in this argument as soon as it was published. The weakness was that Gladstone was the only politician who thought in these terms. Macaulay's article in the *Edinburgh Review* poured scorn on the notion that public bodies could be expected to hold theological views: so far had Tom Macaulay travelled from his Evangelical father. Gladstone himself came to acknowledge that such theology would set him alone in the Commons. But some points may be made in favour of this much-derided youthful essay.

It needed courage to earn, and to face, such ridicule, but courage he had—and many of his fellow-Christians had it too in Victorian England. Such courage gradually earned for the Victorian churches the support of the middle classes; and Gladstone gradually came to see that such support was more important than any legislation. Although he often said that a statesman ought to put his convictions into Bills, and although he was acknowledged as the leading churchman in the House of Commons for more than forty years, Gladstone did not initiate any major reform in the structure of the Church of

England. His lack of creative zeal in this field was an anti-climax after all that he had said and written as a young man. (His book of 1838 had alarmed Keble by appearing to undervalue the 'sacredness' of the existing ecclesiastical arrangements, and he had told James Hope in 1844: 'The purpose of Parliamentary life resolves itself with me simply and wholly into one question: Will it ever afford the means under God of rectifying the relations between the Church and the State, and give me the opportunity of setting forward such a work?') He did not even resist effectively the theological pretensions of the Privy Council, or the interfering legislation of Disraeli's Public Worship Regulation Act, although he denounced them. Paradoxically his greatest political service to the legal security of the Church of England came as an incidental result of his unexpected determination to press on with Home Rule and other radical reforms for Ireland. This drove Joseph Chamberlain, with his following of Nonconformist, imperialist businessmen, into the arms of the Tories, and split the Liberals who otherwise might have dealt radically with the Church of England.[16]

In comparison with the spiritual life of the Church around the Eucharist, however, no Act of Parliament mattered to Gladstone. Many of those whom he had hoped would lead the Church of England through its crisis had gone; yet the Body of Christ was increasing. 'Death and recession, between them, seem to have removed all our most considerable men', he remarked in a letter of 1874: 'and yet the *body* has grown; and, amidst every kind of scandal, grief and danger, I think evidences become stronger and stronger that this singularly constituted and marvellously preserved body has some special work still appointed for it to perform.'

Gladstone was as serious as any clergyman about the spiritual integrity of the Church. He showed this in the sequel to his treatise on Church and State, *Church Principles Considered in Their Results* (1840). This book, like its predecessor, baffled fellow-laymen by its apparent remoteness from current controversies, and it was quickly forgotten by other readers who wanted the skills of professional theology. But as an outline of a basis for Anglicanism by an amateur theologian, it remains impressive more than a century after its writing. It defended the necessity of the visible Church on the ground of the necessity of common action, and in relation to the growth of sympathy and devotion in prayer. It presented doctrines about the sacraments and 'the Apostolical Succession' which had plainly helped at least one busy layman to pray and to act better. Finally, it covered the Anglican debate with Rome in 250 pages remarkable for their care and balance and for their calm hope that, although clear principles

---

[16] Appropriately, Joseph Chamberlain's widow married a parson, Canon Carnegie of Westminster.

prevented the submission of Anglicans to the Papacy as it then was, the unity of Christendom might one day be restored on the basis of 'Divine Truth'.

Gladstone later admitted that he had written this book in a mood of false optimism about the prospects of the Church of England. He had seen the Evangelical and Catholic revivals within the Church, but he had not foreseen the bitterness. As he wrote at the end of his book in 1840: 'I close, at length, this review of the religious position of the Church of England . . . full of the most cheerful anticipation of her destiny, and without the remotest fear either of schism among her children, or of any permanent oppression from the State, whatever may befall the State itself.' The next few years punished such cheerfulness. His eccentric sister Helen became a Roman Catholic in 1842 and his two most intimate friends, James Hope (who revised the 1838 book) and Henry Manning (who revised the 1840 book), both made their submissions to Rome on 6 April 1851.[17] This was Gladstone's most terrible time. In 1851 his heart was already deeply bruised; almost a year before, his little daughter Jessy had died of meningitis. His isolation in public affairs was increased by the opposition which he felt bound to offer against the government-encouraged Protestant hysteria which greeted the Pope's appointment of bishops of England —while in the same period he gave a great deal of energy to denunciations of the cruel misgovernment which held Italy in bondage, particularly in the Kingdom of Naples and in the Papal States. When the Gorham Judgment seemed to strike 'one Baptism for the remission of sins' out of the creed of the Church of England on the authority of the Judicial Committee of the Privy Council, he searched his near-broken heart to see whether it was possible to remain loyal. Yet Gladstone never abandoned his *Church Principles*. The religion stated in that book was the religion in which he lived and worked; and he insisted on climbing out of his deathbed in order to kneel to receive Holy Communion from his son Stephen, who was then Rector of Hawarden.

When Gladstone came to acknowledge that the balance of the argument was against the continuance of the Anglican Establishment in Ireland and Wales (if not in England), and against the Presbyterian Establishment in Scotland, he expressed his change of view in terms as moral and as theological as any which he had used in 1838 and 1840, as well as with inexhaustible statistics.[18]

17 Hope, often called the best-looking man in England, changed his name to Hope-Scott on marrying Sir Walter Scott's grand-daughter in 1853. Manning had been greatly trusted by Maurice as well as by Gladstone.

18 A full study has been provided by P. M. H. Bell, *Disestablishment in Ireland and Wales* (SPCK, 1969).

The argument was never a cool one, based on utility. When he saw that the State could not be expected to endow the church of a minority, he counted it a duty to God to crusade for the disestablishment and partial disendowment of that church. When he saw that the spiritual life of the Church was hindered rather than helped by the patronage of the State, he prophesied (correctly) that the Irish and Welsh Anglicans would gain by independence. He spent much time and money on ensuring that his vast collection of books would be preserved for the use of the clergy and other students at St. Deiniol's Library at Hawarden in Wales. There generations to come could equip themselves for the battle against unbelief. Already in the 1840s his interest in the religion of Scotland (his father and mother were of pure Scottish descent) had caused him to think deeply about the spiritual benefits of independence. He was devoted to the small Episcopal Church in Scotland and took the lead in founding Trinity College, Glenalmond, as a public school for the sons of the Episcopalian gentry. During its early years this school was combined with a tiny college to train priests.[19] He also greatly admired rebels against state control over the Established Church of Scotland, and lectures in London by the chief of these, Thomas Chalmers, drove him to develop his own views of Church and State; Chalmers was admired all the more because he never became a simple disestablishmentarian.

Through all the changes in Church and State, however, Gladstone never gave any support to the common view that the State was a mere police force for the protection of property, and the Church a mere convenience for the spread of respectability. 'We are still a Christian people', he announced firmly in his *Chapter of Autobiography* in 1868. He had been moral as an aristocrat, and he would be moral as a democrat. He was a Tory and he became a Liberal, but he was never a Whig; he never venerated 1688. He used to say that the rejection of the philosophy of John Locke was the beginning of wisdom. That meant that although he abandoned as hopeless the old Tory battle for Church and State, he never abandoned the old Tory ideal of the State as a kind of church; he admired the philosophy as well as the eloquence of Burke.

After his rejection at Oxford in 1865, he became M.P. for South Lancashire, declaring in Manchester: 'At last, my friends, I am come among you, and I am come among you unmuzzled.' So he turned to the people. But even now it was not a complete turn. During the American Civil War he got into trouble by a public indiscretion which showed that he thought that the gentlemen of the South, slave-owners as some of them were, had made a nation in arms against the egali-

[19] See Marion Lockhead, *Episcopal Scotland in the Nineteenth Century* (John Murray, 1966).

tarian but industrial North. What he needed for his almost complete conversion to democracy was an inner conviction that the British people was moral and even religious at heart, like Oxford University. This conviction came as he watched the courage of the workmen of Lancashire when the cotton industry was depressed by the American war. He now believed that the people could be trusted, and that its voice could be heard as the voice of God. The privileged class to which he himself belonged (although he never consented to join the House of Lords) could now be denounced if it was deaf to this voice, the voice which his own oratory in its organ-like plenitude echoed and magnified.

Another development came with his Midlothian campaign, nearly twenty-one years after he had formally joined the Liberal Party. By the series of speeches (developing earlier pamphleteering) which he made against Disraeli's evil policies while he was contesting that Scottish seat in 1879, he awoke the enlarged electorate to the excitement of the issues at stake, and he awoke his own potentialities not only as the Liberal Prime Minister on Disraeli's fall but also as a mob orator; the public chose him as Prime Minister. Many historians have regarded that campaign as one of the decisive dates in the emergence of the politics of democracy. However, the Midlothian campaign was couched in moral terms on a theological basis, as his books had been in 1838 and 1840. Its tradition went back to the anti-slavery agitation led by William Wilberforce. Gladstone had come to acknowledge the justice of William Wilberforce's aim, and he now related the same style, a lay preacher's, to a democracy which would have shocked the great emancipator of the slaves. People in politics laughed at him, as they had laughed at Wilberforce. But 'the People' did not laugh. Believing that the State still had a conscience, he treated the electors of the late 1870s, and the six millions who later became possessors of votes, as a congregation which he summoned to crusades against Turkish atrocities in Bulgaria or against English oppression in Ireland. He always assumed that his vast audience constituted a moral personality; and his attitude did much to make it one, with results which became apparent in 1914 and 1940.[20]

5

There were many disadvantages in this idea of politics, aristocratic or democratic, as public morality. Gladstone's imagination was not

[20] See R. T. Shannon, *Gladstone and the Bulgarian Agitation, 1876* (Nelson, 1963), and J. L. Hammond's classic panorama of *Gladstone and the Irish Nation* (Longmans, Green, 1938).

aroused by subjects which he did not regard as intensely moral. Fortunately for England, finance did become moral in his hands, for he came to regard the reform of taxes and tariffs as a great work of righteousness. But education, for example, seems to have bored him, except in so far as Oxford University could be regarded as an educational establishment.

The great 1870 Education Act was passed while he was Prime Minister; it marked the assumption by the State of responsibilities for the education of the people, and incidentally, while it provided for religion as part of this education, it also provided that no 'denominational formulary' (they were thinking chiefly about the Church of England's Catechism) should be taught at the public expense. Gladstone showed remarkably little interest in it. He allowed W. E. Forster to prepare the Bill with only the vaguest supervision, and the legislation about religion (the 'Cowper–Temple clause') which was so fateful for the future of English Christianity was adopted almost casually by the government during the course of the Commons debates. Gladstone's personal view, to the end of his life, was that undenominational religion in the schools was an 'imposture' or 'moral monster', and he would have preferred to put religious education on an entirely voluntary basis, leaving the churches to instruct their own children. He did not press this view, however, because the topic did not rank high among his priorities. He paid for this casualness when at the next General Election, in 1874, neither Anglicans nor Nonconformists believed that the souls of England's children were safe in his hands; and Disraeli was recalled to power. When Gladstone retired from the leadership for the first time, one reason was that 'I felt myself to be in some measure out of touch with some of the tendencies of the Liberal party, especially in religious matters'. He wished then to concentrate on religion in an interval between Parliament and the grave, but he also indicated that he would be willing to return to Westminster at any time 'with a view to arresting some great evil or procuring for the nation some great good'.

Another subject, pregnant with the future, which failed to command Gladstone's best attention was the Empire. He never liked paying for the Army or Navy. He was Chancellor of the Exchequer during the first period of the Crimean War, but partly because the war embarrassed him he busied himself with domestic matters (notably the Oxford reforms). He liked to think of the Ionian Islands being under British protection, and criticized Palmerston for handing them back to Greece in 1865; but he had no clear views about India or Africa, except that Disraeli's imperialism was immoral. The weakness of his Middle Eastern policy brought bitter criticism to his later years in office. He authorized the British fleet's bombardment of Alexandria as an act of justice, but when he wanted to evacuate the Sudan he chose as his agent an imperialist soldier who became a religious martyr, General Gordon; so that Egypt and the Sudan had to join the Empire.

His taste for moral crusades could lead him to pick up the wrong end of a stick. While Chancellor of the Exchequer he proposed that the earnings of charities from investments should be subject to income tax, because he believed that the exemption of charities from this public duty was immoral—and also that many charities used their assets in an immoral way. The outcry surprised him. Again, when the Pope's infallibility was decreed by the Vatican Council in 1870 he expected many Roman Catholics to share his moral indignation and predicted that the split in the Roman Catholic Church would be far greater than the trouble which had been brought on the Church of England by the Romanizers of 1848 and 1851. He wrote a great pamphlet against the Vatican decrees, and it became a best-seller, but both Newman and Manning were able to answer it because it directed most of its fire at a non-existent enemy. Gladstone argued that every Roman Catholic who was a patriot should denounce the Vatican Council's attempt to interfere with his civil allegiance. But it was precisely in 1870, when the Pope was declared infallible in matters of faith and morals when teaching *ex cathedra*, that the Papacy's temporal power was buried. The real issue, which was whether the Pope was infallible when teaching faith or morals *ex cathedra*, did not receive the attention which it deserved because it did not chiefly engage the eminent pamphleteer's wrath.

Few people in public life thought that Gladstone was insincere, but some criticisms of his style were made by almost everyone. Henry Labouchere's complaint that Gladstone believed that Almighty God had hidden the ace of trumps up his sleeve was widely quoted. Another complaint, made on many occasions in Gladstone's Parliamentary career, was that his speeches closely resembled many sermons in that, however long they might be, the audience was left wondering what the speaker had meant to say. The explanation was advanced that Gladstone had no clear purpose, but was in Disraeli's famous phrase 'inebriated by the exuberance of his own verbosity'. People also complained that, dwelling as he did in this pulpit-like elevation, he did not take the trouble to get to know *them*. He far preferred business to parties, and although he would reply to critics that he never neglected business for the sake of Homer or theology, he could not pretend that he was adept in the social arts of a politician. He could not get interested in the unheroic men who sat on the benches of the House of Commons behind him or who were expected to vote for him in the constituencies. At least, he could not get interested in them one by one. Only when he was addressing them as a mass did his energies quicken and the heavens open. In his old age he was more than ever insistent on his political mission, and refused to give either himself or others the luxury of companionable relaxation. The breaking of the Liberal Party in his closing years was not due solely to disagreement about policies.

Yet what a life it was! When he died men felt that they would not look on his like again, and the psychological secret of his official biography, by John Morley, was that here a comparatively ineffective politician (and an agnostic) was consoling himself by writing about a personality able to shape events to a will forged like steel in the course of prayer.[21] He was always a controversialist, and for this reason might have made a bad bishop. But when we compare Gladstone with a more easily lovable figure such as Stanley, we are struck by the immense superiority of the former's power. This superiority was not due mainly to Gladstone's stronger equipment in application to detail (he would never have made a mess of a commentary on Corinthians), in oratory (he would never have read an old sermon), in financial power (he would never have struck a bad bargain with the Ecclesiastical Commissioners), in virility (he would never have postponed marriage until not far short of fifty years old), and in intellectual force (Gladstone could apply to Stanley's mind the fatal word 'picturesque'). It was due to start in life even more favourable than Arthur Stanley's.

In order to provide for his boys' early education, Gladstone's father obtained from Charles Simeon 'the Rev. Mr. Rawson of Cambridge . . . a good man, of high no-popery opinions'. About a dozen boys formed a little school in Mr. Rawson's parsonage at Seaforth, by 'the pure dry sands of the Mersey's mouth'; Arthur Stanley was later among them, although by that time Gladstone had left for Eton. The two men first met in 1828, when the young Gladstone dined at Alderley Rectory and later invited the young Stanley to a lavish breakfast with strawberries, urging him to enjoy the boating and Latin verses of Eton. When Stanley took the road to Rugby a few months later, it was an indication that his family could not afford the outlook which came naturally to millionaires who could pay for strawberries and Eton out of slaves. And when Stanley began to regard Thomas Arnold as his second father, it was an indication of an emotional need greater than any known by the young Gladstone, who was a completely devoted son—and one of the most privileged men ever to enter British politics.

Gladstone was also Stanley's superior in pious zeal, for his own religion at Eton and Oxford was derived not from any headmaster's preaching but from an Evangelical conversion. The details of Gladstone's spiritual formation cannot be recovered. Both his parents were

[21] See D. A. Hamer, *John Morley* (Oxford University Press, 1968).

devout in an Evangelical way, although naturally they believed that
they knew more than William Wilberforce did about the morality of
slave-owning. A religious influence was also exerted on him by his
elder sister, Anne, who died in 1828. Much of that year was spent
by Gladstone at home, before he went up to Christ Church; and he
had many memorable talks about religion with her. She urged him
to read Hooker's *Ecclesiastical Polity* and spoke to him about baptismal
regeneration, for she was able to include that belief in her mainly
Evangelical theology. In 1832, during a long holiday in Italy, three
shocks added to the force of such pleas for the sacramental element
in Christianity. In January he came across the Italian Protestants, who
were venerated by Evangelicals because they had been the first to be
reformed in the sixteenth century; and he found the reality unim-
pressive. In March he was in Rome, and in St. Peter's he had a vision
of the unity of Christendom as the historic Body of Christ. Six weeks
later in Naples he happened to be examining the Book of Common
Prayer, when his sister's doctrine struck home into his heart: Christians,
converted as they must be, were born again in Baptism and were fed
by the Eucharist. Three years later he wrote: 'I am entirely convinced
that in substance the movement termed Evangelical and that falsely
termed Popish are parts of one great and beneficent design of God, and
that in their substance they will harmonize and co-operate.' In that
comprehensiveness of a religious conversion, both Evangelical and
Catholic, his vast natural assurance was doubled.

Gladstone became a tolerant democrat not because he ever doubted
whether metaphysical truth could be reached by men, but because
of the influence of the Evangelical Gospel which he believed as a
baptized and converted member of the Catholic Church. He would
explain that the Gospel of the God of love had gradually taught him
to love men's liberty. Maurice was one of those through whom he
learned this, although Maurice's theology never satisfied his analytic
mind. In 1856 he wrote to a surprised Bishop of Hereford, apologizing
for his share in the condemnation of the theology of the bishop, then
the notorious Professor Hampden, at Oxford twenty years before. The
immediate cause of this apology was Gladstone's experience of
Maurice's condemnation at King's College, London; both Hampden
and Maurice had been judged unfairly, 'in a condemnation couched
in general terms which did not really declare the point of imputed
guilt, and against which perfect innocence could have no defence'.
But that apology also showed how Gladstone's mind was moving.

Justice now became no less sacred than orthodoxy; criticism, even
when it touched the Bible, should be considered and answered, for
truth could be trusted to vindicate itself. 'The first person who pointed
out to me that there were *some* errors of fact in the Gospels was Dr.

Pusey', he once told a correspondent; 'it was nearly sixty years back.' Freedom, even for heretics, was one of the commands of God. Unity would be restored to Christendom not by the exercise of discipline and not by a stress on morality at the expense of doctrine, but by a free agreement about the truth of the faith. In an essay on 'The Place of Heresy and Schism in the Modern Christian Church', included among his posthumously published *Later Gleanings*, he placed his hope on the fact that 450 millions were already loyal to the great central truths of the Gospel. This was better than 'spurious undenominationalism'. It was 'this mighty modern miracle, this marvellous concurrence evolved from the very heart of discord'. He surprised his fellow-Christians by his willingness to vote for the admittance to the House of Commons of Jews in the 1850s and of the atheist Bradlaugh in the 1880s.[22] His liberality on such issues had an effect all the greater because he was so clearly not one of those M.P.s who all believed in 'a God of some sort or other' (to quote from one of the debates on Bradlaugh). He could write to a Unitarian in 1865: 'I was myself brought up to think . . . that salvation depended absolutely upon the reception of a particular and a very narrow creed. But long, long have I cast those weeds behind me.'

He could not, of course, so liberalize and democratize the idea of heaven as to admit an unrepentant atheist there. But when his book of *Studies Subsidiary to the Works of Bishop Butler* was published in 1896, it was found that at one point his mind had moved away from the concurrence of Christians in his time. He was acutely aware of the difficulties and dangers surrounding speculation about the condition of mankind in a future life, and was careful to insist that this tentative speculation of his should not be treated as a rival dogma. In particular he was anxious not to be mistaken for one of those such as Maurice who might be understood as prophesying a universal restitution which in the end would include the wicked. To the end Gladstone maintained that God's revelation was sterner than men's wishes, that righteousness was eternally against men's wickedness, and that the 'moral government of the world' rested on eternal justice. 'The notion of Universal Restitution is, then, not supported by Scripture, or by Christian tradition, or by any sound philosophy of human nature, which by its constitution tends to an ever-growing fixity of habits.' But, wrapped up in many hesitations and qualifications, Gladstone's guess seemed to be that the soul was not naturally immortal. Those who used their free will in order to reject God and Goodness would not be punished everlastingly. Instead, God would withdraw from the wicked the gift of eternal life which was open to all the righteous.

[22] Walter Arnstein, *The Bradlaugh Case* (Clarendon Press, 1965), was a rich study in late Victorian opinion.

FOR FURTHER READING

The Life and Correspondence of Arthur Penrhyn Stanley, D.D., *late Dean of Westminster*, was compiled in two volumes by Rowland Prothero, later Lord Ernle, 'with the co-operation and sanction of the Very Rev. G. G. Bradley, D.D., Dean of Westminster' (John Murray, 1893). A further volume of *Letters and Verses* appeared two years later, and more letters were included with a memoir by Albert Baillie and Hector Bolitho in *A Victorian Dean* (Chatto & Windus, 1930).

The Life of William Ewart Gladstone was written in three volumes by John, later Viscount, Morley (Macmillan, 1903). Morley's reticence over Gladstone's religion caused some, including Gladstone's own family, to feel that for all its merits this great biography, which won an immense public, failed to give a portrait of the man. A lay High Churchman, D. C. Lathbury, did much to fill the gap on the ecclesiastical side by his sketch of *Mr. Gladstone* (Mowbray, 1907) and his edition of *Correspondence on Church and Religion of William Ewart Gladstone* in two volumes (John Murray, 1910). Many other biographies have appeared, of which the best has been *Gladstone* by Sir Philip Magnus (John Murray, 1954).

6

1828-92.   1828-96

Hort and Benson

1

On 26 December 1882 a Cambridge don wrote to the man who had just been appointed Archbishop of Canterbury. They had been fellow-undergraduates at Trinity College, Cambridge, in 1848. This letter from Fenton John Anthony Hort disturbed Edward White Benson; for it was less a congratulation than a grim warning on St. Stephen's Day, the feast of the first Christian martyr.

'It has become difficult to think of anything but the problems of the present', Hort wrote, describing the 1880s as 'so absolutely new in the history of the world, craving all possible illumination from past experience, and yet hopelessly insoluble except in the spirit of St. Stephen's prophetic welcome of the revolution which was so soon to bring a new heaven and a new earth'. Hort had, we may guess, said much the same thing when they had been undergraduates together, for in 1848 he and Benson had both been as sure as Maurice or Kingsley that the progress of the Church was central to the great expectations of the age, and that faith alone could provide the key to the meaning of the new facts. Now in 1882, the year of Darwin's death, he looked round a Church torn by controversies which were irrelevant to the real challenges; and he was not so sure. He wrote: 'the convulsions of our English Church itself, grievous as they are, seem to be as nothing beside the danger of its calm and unobtrusive alienation in thought and spirit from the great silent multitude of Englishmen, and again of alienation from fact and love of fact;—mutual alienations both.'

Benson replied that he 're-read and pondered much' this warning about the alienation of English religion from the people and from truth. 'Yours was far the most historical and real letter I have had. That is why I am concerned.' Benson invited Hort to visit him and prophesy in Lambeth Palace. He also implied a rebuke for Hort's pessimism and isolation. 'I do not believe that the two alienations of which you speak are *naturally* progressing on us. They may surely yet be arrested. But what if those who have insight prophesy in closets—when they ought to be speaking from the house-tops?' The Archbishop-elect urged the timid don to publish 'a volume of Essays or Discourses'.

Hort's apology was pathetic. 'It grieves me much that I have seemed
to suspend a murky cloud over the prospect. . . . I must doubtless have
given too strong an expression to the anxieties which self-glorifying
choas suggests. . . . So pray forgive my mutterings—articulate speech
on such matters is, I fear, constitutionally denied me. . . .'

'Self-glorifying chaos' is a strange phrase, but a glimpse into the
heart of this introspective, hesitant scholar. Hort probed fearlessly not
only into his own weaknesses (which many other Victorians did) but
also into the facts behind the religious problems of the age. A keen
student of science, he loved botany as his recreation. His store of
classical, biblical, and theological learning was more than Gladstonian.
At different times he had various projects. He would write a history of
the Early Church, in many volumes he once thought, or even a summary. He and Cambridge collaborators would translate all the *Dia-
logues* of Plato. He would write (with his friends Westcott and Lightfoot)
commentaries, both literary and doctrinal, on the whole of the New
Testament; he would himself cover the synoptic gospels, Acts, James,
Peter, and Jude. What he did was to improve greatly the Greek text
of the New Testament, in collaboration with Westcott. But apart from
articles, he published little else. His one general utterance on the basic
issues of Christian belief, his Hulsean Lectures of 1871 on *The Way,
the Truth, the Life*, had not been finally revised for publication when
he died twenty-one years after lecturing, despite a reference in the
Preface to the urgency of the times.

All this learning was, in a sense, 'chaos'. He would not order it in
a book because he was a morbid perfectionist. Any publication must,
be believed, take every relevant fact into account; it must be maturely,
conclusively, judicious. He laid down his life in the love of fact, particularly facts in Greek. It was a don's martyrdom, as in Browning's 'A
Grammarian's Funeral':

> Oh, such a life as he resolved to live,
>   When he had learned it,
> When he had gathered all books had to give!
>   Sooner, he spurned it.

2

Hort was the son of an Anglo-Irish gentleman, a 'Conservative
Whig' in political views, who followed no profession but was an Evangelical and benevolent to the poor. The family migrated from Dublin,
the boy's birthplace, to Cheltenham, then the elegant headquarters of
many leisured and benevolent admirers of the seventh Earl of Shaftesbury. The boy was sent to Rugby School. Tait was headmaster by the

time he reached the Sixth Form in 1844, and the reports on both Sixth Form years noted how 'thoughtful' Hort was.

His own letters show what he was thinking about: his work, his school, his religion. Already a good classical grammarian, he had been captivated by the 'love of fact'. Already devout, he had adjusted the Evangelicalism of Cheltenham to the broader ethos of Dr. Arnold's school. On Easter Day 1846 he wrote to his parents that 'my choice is the Church', but there was by now some tension between the creed of his choice and his parents' piety. A schoolfellow recalled from those days his

somewhat awkward figure and resolute earnest face with the blue eyes, bushy eyebrows, and black straight hair. . . . He was not a boy of many friends, but those he had felt a deep and admiring attachment toward him. . . . He was no great hand at games. . . . Yet I seem to remember his wild rushes at Football . . . plunging into the thick of the struggle.

In October 1846 he went to Cambridge, where he threw himself into the struggles surrounding the decline of religious fundamentalism and of the old social order of landed privilege. He discovered heroes, Coleridge and Maurice. To the latter in 1849 he wrote a long letter about the problem 'which has long been tormenting me' of the never-ending punishment of the wicked. This remarkable document shows the best of Rugby, at the age of twenty-one, struggling with Cheltenham's creed. The letter was also about purgatory, about the devil, and about the punishment of Christ on the cross as the one substitute accepted by the just God instead of every man 'suffering in his own person the full penalty for his sins'. Hort referred to Coleridge's *Literary Remains*, but hoped that Maurice would explain the reference. 'Is there not something strangely significant in the extraordinary language of Coleridge . . . ?'

Maurice wrote an equally thoughtful, but unusually clear, reply to the undergraduate. 'The *starting-point* of the Gospel, as I read it, is the absolute Love of God; the *reward* of the Gospel is the knowledge of that love.' The older theologian opened his heart, confessing that 'every glimpse I have of it has come through great confusion and darkness', confessing, too, the limits of knowledge.

My duty then I feel is this: 1. To assert that which I know, that which God has revealed, His absolute universal love in all possible ways and without any limitation. 2. To tell myself and all men, that to know this love and to be moulded by it is *the* blessing we are to seek. 3. To say that this is eternal life. 4. To say that the want of it is death. 5. To say that if they believe in the Son of God they have eternal life. 6. To say that if they have not the Son of God, they have not life. 7. *Not* to say who has the Son of God, because I do not know. 8. *Not* to say how long any one may remain in eternal death, because I do not know. 9. *Not* to say that all will necessarily be raised out of eternal death, because I do not know....

Not many months after this correspondence, Hort heard Maurice preaching in the chapel of Lincoln's Inn and commented:

It was curious to watch his face looking out into the chapel, with the dark hollows of his deep-set eyes strongly contrasted with the rest of his face in the sort of twilight.... Such a sermon in every respect I never heard; his quiet, deep voice, piercing you so softly and firmly through and through, never pausing or relaxing in its strain of eloquence, every syllable, as it were, weighted with the energy and might of his whole soul (and what a soul!), kept me crouched in a kind of spell, such as I could never have conceived.

Hort received detailed advice from his new hero. The young man should always go back to Plato; 'I never have taken up any dialogue of Plato without getting more from it than from any book not in the Bible.' 'Our modern Socialist questions ... present themselves to you again and again while you are busy with these ancients. And it is a grand thing to read the newspapers by their light, and them by the light of the newspapers.' This advice Hort followed, but so often it meant reading by the light of an oil lamp, a practice which destroyed his sleep and permanently damaged his health. His failure in health accounted for his failure to sweep away all the academic prizes which he and others expected; but he received his honours enough, including Firsts in the examinations and a fellowship at Trinity College in 1852.

By this time his break with his parents' theology was about complete, and he confided to Charles Kingsley that Cheltenham 'maddened' him. By this time, too, his inability to bring his own work to completion had grown ominous. The immense essay which he submitted unsuccessfully for the Hulsean Prize, on 'Evidences of Christianity as exhibited in the writings of the early Apologists down to Augustine inclusive', was thought to demand so much reading and thinking that it trailed off into a series of notes. Fortunately, while meditating on plans to write histories of the Jews from Abraham to 300 B.C., of the Greek philosophers from Thales to Aristotle and after, of the Hellenic world from Alexander to Christ, of the Early Church 'with a view perhaps to writing a great history years hence', and while 'dabbling in Oriental alphabets', he was persuaded by Westcott to edit a Greek text of the New Testament, 'some two or three years hence, if possible'.

He chose to be ordained as a deacon by Samuel Wilberforce. 'I was specially delighted by the calumniated Bishop himself', he told Westcott. He carried on in Cambridge until his engagement in 1857 to

Fanny Holland. It was impossible under the statutes to stay as a married don, and a few days later his college made him Vicar of St. Ippolyts-cum-Great Wymondley, in the countryside near Hitchin. 'I hope to go on with the New Testament text more unremittingly,' he told West-cott, but he also hoped to gain the hearts of his parishioners. With a wife at his side, he was proud to think of himself as more than a grammarian. 'I have never cared much for books', he boasted, 'except in so far as they might help to quicken our sense of the reality of life, and enable us to enter into its right and wrong.'

Hort later regarded his years in a parish as a time of failure. He loved his vicarage, his roses, and his pets; he went round his villagers shyly; he removed the barrel-organ from his church and took endless care over the chants and hymns; he put his massive knowledge, and an agony of effort to simplify and popularize it, into his sermons, some of which were later published. But his son recalled the sad truth. 'It was long after his departure before he revisited the parish, though he was frequently asked to do so; he shrank from going, from an ever-present feeling that he had failed them, that he had not done all that he aspired to do for his flock.' It was, after all, an incredible appoint-ment for one of England's most learned and sensitive scholars, al-though in a pamphlet written soon after his move to St. Ippolyts Hort enthusiastically defended this tradition of putting married clerical dons out to graze in country vicarages.

Shortage of money was one of his problems, and when Macmillan asked for a book for boys on Simon de Montfort, allegedly the founder of the Commons, he turned aside from the Greek New Testament. A learned article was all that resulted. Then he thought of making money by a Greek grammar based on the New Testament. Nothing appeared.

On at least two occasions, however, Hort's refusal to employ his talents in the higher journalism had theological significance. He re-fused to contribute to *Essays and Reviews*, and his place in the scheme was taken by Mark Pattison. 'It is surely likely to bring on a crisis; and that I cannot think desirable on any account.' He also refused to write about Darwin's *Origin of Species* (1859). 'The scientific question is very complicated—far more complicated than Darwin seems to have any idea.' On the other hand, he refused to panic when *Essays and Reviews* or Darwin did cause a crisis. Like Maurice or Tait, he noted that he was more of an Evangelical and more of a High Churchman than the Oxford essayists, but he also (like them) noted who was against them: the sinister combination of Shaftesbury and Pusey. And whatever Samuel Wilberforce might say, Hort was unwilling to con-demn the theory of evolution. 'In spite of difficulties, I am inclined to think it unanswerable.'

What Hort acutally did was to press on with editing the Greek New

Testament, alone for many hours or during visits to the vicarage by Westcott. This study, and all the half-completed other literary work, and the worry over the parish, brought him to exhaustion and 'nerves' in 1860. A century later, it would be called a mental breakdown. Long holidays in the Alps revived him, but he found that he still could not face the parish and he spent most of the period 1863–5 at his parents' home in Cheltenham, taking up geology to cure the boredom of tramps over the Cotswold hills. After this long walk through the Valley of the Shadow, the darkness began to lift. In 1870 he joined the work for the Revised Version of the New Testament. Next year he gave the Hulsean Lectures at Cambridge, complaining to his wife, 'I cannot get up the *brightness* that I want for the subject'. He had resolved to write these lectures without notes or references, 'also no proper names except from the Bible'; but he was very dissatisfied with them as delivered.

He went back to Cambridge as a resident on the March day in 1872 when his hero, Maurice, left it for the last time. But Westcott had returned two years previously, and lived a few doors away in St. Peter's Terrace. In such congenial company, Hort actually published a book, which earned him a Doctorate of Divinity. It was entitled *Two Dissertations*, one of the essays in it being a study in St. John, and the other being on the fourth-century creeds. A Preface summed up Hort's attitude to the creeds and to the councils of the Church, from Nicea onwards, which had adopted them. 'Even the best theological literature of that age, as of every age, contains much which cannot possibly be true, and it is difficult to imagine how the study of Councils has been found compatible with the theory which requires us to find Conciliar utterances Divine.'

So the Cambridge years passed in teaching and committees. He was made Hulsean Professor, and later Lady Margaret's Professor. The Greek New Testament which he and Westcott had been editing since 1853 eventually appeared in 1881, just before the Revised Version of the New Testament in English. He built up a great library of other men's writings, but never managed to write out instructions about what should happen to it on his death. He prepared lectures, some of which were printed after his death.[1] Undergraduates sometimes complained that the term was almost over before Professor Hort had safely surmounted the preliminaries to the announced subject, but among the more studious in Cambridge he became a cult. Armitage Robinson, later Dean of Westminster, recalled: 'He had so seldom failed us, that we felt as if he really knew everything. Of the obscurest book we said, "Dr. Hort is sure to have it"; of the most perplexing problem, "Dr.

---

[1] Examples are the university lectures on *Judaistic Christianity* (Macmillan, 1894), and the six lectures at the new Clergy Training School in Cambridge on *The Ante-Nicene Fathers* (Macmillan, 1895).

Hort knows the solution, if he would only tell"; of any subject, "Dr. Hort will tell you all the literature".'[2]

Twice Dr. Hort told in public. Both occasions were in the service of his scholarly friendship with Lightfoot and Westcott. In 1892 he knew that he was dying. 'With most unusual rapidity' (his son recalled), he wrote for the *Dictionary of National Biography* a full article on the life of Lightfoot; he corrected the proof of this, within three weeks of his death. And on May Day 1890 he preached in Westminster Abbey at Westcott's consecration to be Lightfoot's successor at Durham. During an Easter holiday in Venice, Hort had given anxious thought to this sermon. Back in Cambridge, he had worked on it for all of several nights. When he had to catch the last train to London on the night before the service, he was still writing, while candles were held for him.

What he said was published under the title: *The Sense and Service of Membership the Measure of True Soundness in the Body*.[3] After a long introduction on the Epistle to the Ephesians and its teaching about the Church as the Body of Christ, Hort scarcely had time to do more than mention its relevance to the last decade of the nineteenth century. The main implication was that the sense of *belonging* to the Church was vital. 'The experience of the last few years has shown how little salutary force could permanently be looked for in what is called a Christian world, a realm of habit and language sustained of late for the most part of vague and aimless convention, though permeated by Christian sentiment, and partly derived in the first instance from Christian traditions.' Only a stronger Church, Hort preached, could effectively claim as its rightful province 'the entire world of humanity, because God in Christ has claimed for His Kingdom all things human except the evil that corrupts them'.

If we ask *how* the Church could embrace all life, we have to go back to the Hulsean Lectures of 1871—but then we find that even these lectures are unlikely to convince a sceptical reader today, except perhaps through the attraction of Hort's own character. As Westcott wrote in his Preface in 1893: 'A life so lived, however prolific in literary achievements, is more fruitful by what it is than by what it does.' *The Way, the Truth, the Life* suffers as a piece of argument by being too full of quotations from St. John's gospel, taken as the words of Jesus and used devotionally. Those who are not willing to accept such a use of St. John will find it difficult to follow the argument—or even to see that there is an argument. Hort seems to have assumed through-

---

[2] Gordon Rupp has lectured on *Hort and the Cambridge Tradition* (Cambridge University Press, 1970).

[3] It was reprinted at the end of his lectures on *The Christian Ecclesia* (Macmillan, 1897).

out that he was addressing the converted, although he stated his awareness of 'the prevailing attitude assumed of late years by what is called educated opinion towards the supernatural foundation and the practical authority of Christian faith'. What he did in these lectures was to discuss ways in which Christian conversion and discipleship could be interpreted more broadly than was the custom among Cheltenham Evangelicals.

This demanded a personal statement; and as Hort knew well, 'everything personal,—personal thought even more than personal feeling, if the distinction is possible,—is in a measure absolutely inexpressible.' The exposition suffered from many qualifications, yet the personal vision was communicated. '*Vision*', he wrote in one of the incomplete notes printed at the end of the volume and never incorporated into the text. 'Its three qualities are clearness, completeness, proportion. Vision is essentially personal and individual, involving selection and interpretation. No hearsay can be a substitute. What we have ourselves seen and learned and known is the dominant and the vitalizing factor in all real belief.'

The claim of the Fourth Gospel was that Jesus was more than a teacher or example; and in *The Way, the Truth, the Life*, Hort made clear that his own discipleship had confirmed for him a strong sense of the unique Lordship of Jesus. The early disciples, he wrote, had believed that 'the weight of the world's future rested not on their shoulders but on His', that Jesus was 'the eternal fundamental utterance of Him whose diffracted and remoter utterance is the universe'; and so he believed himself. Yet the whole mystery of Jesus had not yet been fully understood. Further stages in the Way had to be trod; 'for it is His own voice which bids us "rise and go hence", that we may find Him and follow Him elsewhere'. Old truths must be tested and new truths reached, and there would be many casualties to the Church in this struggle. 'Yet so it has been in every great crisis of the Church by which the Kingdom of God has made a swift advance. If we stop to count the falling or fallen, no battle will ever be won.' Hort did not 'fear for the fate of the costly truth itself', for 'no faith founded on truth can ever die except that it may rise to a better life'. In more than one passage he dwelt on the excitements of undergraduate days, when many roads to the truth and life seem to lie open before young men; but he was able to state the mature experience of his own life. In this life, honest study had made showy triumphs impossible, but precisely this dedication to the truth had been for Hort the way of discipleship. He said, and it was his own epitaph: 'The pursuit of truth begins in a sense of freedom. We almost make truth itself the symbol of freedom for the workings of our minds. We are slow to learn that truth is never that which we choose to believe, but always that which we are under a necessity to believe. In proportion to the earnestness of the pursuit we discover that we must needs be servants where we thought to be masters. A life devoted to truth is a life of vanities abased and ambitions forsworn.'

In the sermon on May Day in the Abbey, and in these lectures, the vision of Christian undergraduates in 1848 came back. The grammarian had at last begun to turn his notes into the literature he had dreamed of writing, and we may leave him here.

> Here's the top-peak; the multitude below
> Live, for they can, there:
> This man decided not to Live but Know—
> Bury this man there?

3

Benson, who had that correspondence with Hort on becoming Archbishop of Canterbury, was a very different man. His besetting sin was not the scholar's shyness, although like Hort he suffered long periods of depression about the Church and about his own life in particular. His weakness was a foul temper, which became a public talking-point while he was a schoolmaster. He also suffered from neuralgia. But he was a great ecclesiastic, in public the very model of the self-composed Prince of the Church; and his love of church history as the great setting of his active life led him into doing, in moments snatched from an administrator's busy years, something which the secluded Hort never did. He wrote a big, scholarly book, replete with a flowery narrative and copiously learned footnotes.

In this self-controlled way the Archbishop seems to have been a manic depressive. Both the bitterness leading to explosions of fury and the excitement leading to visions of glory had their origins in a strange boyhood. He was born in 1829, the son of a Birmingham manufacturer of chemicals. His father was an Evangelical, a total abstainer from alcohol and totally unworldy. He did not gain much from his inventions, and what money he did make he invested in the British White Lead Company, which went bankrupt. He died the next year, 1843. His partners graciously allowed his widow to remain in the little, insanitary house next to the abandoned works with a small annuity, in exchange for a profitable patent for manufacturing cobalt. The son reacted to all this by developing a grasp of details and by accepting the High Church influence of an uncle. In a tiny office in the silent factory he established his own oratory, where he said the monastic offices every day. The practical sense was to ensure his success in life; the High Church piety was a release into the Christian centuries out of orphanhood and poverty.

He found his escape through King Edward's School, Birmingham, and he found his hero in his headmaster, James Prince Lee, who had taught at Arnold's Rugby. Each morning he would walk to school with a boy named Lightfoot. He was a schoolfellow with a boy named Westcott. He used to say that his ambition was to be a canon of a cathedral. When Prince Lee began his (disastrous) time as Bishop of Manchester, Benson organized the gift from his pupils, and in the same year, 1847, he planned with Lightfoot, who had preceded him to Cambridge, a society for holy living and for the Christian education of the poor. 'Let us determine while our hearts are still warm, and unchilled by the lessons of the world, to teach the *Poor*.' 'Doubtless there is high and holy work for heads and hearts and hands in the generation to come,' he told his journal. But he sent his mother a shocked remonstrance when she suggested that she might take part in the manufacture of cobalt herself.

His work was almost frustrated when his mother died in 1850; with her, his slender financial backing ended. The house in the Birmingham Lead Works had killed off his sister Harriet by typhus, and his mother, who had nursed her, had died of heart-failure the next night. He returned to Trinity College, and his face, always pale, told his story; but a bachelor don, the Bursar of Trinity, Francis Martin, spotted him walking disconsolately across the Great Court. He invited him to his rooms and assured him that he would be responsible for financing the rest of his undergraduate course; he also supported the rest of the boy's family. So his life proceeded, and fortunately for him it was untroubled by religious doubts. On his mother's death he refused to allow his youngest brother to be made the heir of a rich uncle, for that uncle was a Unitarian. He was appointed to a well-paid post on the staff at Rugby; elected a Fellow of Trinity (but he did not reside much in Cambridge); and ordained as a schoolmaster.

In 1858, while Hort was trying to settle at St. Ippolyts-cum-Great Wymondley, the chance of a lifetime came to Benson. A fund to perpetuate the memory of the Duke of Wellington, under the close patronage of Albert the Prince Consort, was devoted to the education of the sons of army officers. On the recommendation of Frederick Temple, Benson was appointed the first Headmaster of Wellington College. He was sent to Germany, to study the best methods. He returned convinced that, whatever Prince Albert might think, the ecclesiastical and classical tradition of Rugby already provided all that was wanted to make a school out of the new red-brick imitation of a French château on Bagshot Heath, to which the nearest building was the Criminal Lunatic Asylum at Broadmoor. He made only one last-minute preparation for the battles which would be needed to build this new Rugby. He married his cousin Mary Sidgwick, a girl whom he had loved for years while he had been boarding with her parents in Rugby. She was aged eighteen. She would make a home for him in what he called the Master's Lodge at Wellington College; and she would be his first pupil.

He had, or took, the entire control of the new school in his hands. He defied his governing body, and was habitually on the brink of resignation. The building of the chapel was his first love, but every detail of school life received his stern and often angry attention. He ruled through terror, but he knew his masters and boys thoroughly and could be intimately gracious when he chose. He and his young bride would say good night to them all. Long afterwards the boys would remember his theatrical entrances into the chapel, his mingling with the mighty on Speech Day, his handsome grey face which could flush so easily; and the masters would remember his rebukes and tearful reconciliations. 'He saw so vividly the beautiful thing he meant to create.' 'To act with him was like being in a sort of solemn and joyous drama.' 'No one could see Benson at Wellington without feeling that he loved his position. He loved, as he loved all through his life, the work of organizing down to minute detail. He loved and idealized the place. . . . He passionately loved teaching', wrote his successor in the headmastership. Benson made Wellington College, in conception a monumental charity, one of the most distinguished and most expensive schools in England.[4]

But what had become of his dream of a society for holy living, 'to teach the *Poor*'? In 1869 his appointment as an honorary Prebendary of Lincoln Cathedral revived the prayer in him. 'Lord,' he wrote in his journal, in the Victorian manner, 'Thou knowest how from a child Thou hast put into my heart deeply to love the beauty of Thy house —and how earnestly in all the minsters of England I have prayed that Thou wouldst raise up once more the Spirit whereby they were once builded. . . .' In the same year he refused to follow Temple as Headmaster of Rugby, feeling that his next post ought to be one where he could 'give manhood to men—if God only fit me to do so'. Three years later the call came, and he was Chancellor of Lincoln Cathedral. The income was half his salary as a headmaster, the duties were vaguer, he left Wellington in tears; but at last he was a canon of a cathedral, with an opportunity to teach the poor. And he was free of the school's governors, whose worldliness had recently almost broken their headmaster's strained nerves.[5]

[4] See David Newsome, *A History of Wellington College, 1859–1959* (John Murray, 1959).

[5] David Newsome, *op. cit.*, pp. 165–70, recounts how they tried to prevent Benson from expelling three boys who had had carnal knowledge of a domestic maid during the holidays.

He threw himself into Lincoln, instructing ordinands, preaching in a crowded cathedral, befriending the humbler citizens who had previously known little contact with the great church up the hill. His power of vision once more glowed. A cathedral should be the centre for an evangelism which reached into all the world.

I firmly believe [he wrote in 1873] that there is now no greater need for the Church of England, which (so far as I can see) is now charged with the world's Christianity, and must make herself truly Christian first, than this English order of Missioners in close filial union with Bishops and Mother Churches. . . . We want the social dispersion and the central fire.

So much was involved beyond a new theological college and a new night school. And by now many others knew it. He was asked to return to Cambridge, to be Bishop of Calcutta, to be the first Bishop of Truro. He accepted the last call. After four years at Lincoln, it was once again what he needed: a call to inaugurate. Disraeli commented, 'Well, we *have* got a bishop!' Dean Church, who arranged his consecration at a great service in St. Paul's, wrote to him: 'I hope you may be permitted to add in Cornwall another of the many victories which the revived English Church has achieved, and which, in spite of disasters and menacing troubles, make it the most glorious Church in Christendom.'

Carving Cornwall out of the ancient diocese of Exeter was, in fact, ideal work for one who thus combined a romantic heart with a love of administration. Many of the Cornish parish churches had slept through the centuries, while Methodism had recently provided what religion there was. Benson did all that he could to put new life into them and into their usually poor and lonely, often broken-hearted or queer, parsons. His optimism was like the sunshine on their moors, his eloquence like the incessant sea on their rocks; and everywhere he expounded the examples of the local saints. His daughters needed educating, so he founded Truro High School for girls, and was at work on a similar grammar school for boys. 'You have no idea what life is becoming to me', he wrote to a friend; 'a humming top is the only thing that resembles it: perpetual motion, very dizzy, hollow within, keeping up a continuous angry buzz.'

At the centre of this buzz was a wooden shed, his first cathedral. There at 10 p.m. on Christmas Eve 1880 he presided over a Festival of Nine Lessons and Carols, designed on medieval precedents but intended to get the men out of the pubs.[6] He already had Truro Cathedral in his heart. He was his own dean at Truro, and he was not likely to neglect the opportunity. (It had been the prospect of building up

[6] The service became famous when it was adapted by Dean Milner-White at King's College, Cambridge, in 1918, and first broadcast in 1928.

Anglican cathedral life in India that had most tempted him to become Bishop of Calcutta, until he had realized the difficulties of educating his children.) J. L. Pearson designed Truro Cathedral's granite and marble, an admirer gave £40,000, and the foundation stone was laid in 1880. 'People are saying, "the first Cathedral founded since the Reformation" ', he boasted in his journal. 'Has any been founded (one or two have been translated) since the Conquest?' He consecrated it seven years later.

But black clouds of depression still rolled over him. He was desolated by the death in 1878 of his eldest son, the brilliant Martin, while a boy at Winchester. He never fully recovered. 'Martin's death remains an inexplicable grief—every day—to see into that will be worth dying,' he wrote ten years later.[7] In his journal for 16 September 1882 he noted: 'Such reasons for thankfulness and yet this invincible depression within. Maybe these very short nights of sleep, but scarce seems so.' The years at Truro also had their depressing side for Benson in his professional life. As the junior bishop he could not belong to the House of Lords, and in more specifically clerical discussions he was frustrated under Archbishop Tait, who used to sink back in his chair with a good-humoured smile when Benson was ecstatic with some Wilberforce-type vision of ecclesiastical revivalism.

On Tait's death he was an obvious possibility for Canterbury. Gladstone and his adviser, Dean Church, considered him sufficiently sound in churchmanship; the Queen remembered his work with Prince Albert in founding Wellington College; he had won a victory in Cornwall. But one trouble about Benson was his age: he was only fifty-three. Would the other bishops, who were all older, work under him? Would it be wiser to appoint Bishop Harold Browne of Winchester as a stop-gap? Yet Browne was seventy-two and unwell; Gladstone wrote to assure him that only his age had prevented his promotion. His comparative youth having been accepted, Benson's temperamental handicaps remained. Tait had been an administrator; Benson was a creative pioneer. Tait had enjoyed a fight; the more artistic Benson was easily thrown by opposition into another of his depressions. The post of Archbishop of Canterbury had been made by Tait into a Parliamentary office, and at that time Parliament was still the only effective instrument of ecclesiastical legislation; Benson had no Parliamentary experience. After hesitations which seem to have been genuine and to have persisted, Benson accepted. His son Arthur commented some forty years later: 'I am by no means sure that it was not the greatest mistake of his life. He yielded perhaps to what had always

<hr>

[7] A memoir of Martin White Benson, and also a chapter on James Prince Lee, were included by David Newsome in his *Godliness and Good Learning* (John Murray, 1961).

been a temptation of his, the love of ruling. But I do not think that he had by then a wide enough outlook upon the world; indeed, I do not feel that he was interested so much in life as in the mould of institutional religion into which it could be run.'[8]

From now on, however, he ruled in the House of God. He slept about five hours a night, with many vivid dreams of ecclesiastical subjects. He slaved and fussed over the details of administration. His recreations were a landlordly life at Addington Park, tours of historic (and if possible, ecclesiastical) sites in Europe, and work on his *Cyprian*. He entertained lavishly. His servants were many and dedicated. 'His feeling about the splendours of the Church was that they were a stately heritage, which it was right and proper to enjoy, and he had not the faintest sympathy with—only horror for—Socialistic ideas,' Arthur Benson recalled. But Arthur also remembered that his father was seldom happy except when immersed in work. 'His thoughts naturally turned to what was unsatisfactory or painful, in prospect and retrospect. He would reflect how little use he had made of his opportunities, or sink beneath the oppressive thought of some difficult or delicate task which overshadowed him.' Another glimpse of his father was left by Arthur. 'Papa always felt the need of economy at an inn. . . . He would have liked to be comfortable, but didn't know how, I think his fear of waste was so strong.'[9] What scars had been left by the Birmingham boyhood?

4

'The Church of England has to be built up again from the very bottom,' the new Archbishop of Canterbury wrote in his journal in June 1883. 'It is the lower and lower-middle classes who must be won.' It was the 1848 dream, to see the people in the cathedrals, 'to teach the *Poor*'. But in fact Benson did little in this direction. Instead, he took to the ceremonies surrounding the old Queen like a duck to water, and grappled less successfully with his new role in the House of Lords, a body which, we are told, seldom loves one who is either prelatical or schoolmasterly in manner. He was uneasy in the sphere where Tait had excelled, lamenting in 1891, when Parliamentary difficulties delayed a Clergy Discipline Bill: 'I know so little of how any of these things are done.' This lack of Parliamentary skill was a serious deficiency in the circumstances. For example, urgently needed reforms in the patronage system in the parishes were not enacted by

[8] A. C. Benson, *Trefoil* (John Murray, 1923), p. 281.
[9] *The Diary of Arthur Christopher Benson*, ed. Percy Lubbock (Hutchinson, 1926), p. 30.

Parliament until 1897, despite Benson's pleas throughout his Primacy. His first Parliamentary defeat came during his first year as Archbishop. Men were to be allowed to marry their deceased wives' sisters, despite the Church's prohibition founded on the Old Testament. Then came the threat of something worse. On 13 June 1884 he found Gladstone 'surely "advancing" fast into revolution'. Would the radical old man, or Joseph Chamberlain who seemed to be his destined heir as the Liberal prophet, disestablish Anglicanism in England as well as on the Celtic fringe? On 12 December 1886 the Archbishop observed 'the Church steadily losing ground with the Crown, with Cabinets, with the House of Commons, while she is steadily winning the people and the poor.' Even the Conservatives slighted him. On 15 August 1895 he lamented that Lord Salisbury had failed to consult him about who should be the new Bishop of Rochester; indeed, the new bishop himself had not discussed the matter with him.[10]

Benson, however, took care to win the friendship of sympathetic aristocrats. Adeline, Duchess of Bedford, became one of his closest friends, and under her marshalling ladies of high social position gathered regularly for devotions in Lambeth Palace Chapel. In July 1888, while staying with Lord Carnarvon, the Archbishop meditated in his journal:

One has nowadays great heartaches in these glorious homes, with their strong heads, real pillars of the civilization that now is, and their most delicate stately women, and children whose sweet proud curves of feature show the making of many generations and readiness for responsibility from almost tender years: are all these glories going to keep together? If not how will they go down? By brute force, or by silent self-exilings?

Next year he had to record a rather less generous tribute to the Church from 'an old Duchess', who laid hold of his arm in the garden of Marlborough House, saying: 'I shall hold by the Church—until you are disestablished—which you will soon be.'

Despite the changes which he labelled Socialism and Agnosticism, Benson was on the whole master of his familiar ecclesiastical world, and anxious to build up the Church as a bulwark against these menaces. What he wrote about St. Cyprian in his big book was true of himself:

We need not look to him for Theology proper, for doctrinal refinement, for the metaphysic of Christian definition. We shall find him busy with moral conditions, the work of grace, the bonds of union: the sanctification of life through the sacraments, the remodelling of life through discipline; the constitution of the Church in permanence, the transforming social influences

[10] This was Edward Stuart Talbot, who had been the first Warden of Keble College, Oxford, and who became Bishop of Winchester, 1911–23. His biography was written by Gwendolen Stephenson (SPCK, 1936).

which are to control the application of power and wealth, to charge science again with the love of truth, art with the love of beauty, and to create a new benevolence.

What the Archbishop found in his hero, others found in him: 'the devotion of his gifts, acquirements and positions to the work and life of the New People as they grew in Christ.'

A typical act was his opening of the House of Laymen in 1886, a consultative body without legislative power, but one drawn by election from all the Diocesan Conferences in the Province of Canterbury. (York followed in 1892.) It was an innovation which had resulted from a 'memorial' from Cambridge theologians headed by Westcott, and which Benson in his inaugural address justified by a reminder that 'before the Italian Church over-rode all such promises, St. Cyprian promised the faithful laity that he would without their assent do nothing'. It was a turning point in the history of the Church of England, this summoning of just over a hundred laymen; for it was the beginning of the recognition by the Church of England that Parliament was no longer the adequate voice of the laity.

Another innovation Benson contemplated, but without result. Willing to imitate Rome in this at least, he wanted a body of cardinals for the Church of England: 'the appointment of four or five bishops, to give at least an annual fortnight of conference, with nothing else to do, on matters proposed by the Archbishop—or otherwise found necessary. These to be named by the Archbishop.' One difficulty here was that the most desirable cardinals disliked the thought of such meetings; Lightfoot was reluctant to leave Durham, and Temple in London was reluctant to treat others as equals. Benson, after abandoning the idea that men who were not bishops might be included instead, was left alone to carry the burden of leadership in a situation which he described in his journal for 1888: 'so full of fears, self-misgivings, anxieties, perplexities—such sorrows threatening, such sorrows present, such openings for great mistakes . . . the clergy so depressed'.

Benson could probably have done little to lift this depression, even with the aid of a college of cardinals. The psychology of the clergy reflected a sombre mood in the nation, where the boom which had brought prosperity to the 'workshop of the world' had receded with the slumps of 1876–9 and 1883–6. The agricultural depression distressed the countryside where most of the clergy lived. The operation of the Education Act of 1870 was by now making it clear that the Church of England was no longer the nation's schoolmaster, and the Liberation Society pressed for disestablishment while party strife tore the Church apart. In brief, Tait's prestige had not removed the real problems. However, in his self-pitying journal, which served much the same purpose as Shaftesbury's, Benson certainly exaggerated the dangers of the Church because of the depression and fears within him. On public occasions the Church, and the Archbishop as its spokesman, could, indeed, err like Shaftesbury in the opposite direction of over-excitement and sheer arrogance, as when the bishops met in the Lambeth Conference in this same year, 1888. 'We have realized, more fully than it was possible to realize before', they declared in their Message, 'the extent, the power, and the influence of the great Anglican Communion. We have felt its capacities, its opportunities, its privileges.' But there were some solid grounds for sober confidence. When Gladstone was talking with Lord Morley at Biarritz on Christmas Eve 1891, he made a remark which reflected the true situation in England. 'The establishment', Morley noted, 'he considers safer than it has been for a long time.' And that something was due to Benson was implied by Gladstone's grumble (to his son) in 1894: 'painful indeed is the Archbishop's establishmentarian fanaticism'.

In answer to the dangers which did confront the Church, Benson was able to do something characteristically his own. His own sympathies were obviously High Church, but he was determined 'not to make the Evangelicals feel uncomfortable'—for fear, as he confessed to his friend A. J. Mason, that the Evangelicals would leave, and with them the Establishment would be lost. He seemed to his intimates nervous and ashamed about his own love for ritual and about his great knowledge of its history. But as it was, his scholarship enabled him to pluck the nettle of the problem about what practices connected with the celebration of the Holy Communion were, or were not, lawful in the Church of England.

Edward King, Bishop of Lincoln, was now accused by the Church Association of illegal liturgical practices. It was the most dramatic lawsuit in this field in this century—and not only because Edward King was a bishop. For King was Keble's successor as the High Anglican saint. As Benson himself noted, 'he is adored at Lincoln'. Scott Holland wrote about this man who was accused of having candles lit on the altar:

It was light that he carried with him, light that shone through him, light that flowed from him. The room was lit into which he entered. It was as if we had fallen under a streak of sunlight that flickered, and danced, and laughed, and turned all to colour and gold. Those eyes of his were an illumination. Even to recall him for an instant in the bare memory was enough to set the whole day alive and glittering.[11]

[11] *A Bundle of Memories*, p. 48. King taught pastoral theology at Cuddesdon Theological College, 1858–73, and then as professor in Oxford. He was Bishop of Lincoln, 1885–1910. A modern portrait is to be found in Lord Elton, *Edward King and Our Times* (Bles, 1958), supplemented by Owen Chadwick, *Edward King, Bishop of Lincoln* (Friends of Lincoln Cathedral, 1968).

The trial of Bishop King was also dramatic because Benson reluctantly decided to turn the complaint into a legal case where he would himself be judge, with other bishops as assessors. Rather to everyone's surprise, the Judicial Committee of the Privy Council recognized his right to do so, although there had been no precedent for an archbishop trying one of the bishops since a scandalous Bishop of St. David's had been deposed in 1699. The deeply learned historian William Stubbs, who was then Bishop of Oxford, muttered to himself that this was merely an archbishop sitting in his library, but most churchmen were delighted by Benson's judgment when it came. This delight was not because all churchmen proposed to act on every word of the Archbishop. To the pleasure of the Anglo-Catholics he accepted candles on the altar, the Eastward position of the priest facing the altar, the singing of *Agnus Dei* after the consecration, and the reverent ablution of the vessels, but he ruled against the other High Church practices of mixing wine and water ceremonially, standing so that the people could not see the consecration, and making the sign of the cross when absolving or blessing; and these practices continued. The main effect of the Lincoln Judgment, delivered in November 1890, came because this compromise was well argued legally, and was well illustrated on a theological and liturgical basis, by an archbishop known to be in love with ecclesiastical tradition. In particular, High Churchmen were delighted that Benson reversed a judgment of the Judicial Committee (against the priest's Eastward position in 1871) because careful consideration had persuaded him to set the history of Church higher than the Privy Council.

'It is the most courageous thing to have come out of Lambeth for the last two hundred years', said Dean Church. More important still: the Judicial Committee accepted it. Ever since 1871, if not before that the committee's competence in liturgical questions had been denied or doubted by many churchmen, so that the Church of England had in practice possessed no final court. The acceptance of the Lincoln Judgment now opened up the prospect of the Church putting its own house in order through a system of ecclesiastical courts, although no further step could be taken at the time because Parliament was as yet unwilling. Benson, who had made the decision to try the case himself before he had been sure of the Judicial Committee's attitude, was showered with congratulations.

Randall Davidson said after his death: 'I have often asked myself what was the secret of his great power. . . . I should put first . . . his peculiar grasp of the great underlying religious principles of the Church's life.' Davidson had in mind the Archbishop's ability to use church history as the touchstone of nineteenth-century problems; it was all very different from Tait. Next to the Lincoln Judgment, the most notable display of this power was Benson's *Cyprian*. Begun as a safeguard against rusting as a scholar while he was running Wellington College, it was continued as a hobby; but the minute examination of the problems of the scholarly Bishop of Carthage, a high episcopalian and rigorous disciplinarian who was martyred in 258, was believed to be relevant to Truro or Canterbury. As his research assistant, Alexis Larpent, wrote later: 'Cyprian could be consulted about schism, conciliar assemblies, appeals, questions of doctrine, discipline, even of ritual, and above all on the great question of our day—the reunion of Churches.' St. Cyprian had argued that one's eternal salvation depended on one's loyalty to the local branch of the Catholic Church; and that each branch depended on its bishop, who (rather than the Bishop of Rome) had inherited the Lord's promises to St. Peter. These ideas were scarcely possible for an archbishop under Queen Victoria; but Benson enjoyed playing with them in hours snatched from the business at Lambeth or when tempted to depression during his holidays.

St. Cyprian had stood up to Pope Stephen of Rome (who had urged on him the validity of schismatics' baptisms), and Benson used that fact in his attempt to paint the third century as essentially Anglican. 'Cyprian and his times', he wrote, 'were as innocent of presbyterian and of congregational, as they were of papal, catholicity.' In September 1896 Benson received his own challenge from Rome, in the shape of Leo XIII's Bull *Apostolicae Curae*, which described the ordinations of the schismatic Anglicans as 'absolutely null and utterly void'.[12] Benson immediately set about the arrangements for a scholarly reply. He died before this could be published, and also before the Lambeth Conference of 1897 could be held as an even more effective response. He had planned to celebrate the thirteen-hundredth anniversary of the landing of St. Augustine, the first Archbishop of Canterbury, by gathering Anglican bishops from all over the world, and he seems to have half-hoped that this conference would formally recognize a world-wide status for the throne of St. Augustine.

But his was a perfect end. After putting almost the final touches to his labour of thirty years on his *Cyprian*, he conducted a successful tour of Ireland, and found the disestablished Church in surprisingly good heart. On his way back he stayed with the Gladstones at Hawarden and enjoyed animated conversations with the statesman who called him to Canterbury. On Sunday 11 October 1897 he went to Matins in Hawarden parish church, and soon after the beginning of the service had a fatal heart attack. He was aged sixty-seven. He was the last archbishop to be buried within Canterbury Cathedral, where his grave

[12] See John Jay Hughes, *Absolutely Null and Utterly Void* (Sheed & Ward, 1968).

lies beneath the carved list of the chief pastors of England since St. Augustine.

5

Apparently it was a life much more successful than Hort's. But there was a disturbing epilogue.

What wounds did Benson inflict on the minds of the wife and children whom he adored? His beloved Minnie, to whom he had written an ardent love-poem when she was eleven, and whose life was to be largely emptied of meaning when she was widowed at the age of fifty-five, wrote a journal as he did—but hers was more intimate, and more poignant. In that journal, she looked back on the early days of her marriage.

An utter child, I danced and sang into matrimony with a loving but exacting, a believing and therefore expectant spirit, twelve years older, much stronger, much more passionate, whom I didn't really love. But let me try to realise how hard it was for Edward. He restrained his passionate nature for seven years and then got me, this unloving, weak, unstable child. I know how disappointing this must be to him, how evidently disappointed he was. How hard for him, full of all religious and emotional thoughts and yearnings. They had never really awoke in me. . . .[13]

At Wellington College this ill-matched pair, the debutante and the headmaster, bickered, but mostly she submitted, blaming herself when she failed to keep up with his ecclesiastical and physical vitalities, or when she dared not offer comfort when he was irritably depressed. Gradually, through this self-giving humility, she became the Victorian 'good wife' and developed into the capable mistress of his palace at Truro, then of Lambeth and Addington. Her intelligence was certainly high. When the brilliant Mandell Creighton met her in 1884, he described her as 'Mrs. Benson, wife of the Archbishop of Canterbury, who, strange to say, is one of the wittiest and most amusing ladies I ever talked to'. But her journal shows that she was slow to lose her fear of her husband. Fifteen years after her marriage she passed through a crisis of personal faith. She confided her doubts in a woman friend, not in her husband; and the simple, calm religion which she then worked out for herself seems to have owed little to his excited churchmanship, although she always supported and honoured the Church of England. Her intimate friend was Lucy Tait, the other archbishop's daughter; 'it was impossible to think of them apart'.[14]

The children were devoted to her, while they could never entirely

[13] E. F. Benson, *Mother* (Hodder & Stoughton, 1925), pp. 12–13.
[14] E. F. Benson, *Final Edition* (Longmans, Green, 1940), p. 13.

relax in their father's always educational and moralizing company. But something went wrong in their formative years; and although all three boys, Arthur, Hugh, and Fred, wrote many books which seemed to be self-revealing, and although both Arthur and Fred wrote about their sister Maggie, we are in the position of not knowing exactly what was the trouble. We may guess in a vaguely Freudian way. None of the children married. Arthur, the don, was subject to his father's fits of manic depression, but more acutely and for years at a time. Hugh was another strange creature, uneasy as a parson and monk in the Church of England and as a curate of the Roman Catholic church in Cambridge; he came alive when he poured out his dream of the Catholic past as a preacher and as a novelist. Fred (E. F.) was the most sociable and successful of them all, and some of his novels were best-sellers, but he became serious when treating the romantic days of male youth. Maggie, intellectually as able as any of the sons, was confined to an asylum with a persecution complex and homicidal mania. While insane, her special hatred was reserved for her mother.

We know also that none of the children ever lost their fascinated interest in their father. Arthur wrote his biography in two large volumes, and had vivid dreams of him throughout his life. Hugh, who edited a posthumous collection of his prayers and hymns, kept much of his library (unopened) in his home, and when he died he bequeathed that home, Hare Street House, Buntingford, in Hertford-shire, to be the country home of the Roman Catholic Archbishops of Westminster; he remembered what Addington Park had meant to an Archbishop of Canterbury. Fred supervised the posthumous printing of the Archbishop's *Cyprian* although he knew nothing whatever of the subject, and more than thirty years later wrote some lighter-hearted reminiscences of him.[15] Maggie made herself responsible for the publication of the Archbishop's book on the Revelation of St. John the Divine, grew absorbed in interpretations of the Divine's visions, and set herself to imitate her father in as many little ways as possible, before she went mad.[16] So in the grave Benson continued the dictatorship which had elevated or darkened life for his family.

It was not a rule which convinced them about the religion so dear to his heart. Two of the children (Martin the devout schoolboy, and Nellie) died immature. The others did not grow up as orthodox Anglicans. Maggie wrote a strange *Venture of Rational Faith* (1908) before madness overtook her. The happier Fred was worldly, while Hugh expressed in fiction the very spirit of Rome at its most romantically arrogant, thus fulfilling the forebodings which the Archbishop poured out in his journal on Christmas Day 1887.

[15] In E. F. Benson, *As We Were* (Longmans, Green, 1932).
[16] See A. C. Benson, *Life and Letters of Maggie Benson* (John Murray, 1917).

How do I know that the grumbling at the pressure of sermons, of speeches, all God's holy works of different kinds, of correspondence on church matters and clerical details (and I *do* express myself too freely on such matters and all the faults of the clerical character as they *deploy* before me) may not be the cause of my not having the greatest joy of all joys—the seeing my own sons devote themselves to Holy Orders? This is what I always most wished, and this seems little likely to come to pass. Have I myself to thank that *we* do less for God's service than many, many placed in positions where such service would be impossible to procure?

Although Hugh was ordained by his father, the 'clerical details' of life in the Church of England could not satisfy his ardent imagination.[17]

Arthur Benson, Hugh's elder brother, taught at Eton but would not be ordained. He would not even consent to stand for the head-mastership when virtually assured of election. Instead he retired to Cambridge, where he found a new life as a popular essayist with a tone of gracefully sympathetic melancholy, and as a Fellow (later the Master) of Magdalene College. 'To the last of his days he was nowhere quite so much at his ease . . . as with the Church.'[18] But he could not carry out the work which his father had designed for the dead Martin and which Hugh had now laid down; for he could not bring himself to believe the full orthodox creed. His own personal beliefs were expressed in a nostalgic and vague whimsy. He remembered how alarmed his father had been when any wind of scepticism had come near by accident; and how he had himself been distressed by religious doubts when an undergraduate at Cambridge in the early 1880s. And he concluded that his father had sent his sons into the world unprepared for this battle because he had himself refused to face the full challenge of the modern world's alienation from the historic Church.

Arthur Benson's verdict on his father did not apply to the more open-minded Hort. And the Archbishop himself seems to have felt that Hort's martyrdom for the truth's sake had been a life of the quality needed. The world's lamps were being extinguished for him, he wrote to Westcott when Hort died. 'I wish I could *feel* that the coming school at Cambridge was as gallant, as devoted to the truth, as ready to suffer in the flesh for it, as the old school. But *you* are hopeful, and always God is true.' For all his love of the Christian past, Archbishop Benson knew uneasily that the Christian future would depend on others thinking God true.

[17] See A. C. Benson, *Hugh: Memoirs of a Brother* (Smith, Elder, 1915).
[18] Percy Lubbock, *The Diary of Arthur Christopher Benson*, p. 30.

FOR FURTHER READING

His son Sir Arthur Hort compiled *Life and Letters of F. J. A. Hort* in two volumes (Macmillan, 1896).

His son A. C. Benson compiled *The Life of Edward White Benson, sometime Archbishop of Canterbury,* in two volumes (Macmillan, 1899), with a later, more informal, supplement, *The Trefoil* (John Murray, 1923). In this chapter, dates have been attached to previously unpublished extracts from the Archbishop's journal which is preserved at Trinity College, Cambridge.

1828 – 1889.   1825 – 1901.

Lightfoot and Westcott

1

When Joseph Barber Lightfoot died in 1889, the great see of Durham which he had occupied remained vacant for an unusually long time. Behind the scenes Queen Victoria and Archbishop Benson were insisting on the claims of Brooke Foss Westcott, while others—and the Prime Minister, Lord Salisbury, was among them—maintained that the experiment of sending a scholar to industrial Durham, although it had been successful in Lightfoot's case, should not be risked with Professor Westcott. The elderly professor's reputation was that of an earnest but obscure mystic whose most intelligible work had been in a field which appeared to be remote from the Durham collieries: the revision of the Greek text of the New Testament. Eventually the Archbishop persisted in his refusal to take seriously one bishop whom the Prime Minister had in mind for promotion to Durham ('a shrimp in comparison with the predecessor he would be invited to follow') or another (his 'self-opinion mars fatally an otherwise interesting character'); and the Queen had made up her mind.[1] Westcott was enthroned in Durham Cathedral on Ascension Day, the festival on which Lightfoot had been enthroned eleven years before. When he died in 1901, the twenty-two years of these two scholar-bishops were recalled as a golden age, and their work still deserves to be remembered, for it shows that by the end of the nineteenth-century the alienation of the Church of England from the English people was not so far-reaching as Hort and Benson feared in their times of gloom. The story of Lightfoot and Westcott is also worth recalling because, with Benson, these men constituted an amazing gift to the Church from the one school, King Edward's School, Birmingham, and virtually from the one headmaster, James Prince Lee; and because, with Hort, they constituted the Cambridge theological triumvirate.

---

[1] Benson's Journal for 10 February and 5 March 1890. The bishops thus dismissed were the eloquent William Boyd Carpenter of Ripon and the learned John Wordsworth of Salisbury.

2

Their story does not take long to tell, for both lives were spent mainly in the quiet work of education.

The son of a Liverpool accountant, Lightfoot found himself orphaned like Benson, but in more comfortable domestic circumstances when the family moved to Birmingham. At Trinity College, his school-fellow Westcott supervised some of his classical studies, and, like Westcott, Lightfoot obtained the highest classical and mathematical honours. He never married, and in academic peace from 1852 he was a resident Fellow of Trinity, becoming in Tait's words 'a man of really humble mind, of great learning, and perfect scholarship'. He worked for his college as a tutor and for his university as a professor, but his real work was done in his study in the Great Court as the light burned by night during term, and as he read and wrote steadily through the vacations. From this Cambridge base he made contact with all learned Europe, almost entirely by reading and writing. He was fluent in Hebrew, Latin, Greek, French, German, Italian, and Spanish, and had a working knowledge of Syriac, Arabic, Ethiopian, and the Coptic dialects. 'Does it not sometimes happen to you', he once innocently asked a young clergyman, 'that when you have read a book you forget in what language it was written?'

With a knowledge deeper even than Hort's went an apparently complete lack of emotional oddities. His manner of life was that of a recluse, apart from excursions to cheer the college boats, to sit on university committees, to preach before Queen Victoria, or to examine ordinands for Tait. He had, so far as we know, no dark doubts about the Christian faith or about the scholarly life. In his scholarship he had no pet theories. In the composition of his lectures and books he suffered no inhibitions. He set himself to recover the history of Christianity in its first three centuries. He wished to get at the facts, and incidentally he was confident that the facts would vindicate everything that mattered in Christianity's historic faith. But he would not get entangled in the controversies of the day, and it was his refusal to co-operate that dissuaded Westcott and Hort from attempting a volume which could be offered to the public as an alternative to *Essays and Reviews*. Characteristically, he made his only extended contribution to doctrinal theology by leaping to the defence of Christian scholars such as Westcott when they had been attacked in an anonymous best-seller called *Supernatural Religion*. Seven articles by Lightfoot in the 1870s pulverized that showy but ill-informed work by a retired Bombay merchant, W. R. Casels.

This dry student was encouraged to develop more of a preacher's fluency—although he was never really fluent—when Gladstone gave him a part-time canonry at St. Paul's in 1871. He became attached to his colleagues, Dean Church and Canon Liddon, much as he deplored their Tractarian interpretation of church history. He was more than ever assured about the Church of England's mission by their success in both spiritualizing and filling Wren's cathedral 'at the centre of the world's concourse'—the words with which he dedicated his work on St. Ignatius to Liddon.

His commentaries on St. Paul formed another Anglican glory. They were the work of an historian, but unlike Stanley's *Corinthians* they were the work of an historian with an enthusiasm for the exact meaning of the Greek. 'The prevailing characteristic', as Hort later noted, 'is masculine good sense unaccompanied by either the insight or the delusion of subtlety.' In addition to much detailed exegesis they were generally significant, in two ways. First, they answered the Tübingen school, which under Ferdinand Christian Baur had reconstructed the life of Paul in order to emphasize a profound conflict between him and the other apostles under Peter and James. Lightfoot's (and Westcott's) tendency was to sustain the theme of the Acts of the Apostles that Peter, James, and Paul had been fellow-apostles of the one Lord, with differences but with a common Gospel. And Lightfoot's commentaries were also conceived as a reply to innovators who claimed the label 'Catholic'.

Lightfoot brought a new wealth of equipment to the traditional Anglican answer to Rome: the apostolic Gospel was simpler and stronger than the developed Roman Catholic system of dogmas, and apostles such as Paul had certainly not regarded Peter, let alone any Bishop of Rome in the centuries to come, as the infallible Vicar of Christ. Without naming them Lightfoot also answered men such as his own colleagues at St. Paul's, who held that the 'apostolic ministry' had been handed on by the apostles to the bishops and by them to priests and deacons episcopally ordained. Lightfoot taught that the government of the Church by bishops had emerged out of a more fluid situation. The crucial points for him were that the 'elders' or 'presbyters' mentioned in the New Testament were not called priests, so as to avoid confusion with paganism; and that they *were* also called 'bishops'. The Church described in the New Testament was, Lightfoot believed, a new start in the history of religion. It was a start made by Christ alone, who had, however, not laid down a detailed church order. As Jerusalem fell to the Romans, the Jerusalem church over which James the brother of the Lord had presided was scattered; and James, Peter, and Paul were all martyred. Thus it became necessary to have a new focus of Christian leadership, to replace Jerusalem and the apostles. The local churches had already imitated the Jewish synagogues in appointing 'elders', and gradually, under the pressure of circumstances, one of these elders became overseer or bishop in each place. As Lightfoot put it: 'the episcopate was formed not out of the apostolic order by localization but out of the presbyteral by elevation: and the title, which originally was common to all [the presbyters], came at length to be appropriate to the chief among them.'

When Lightfoot was elevated from the presbyterate, the shrewder Nonconformists took pleasure in pointing out that as a bishop he was not the successor of the apostles. Lightfoot could, however, reply that he had always maintained that the development of episcopacy had been under divine guidance and in 'the Apostolic Age'. He thought it had first developed in Asia Minor, where the apostle John had given firm leadership to the churches. The succession of bishops had first been thought of as succession in the work, not in the laying on of hands. Lightfoot recalled how the presbyters of Alexandria for long consecrated their own bishop, and how it was not until a church council in 314 that this practice was forbidden. Moving to more recent times, he deprecated any extravagant claims for episcopacy. He was glad that at various points in its history the Church of England had been very friendly with non-episcopal churches, and until 1662 had allowed some ministers not episcopally ordained to be incumbents of parish churches and cathedral dignitaries. Lightfoot's conclusion for the nineteenth century was clear. It was both possible and necessary to preach the apostolic Gospel in the apostolic Church. The Church was based on the Gospel, not on government by popes or bishops; but the bishops should lead the Church.[2]

3

Despite the credit which came to him for these scholarly labours, Lightfoot refused to stand for the senior (Regius) Professorship of Divinity at Cambridge in 1870. He wanted to see Westcott elected and thus able to return to academic work after years of frustration. For Westcott, like Hort, had sacrificed his residence as a Fellow of Trinity to marriage.

Three years older than Lightfoot, Westcott was the son of a leisured, if not particularly affluent, capitalist like Hort's father. It was remembered that his father was a man of retiring disposition, and lived for the most part a quiet home life, being devoted to scientific pursuits.

[2] J. B. Lightfoot, *The Christian Ministry* (Macmillan, 1901), contains the famous Dissertation appended to his *Philippians* with some later explanations. For a more recent survey of the evidence by a Cambridge scholar, see William Telfer, *The Office of a Bishop* (Darton, Longman, and Todd, 1962).

Chartist demonstrations in Birmingham awakened a boyish interest in social questions; and James Prince Lee gave him the intellectual equipment needed for a contribution to social progress.

'A schoolmaster or a clergyman?' the young man wrote to his future wife. He became both. After a period recalled as 'torturing scepticism', he was ordained by Prince Lee as deacon and priest in 1851, although he was disappointed by the coldness of the proceedings. Next year he finally gave up his life as a tutor in Cambridge, to teach classics at Harrow under C. J. Vaughan. The cause was 'Louey' Whithard, with whom he had fallen in love while at school. They had met when he had rescued her brother from a bully. She took the extra name Mary at his request when she was confirmed, and he always called her Mary, in a married life of great devotion and fertility. Seven sons and three daughters were born, and they lived frugally. Westcott, who dreamed of founding some sort of monastic order for Christian families, spent little on himself. It was only when his sons had pooled their pocket money for this gift that he was persuaded to fulfil his ambition to buy a tricycle, on which, followed by the boys on bicycles, he would visit nearby churches.

He published some theology, in addition to the work which he now began with Hort on the Greek Testament. He expressed alarm to Hort lest their revision of the Greek text should encourage a new theology; but Hort persuaded him to work on. However, his was an orthodoxy enriched by a golden setting—or (as his critics used to say) obscured by a dense fog of rhetoric.[3] To the end of his life Westcott maintained that 'the whole life of men points to the answer which Christianity has given'. He could not argue that Greek thought was identical with Christianity; for 'the assumption of humanity, not for a time, but for ever, by the Word, who is God, was a truth undreamt of till it was realized.' But he did believe that the thought as well as the language of the New Testament was close to Plato's, so that 'the work of Greece . . . lives for the simplest Christian in the New Testament.'[4] One of his favourite theologians was Benjamin Whichcote, the gentle Christian Platonist of seventeenth-century Cambridge. When Newman remembered in his *Apologia* how he had been 'carried away' as a young man by the Christian Platonists of third-century Alexandria, he might have been summing up Westcott's own theology. 'The exterior world, physical and historical, was but the manifestation to our senses of

---

[3] Articles of the Harrow years on Aeschylus, Euripides, and Plato were to be collected with other papers to form *Essays on the History of Religious Thought in the West* (Macmillan, 1891). They had the theme that the Greeks had prepared the way for Robert Browning's Christianity.

[4] These quotations come from Westcott's *The Gospel of Life* (Macmillan, 1892), pp. xxii, 252, 113.

realities greater than itself. Nature was a parable: Scripture was an allegory: pagan literature, philosophy, and mythology, properly understood, were but a preparation for the Gospel.'[5]

Other books of the Harrow years reflected the young Westcott's stature as a teacher of the New Testament, and one, *The Gospel of the Resurrection* (1866), showed the personal faith which he had reached through his period of doubt. It was a book which announced not a dogma but an experienced mystery, the mystery of the flesh of Jesus common with ours, yet in resurrection lifted above our limitations. 'Wild as my doubts are, I cannot but feel that the N. T. "finds" me', he had written in his journal for 1849, 'and that with its deepest mysteries—but as *mysteries*, not as *dogmas*. Why should we be surprised at the fiery trial of scepticism? I should more reasonably doubt my safety, if I did not doubt.' A little later in the same journal, Westcott noted: 'Faith is an intuition—a momentary acknowledgment of the heart, spontaneous and perfect.'

For the ultra-orthodox, this could not be enough. The great Canon Liddon dismissed Westcott as 'a thoughtful Latitudinarian, covered all over with a thin pietistic varnish, which has the effect of leading the *Record* and other Low Church persons to suppose that he is a variety of Evangelical'.[6] But this was the Gospel which he preached to the Harrovians—and which he implied in a private talk with a despondent Prince Lee during 1865. Lee had been talking about Arnold (whole letters to him he had just burned, explaining enigmatically that they witnessed to great differences between them), about Newman (who had 'trifled with his reason until he had lost it'), and, with his eyes filled by tears, about death. 'People quote various words of the Lord as containing the sum of the Gospel', he said to Westcott, but to him the best was the text: *Fear not, only believe.* What Prince Lee had in mind was a fundamentalist belief.[7] But 'Lord I believe', Westcott quoted in reply; 'help thou mine unbelief.'

He was thankful to accept a canonry at Peterborough in 1869 as an escape from the Latin and Greek proses of Harrow. He would unlock the cathedral at night and pray, the only mortal man in it; and one

---

[5] An Oxford scholar, Charles Bigg, composed a learned but deeply felt portrait of *The Christian Platonists of Alexandria* (Clarendon Press, 1886). In Cambridge the Platonic influence owed more to a more recent pundit, S. T. Coleridge. See David Newsome, *Bishop Westcott and the Platonic Tradition* (Cambridge University Press, 1969).

[6] G. W. E. Russell, *Dr. Liddon* (Mowbray, 1905), p. 77.

[7] In *The Claims of the Bible and of Science* (Macmillan, 1863), p. 138, Maurice had protested against a claim by Prince Lee that 'the very foundation of our faith—the very basis of our hopes—the very nearest and dearest of our consolations are taken away from us when one line of that sacred volume, on which we base everything, is said to be unfaithful or untrustworthy.'

fruit of the peace of these years was his commentary on St. John, part of the *Speaker's Commentary* on the Authorized Version. He argued that the fourth gospel, and before it the last book in the printed Bible, were both written by the apostle John to convey his vision of the cosmic, triumphant Christ. The teaching in the gospel was authentically Christ's, remembered although not at first understood. St. John, as he meditated on it, found it correcting his own over-hasty teaching that the Lord Jesus would come back to the earth soon. Westcott, however, resigned this Peterborough canonry suddenly in 1883, when the Bishop complained that he was neglecting his duties in the diocese.[8] Gladstone came to the rescue with a canonry of Westminster.

His Cambridge professorship was his main task for twenty years. He believed that the university was called 'to inspire men with a sense of their sovereign grandeur' and that 'no nation, no church . . . was ever called to fulfil a greater work than that to which the English nation and the English church are now summoned'.[9] He became a Fellow of King's, where he used to hold a religious discussion on a Sunday afternoon, and a Cambridge University Church Society was founded under his patronage. But his chief interest was in the red-brick Divinity School, which was built in his time. There he presided over the teaching of the Bible and the early Christian centuries and over the beginning of the Theological Tripos as an examination for undergraduates. Accepting much of the work himself, he persuaded a growing number of bishops and Oxford theologians to institute a standard examination for those to be ordained, virtually replacing the tests by the Examining Chaplains which had greatly varied from diocese to diocese. His initiative also led to the formation of a Clergy Training School in Cambridge; it was his wish that ordinands should do all their work based on their own colleges, but after his time the scheme developed into a seminary, Westcott House. He also did all that he could to encourage both the new Cambridge Mission to Delhi for dialogue with educated Hindus and the 'university extension' movement for adult education in England. It is, however, clear that in Cambridge as at Harrow many were confused by his actual teach-

[8] This was Magee, an eloquent Irishman with a zest for displaying his logical powers in ecclesiastical controversies. Victoria once described him to Disraeli as 'the finest preacher the Queen has ever heard out of Scotland'. A consistent individualist and a stout Tory, his most famous remark was that he would rather see England free than England sober; however, unlike his patron Disraeli he had sufficient faith in the Church of England to think that it would survive if set free. 'Disestablishment', he wrote privately in 1876, 'will very nearly drown us; but it will kill the fleas.' He was appointed Archbishop of York while Westcott was Bishop of Durham, but soon died. See J. C. Macdonnel, *Life and Correspondence of William Connor Magee* (Isbister, 1896).

[9] *On Some Points in the Religious Office of the Universities* (Macmillan, 1873), pp. 19, 69.

ing, if they had the patience to listen. When he died Scott Holland, who loved him, recalled his famous conversation with a pupil. 'Thank you! Thank you, Dr. Westcott! You have made that perfectly clear to me!' 'Oh! I hope not! I hope not!'[10]

These were also years of writing.[11] Always he returned to the thought that the humanity of Jesus drew 'all men' and took all humanity into God. Everywhere in history there was self-sacrifice and a priestly prayer, but these were perfectly consummated in Jesus. When he read the biography of Maurice he wrote: 'I never knew before how deep my sympathy is with most of his characteristic thoughts'. But he shared, too, Maurice's sense of the inadequacy of words, and wrote: 'Lord Shaftesbury's has been a noble life, and complete in its way, though I wish he had left Theology alone. To study that we want an unusual endowment of modesty.'

4

When Lightfoot became Bishop of Durham at the age of fifty-one, it was hoped that he would carry on as a scholar and teacher, and men recalled another Joseph: Bishop Butler. Being a bachelor don now possessed of a large income, he turned Auckland Castle into an informal college. Under his eye an Auckland Brotherhood of young men from Oxford and Cambridge read, talked, played football, visited homes, and said prayers in the great chapel in preparation for a curacy. Some of them could afford to be a curate without any stipend, just as Lightfoot refused all payment for them; six or eight at a time were his guests. Not many of these young men stayed long in County Durham, but Lightfoot ordained 323 deacons in ten years.

He also brought his scholarly work to a splendid completion. He was resolved to set in order the materials for the history of the Church in the century after the apostles' deaths. This task involved a minute examination of the evidence, much of it fraudulent, much of it discovered only in his lifetime, before a lucid narrative could be made. No difficulty daunted him. He had published an edition of the Epistles of St. Clement (one authentic, the other not) in 1869, with the same care as he had lavished on the Epistles of St. Paul, and he was revising his *Clement* to the end of his life, as fresh evidence came to light. The scholarly work of his Durham years was to complete this Cambridge material, particularly by an examination of the seven

[10] See Owen Chadwick, *Westcott and the University* (Cambridge University Press, 1963).
[11] See C. K. Barrett, *Westcott as Commentator* (Cambridge University Press, 1959).

letters attributed to St. Ignatius of Antioch, who was martyred in Rome at the beginning of the second century. These were documents of importance to theologians. 'As to the Episcopal system, I founded it upon the Epistles of St. Ignatius', Newman remembered; on the other hand, radical Germans detected forgery. With an unprecedented thoroughness in studying both these letters and their background, Lightfoot established their authentic text and placed it in the context of an account of the whole period, including an equally careful edition of the story of the martyrdom of Polycarp, Bishop of Smyrna. Two volumes of his *Apostolic Fathers* were published in 1885, and the third in the year of his death. In an act of thanksgiving he paid for the building of a new church in Sunderland, dedicated it to St. Ignatius, and consecrated it after a sermon by Westcott.[12]

None of this achievement surprised anyone who knew the orderly power of his educational influence and academic work, or the resources of his library and memory. 'From strength to strength' had been the text upon which Westcott had preached at his consecration as a bishop. Nor was Cambridge surprised when young men felt a reverent affection for this ugly, shy, endlessly learned bishop. A member of the Auckland Brotherhood recalled: 'Lightfoot had no beauty of face or form, but he had a most gorgeous smile, and when this came, it lit up his face like a glory. . . .'

Less expected was his effectiveness as a Victorian apostle. His pastoral work in County Durham interested him far more than the national problems of the Church. He never seems to have hesitated to sacrifice to it any prospect of becoming Tait's successor or Benson's closest counsellor at Lambeth. Under his predecessor, Charles Baring, the population had grown, and with it the number of churches. The policy of church-building now flourished: forty-five were erected in ten years. Lightfoot's *Leaders of the Northern Church* (1890) was a series of portraits of Aidan, Hilda, Bede, and other early English missionaries based on sermons preached at churches dedicated to them. But what had been lacking was a strong diocesan organization, and this Lightfoot set himself to supply. He successfully carried through the division of the diocese when the new see of Newcastle was created (with Samuel Wilberforce's son Ernest as its first bishop). Within the more manageable area left to him, he threw himself into confirmations in a style astonishing in a scholar who was heir to the Prince Bishops of Durham. He created a new archdeaconry, multiplied the rural deans, reorganized and increased the finances, confirmed tirelessly, and encouraged the laity both to speak in the councils of the Church and

[12] A convenient introduction to the task of setting Lightfoot's scholarship in a more modern context is provided by *Early Christian Fathers*, ed. C. C. Richardson (SCM Press, 1953).

to assist the clergy in preaching and visiting, then a startling innovation.

The combination of diocesan and academic work was fatal. During Lightfoot's journeys about his diocese, or in his August holidays, his mind would be at work on his writing. He would write before Matins and breakfast; he would write late at night, falling asleep at his desk. His studies of Ignatius and Polycarp turned out to be his own martyrdom, yet his recreation was to write a history of Auckland Castle, the oldest episcopal residence in England. When the strain of the Lambeth Conference of 1888 was added to such overwork, his heart collapsed. After a brief recovery, he died next year.

5

So it was that, against all his own expectation, Westcott was summoned to spend the last years of his life in carrying on his friend's leadership of the diocese of Durham. And he, too, was far more successful than others expected. He succeeded partly because he limited himself. He did not attempt to create a new organization; he did not attempt to write books of original scholarship; he did not often trouble to read other men's books. Although he kept up the Auckland Brotherhood, he did not live with the young men as Lightfoot had done. But he succeeded also because the humility of this elderly professor made its impression. His favourite drink was weak tea, and when he had to use the episcopal carriage he sat miserably with his back to the horses. When he addressed the privileged, he could preach what he practised, describing 'anything which costs more either in money, or in time, or vital energy than it contributes to his power of service' as, for a Christian, a 'culpable luxury'.[13] His devotion to duty was such that he preferred a meeting of rural deans to Archbishop Benson's funeral in Canterbury. When his wife died, he had left her bedside because he had an engagement to consecrate a churchyard in the presence of a miners' brass band.

He could be down-to-earth, and was fed with practical information about social conditions by the Vicar of Gateshead, but it may be doubted whether the eloquence of Westcott was understood much more readily by the workmen of County Durham than it had been by the schoolboys of Harrow. (Had the congregations understood everything in the sermons which Lightfoot had written out with such care?) What counted was what he was. In his old age Westcott's leonine head and eager eyes conveyed a memorable impression of the attraction of the unseen world, yet he, a man of books, loved to quote the dictum of Benjamin Whichcote: 'I act, therefore I am.' In his

13 *The Incarnation and Common Life* (Macmillan, 1893), p. 134.

first address to his Diocesan Conference, he said: 'I know the attractions of the pursuit of speculative and of historical criticism, but these are wholly subsidiary to action, which is the characteristic of man. The Gospel which is committeed to believers claims to have the power to deal with every practical question of human conduct for the manifestation of God's glory; and friends and foes alike have a right to demand that this claim should be vindicated on the broad fields of life.' He never became a man of action, but men were impressed by his feeling that he ought to be one.

On 1 June 1892 Bishop Westcott's reputation proved to be already strong enough to win for him his most memorable success on the 'broad fields'. A fall in the price of coal had led the colliery owners to reduce wages by $12\frac{1}{2}$ per cent, but the trade union, the Mining Federation, had insisted on $7\frac{1}{2}$ per cent as the maximum. The result had been a stoppage of work by about 10,000 men, reducing most of them to destitution and damaging the whole of the North. Ignoring cynical protests that he was a capitalist but no economist, Westcott proposed a compromise. Work should be resumed on two conditions: that there should be an immediate reduction of only ten per cent in wages, and that the question of any further reduction should be referred to a Wages Board, to be established with full powers to deal with this and all future differences as to the increase or reduction of wages. Although both sides were by now desperate for a compromise, the formula was far from being obvious; the owners had increased the reduction to $13\frac{1}{2}$ per cent, and the bitter miners did not trust the idea of a Board for conciliation. Westcott went from group to group, mediating, during a Saturday afternoon when representatives of Capital and Labour conferred together and separately in Auckland Castle. A crowd around the palace set up a mighty cheer for the bishop as well as for the miners' leaders when the end of the strike was announced.[14]

His success as an arbitrator spread Westcott's reputation so widely that he was asked to be the chief speaker at a demonstration of the unemployed in Trafalgar Square. He refused, but he was glad to be President of the more middle-class Christian Social Union founded in 1889, and his preaching was now borne along on a tide of a reforming optimism. In a preface to a book of sermons, he announced that 'there is a growing tendency to judge conduct by reference to the whole, and to the eternal; to subordinate personal to social interests'.[15] The sermons breathed an atmosphere of trust. As the reviewer in the

[14] See G. F. A. Best, *Bishop Westcott and the Miners* (Cambridge University Press, 1967).
[15] *Christian Aspects of Life* (Macmillan, 1897). For one of the tendencies which Westcott had in mind, see Melvin Richter, *The Politics of Conscience: T. H. Green and His Age* (Weidenfeld & Nicolson, 1964).

Yorkshire Post noted: 'He is not content to explain Christian duty and urge its performance: he always suggests in some subtle way that men only want to know their duty to discharge it.' Two other collections of sermons (*The Incarnation and Common Life* and *Lessons from Work*) appeared, in the same mood. Various challenges to the Church were mentioned, only to be classed as opportunities, for the Gospel could never be defeated. The nineteenth century seemed to be ending in an evening of glory. Typical was the parable of the Alpine sunset which closed a Whitsun sermon in 1891.

We gaze on the vast bare rocks and snow-slopes transfigured in a flood of burning light. In a moment there falls over them an ashy paleness as of death, cold and chilling. While we strive to measure our loss a deepening flush spreads slowly over the mountain side, pure and calm and tender, and we know that the glory which has passed away is not lost even when it fades again from our sight.

Westcott was surprisingly popular both with the miners and with the gentry of County Durham. This very popularity indicates that he was not ruthless in his demands for change. On the contrary, he was a scholar in his seventies, 'pure and calm and tender', who had not been particularly interested in social questions while a schoolmaster or professor. The Christian Socialism which he expressed was something of an enigma to contemporaries. They knew that it was not the Socialism of Karl Marx or the Independent Labour Party. They also knew that public control was increasing now that politics increasingly depended on the working-class vote, and they wanted to know how a churchman who was in favour of this kind of semi-socialism differed from, say, Joseph Chamberlain. Westcott could be as disappointing as Maurice himself when he had to answer political questions. He, who had so often preached about peace between the nations, refused to follow Pope Leo XIII in condemning the British attack on the Boers. 'It was impossible for us to submit to arbitration the fulfilment of our imperial obligations.' Yet it would be wrong to conclude that this elderly bishop caused no alarm among conservatives. The 'Socialist tendencies of the speeches which he has made since he became a bishop' were enough for Lord Salisbury to scotch the Queen's suggestion that he should be made Archbishop of York in 1890. The fact—heartening or alarming, according to one's taste—was that this theologian with one foot in heaven was prepared to preside at conferences about social questions drawing management and labour to Auckland Castle, to inspect the housing of the poor as he went about his diocesan duties, and to praise the motives of trade unions and co-operatives. Many of the tributes after his death in 1901 came from manual workers, and many of the Christian Socialists who were far more radical than he was knew that their cause had gained from the glamour of his example.[16]

At the annual miners' service in Durham Cathedral a week before his death, he summed up his message, explaining that 'it is not likely that I shall ever address you here again.' It was a message about the love of Christ.

Try by its Divine standard the thoroughness of your labour and the purity of your recreation, and the Durham which we love, the Durham of which we are proud . . . will soon answer to the heavenly pattern. If Tennyson's idea of heaven was true, that 'heaven is the ministry of soul to soul', we may reasonably hope, by patient, resolute, faithful, united endeavour, to find heaven about us here, the glory of our earthly life.

6

Both Lightfoot and Westcott repeatedly stressed the Christian foundation of the Victorian age. 'Our civilization both in its gentleness and in its strength is due to the Christian faith and has been supported by Christian institutions,' Westcott claimed, adding that 'whatever we owe to non-Christian sources comes to us through a Christian atmosphere and is steeped in Christian thought'.[17] The two men worked in the moment which Hort and Benson feared might be passing: the moment when the Christian culture of England was broad enough to include the new scientific spirit, the new internationalism, and the new industrialism, but had not yet disintegrated into a pluralism without a public philosophy.

Like Benson, they drew strength as bishops from their work as historians. Lightfoot would describe church history as a 'cordial for drooping spirits'. Westcott wrote: 'When once we can feel that faith in the risen Christ has not only conquered all opposing forces in each past crisis, but preserved in each case and incorporated into itself all that which gave real vitality to the opposition which it encountered, our own courage will be quickened.'[18] And, like Benson, they felt that they were standing within this great tradition. The Cambridge which they knew was a university astir with many new intellectual ambitions, but it was still a Christian, indeed a clerical, place. Attendance at chapel was compulsory, and tutors would justify it on the ground that most of the young men were used to their public school chapels and to

[16] See A. R. Vidler, 'Westcott's Christian Socialism', in *F. D. Maurice and Company* (SCM Press, 1966), and Peter d'A. Jones, *The Christian Socialist Revival* (Princeton University Press, 1968).

[17] *The Gospel of Life*, p. 54.

[18] ibid., p. 282.

family prayers. Few of the dons publicly confessed unbelief. The best undergraduates were uneasy about their lives of privilege and alert to the challenge of the slums, which often reached them through clergymen. As Bernard Shaw (who in *Candida* achieved a brilliant character-study of a Christian Socialist) wrote in his Preface to *Plays Pleasant*: 'Religion was alive again, coming back upon men, even upon clergymen, with such power that not the Church of England itself could keep it out.' And the Durham which these two bishops knew was a county astir with the new Labour movement, but religious at heart, aware of the danger and disease which the miners faced, aware of the strength which came to their hard lives from the intense community life of the village at the pithead, aware of the more glorious world which might be glimpsed in the cathedral or the parish church or (more probably) in the hymns of the Methodist chapel. Trade unionism in the nineteenth century was not yet organized for the long strike or for the political campaign; the union was still in many respects like a church, and was often led by workers whose characters and minds had been developed in the churches and chapels. Of course these bishops were aware that the tradition was under attack, but they assumed that it could be defended. For example, when Lightfoot was taunted with being too 'earnest' in replying to the sceptical author of *Supernatural Religion*, he replied very sternly:

I am indeed in earnest, as I believe him to be. But it seems to me that the motives for earnestness are more intense in my case than in his; for (to say nothing else) as I read history, the morality of the coming generations of Englishmen is very largely dependent on the answers which they give to the questions at issue between us.

Lightfoot and Westcott thus believed that the Christian civilization around them could be preserved by 'earnest' work. The scholar, having done his duty among the books, could do it among the miners. But the moment in which they worked passed. In the ancient universities, clerical fellows of colleges became rarities once the legal monopoly of the Church of England had been broken, and the faculties of Divinity never grew large or dominant. In twentieth-century County Durham labour did not need, or did not think that it needed, episcopal inspiration or clerical charity, and although religion seemed a little stronger in the North East than elsewhere in England the Victorian expansiveness of church life proved a burden to maintain. Hensley Henson, when Bishop of Durham in 1931, refused to contribute to a volume of eulogy for Lightfoot. The revolutionary changes since 1889 had, he wrote, 'destroyed knowledge of, and interest in, all, even the greatest, of the figures which belong to the previous epoch'. In particular Henson blamed Lightfoot for the division of the old see of Durham, and complained that 'his multiplication of small Mission buildings . . . has created embarrassments and difficulties which are now very grave'.[19]

We need not be so grudging. We can see why such great men, standing as they thought at the beginning of an era when Christianity could be reconciled with modern knowledge and modern labour, had a fellow-feeling with the Christian thinkers in Alexandria who had hoped and worked for the reconciliation of Christianity with Hellenism. But we need not share the belief, to which they were inclined, that the faith and morality of future generations of Englishmen depended on the particular arrangements and arguments which they used in defence of a slightly revised version of James Prince Lee's religion. For not all the arrangements and arguments have lasted; yet in the twentieth century some Christians survive. If it is generally agreed that the churches built and the clergy recruited to serve the workers of County Durham represented a heroic effort by the Victorian Christians, it is not agreed that the Victorian pattern of church life must be imitated, or even envied, by a later generation. If it is generally agreed that the scholarship of Lightfoot won a permanent victory over some of the Germans of the nineteenth century, and that Westcott's mysticism did open up the mind of St. John, it is not agreed that the Lightfoot–Westcott religion was watertight—or that the Revised Version of the New Testament was of much permanent value. Nor is it agreed that the Victorian Establishment which these two bishops adorned reflected all the life of the first and second Christian centuries. It cannot escape notice that, partly because Hort never got round to writing on the synoptic gospels, the great Cambridge trio never considered Jesus himself at any length: Jesus, who was not a Platonist and not an Anglican.[20]

What remains, now that the moment has gone, is chiefly the personal example. When Westcott wrote a prayer 'for Truthfulness' to be used by the uncomprehending boys in his house at Harrow, he was showing the spirit in which Christians, perhaps more courageous than he was, would have to carry on the intellectual task.

Almighty God, Who hast sent the Spirit of Truth unto us to guide us into all truth, so rule our lives by Thy power, that we may be truthful in word, and deed, and thought. O keep us, most merciful Saviour, with Thy gracious protection, that no fear or hope may ever make us false in act or speech. Cast out

[19] *More Letters of Herbert Hensley Henson*, ed. E. F. Braley (SPCK, 1954), pp. 69–72.

[20] See Henry Chadwick, *The Vindication of Christianity in Westcott's Thought* (Cambridge University Press, 1961), and for the background, Stephen Neill, *The Interpretation of the New Testament, 1861–1961* (Oxford University Press, 1964).

from us whatsoever loveth or maketh a lie, and bring us all into the perfect freedom of Thy truth: through Jesus Christ, Thy Son, our Lord.

When Westcott voiced a generalized sympathy with the Durham miners, he was setting an example which other Christians would have to copy while being more detailed, and therefore more controversial, in the solutions which they offered to the grim problems of industrialization. He was acting out the prayer which he had taught at Harrow:

Blessed Lord, who for our sakes was content to bear sorrow and want and death, grant to us such a measure of Thy Spirit that we may follow Thee in all self-denial and tenderness of soul. Help us, by Thy great love, to succour the afflicted, to relieve the needy and destitute, to comfort the feeble-minded, to share the burdens of the heavy-laden, and ever to see Thee in all that are poor and desolate.

FOR FURTHER READING

There is no biography of Lightfoot apart from Hort's article in the *Dictionary of National Biography*, but a collection of 'memoirs and appreciations' was put together while some of those who had known him survived: *Lightfoot of Durham*, ed. G. R. Eden and F. C. Macdonald (Cambridge University Press, 1932). Some details about his episcopate are in the anonymous *Bishop Lightfoot*, with a Preface by Wescott (Macmillan, 1894).

Life and Letters of Brooke Foss Westcott, D.D., D.C.L., sometime Bishop of Durham, were compiled by his son Arthur in two volumes (Macmillan, 1903). A. C. Benson included informal sketches of Lightfoot, Westcott, and other Cambridge men of the time in his *Leaves of the Tree* (Smith, Elder, 1911). But slightly fuller footnotes than usual have been supplied here, since no comprehensive study of the theology of Lightfoot and Westcott has yet appeared.

8

1843-1901 *1848-1930.*

Creighton and Davidson

1

On St. Mark's Day, 1891, two bishops were consecrated by Arch-bishop Benson in Westminster Abbey. One was Professor Mandell Creighton, to be Bishop of Peterborough. Six years later, when Benson died, the Prince of Wales, the Archbishop of York, and others wanted to see this brilliant man at Canterbury. He was appointed instead Bishop of London. A little less than ten years after his consecration, however, a stomach ulcer killed him. The other new bishop kneeling beside Creighton at that service in 1891, Randall Thomas Davidson, rather disapproved of him, and wrote some severe words about him privately after his death.

A great many people who knew him well found it difficult not to believe him to be a cynic, and there were those who doubted his real hold upon the dog-matic side of Christianity. This last was probably due to his endeavour, mis-taken and unsuccessful as I personally think it was, to appear as a finished man of the world with social experience and social gifts, who could meet other men of the world on equal terms.

Creighton, unlike Davidson, was reluctant to become a bishop, for the simple reason that he wanted to read. Two years after his con-secration he wrote: 'My life has been that of a man who tries to write a book, and is the object of a conspiracy to prevent him from doing so. It is quite true that no one cares to read my book, but that has never interfered with my pleasure in reading for it.' When a lady attempted to console him with the remark that 'after all, men are more interesting than books', he commented: 'Doubtless this is true, but you choose your own books, and you must take your men as you find them.' He used to say that he wanted his epitaph to be: 'He tried to write true history.' In fact, after his death men said more flattering things, and the chorus of praise swelled when his widow published his *Life and Letters* in 1904. Randall Davidson added after his comment just quoted: 'I know of no instance in which the publication of a public man's biography has so greatly raised him in the estimation of good and thoughtful people.'

Creighton's great book was on the Renaissance popes, and he resembled them in some ways. He shared all their love of learning. 'The formula which most explains the Church of England is that it rests on an appeal to sound learning' was one of his many donnish sayings. He was close to them in his love of Italy, tradition, art, and ceremonies. The Archdeacon of London described him sniffingly after his death to a journalist: 'Although in doctrinal opinions a very Broad Churchman, he had great sympathy for medieval ritual and all kinds of pomp and magnificence'.[1] It was a combination which caused Lytton Strachey to toy with the idea of making him the fifth and last of the *Eminent Victorians*.[2] Yet Bishop Creighton was out of tune with his own age, as the popes had not been out of tune with theirs; for in the last days of Queen Victoria an effective churchman had to be thoroughly earnest. 'He's too clever', chuckled Archbishop Frederick Temple after one of Creighton's after-dinner speeches. To Creighton, the essentials of Christianity seemed simple and sure, so that everything else could be treated as material for objective research or donnish humour. This should be remembered as the context of his remark about the Anglican appeal to sound learning. He said:

The Church of England seems to me to have a very decided position of its own—the noblest which can be taken by any institution, but through its very loftiness easily capable of misrepresentation and of misunderstanding . . . The Church of England puts to one side all that is irrelevant, it shuns definitions about questions which arose from mere human curiosity, it is chary of denials in matters where affirmation and denial are alike impossible . . . It is this characteristic which has led to the groundless assertion that the Church of England expresses a compromise. Sound learning must always wear the appearance of a compromise between ignorance and plausible hypothesis . . . It is the function of learning to assert what is known, and to leave perverse ingenuity steadily alone.[3]

Randall Davidson, although a Broad Churchman like Creighton, had developed a manner always 'good and thoughtful', consistently 'earnest and reverent' (another of his favourite phrases). He took seriously what churchmen took seriously, although he also took seriously the English layman's dislike of medieval magnificence in the clergy. He was, as a result, trusted in the Church as Creighton never was. If he was somewhat ponderous, so were they. If he was no scholar,

---

[1] C. H. Dant, *Distinguished Churchmen* (Treherne, 1902), p. 44.

[2] Strachey did eventually write a little essay about Creighton, in *Life and Letters* (June 1929). It had some good phrases, e.g. about the *History of the Papacy:* 'The biscuit is certainly exceedingly dry, but at any rate there are no weevils in it.' But the essay was a damp squib.

[3] Mandell Crighton, *The Church and the Nation* (Longmans, Green, 1901), pp. 250–1, 258–60.

their own churchmanship did not rest on the appeal to sound learning. The charge usually made against him during the first half of his life was not that he was too clever, but that he was too ambitious. After a slow start he had gone to Lambeth as Archbishop Tait's chaplain at the age of twenty-nine. Since then he had remained at the centre of Church and State as Dean of Windsor, and in 1891 he was being consecrated as Bishop of Rochester. He had already developed a stomach ulcer, and eleven days after his consecration it confined him to his bed. (The next six months were the only period after his ordination when he found time for systematic reading.) He was transferred to the less arduous see of Winchester after four years. Weak health was the reason why he was not made Bishop of London in 1897, and why he refused to be Creighton's successor there in 1901. However, after Creighton's death Davidson's was the only possible name for Canterbury. 'I do know the ropes', as he said. He was the pope of the Anglican world for a quarter-century, and he died full of honours at the age of eighty-two.

2

Mandell Creighton was born in Carlisle, and wrote a book about its history. His father and grandfather had been carpenters, and his father's furnishing and decorating shop was a few yards from the cathedral over which Tait presided as dean. His mother died when he was seven years old, and the home over the Castle Street shop now possessed few signs of happiness, or books, pictures or other inducement to the young Mandell. The boy's chance came through the grammar school close by the cathedral. There he was nicknamed 'Homer', and from there he won a scholarship to the King's School which was part of Durham Cathedral. It seems to have been the historic beauty of Durham and its choral services that turned his thoughts to ordination. In 1864, having recently left school, he wrote an immense letter to his successor as head of the school, thus recording his eloquence as a young moralist in the high Arnoldian style.

He won a scholarship at Merton College, Oxford, and a further nickname: 'the Professor'. He was now a definite High Churchman, with severe views about the slack ritual in Carlisle Cathedral; he was also a passionate friend of fellow-undergraduates. 'Of course at a certain age', he wrote to a fellow-student, 'when you have a house and so on, you get a wife as part of its furniture. . . .' He took the orthodox classical course, and after his Firsts turned to history, becoming a Fellow of Merton in 1867 and hastily reading history books in the evening in order to lecture on them next morning. He was by now a clever, flippant, and sarcastic talker, with a taste in wine, in silk ties, in Morris wallpapers, and in blue china plates. He was strict with the college servants. He went through no religious crisis in an Oxford which was now growing more and more lay and sceptical. He did not trouble to read Darwin, and considered the controversy 'amusing'. The fellowship which he held entailed an obligation to be ordained, but he was not made deacon until 1870, and then he made little specific preparation. He said about this time that it was the habit in Oxford to assume that a man who took Holy Orders must be either a fool or a knave; and people could not call him a fool. But perhaps he exaggerated his wisdom.

At one of Ruskin's lectures next year he noticed a girl wearing a yellow scarf. The fellow-aesthete was Louise von Glehn, the daughter of an Esthonian merchant who had settled in England. Three weeks later he was engaged. It was now that his life began to be more than the life of an ordinary Oxford tutor. His bride was enthusiastic about Italian art, and with her encouragement he formed the intention to write a history of the subject, at a time when the Italian Renaissance was only beginning to be familiar to educated Englishmen. He taught her Italian; she taught him German; they visited Italy in a shared ecstasy. He explained religion to her, and found it difficult. What he did see was that the religious liberalism of Stanley and Jowett was inadequate. After hearing Stanley preach, he told Louise that 'the wording was all that could be wished: my objection was to the contents, viz. that there were not any.' He questioned whether a sermon by Jowett could 'make a practical system to set before the heathendom of England, and be a moral engine to elevate society'. He grew uneasy, but impressed, when Louise proposed to visit the poor. By the time he was ready to be a priest, in 1873, he was so nervous about the examination before ordination that he wrote to the archdeacon offering to withdraw.

The don's life continued for another year, until a vicarage where his college was the patron, and where the income was exceptionally good, fell vacant. He decided to go. He was growing bored with being a 'teaching drudge', and wanted to put all his energy into the study of one historical subject. Somehow he would buy or borrow the necessary books. The place was Embleton, on the coast of Northumberland, a quarrymen's village notorious for immorality and consisting of six hundred people, almost all in one-room cottages, with about eleven hundred other souls in the bleak countryside around.

The success of Creighton's ten years as a parish priest was both academic and personal. He finished two volumes of his history, and did most of the work for three more. He added a study of the Elizabethan Age, a biography of Simon de Montfort (poor Hort's project), many book reviews, and some coaching of pupils for the sake of the

money. And in the afternoon he and his wife would visit the
parishioners, entering into their lives with a human, pastoral kindness
which few had suspected in the Oxford historian. The vicarage with its
fortified peel tower, built as a protection against raids from Scotland,
was a home where an adequate domestic staff functioned and a young
family grew up in happiness—although Creighton insisted that his was
the will around which the home revolved. The ancient church was
the place where Creighton learned to preach extempore, usually with
a moral application, but based on a simple exposition of the Bible,
avoiding critical and controversial questions; it was a pulpit style to
which he adhered for the rest of his ministry. He acquired other
duties, but he had no ambition to take a prominent part in ecclesiastical business or theology. 'I don't like talking about religious matters',
he would protest.

His work on the Papacy from 1378 was based on some original
sources, but the Vatican's archives were still closed. He used mostly
German scholarship, so that Embleton's distance from the conversation of historians did little harm. Enough of Creighton's original intention to write about Italian art remained to give a special zest to his
descriptions of the cultural background in the Renaissance, but his
down-to-earth history belonged to another world than Walter Pater's
Renaissance (1873). 'When events are tedious, you must be tedious' was
his motto. Enough of his worldliness remained to make him a master
storyteller of the politics in which the Papacy was all too deeply involved, and to make him refrain from denouncing the popes—although he freely denounced idle undergraduates or debauched
villagers. About the Borgia family, Creighton wrote that 'they have
become legendary as types of unrestrained wickedness and it is difficult to judge them fairly without seeming to palliate iniquity.' But
he did judge fairly, even tenderly, and thereby shocked many Victorians.[4] About a pope who was deposed for the grossest immorality
(the subject of a famous passage in Gibbon), he would say: 'it is
difficult not to feel that John XXIII had hard measure dealt to him
in the exceptional obloquy which has been his lot.' Even this amount
of ethical judgment in Creighton's history may look strange to
twentieth-century eyes, but his attitude was one of sovereign impartiality. Stanley's taste for picturesque edification was not Creighton's
conception of the historian's task. 'There is no reason why anyone
should want to know about the past', he wrote to a friend; 'but if he
does, he can have such knowledge as exists, not fancy pictures.'

[4] This was a time when Westcott had to mention *The Grammarian's Funeral*
with the qualification that 'there is, perhaps, little in the literary history of the
Renaissance to justify the picture which Browning has drawn'. *Essays in the
Religious Thought of the West*, p. 271.

Creighton's impartiality won his praise from scholars on both sides of the Catholic–Protestant chasm, but brought about a memorable correspondence with the Roman Catholic historian, Lord Acton.[5] Acton knew more about the subject than any Englishman except possibly Creighton himself, but he approached it with a passionate commitment to a cause. Precisely because he was a devout Roman Catholic, he was ashamed of the Renaissance popes; and his indignation about their immorality and their rejection of reform got mixed up with the despair which he felt (with his friend Gladstone) at the insistence of the nineteenth-century popes on being both infallible and obscurantist. Creighton seemed to him, as to Davidson, insufficiently serious.

Acton reviewed the first two volumes quite favourably, but in a private letter of 1882 the peer condescendingly warned the vicar that more theology was becoming inevitable as his history progressed towards Luther. 'You will not escape theological exposition when you come to the explosion at Wittenberg, the negotiations of Augsburg, the debates of Trent. . . . There are two questions, What made Luther? and What made him so strong? which occur in the introductory period, and have never been satisfactorily answered.'

When Creighton published his next two volumes, five years later, he was a professor editing the *English Historical Review* and he sent the volumes to Acton, expecting (no doubt) similar treatment. Instead, Acton wrote a review which was an outright attack. One charge was intellectual superficiality. 'The author prefers the larger public that take history in the shape of literature, to scholars whose souls are vexed with the insolubility of problems and take their meals in the kitchen.' With this went a moral accusation. 'He is not striving to prove a case, or burrowing towards a conclusion, but wishes to pass through scenes of raging controversy and passion, with a serene curiosity, a divided judgment, and a pair of white gloves.' Creighton was angry in response to Acton's 'furious passion', but then cooled off and persuaded Acton to remove some of the more personally hostile passages from the review. He did not, however, persuade Acton to modify his condemnation of the history's indulgent description of the popes on the eve of the Reformation.

In particular, Acton was furious that Creighton appeared to condone the Papacy's involvement in the Inquisition, and he wrote to rebuke Creighton privately.

You say that people in authority are not to be snubbed or sneered at from our pinnacle of conscious rectitude. I really don't know whether you exempt them because of their rank, or of their success and power, or of their date. . . . I cannot accept your canon that we are to judge Pope and King unlike other

[5] See David Mathew, *Lord Acton and His Times* (Eyre & Spottiswoode, 1968), pp. 329–35.

men, with a favoured presumption that they did no wrong. If there is any presumption, it is the other way, increasing as the power increases. . . . Power tends to corrupt, and absolute power corrupts absolutely. Great men are almost always bad men, even when they exercise influence not authority: still more when you superadd the tendency or the certainty of corruption by authority. . . . The inflexible integrity of the moral code is to me the secret of the authority, the dignity, the utility of history.

Creighton's reply was impenitent. What he had meant was that

Anyone engaged in great affairs occupied a representative position, which required special consideration. Selfishness, even wrong-doing, for an idea, an institution, the maintenance of an accepted view of the basis of society, does not cease to be wrong-doing; but it is not quite the same as personal wrong-doing: it is more difficult to prove, and it does not equally shock the moral sense of the doer. The acts of men in power are determined by the effective force behind them of which they are the exponents: their morality is almost always lower than the morality of the mass of men; but there is generally a point fixed below which they cannot sink with impunity.

Creighton is generally thought to have won this argument against Acton's insistence on 'morality as the sole impartial criterion of men and things'; and in personal terms, his achievement of sympathy with the holders of power without ever losing sight of the sacredness of liberty is rightly considered a major victory over many easy prejudices. Nevertheless, Creighton's limitations were revealed by this correspondence with Acton. This don had far less experience of men of power than the aristocratic and widely travelled Acton had accumulated, and less insight into the deeper currents of past and contemporary societies. He therefore had far less appreciation of what was at stake when the eminent earnestness of the Victorians was compared with the pleasure-seeking of the Borgias (or of Edward VII). Above all, this vicar, although he died as a bishop in the same year as Westcott, never really understood the Evangelical basis of Victorian morality; indeed, he never understood any form of religious passion.

In his history his best portrait was of the character of Aeneas Sylvius Piccolomini, the man of letters who became Pius II without losing his literary *panache* or his frank worldliness. Creighton confessed that Aeneas had sinned in his climb to the Papacy, adding: 'In those days chastity was a mark of a saintly character, and Aeneas never professed to be a saint.' The great dream of Aeneas as pope was that Christendom might unite in another crusade against the Turks, and Creighton's own great dream was that Christian England might be revived for the twentieth century—but as Hensley Henson pointed out in a sermon on Creighton's death, neither Pius II nor Mandell Creighton had always viewed themselves as crusaders. As a verdict on Creighton's own life, Henson quoted his words about Pius II: 'Had he been less of a student, had his mind been less fertile, he might have concentrated his energies more successfully on one supreme object.'

Two other characters whom Creighton understood intimately, and about whom he wrote excellent short books, were Cardinal Wolsey and Queen Elizabeth I: clever people, whose object was a political unity. When dealing with the crisis of the Reformation he admired Erasmus, the moderate devoted to a gentle ethic, to a simple piety, and to humane studies. He liked to think that the Church of England was at its heart Erasmian. He held no key to the mind of Luther, about whom he himself wrote that 'his whole being depended on the consciousness of a relationship to a loving God'; and it was probably fortunate for his reputation that other duties overwhelmed him before his history had progressed far into the Reformation. He understood only that the Papacy had been foolish to refuse a cautious reform and a limit to its own financial appetites. With more elasticity, he thought, the fabric of Christendom might have been preserved. He once confessed:

If the Pope would have left off pillaging Germany, I believe that 'Justification by faith only' would have created only a languid interest . . . I can never ask myself first: 'What mighty ideas swelled in the hearts of men?' but: 'What made men see a chance of saving sixpence, or gaining sixpence, or escaping from being robbed of sixpence?'[6]

There was something undeniably paradoxical about the man who had won an international reputation for his smooth narrative of the Renaissance Papacy working as a vicar in Northumberland, and Creighton came to feel this himself. In 1884 he accepted an invitation to be the first Dixie Professor of Ecclesiastical History at Cambridge. Next year he was made a canon of Worcester, and in that cathedral he contentedly spent his vacations. During term he showed Cambridge that there was little difference between the sacred and the profane. 'Theology has become historical, and does not demand that history should become theological', he declared. 'Ecclesiastical history must be pursued in exactly the same way, and with exactly the same spirit, as any other branch of history.'

3

After seven years, the blow fell. As he wrote to a friend: 'A bishopric is to me personally after the flesh a terrible nuisance. But how is a man to refuse the responsibilities of his branch of the service?' As he listened

[6] Owen Chadwick has lectured on *Creighton on Luther* (Cambridge University Press, 1959).

to the regrets of his fellow-historians, he knew that his whole existence must be transformed. To another friend he now wrote that 'my position in life is changed. It is no longer to *teach*, but to *edify*. I have no longer to startle people out of self-complacency, but to be kindly, sympathetic, humble and helpful.' As a bishop he acted on the assumption that 'mankind want a religion: and it is as a religion that Christianity works in the world.' Although he had never used the Athanasian Creed at Embleton, he insisted on its regular use in his diocese. The scholar who had exercised his wit in order to tease Hort over dinner in Emmanuel College poured out a more disciplined kind of conversation for the benefit of the country clergy. He lectured to the working men of Leicester or Northampton, he smoked with the young men in the houses of the gentry, and he was (as his wife recalled) 'determined to like' Peterborough. After six years of it, he told a friend: 'I can truly say that I am happy, not through my public activities, or my social powers, but through growing sympathy in little matters with children, with the young, with the sorrowful, the tempted, the perplexed.' Perhaps so; anyway, Mrs. Creighton was happy. She quickly became the most formidable bishop's wife in England. In the biography of William Temple it is recorded that when Creighton was passed over for Canterbury in favour of William Temple's father, a schoolboy at Rugby commented: 'What a sell for Mrs. Peterborough!'

At this stage Creighton kept up some academic work. The fifth— and, as it turned out, last—volume of his *Papacy* appeared, together with books made up of Cambridge lectures on Elizabeth I and his Hulsean lectures of 1893–4 on *Persecution and Tolerance*. Creighton's Hulseans concluded that liberty is 'only secure under the guardianship of the Church; for the Church possesses the knowledge of man's eternal destiny—which alone can justify his claim to freedom.' A few months later he was delivering his Primary Charge to his diocese, again emphasizing liberty: 'the great question for the modern world to determine is how men are to be fitted to bear the heavy burden of liberty'. The message of the Church was indispensable to true progress: 'the service of men without the service of God becomes an intolerable burden.' Nothing is more striking than to see the confidence with which Creighton, while pleading for liberalism within Christianity, ignored the basic secularization which Hort, for example, had discerned in English life. 'The truth of Christianity is apparent in the Christian life: and all the conceptions which support the non-Christian at the present day are of Christian origin, and owe their power to the vitality of the Christian faith. Current morality, philanthropy, high aims in politics, ideas of progress, of liberty, of brotherhood—what you will—owe their position to Christianity.' Equally striking was his failure to perceive, when he represented the Church of England at the coronation of the Tsar in Moscow in 1896, that Holy Russia was doomed as surely as the Renaissance Papacy.

His promotion to London in 1896 seemed natural, yet it was a mistake to give Creighton the busiest diocese. He felt that he had to talk as cleverly as possible on all the occasions when the Bishop of London was wanted and when his predecessor, Temple, had often been gruff or rude. He delivered 294 sermons and addresses during 1897. But his life as a student was now closed. Nor did he now enjoy many opportunities to influence individuals; he always had to rush on to another engagement or to write another administrative letter.

The mistake of imposing such duties on Creighton became murderous when he got involved in disputes with Anglo-Catholic ritualists. In London there were Anglican priests who put an almost Lutheran religious passion into the revival of the ceremonies which had been familiar to the Renaissance popes. Creighton could not understand such a reverence for historical precedent when it clashed with what had become the master-theme of his speaking and writing: the unity of the English Church with the English State under law. His predecessor, Temple, had in practice allowed such eccentrics to go their own way, while not troubling to conceal his contempt. Now Creighton set himself to bring the diocese to order, and this aim caught him in a dilemma because of his character. If he had cared less for order, he would have put good will above it, as his successor Arthur Foley Winnington-Ingram was to do.[7] If he had cared less for liberty, he would have prosecuted the rebels as Tait had done—or would at least have forbidden their practices firmly, as Davidson was then trying to do in the diocese of Winchester. What he did was to plead with them to accept order freely, for the sake of peace. And his health, poisoned by the overwork and anxiety, was certainly not improved by a foolish decision to which he adhered obstinately. He not only insisted that the officials throughout his diocese, including the suffragan bishops, should refer all substantial questions to him; he also declined to employ a single secretary. He would dictate some letters to his chaplain or to his daughters, but he wrote most of them with his own hand, often during meetings. His filing system was therefore mainly in his head.

This scholar who pretended to be a man of the world was tormented by the unimportance of the disputes which added to the burdens on

[7] Winnington-Ingram was a charming and tireless friend and pastor, and a speaker able to fire East or West London audiences with the idea that Christianity was a glorious and delightful adventure. He succeeded Hensley Henson as Head of Oxford House in Bethnal Green in 1888. The love which he gave and received was such that no one was surprised when Temple invited him to be Bishop of Stepney in 1895, and his administrative slackness would not have mattered so much, had he not remained Bishop of London for so long (1901–1939). See S. C. Carpenter, *Winnington-Ingram* (Hodder & Stoughton, 1949).

his desk. 'It has been a permanent feature of the English people to show themselves incapable of theology', he lamented to his clergy. 'We have had contention enough, but we have contended not about ideas, but about external things. Englishmen cannot grasp an idea. . . .' But he allowed himself to be dragged down into these trivialities because he thought that he had incurred the obligation by agreeing to be an English bishop. He was the most patriotic of men, and called himself a 'fanatical' Anglican. 'I very much wish to have ecclesiastical matters raised above trivialities', he wrote, 'to a conception of the mind and intention of the English Church—the noblest exhibition of Christianity and therefore the most difficult to maintain'. In this context he would provocatively say, 'I am not ashamed to own that I am an English-man first and a Churchman afterwards', before explaining the epi-gram: 'Church and State are the nation looked at from different points of view.' He hoped that when he had disposed of the trivialities he would live to see the nobility. In February 1899 he recorded what he had done in less than two years. He had worked through, and re-vised, all the services used in more than two hundred churches. 'All services that went beyond the Prayer Book have practically ceased.' He concluded:

Speaking generally, I have found a reasonable readiness to obey except on these points—(1) carrying the Communion to sick persons, (2) the ceremonial use of incense, (3) the introduction of lights at the Gospel. Of these I have remitted (2) and (3) to the Archbishop, who will soon hear the pleadings and pronounce decision.

The Archbishop was, however, the very man whose policy (or lack of it) while Bishop of London had brought such anxieties to his successor. In knowledge of, or interest in, ecclesiastical history Frederick Temple was no true successor to Benson, and his verdict, when it came, was based simply on the Act of Uniformity then 340 years old. That Act had prohibited any ceremony not ordered in the Prayer Book. The Anglo-Catholic incense and processional lights had not been so ordered; therefore, they should cease. The next year Archbishop Temple delivered an equally simple verdict on the practice of 're-serving' the consecrated bread and wine for carrying to the sick (or, in some very High churches, for adoration). The Prayer Book was enough. 'The Church of England does not at present allow Reserva-tion in any form.'

Even the aged Temple, in delivering this judgment in 1900, recog-nized that it might be thought desirable to alter the law which he stated, although he took no steps in that direction. Creighton went further than this. To his historical imagination and broad sympathy, Anglicanism was a living thing. 'Progress can only be made when all that is good in the past is retained,' he wrote to a prominent High Churchman, adding: 'we do not want to subvert 1559, but to absorb it, and go beyond it.' In another letter to the same correspondent, he recalled a conversation with Hort in Cambridge.

I remember that I was once trying to find a title for a book about English Church history from 1534–1662. I was talking about it to Dr. Hort, who said, 'the true title would be *Experiments in Anglicanism;* but that would not do.' That is quite true, and the experiments are not yet finished. There was a lull from 1662 to 1832; now we are in the thick of a period of revision of them.

However, in the same letter he argued that Italianate ritualism in the Church of England was 'a systematic attempt to organize the Church beyond the limits of organization which Englishmen will endure'. And Creighton added: 'Englishmen are religious; they have consciences, which the Latin peoples have not in the same degree.'

For his own patriotic reasons, therefore, Creighton defended his Primate and attempted to enforce the decisions in the churches of London, remarking to one indignant High Churchman that 'the Catholic Church must go into the waste-paper basket'. However, his lack of zest was disclosed in another widely reported remark: 'If they want to make a smell, let them.' He vetoed two proposed prosecutions. In the feverish atmosphere he feared that some Anglo-Catholics would leave and wreck the Church of England, and thus ruin 'this ancient Christian land'; and it sickened his heart. But even this fear brought out the historian in him. He observed to his chaplain that the nineteenth century had been one of the greatest ages in all history, next to the thirteenth century and the Elizabethans. It had been the great philanthropic age, when everybody was eager to do good to others. But he added then that most people had made the mistake of wishing only to do good in their own particular way; and in a more flippant mood on a previous occasion he had declared that 'no people do so much harm as those who go about doing good'.

Amid such quips, a great weariness had settled on his inner life. Although he was not more than fifty-seven years of age, he told his wife that he had a horror of working on like Archbishop Temple, and an equal horror of retiring from work in exhaustion. When he suffered a severe haemorrhage on 8 January 1901, he 'did not seem as if he wished to live'. It was over within a week. He was buried in the crypt of St. Paul's, with Davidson representing the Queen at the funeral. The Anglo-Catholic ritualists mourned their bishop and carried on their practices. The next year Lord Rosebery said of the man who had thus allowed himself to be killed by trivialities: 'I think that the late Bishop of London was perhaps the most alert and universal intelligence that existed in this island at the time of his death'.

4

Creighton's ancestors had been Scots. Randall Davidson was of pure Scottish blood, his father being a timber merchant in Edinburgh. He was born in 1848, and baptized in the Church of Scotland, but was sent to Harrow for his education. There he was confirmed as an Anglican and brought under the influence of Westcott, his housemaster for part of his schooldays. ('We had a very learned sermon from Westcott this morning', he wrote home, 'which might possibly have been intelligible had one been thoroughly well up in the Ecclesiastical histories of Rome, Greece and Syria for the first 5 centuries A.D.') In 1866 he was more or less crippled by being shot in the back by accident, and this accident accounted in large part for the disappointment of his time at Oxford. 'A poor, rather feckless, but aspirant invalid undergraduate' was how he remembered himself later. Creighton was one of his tutors in history, but took no particular interest in him.

After collecting his Third at Oxford, Davidson spent the next three years trying to recover his health and to read some theology. He had intended to be ordained for some time, and he made an earnest and aspirant curate for three years in Dartford in Kent. Any trace of fecklessness had already gone; his nickname was 'the Dean'. Then early in 1877 he had his chance. He had known Craufurd Tait intimately at Oxford, and it was at Craufurd's suggestion that Archbishop Tait invited him to be his Resident Chaplain at Lambeth. 'I am now bound to see and do everything', he wrote to his father after a few weeks. 'I am certainly enjoying my life here hugely and making many friends.' Not many months later, he proposed to Edith Tait, aged nineteen, and was accepted. 'Now all is smooth, and utterly happy', he wrote to his own father. Randall and Edith Davidson had no children, but she was the perfect hostess in one ecclesiastical residence after another.

Such a son-in-law became indispensable when the weary old man was bereft of wife and son, but it was anyway Tait's practice to delegate as much as possible of his correspondence. So while in his thirties this chaplain had the experience of writing many letters which shaped Anglican history, and of conducting confidential negotiations with the bishops. He was recognized by honours such as a chaplaincy to the Queen. When the Archbishop himself died in 1882, Davidson sent the Queen an account of the deathbed which 'greatly touched' her. 'Would it suit you to come and see me on Saturday?' she asked. He came; he saw; she was conquered. Soon Davidson was interviewing Mrs. Browne, on the Queen's instructions, to discover whether Bishop

Browne was fit enough to succeed Tait; was deciding that he was not; and was recommending to Victoria names of possible bishops and deans. Next May he was Dean of Windsor, at the Queen's command.

In St. George's Chapel in Windsor Castle, he presided smoothly over the four canons, half of whom had been appointed before he was born, but his chief duties were in the Royal Household. Here the young Scot, who had been a curate six years before, succeeded the great Dean Wellesley as the Queen's intimate counsellor in all ecclesiastical and spiritual matters. In 1883 Victoria had just lost John Brown, the Highland servant who had to some extent been a substitute for Prince Albert, and many were the talks between the old queen and the young dean about life beyond the grave. 'She asked me', he wrote, 'whether there ever came over me (as over her) waves or *flashes* of doubtfulness whether, after all, it might be all untrue.'

Davidson was a tactful courtier, but early in 1884 the Queen proposed to publish another volume of her journal of her life in the Highlands. One volume of *Leaves from the Journal* had already appeared. Since all the other courtiers were afraid to anger her, it fell to Davidson to express the view that the first volume was enough.

Your Majesty will readily understand [he wrote] that such a spirit of ready response to the gracious confidences so frankly given, is not always to be found, and I should be deceiving Your Majesty were I not to admit that there are, especially among the humbler classes, some (perhaps it would be true to say *many*) who do not show themselves worthy of these confidences, and whose spirit, judging by their published periodicals, is one of such unappreciative criticism as I should not desire Your Majesty to see.

The Queen asked for a withdrawal and apology. The Dean refused, and offered his resignation instead. A fortnight of silence followed. Then Victoria sent for him on another matter and nothing more was heard of the proposed book. In a young man with Davidson's delight in the favour of the great, such honesty was very brave indeed; and when he returned to Lambeth as Archbishop, *The Times* justly commented that he had kept his feet in slippery places.

In addition to these duties in Windsor Castle, he was consulted almost daily by Archbishop Benson. The Benson family regarded Davidson as serpent-like in his wisdom, but the visionary archbishop frequently gained from the more worldly dean's advice about the personalities involved in church politics. In these same years, Davidson's grasp of the history of the Church of England was further strengthened by his work (helped by William Benham) on the *Life of Tait* which appeared in two volumes in 1891.

Queen Victoria and Archbishop Benson made private comments about his ambition, but they knew that such a man should be himself a bishop. Various sees were discussed, among them Durham and Winchester, but the Prime Minister of the day, Lord Salisbury, offered him a humbler choice, between Worcester and Rochester. Davidson chose the latter diocese, 'containing, as it does, all South London'. No historic palace was attached to the diocese of Rochester at that time, so he lived in the midst of his urban work, in Kennington Park Road. Bishop Ridding of Southwell wrote to him: 'Leaving your fatness, your sweetness, your good fruit and wine, to be promoted over such a forest—what a plunge from the comfortable to the un!'

Davidson does not seem to have enjoyed the exchange. Later he recalled his visits to the parishes of South London. 'Life in those parishes, and the almost insuperable obstacles to making it religiously bright and buoyant, weighed upon my thoughts by day and night.' To his despondent clergy he would quote Westcott's words: 'It is the office of the State to give effect to public opinion, it is the office of the Church to shape it.' But fair words were not enough. His stomach ulcer brought on him three other grave illnesses, and, knowing how much evening work was essential in South London, he had no hesitation in accepting the invitation to move to Winchester in 1895.

Life in Farnham Castle, the historic seat of the Bishops of Winchester, was more congenial than life in Kennington Park Road, but the new diocese, if properly worked, was itself no light task, as Samuel Wilberforce had found; it still included the present dioceses of Guildford and Portsmouth. Such routine labours, after the failure of his time in South London, told on the sick man, who at Windsor had been so sure and so eager. Prominent laymen when they had been in conversation with him usually united to praise his good sense, but once Sir Edward Grey happened to share a silent railway carriage with Sir Michael Sadler and the Bishop of Winchester. When Davidson had got out, Sir Edward asked Sir Michael: 'Who was that bishop with such a puzzled face?' Both in South London and in the country parishes of Hampshire and Surrey, Davidson seems to have sensed that the Victorian religious boom was over.[8]

Winchester diocese was (like Durham or Peterborough) largely exempt from London's liturgical extremes, but Davidson stirred up trouble for himself by issuing a detailed prohibition of Anglo-Catholic practices. Many of his clergy protested, and rather feebly he had to say that the notice which had been issued as *The Bishop of Winchester's Directions to Incumbents* was merely advice. In his first few months at Winchester his law-enforcing policy brought him into a dramatic collision with Father Dolling, an Anglo-Catholic priest (and Irishman) who was doing heroic and popular work as the Winchester

[8] For reflections about this by one who was Rector of Rugby and later Dean of Windsor, see A. V. Baillie, *My First Eighty Years* (John Murray, 1951), p. 149.

College Missioner to the slums of Portsmouth. The immediate point at issue was Dolling's habit of praying for the dead, as emotionally as he preached to the living. An altar was to be specially dedicated for this practice at Requiem Masses. Confronted by this altar, Davidson acted to uphold the law which appeared to forbid Requiem Masses. He was as benevolent as possible, but he did not speak the same language as the slum priest, who resigned in a blaze of publicity.

Any puzzlement on Davidson's face was not eased by the embarrassment of his position when Archbishop Benson died. Lord Salisbury brutally pointed out to the Queen that her favourite 'was not distinguished at the University (he only took a third class); he has had no important pastoral cure; he has not published any work of note except the biography of his father-in-law; his speaking and preaching, though good, are not of unusual merit; he is the youngest of all the Bishops on the English Bench.'[9] But the Queen wanted him to return to Lambeth Palace at once, and Frederick Temple—the Grand Old Man who was appointed by Lord Salisbury to serve for a few years as Archbishop, despite the Queen's complaints about his manners— believed that immediate promotion had been Davidson's wish also. In the event Davidson, who had been prominent in the central decisions for nearly twenty years, and who was the heir-apparent, found himself cold-shouldered by Temple. 'Mind you keep me in touch so far as you can with what goes on', he wrote to the Archbishop's chaplain, 'for to me it is the strangest of all the changes in my life to find myself out in the cold. . . .' Only his friendship with royalty now enabled him to see behind the public stage. Thus he was prominent when Queen Victoria died at Osborne (in his diocese), and he planned the next Coronation as the intermediary between the invalid king and the aged archbishop; during the ceremony in the Abbey, he was Frederick Temple's prompter and guide.

Embarrassment increased with the funeral of Father Dolling in an Anglo-Catholic church in London in 1902. One of the greatest crowds in the history of the East End then heard the new Bishop of London, arrayed in black cope and mitre for the Solemn Requiem Mass, eulogising the faithful priest who had walked so closely after Jesus Christ. 'When everybody else had given a man up, it was always said, "Dolling will take him".' So Winnington-Ingram declared; and Davidson seems to have felt deeply the stigma of being the bishop who had 'driven Father Dolling out'. Dolling was buried in Woking, next to the grave of Father Mackonochie who had featured as a rebel in the story of Tait.[10]

[9] *Letters of Queen Victoria*, third series, ed. G. E. Buckle, vol. iii. (John Murray, 1932), p. 99.
[10] See Charles Osborne, *The Life of Father Dolling* (Arnold, 1903).

At last, two days before Christmas 1902, Frederick Temple died. The casual Balfour was then Prime Minister. He simply wrote to Davidson: 'I mean to propose your name to H.M. for Canterbury. From conversations I have had with him, I have no doubt that he will agree. But, what next?' Davidson replied suitably to this 'momentous and most solemn intimation', and plunged with zest into the correspondence and discussions which Temple had neglected. He and his Edith were back where they belonged; and those near to him noted that it was not long before the weak health grew strong, and the puzzled face assumed a look of calm, wise dignity. Power suited Randall Davidson.

5

As Primate, he naturally reverted to Tait's habit of paying the closest possible attention to the politics and the politicians of the day. He had already made his mark on the House of Lords by arguing the case for curbs on the drink trade against a Conservative government which valued the support of the brewers; and when the Liberals, backed by open Nonconformist support, swept into power in 1906, he became very busy with all the negotiations which surrounded their vain attempts to pass an Act of Parliament curbing the church schools.[11] His course was not easy. Because the Nonconformists urged temperance, many in the Church of England wished to defend the liberties of public houses. Even stronger was the Anglican defence of church schools; Edmund Knox, the staunchly Evangelical Bishop of Manchester, led a great demonstration in London, and the House of Lords threw the government's Bill out.[12] Davidson suggested various compromises on education, only to be defeated by the ardour on both sides. Eventually the Conservatives' 1902 Act remained in force, although it proved less effective than had been hoped (or feared) in propping up the church schools. Most of these schools were nineteenth-century buildings, and many of them were in villages; but no public

[11] The Conservatives under Balfour in 1902 when creating the Education Committees of the county councils had authorized them to meet the running expenses, including teachers' salaries, of 'voluntary schools' which allowed them to appoint one third of their managers. Such subsidies were to be allowed even when these schools continued to give denominational instruction, and even when there was no alternative local authority school. About 8,000 areas, many of them in Wales, had a single school, controlled by the Church of England.

[12] Edmund Knox wrote *Reminiscences of an Octogenarian* (Hutchinson, 1935). He was the father of the brilliantly rebellious Ronald, who was a convert to Roman Catholicism in 1917, and glimpses of the home occur in Evelyn Waugh, *Ronald Knox* (Chapman & Hall, 1959).

money could be spent on their material improvement. It was all too reminiscent of John Keble. Although when the century began there were almost two and a half million children in the 'voluntary' schools, by 1938 the number had almost halved.

Davidson was a force in such debates, but it is clear, if not edifying, that he gained much of his prestige with the statesmen by refusing to join most of the agitations which attempted to bring moral pressure on them. Thus when asked to join a protest against the British share in the opium trade in China, the Archbishop replied: 'I have no wish personally to promote the continuance of a trade which is undoubtedly productive of much evil, though apparently, in the opinion of many wise observers, it is also productive of a great deal that is wholesome and good.' When asked to receive a deputation of unemployed men who had marched to Lambeth from Leicester, he refused: 'I should master those facts better were I to study them in writing'. He also refused to act as host to a demonstration from Manchester in defence of church schools: 'we could not have a camp at Lambeth'.

The absence of drama was itself what he sought. England under Edward VII possessed many assets, but these did not include a sense of proportion. The Protestant bitterness over incense and candles in church, and the Romanizing romanticism which defied the law, were only parts of an overheated atmosphere in the nation. Davidson, doing the safe, sensible, and boring thing, moderated passions over denominational influence in the schools (at a time when almost half England's children left school at the age of fourteen); over the opposition by the House of Lords to the popularly elected government; over the prospect of civil war in Ireland as Ulster, egged on by some Conservative politicians, reacted to the Liberal policy of Home Rule. His shrewdness helped the Church of England to appear as one of the country's respectable and reliable institutions. It was no mean feat at a time when the victorious Liberals, inspired by the Nonconformist conscience and electoral support, pressed on with the disestablishment of that Church's four dioceses in Wales. Amid great excitement the Lords rejected Welsh disestablishment, and the Government had to force it through over their heads, under the Parliament Act of 1911. In England the dream of a union of Church and State survived remarkably well; and the supply of clergy was one barometer. True, it declined from 814 new deacons in 1886 to 587 in 1907, but the Lambeth Conference of 1908 had little doubt that the main cause of the decline was financial, and proposed remedies. The bishops certainly did not foresee the figure of 420 new deacons sixty years later. In 1913 they decided that in seven years' time all ordinands in the Church of England must normally be graduates. Only a few small back doors into the priesthood were to be permitted, such as the house at Kelham where the Society of the Sacred Mission had begun training poor boys. The Church was to be staffed by educated gentlemen.

Such stability in England had its consequences in the world-wide Anglican Communion, which was in those days the spiritual equivalent of the British Empire (with some citizens of the former American colonies). Tait and Benson had sustained much correspondence between Lambeth and the Anglican globe, but Tait was an old-fashioned defender of the ecclesiastical as well as the secular rights of the English Crown in the colonies, while Benson's romantic idea of the status of Canterbury aroused American and other suspicions of a new Papacy. Davidson did not fall into either trap; instead, he was the first successor of St. Augustine to visit Canada and the United States, in 1904. He went as the guest of the financier, J. Pierpont Morgan. In London in the summer of 1908, he had his reward, when a Pan-Anglican Congress included clergy and laity with the bishops attending the Lambeth Conference. The congress resounded with oratory about the opportunities before Anglicanism, and impressed on the English mind the fact that the National Church had somehow become the mother of a multicoloured family. Nor was the Archbishop's blessing confined to the members of his own international denomination. He bravely agreed to address the World Missionary Conference at Edinburgh in 1910, the assembly which is usually reckoned the beginning of the modern ecumenical movement; and he did so in optimistic terms about the coming of the Kingdom of God.

Under Davidson, the teacups of the Church of England were still rattled by internal storms, but he made it his business to see that nothing much was spilt. A Royal Commission on Ecclesiastical Discipline was appointed in 1904 in order to study ways of breaking the deadlock caused by the Anglo-Catholic clergy's defiance of Archbishop Temple's interpretation of the liturgical law. Davidson submitted a masterly memorandum on the tedious history of the question, and did as much as the chairman, Lord St. Aldwyn, to secure the unanimous recommendation of the two main conclusions. 'First, the law of public worship in the Church of England is too narrow for the religious life of the present generation. It needlessly condemns much which a great section of Church people, including many of her most devoted members, value. . . . Secondly, the machinery for discipline has broken down.' The report recommended that Letters of Business should be issued by the Crown in order to enable the clergy in their Convocations, taking counsel with laymen, to begin the overdue revision of the Prayer Book; and that new ecclesiastical courts should be set up. Other proposals included the repeal of the Public Worship Regulation Act of 1874 and the reservation to the bishops of the right to decide appeals on doctrinal questions. And all the proposals were accepted by Parliament. Although nothing very much was done in the Church (indeed, the 'anarchy' grew worse), this report meant that there would never be another Mackonochie or Dolling case. Davidson had very few inflexible policies of his own, perhaps only one: to keep the Church of England together, despite the menace of an Anglo-Catholic exodus which had so deeply worried Creighton. While Davidson did not expect to see all the Anglo-Catholic demands granted, he accepted some concessions as inevitable.

A second triumph in ecclesiastical politics—if 'triumph' can mean the reduction of tension—now came to Davidson. An Oxford clerical don, J. M. Thompson, published a book denying the historicity of some of the miracles of the New Testament, and drew on himself the censure of the Bishop of Winchester (Edward Talbot, who was Visitor of Magdalen College where Thompson was Dean of Divinity) and the Bishop of Oxford (Charles Gore, the Anglo-Catholic leader). A doctrinal crisis broke out, for the Anglo-Catholics, so recently under attack for their ceremonies, leapt to the defence of the creeds against the Modernists; and one evening at Lambeth in February 1914 Davidson had to cool Gore down by threatening to resign. As he noted at the time: 'I had some grave talk with Gore about Church affairs. I spoke of the possibility that I am myself growing to be out of touch with the strongest advances in the Church. . . . And I said that I should not remain at the helm if I found myself trying to steer a course clearly contrary to the best Church of England feeling and spirit.' Next morning Gore told Davidson: 'I am profoundly convinced, with a certainty that is unshakeable, that the very greatest disaster that could at this time befall the Church would be the loss of you from Lambeth.'

Davidson therefore got his way. The bishops had been asked by Gore to denounce disbelief in the virgin birth or physical resurrection of Jesus as being incompatible with a sincere acceptance of the obligations of a clergyman of the Church of England; but Davidson feared that such a declaration, if made without any qualification, would render the position of 'quite a large group of our best and most thoughtful clergy' untenable. He remembered what Frederick Temple had written to his own master Tait: 'If the conclusions are prescribed, the study is precluded.' Although he never confessed to any personal difficulty in accepting miracles, he did not wish to drive any Temple of the twentieth century out of the Church of England, any more than he wished to drive out Charles Gore. The resolutions as passed by the bishops in April 1914 therefore endorsed Gore's insistence that 'the denial of any of the historical facts stated in the Creeds goes beyond the limits of legitimate interpretation'; but they also stressed 'the need of considerateness in dealing with what is tentative and provisional in the thought and work of earnest and reverent students'—a very Davidsonian touch. The outcome satisfied the Archbishop. A secularized Thompson went on to become a history don, the author of standard works on the French Revolution; but almost all the other Modernists remained earnestly and reverently in the Church of England. And Davidson remained at the helm.[13]

A third crisis in the small world of Anglicanism arose in 1913 when a conference of missionaries under the chairmanship of the mildly Evangelical John Willis, Bishop of Uganda, studied a proposal for a federation of the missionary churches in East Africa and together received Holy Communion from the bishop's hands. A neighbouring bishop, the Anglo-Catholic firebrand Frank Weston, promptly exploded and fired off the following indictment to Davidson: 'We, Frank, by Divine Permission Lord Bishop of Zanzibar and East Africa, do by these presents accuse and charge . . . the Right Reverend Father in God John Jameson, Lord Bishop of Uganda, with the grievous faults of propagating heresy and promoting schism.' Weston demanded that 'You and not less than twelve of Your Grace's comprovincial Bishops' should act as judges. Both Weston and the accused Willis returned to England to see Davidson, who refused to get excited and referred the whole matter to other Anglican bishops overseas, including a Consultative Body which had been set up by the Lambeth Conference. Scholars were also set to work to establish the Anglican attitudes to episcopacy, thought by Weston to be seriously in danger although to him the bishop was the 'Christ-given centre of union.[14]

In the end, Davidson pronounced. He virtually declared that the proposal for a missionary federation had been admirable in its intentions but deficient in its theological care, and that the joint Communion had been admirable in its motives but should not be repeated. Neither side was now entirely happy, yet neither side was excessively angry. And since the date was now Easter 1915, most men found it difficult to remember why either side had been so excited.

[13] See J. M. Thompson, *My Apologia* (Alden Press, Oxford, 1940). The kind of theologian that Davidson trusted is portrayed in G. H. Harris, *Vernon Faithfull Storr* (SPCK, 1943). Canon Storr was the spiritual leader of the Liberal Evangelicals.

[14] See, for example, A. J. Mason, *The Church of England and Episcopacy* (Cambridge University Press, 1914). But *Episcopal Confirmation and Ordination*, ed. J. W. Hunkin (Cambridge University Press, 1929), was a collection of documents designed to contradict Mason's High Church thesis. What remains is Weston's example of pastoral courage and perseverance in Africa: see the biography of *Frank, Bishop of Zanzibar*, by H. Maynard Smith (SPCK, 1926).

6

Like most members of the English ruling class, Davidson had no idea that the world war was coming; but when it came, like them he behaved well. As a patriot he refused to get entangled in Archbishop Söderblom's efforts in Uppsala to use Sweden as a meeting-ground between the two camps. On the other hand, with an independence which aroused some surprise, he also refused to put his authority behind the war effort as many of the politicians and most of the public conceived it. His biographer—George Bell, who was to make a more public, and therefore even more unpopular, stand during the second world war—has recorded in detail how Davidson refused to encourage hate of the Hun; how he pleaded against lying propaganda, the use of poison gas, and reprisals against German civilians; and how he forbade the clergy to enlist as combatants. When in 1915 he was urged to lead a National Mission, he threw aside his caution and did give a lead to this ambitious enterprise, which was sub-titled 'of Repentance and Hope'. To some, the whole conception seemed too grandiose; to others, it was too sober a contribution to the glorious fight. Davidson was convinced that England must fight, but fight with clean hands. This gave him a great theme at a great hour. The Vicar of Ramsgate wrote to Mrs. Benson, describing the scene in Canterbury Cathedral when the Archbishop addressed his clergy. 'The first impression one got of *him*—and it remained strong to the end—was Power: he seemed to have regained completely mental and physical strength, and sureness of grip. He was quite certain of his message. . . . It was all very deliberate, very simple, very grave.'

Here, then, was Creighton's 'ancient Christian land' being tested as it had not been through the long peace of the nineteenth century. In the trenches the Church could not avoid meeting the consequences of its failure to baptize the English industrial revolution; nor could it escape acknowledging that the Victorian religious revival had insufficient strength to meet the shock of one of the great agonies in world history. The clergy who volunteered as chaplains to the Forces experienced, as they had not done amid the routine of their parishes, the alienation of Englishmen from the Church. They found that 'the padre' was an isolated, useless figure in that world of khaki, mud, the shadow of death, and pathetically endless talk about sex, unless they commended their Gospel by lives of exceptional appeal.

They had to do it in bitter places. In 1903 Mandell Creighton's son Oswin, then an undergraduate, had heard Bishop Gore preach in Oxford. He had then written home: 'He preached an admirable sermon on religious doubts and difficulties, but did not seem to make it very clear how to get over them. It is strange how nearly half the people I meet here have doubts, or say they have, and I am not conscious of ever having had any myself.' Now Oswin Creighton became a much loved padre and was killed in April 1918, but not before he had written:

The Church . . . has degenerated either into emotional ritual, or hymn-singing, or secluded and entrenched piety. . . . It neither understands the world nor touches it at any point. . . . The war reveals that the Englishman is the best hearted, most enduring, and most ignorant and least original man in the world. The work of the Church is to help him build up what he has not got on the basis of what he has.[15]

Other priests such as 'Tubby' Clayton, whose hostel for troops at Poperinghe was the first base of the Toc H movement, had a vision of the Church as a brotherhood holding the secret of a world at peace.[16] Within this brotherhood, class distinctions must go. The bishops must no longer lord it over the clergy; the clergy must no longer lord it over the laity. The priest was still someone special, but as a representative of the suffering Christ, as a spiritual leader. The new aspirations of social reform must be welcomed by the Church, because they could build a new age, the age of democracy. The new knowledge of science must be joined to the Church's belief, for it was God's new revelation. Almost incidentally, the padres added that the division of the Church of England into ecclesiastical parties must be ended. They virtually mutinied against control by a stoutly Evangelical ex-missionary bishop, Taylor-Smith, who was Chaplain-General from 1901 to 1925; and a much broader-minded Evangelical, Bishop Llewellyn Gwynne, had to be summoned from Khartoum to be their pastor as Deputy Chaplain-General in France.[17]

But the problems which all this wartime stirring raised seemed far from simple to the leadership of the Church of England. For example, Davidson had to cope with a fresh doctrinal crisis brought about by the nomination of Hensley Henson to be Bishop of Hereford in 1917. Henson was a firm Conservative in politics, but Lloyd George believed that his theological liberalism ought to be rewarded. There was an outcry from those who thought Henson too liberal. The story belongs to our study of Henson; here we can only note that Davidson's shrewdness in the affair may be contrasted with Samuel Wilberforce's

---

[15] *Letters of Oswin Creighton, C.F.*, ed. Louise Creighton (Longmans, Green, 1920), pp. 2, 232–3.
[16] See Melville Harcourt, *Tubby Clayton* (Hodder & Stoughton, 1953).
[17] See E. L. Langston, *Bishop Taylor-Smith* (Marshall, Morgan & Scott, 1939). H. C. Jackson has written a biography of Gwynne, *Pastor on the Nile* (SPCK, 1960). F. B. Macnutt edited a fascinating book of essays by army chaplains, *The Church in the Furnace* (Macmillan, 1917).

blunders when another 'heretic' had been nominated Bishop of Hereford. First the Archbishop tried to get the Prime Minister to withdraw the nomination; an industrial see would be better. Next he tried to get Henson to refuse to go to such a 'little country place'. He then tried to get Henson to declare his theological orthodoxy, only to be met by a refusal like Hampden's to Wilberforce. But ultimately Henson yielded, because he feared that the Archbishop actually would resign, rather than agree to consecrating a heretic as a bishop. As an epilogue to the story, Davidson had to persuade Henson to devote himself to quiet work in his diocese until the storm had blown over. Looking back over all this, Davidson used to refer to the 'Hereford scandal' (as others called it) as the most anxious crisis in his whole time at Lambeth.

We may note also that it was Davidson who took the responsibility for ordaining Frederick Temple's son William, who was suspected of heresy. But Davidson's defect was that he was no theologian. 'The essence of kindness and sanity—without a glimmer of inspiration' was how William Temple described him to his mother in 1908. In all the basic questions which agitated sincere minds about the truth of Christianity, his policy was to preserve both the unity of the Church of England and the liberty of the 'earnest and reverent' scholars who might (he hoped) in due course, after their mysterious researches, reach conclusions which would support his own 'very simple, very grave' piety—and the piety of the English layman. He had himself little idea about how a constructive theology might emerge. Essentially his was the same attitude as his father-in-law's, with the additional emotional fact that, while Tait had been Tutor of Balliol, to the end of his life Davidson smarted under the memory of his failure at Oxford; his suspicion of dons came out in his assessment of Creighton.

Despite his theological limitations Davidson eventually agreed with the argument of Dr. Howard Burge, then Bishop of Oxford, and with Will Spens the lay theologian at Cambridge that an Archbishops' Commission on Doctrine should be appointed with the following Reference: 'To consider the nature and grounds of Christian Doctrine with a view to demonstrating the extent of existing agreement within the Church of England and with a view to investigating how far it is possible to remove or diminish existing differences.' This was at the turn of 1922–3, and Davidson would probably not have consented to a policy which he believed to be fraught with the danger of further controversies, had not the Modern Churchmen's Union then seemed at the height of its promise (or threat).[18]

[18] When Henry Major delivered lectures on *English Modernism* at Harvard in 1925, he was full of confidence that his simplified Christianity would appeal to enlightened people wishing to reconcile religion and science. His lectures were published by Harvard University Press (1927). In the same year Percy

J. B. Lightfoot by W. Richmond

F. J. A. Hort by J. Hood

B. F. Westcott by W. E. Miller

A. P. Stanley by H. N. Ring

Mandell Creighton   Randall Davidson

E. W. Benson   Charles Gore

The Union had sponsored a particularly controversial conference on 'Christ and the Creeds' at Girton College, Cambridge, in 1921. The conference had thrown Gore and others deep into renewed anxieties lest the fundamental Christian beliefs were being betrayed by Anglican clergymen; Henson had himself been shocked. Davidson had at last seen that the time had come for the 'earnest and reverent' to confer on a rational basis and under official auspices. Burge and Temple were to be the two bishops on it. The Archbishop did, however, take care to discourage the plan that this commission might issue an authoritative statement. He had no wish to bequeath to his successors new problems about the judicious interpretation of official documents after troublesome quarrels between intellectuals and fanatics. What he could not foresee was that by the time that this commission reported, in 1938, men would have lost interest in theological controversies, and even in an honestly truthful theological reconstruction, because the clouds of another world war held their frightened eyes.

The appointment of a commission did not itself provide the profoundly and thrillingly Christian vision of God which the padres had hoped for in the trenches, but forty years after Hort's warning to Benson it was a move by the Church of England to counteract its alienation from Englishmen and from facts. Davidson also presided over the creation of the National Assembly of the Church of England, which was not quite the thoroughly Christian rebirth of fellowship for which the enthusiastic prayed and campaigned, but which was something.

The advisory Houses of Laymen, starting in 1886, had been on a provincial (Canterbury and York) not national basis; and although the Representative Church Council, over whose birth Davidson had presided during the first year of his Primacy, had combined the clergy and laity of Canterbury and York, it had never been given legal powers. Davidson had shown little impatience to alter that situation; he was too much the heir of Tait and the *protégé* of Queen Victoria to be a democrat. But the campaign against the disestablishment of the Church of England's dioceses in Wales led to increased demands that the relationship of Church and State in England should be made more defensible by giving a clear legal status to the clergy and laity elected by the English dioceses, and by clearly assigning to them the chief responsibility for the Church's spiritual life. The Representative Church Council had resolved in 1913 'that there is in principle no inconsistency between a national recognition of religion and the

---

Dearmer and Vaughan Williams published *Songs of Praise*, a new hymnal very different from their Anglo-Catholic *English Hymnal;* it put Major's creed to music. Dr. Alan M. G. Stephenson has in preparation a study of Major and modernism.

spiritual independence of the Church'. An Archbishops' Committee on Church and State had been appointed under Lord Selborne, and had unanimously reported in 1916 that the Representative Church Council should be given legislative powers, subject to the possibility of a Parliamentary veto.

When the ardent young William Temple led the 'Life and Liberty' campaign for the enactment of this committee's recommendation, the Archbishop was as usual cautious. He had a special reason for caution: he regarded it as an unwise attempt to distract the attention of the Church from the graver questions of 1917. He was, however, gradually persuaded that the solid opinion of the Church which he loved was in favour of doing something about the matter, sooner rather than later; and that the Parliament which he also served was not against it. Eventually he got the proposal through with a characteristic argument. He did not appeal to a new vision of Christian brotherhood. Instead, he quietly explained that the pressure on the time of Parliament had become so great that it was difficult to secure attention for the legislation necessary to the smooth running of the Church. He made it sound a technical matter, on which all sensible experts were already agreed; and the Church Assembly was born with little opposition, except from a minority which feared the consequences of the lessening of Parliament's control over the National Church.

There were, in fact, only two major obstacles to be surmounted before Parliament passed an Enabling Act to recognize the powers of the Church Assembly (in the same summer of 1919 in which the final arrangements were made for the disestablishment of Anglicanism in Wales). The first dispute was the occasion of Gore's resignation as Bishop of Oxford. Gore insisted that the laity who sent representatives to the Diocesan Conferences (which were to elect the laymen sitting in the new Church Assembly) must be communicants. Davidson and the overwhelming majority insisted that it was enough for them to have been baptized, if they were resident in the parish or worshipped regularly in its church. This dispute over the composition of the parish churches' Electoral Rolls was an ominous indication that two ideals were still clashing in the Church of England: the ideal of the Church as the Body of Christ fed by Holy Communion, and the ideal of the Church as the Christian nation.

The other dispute concerned the nature of the Parliamentary veto over the 'Measures' to be passed by the new Church Assembly. It was at first proposed that the two Houses of Parliament should appoint an Ecclesiastical Committee which would advise the Crown to give its assent to a Church Assembly Measure 'unless within forty days either House of Parliament shall direct to the contrary'. In answer to an objection by the Lord Chancellor, the Archbishop quickly agreed that after advice by the Ecclesiastical Committee a definite 'Address' to the Crown from each House of Parliament should be necessary before a 'Measure' received the Royal Assent. This concession, which seemed harmless enough at the time to an archbishop confident that Parliament was on his side, made more likely the prospect which he had always striven to avert: the prospect of the House of Commons joining a controversy about legislative proposals which reflected the conflict of ideals in the Church of England.

7

Thus were sown the seeds of the Church of England's humiliation in 1927–8. Davidson would have been wiser had he resigned in 1923, the twentieth year of his Primacy and the seventy-fifth of his life. He was then at the peak of his prestige. He had appointed the Doctrine Commission to work towards a theological reconciliation. The Church Assembly, sitting regularly from 1920 onwards, had begun to tackle administrative problems such as the reform of patronage in the parishes. The Lambeth Conference of bishops in 1920 had issued an epoch-making 'appeal to all Christian people' for unity, and Lambeth Palace had been the scene of earnest, if abortive, conversations about reunion between Anglicans and Free Churchmen, in striking contrast with their bitter quarrels over education before the war. Other conversations were going on with Roman Catholics, at Malines in Belgium under the wartime hero Cardinal Mercier. The conversations had no official status. Davidson was too canny to be unaware of the continuing force of No Popery. Even if he had been slow at this point, eager Protestants such as Henson had warned him loudly enough. On his side, Cardinal Bourne of Westminster had no intention of seeking any recognition of the Anglican heretics. But these Malines conversations looked forward to a day when some fellowship and even union might be renewed between separated Christians without any sacrifice of conscience, and Davidson had been wise not to impose a veto.[19]

All over the world Anglicans and others now looked to Lambeth Palace for prudent counsel, and Cosmo Lang, Archbishop of York, was waiting to provide such counsel himself, as Davidson had waited

[19] Even had he wished to do so, he would have been checked by his healthy respect for the leading instigator, the Anglo-Catholic aristocrat Lord Halifax, a wily and inflexible saint. J. G. Lockhart's biography of *Viscount Halifax*, 2 vols. (Geoffrey Bles, 1935), shows the strength of the Anglo-Catholic movement under such lay leadership, the nearest twentieth-century equivalent to the great Lord Shaftesbury. But it also shows why this Lord Halifax's son, the Foreign Secretary who was also a devout Anglo-Catholic, was not well trained to understand Adolf Hitler.

during the Primacy of the aged Frederick Temple. But no Archbishop of Canterbury had ever resigned, not even George Abbot who accidentally killed a man while hunting in 1621; and Davidson in 1923 was flattered by all those whose voices he heard. He stayed on.

Disaster did not strike when it might have been expected. The Church of England was largely out of touch with the working class, and many anachronisms lingered in its own system. Davidson, for example, had only vague sympathies with Labour, and all that the man in the street knew about him was that his income was £15,000 a year. Another well-known 'fact' about the Church of England was that the Ecclesiastical Commissioners 'owned' brothels in Paddington. In reality the Archbishop of Canterbury had to meet almost all his official expenses out of his income, while the Commissioners had no control over the use of the houses leased from them in Paddington. But the man in the street was shrewd in his suspicions. Like their predecessors, the Davidsons kept a large domestic staff at Lambeth; and like other landlords, the Commissioners had taken inadequate precautions against the abuse of leases.

However, Archbishop Davidson was wise enough to see that the Church of England should not identify itself with the employers. During the General Strike of 1926, in agreement with other Christian leaders, he issued an appeal for reconciliation. Sir John Reith at the B.B.C. refused to broadcast it, and Winston Churchill refused to print it in the Government newspaper, the *British Gazette*, because it included proposals that the Government should subsidize the depressed coal industry and that the mine owners should cancel the lowering of wages. Davidson surprised everyone, including it would seem himself, by this readiness to lend some support to the pro-Labour sentiments of colleagues such as William Temple; so much so that he found himself privately dreading a battle of 'the Church plus the Miners on the one side and the Government on the other side'. In such a battle, as he wrote to the Bishop of Lichfield, 'I should find it difficult to say where my allegiance lay'. From him, it was a warm tribute to Socialism.

So, in the 1920s the Church of England scraped through a social crisis, rather more successfully than the Conservative Party with which it had often been identified in the 1900s. Nor did disaster come immediately because of a lack of radical reform within the Church. It is true that the continuing decline in the parishes caused some ineffective worry. R. H. Malden, the Editor of *Crockford's Clerical Directory*, wrote in one of his famous Prefaces, in 1927:

If the history of the last ten years is continued for another ten the effective maintenance of the parochial system will have become impossible in all but a few favoured localities. Anything which may fairly be called the Church of

England will have ceased to exist and its place will have been taken by the sporadic activities of a denomination.[20]

But Malden's diagnosis was based on the statistics that 550 parish priests were dying or retiring each year and only 350 being recruited; and immediately it had been made, there was an upward swing in the figures. On the whole, the Church under Davidson was not aware of the depth of its crisis; it could still point to parsons and parishes obviously successful.[21]

Opposition delayed into the 1930s obvious reforms such as the stopping of the sale of advowsons (the transfer of a parish from one patron to another for money) and the creation of Diocesan Patronage Boards. Three committees (in 1902, 1924, and 1933) reported that, as a first step towards financial rationalization, the Ecclesiastical Commissioners created in the 1830s should be merged with the body known as Queen Anne's Bounty, dating from 1704, for the work of the two offices for the parishes overlapped in the most confusing way; yet nothing was done. One problem was that there were too few bishops to give adequate leadership. A Church Assembly Commission in 1922 reported that fifteen dioceses needed dividing. In the end only four were split, with the creation of the new dioceses of Leicester, Blackburn, Derby, Portsmouth, and Guildford. If more bishops had been made, it would have been expensive: in 1921 bishops were averaging £4,000 a year plus palace, no less than ten times the average for the incomes of parochial incumbents. However, Davidson and most of the leadership of the Church were content to carry on as if no radical innovation was needed, and the price of this delay was not fully exacted until the 1940s.

Disaster came, instead, in the very sphere where Davidson, like Tait, took pride in being expert: the handling of the Parliamentary business of the Church.

The process of liturgical revision led, after immense discussions, to the final draft of a Revised Prayer Book in 1927. This was supported by all but four of the forty-three diocesan bishops and by almost all the Diocesan Conferences; it was adopted by the Church Assembly; it

[20] Malden, an Etonian who became Dean of Wells, expressed his observations and prejudices with a pungent pen. See his (anonymous) *Crockford Prefaces: The Editor Looks Back* (Oxford University Press, 1947).

[21] *Well Remembered*, the autobiography of Claude Blagden who was later Bishop of Peterborough, happily describes his work as Rector of Rugby, 1912–27 (Hodder & Stoughton, 1953). Oliver Tomkins, *The Life of Edward Woods* (SCM Press, 1957), describes the ministry of a liberal Evangelical who was an immensely popular pastor in Cambridge and Croydon, and later Bishop of Lichfield. For the ecclesiastical decline of Rugby since Blagden's day, see Roger Lloyd, *The Church of England in the Twentieth Century* (SCM Press, 1966), pp. 525–7.

was approved by the House of Lords. Then, on the night of 15 December, the 'Measure' from the Church Assembly was vetoed by the House of Commons, by 238 votes to 205, although a majority of English M.P.s voted in favour and all Roman Catholics abstained. In a sense, the defeat in the Commons was not the Archbishop's fault, for the House was swayed by the No Popery eloquence echoing a vanished age and by the feebleness of the M.P.s who tried to explain why the proposed Prayer Book, although it recognized many Anglo-Catholic practices, was not a capitulation to Rome. But Davidson by now possessed such a hold on the Church of England that the adoption of a policy which led to such a defeat did indicate a slackening of his grip on diplomacy and power; and the fatal mistakes which were made by the Church of England under him did show the gaps in the equipment which he had gained from Tait's Lambeth and Victoria's Windsor.

The first mistake was to concentrate on pleasing the Anglo-Catholic experts who wanted the liturgy enriched, instead of attempting to please the people by a radical simplification of worship, of the kind which the padres at the war had begun to desire. Placating liturgiologists was in itself a tricky business; two of the leading experts, the very learned Darwell Stone at Oxford and the very elegant Eric Milner-White at Cambridge, made no secret of their contempt for the half-baked proposals which emerged. And in the event, the liturgical fashions which seemed so desirable in the 1920s declined fairly rapidly, because the most pastorally minded of the Anglo-Catholics themselves saw the need to make worship more corporate and more contemporary. As things turned out, it would have been wiser to heed those who wanted a collection of far simpler services, as an optional alternative to the 1662 book; such a modernization would have aroused controversy, but unlike the controversial proposals which were put forward in 1927–8 it might have caught the imagination of laymen. However, Randall Davidson was not really at home in these questions. He left the advanced liturgiology to the Bishop of Truro, Walter Frere of the Community of the Resurrection, the first monk to become an Anglican bishop; and he smiled at Frere's enthusiasm, as Tait had smiled when Benson came up from Truro. He also left the popular appeal to rather alarming progressives such as William Temple; for the 1662 Book fed his devotional life satisfactorily. Davidson, who had no personal experience of responsibility for popular worship, believed that what was needed was the enrichment of 1662 in response to pressure, in order to get a new Prayer Book which could be enforced.[22]

[22] See F. L. Cross, *Darwell Stone* (Dacre Press, 1943); Philip Pare and Donald Harris, *Eric Milner-White* (SPCK, 1965); and *Walter Howard Frere*, ed. C. S. Phillips (Faber & Faber, 1947).

The second mistake was a failure to try out the proposals in an experimental period in the parishes. When the Church of England took up revision again in the 1960s this seemed the obvious way, but in the 1920s the Church burned its fingers because it proposed that the Revised Prayer Book should be enforced before it had been tested. Very few people in the 1920s suggested anything else, and the Archbishop was not among them. This mistake was part of the whole authoritarian approach of the period in which Davidson's mind had been formed. It was taken for granted that changes in the Church were discussed among bishops and scholars, among the weightier clergy, and even among the unusual laymen who sat in the Church Assembly. A compromise was hammered out in the course of these debates, and it was the function of the Diocesan Conferences to approve the outcome. Once the changes—or the refusal of any change—had been agreed among the people at the top, it would be imposed on the whole Church, if necessary by legal sanctions. No really creative role was allowed to the congregations, although the Parochial Church Councils had been set up at the same time as the Church Assembly; and the priest in the parish was usually the target of suspicion from his betters who feared that he might be 'eccentric' or 'extreme'. Worship could not spring out of the local situation; it must be regulated, if not by an Act of Parliament, then by a Measure of the Church Assembly. This account of the motives of the framers of the Prayer Book of 1927 is, of course, oversimplified; not one of them would have used exactly these words. But as a sketch of an attitude, it has the substance of the sad truth about the leadership of the Church of England under Davidson. When Protestant fanatics in the House of Commons claimed to speak for the silent laymen of the Church of England, the Archbishop could not argue that these laymen had already spoken for themselves.

The third mistake was a failure to acknowledge that there could be a clash between Church and State. So many crises had been averted by diplomacy since Tait had gone to Lambeth in 1868, and Davidson had been so conspicuously successful in smothering controversies, that the Church of England in the 1920s walked into the trap. As Henson, who had owed so much to Davidson's diplomacy in 1917, wrote in his journal after the crisis of 1927: 'It was one of those occasions on which his opportunism failed. The lifelong habit of "getting round" difficulties, instead of facing them, hardly prepares a man for the handling of a crisis. And the Church is now confronted by a crisis, the gravity of which can hardly be exaggerated.' Even when the trap had sprung on that December night in the House of Commons, the Church of England came back in 1928 for further punishment. Minor modifications were made in the Church Assembly's proposals, particularly in the regulations about 'Reservation'; and back they came for another defeat in the House of Commons in 1928. The modifications would probably have been effective had they appeased Protestant prejudices by leaving the Holy Communion service substantially unaltered, and by making no formal provision for the 'Reservation' of the consecrated bread and wine after the service. Archbishop Lang, who came from an Anglo-Catholic background, was in favour of such a concession to the Protestant M.P.s. But Davidson was convinced that the House of Commons did not really expect the Church to make a concession of this nature, which would have left the Church still confused over what was or was not its law about Holy Communion.

What was to be done now? The bishops agreed to a statement.

It is a fundamental principle that the Church—that is, the Bishops together with the Clergy and Laity—must in the last resort, when its mind has been fully ascertained, retain its inalienable right, in loyalty to our Lord and Saviour Jesus Christ, to formulate its Faith in Him and to arrange the expression of that Holy Faith in its forms of worship.

A mildly defiant act was undertaken: the 1928 Prayer Book was printed for use in churches, with a notice in each copy which reminded its users that it was not authorized for use. But Davidson still refused to agree that a divorce was desirable between Church and State. In his last speech to the Church Assembly, he pointed out that many of the M.P.s who had voted against the revision had 'believed, however mistakenly, that they were voicing the real underlying wish of a majority of Church folk in England'; and he declared his hope that the House of Commons would return to its reasonable spirit when it could be shown that the Church of England was united. He resigned the Archbishopric of Canterbury, becoming Lord Davidson of Lambeth, not because of this Parliamentary catastrophe, but because he wanted Lang to preside over the Lambeth Conference of 1930. His chief worry seems to have been a fear of boredom, now that his daily mail would be drastically reduced after so many years at Lambeth.

Henson in his journal sardonically noted the contrast between the tributes, verbal and financial, which now flowed to the aged Davidson and the lack of sentiment with which the House of Commons had thrown out the two Prayer Books. But Davidson himself seems to have felt nothing very strange in this, and did not intend his soul to be troubled because Anglo-Catholicism was not clearly legalized. The real issues for him did not lie in the sanctuary, and the Church of England which he knew in his bones was not very much disturbed by the Prayer Book crisis. He had been ordained knowing little about such matters, and the fact that the completion of liturgical revision had been delayed for twenty years after the recommendation of it (by the

St. Aldwyn Commission at the beginning of Davidson's Primacy) itself says something about his sense of priorities. A positive conviction, as well as his caution, determined his attitude; it was not merely that he had grown used (as one critic said) to 'sitting on the fence with both ears to the ground'. Before, during, and after the horrors of 1914-18, he shared the belief of his fellow-Victorians that the preservation of the Christian character of the nation was what mattered. He also shared the belief of his master, Tait, and of the other Rugbeians in Thomas Arnold's tradition, that the legal establishment of the Church of England as the comprehensive 'Church of the English people' would do more for the Christian character than any enriched church services could do. Davidson was no intellectual, but we should remember that this was also Creighton's basic attitude. He was no mystic, but he could invoke the spiritually impressive name of Westcott.

He presented the Church which he knew, and for which he was prepared to fight, in his charge to the diocese of Canterbury in 1912. His addresses on that occasion were printed as *The Character and Call of the Church of England*, and under such a title are open to criticism.[23] But in these addresses Davidson quoted from his old schoolmaster, Westcott, words which summed up his own belief that nothing vital was at stake in either the liturgical or the scholarly controversies of the day.

The English Reformation corresponds with the English character which is disinclined to seek the completeness of a theological system. It looks to finding truth through life other than through logic, for truth is not of the intellect only. It is patient of hesitation, indefiniteness, even of superficial inconsistency, if only the root of the matter can be held firmly for the guidance of conduct; for spiritual subjects are too vast to furnish clear-cut premises from which exhaustive conclusions can be drawn.

He applied these words to the proposals to disestablish Anglicanism in Wales. He resisted such proposals (as did Creighton), but he calmly, if unconvincingly, explained that the demand by the Liberal Party was due to 'lack of adequate knowledge'. He added: 'Never let anyone imagine that we regard the proposals as threatening the actual life of the Church.'

'Truth through life . . . held firmly for the guidance of conduct.' There, in Westcott's phrase as invoked by the Archbishop in Canterbury Cathedral, was the formula which most explained the Church of England which he led; and there, in Randall Davidson, was one exception to Lord Acton's rule that great men are almost always bad men.

23 'Here, one would have thought, would have been an opportunity for a little Christian teaching', one ecclesiastical historian who became Bishop of Ripon has written. J. R. H. Moorman, discussing 'Archbishop Davidson and the Church' in *Theology* (July, 1956), p. 275.

FOR FURTHER READING

His widow Louise edited *Life and Letters of Mandell Creighton, D.D. Oxon. and Cam., sometime Bishop of London*, in two volumes (Longmans, Green, 1904). W. G. Fallows, Bishop of Pontefract, supplied an assessment and some fresh details in *Mandell Creighton and the English Church* (Oxford University Press, 1964).

G. K. A. Bell, his former chaplain, wrote the life of *Randall Davidson, Archbishop of Canterbury*, with outstanding skill in two volumes (Oxford University Press, 1935), and added a reflective Preface to the 1952 edition. There was also a memoir of *Edith Davidson of Lambeth* by 'M.C.S.M.', in fact Mary Mills (John Murray, 1938).

9

1853-1932   1863-1947.

Gore and Henson

1

If the comprehensiveness which Davidson had inherited through Tait from Thomas Arnold was not to be the basis of the Anglican fellowship—at least, not in the form in which Davidson, Tait, or Arnold stated it—what, then, was to be the basis? In the first year of the twentieth century, two men with opposed interpretations of Anglicanism served together in Westminster Abbey as canons: Charles Gore and Herbert Hensley Henson. Gore was High, and Henson was Broad. It was the contrast between Wilberforce and Tait forty years or so before, but with a new tension.

Henson himself connected the tension with the contrasts in their formation, socially and emotionally. Gore was a Christian Socialist; 'the Socialist Party at Mass' was Henry Major's summary of his influence. Henson, who was a Protestant Conservative, wrote:

Gore's sympathy with the suffering and oppressed was deep and generous, but he ever felt more keenly for classes and descriptions of men than for individuals, and he seemed to me inadequately sensitive to the personal rights of those from whom, whether on religious or on economic grounds, he differed. His natural ardour of temperament led him to express his opinions with an enthusiasm and vigour which did undoubtedly commend them to public acceptance, but were not always sufficiently regardful of public law and private right. By birth and breeding Gore was an aristocrat, and took an aristocrat's view of legal obligations and personal rights. I was from the middle class, in which these things have been most highly esteemed, and by which they have been most valorously championed.

But here, for once, Henson was lacking in candour. He was far from being a typical member of the comfortable middle class. His own experience of humiliating poverty and introspective despair had led him in the days of his success to fight so 'valorously' for the right of the individual against Church or State.

Gore, who expressed alarm at Henson's appointment to Westminster, regarded him as another Stanley: a friend of heretics. Henson, who took pride in having bought Dean Stanley's writing table, regarded Gore as a fanatic unsuitable for Westminster Abbey or for the Church of England.

He was, indeed, of the stuff of which the great leaders of the Counter-Reformation were fashioned [Henson wrote], though far too morally sensitive and too widely read to endure the compromising ethics and uncompromising dogmatism of the Church of Rome ... Gore was wont to emphasize the duty and value of 'corporate thinking', but what he really understood by the odd phrase was not really thinking at all, but surrender to his own domineering will.

Yet Gore never allowed his many controversies with Henson to lead him to think that Henson was dishonourable. 'I think he is a most lovable creature, though I own I am always a little nervous when I open *The Times* in case he should be writing something in it about me.' For his part Henson wrote that 'we were temperamentally opposed, but this opposition never affected the admiration which I felt for his remarkable courage and ability, nor the affection with which I regarded his person'. When Gore died, Henson gave this verdict: 'I judge him to have been the most considerable English Churchman of his time, not the most learned, nor the most eloquent, but so learned, so eloquent, so versatile, and so energetic that he touched the life of his generation at more points, and more effectively, than any of his contemporaries.'

2

Gore's birthplace in 1853 was in Wimbledon. The garden had forty acres, and the old Whig conventions were apparently permanent in the drawing room. His parents were descended from the Earls of Arran and Bessborough. But when he was eight or nine, Charles Gore came across a novel praising the conversion of a Roman Catholic priest to a sound Protestantism like the religion of Wimbledon. The boy felt instinctively attracted to the sights and sounds depicted in the earlier chapters, and about this time he began to preach to his sister in the nursery. He was sent to Harrow and emerged as a scholar in a school dedicated to athletics. In 1861 he heard Westcott preach in the Harrow chapel on *The Disciplined Life*. It was a mainly historical sermon, telling the boys about St. Antony in the desert, St. Benedict and his monks, St. Francis and his friars, and St. Ignatius and the Jesuits, but concluding with a question whether 'the Saxon race' was not now summoned to accomplish the ideals of asceticism in a nineteenth-century way. The schoolboy who heard that sermon founded the Community (first 'the Society') of the Resurrection as an Anglican religious order for men twenty years later.

In Oxford he did so well in the Greats course of classics and philosophy as a Balliol undergraduate that his election to a fellowship at the college next door, Trinity, was natural. But it soon became evident that Gore would not spend his life as a classical tutor. He was not merely 'eloquent and well-connected', as a cynical colleague noted; he was also a pastor already. He was ordained, assisting as a curate first in Bootle and then in the Liverpool church of Bell Cox, one of the priests who had been imprisoned under the Public Worship Regulation Act. In 1880 he went to teach the ordinands at Cuddesdon College; and he was the obvious man to appoint as the first Principal when on Pusey's death it was resolved to establish as a memorial an Anglo-Catholic centre in Oxford. Many of Pusey's disciples feared that the university was fast becoming secular, and resolved that Oxford should contain at least one citadel of the Faith: Pusey House. In order to allay some of the suspicions of the university, the Principal's assistants were termed Librarians. The term was not entirely inappropriate, for Pusey's vast collection formed the nucleus of a theological library. Newman wrote to Gore: 'I indulge the welcome thought that, in promoting the interests of his School, you will eventually be advancing Catholic Truth as held and taught at Rome.'[1]

In the 'Puseum' Gore continued to exercise a great influence on sympathetic young men. During the vacations he joined a group of theological dons who would discuss and pray together in a country rectory, the 'Holy Party'. Theirs was a Catholicism which, unlike Newman's, leaped with confidence into the questions of the hour. The needs of India held Gore's imagination and the Society of the Resurrection in Oxford was linked with the Brotherhood of the Epiphany in Calcutta; but he did not neglect the needs of England's workers, and began the Oxford branch of the Christian Social Union. And in order that the tradition expounded by Pusey should be brought into relationship with the English philosophy of the day, Gore edited in 1889 a volume called *Lux Mundi*.

This book, which seems so remote from later storms, was controversial at the time because its occasional concessions seemed to some conservatives to open the floodgates of heresy. The Oxford University Press refused to publish it: it was printed in Oxford, but the publisher John Murray had to take the odium and the profit. When it appeared, it broke the heart of Pusey's biographer, Henry Liddon, who died within a year (but still left Gore as his chief executor). While he was a bishop Gore was still followed by echoes of this controversy; the eccentric Anglican monk Father Ignatius would interrupt meetings with protests that the bishop was not sound on the Trinity. Even the mature Henson, who never sought the approval of the Anglo-Catholics, was to waver under similar attacks. Gore in his mid-thirties was badly

---

[1] 'Tho' it is not your purpose' was added as an afterthought. Quoted in *Newman: A Portrait Restored*, ed. John Coulson (Sheed & Ward, 1965), p. 63.

shaken. He took every opportunity to show how orthodox his theology was; and, having survived the accusations of heresy, he developed what S. C. Carpenter called a 'Never Again Complex'.

Lux Mundi was a series of studies in 'the religion of the incarnation'. It included an essay on the Atonement by Arthur Lyttleton, and this held much of the Evangelical Gospel.

> The cross was, on the one hand, the proclamation of God's ordinance against sin, on the other it was the response of man at length acknowledging the righteousness of the condemnation. . . . He must pass through this last and most awful human experience . . . because by the victorious endurance of it alone could the propitiation be accomplished. . . . If this is mysterious, irrational, transcendental, so is all morality; for at the root of all morality lies the power of self-sacrifice, which is nothing but the impulse of love to make a vicarious offering for its fellows, and the virtue of such an offering to restore and to quicken.

Yet Arthur Lyttleton rejected the Evangelical theory that the essential work of the cross was to substitute the *punishment* of Jesus for our punishment. Moreover the Mauricean connection between the cross and the common morality of men, brought out in that last sentence quoted, was a part of the book's main tendency. *Lux Mundi* went much nearer than the Evangelicals liked to concentration on the crib, and it seemed to expect the light shining in Bethlehem to be welcomed by the world. It was all very different from Henry Liddon's description of religious work in the Oxford of his old age: 'combing the hair of a corpse'.

The tone was set by Henry Scott Holland's opening essay on faith. Faith is a whole-hearted surrender to Jesus Christ, an act of the deepest personal will showing that we recognize that we, too, are all sons of God. Surely this enthusiastic kind of faith will appeal despite 'the exciting transformation which has passed over the entire surface of our intellectual scenery'? Aubrey Moore proceeded to expound the doctrine of God: a 'severe' God (here he drew on Dean Church), but *not* an immoral one (like Lyttleton, Moore quoted with approval J. S. Mill's words: 'I will call no being good, who is not what I mean when I apply that epithet to my fellow-creatures'). The reality of this good God of Christian belief is, Moore claimed, attested both by the verdict of man's conscience and by the character of nature. God is revealed everywhere (or nowhere—as even Moore added). If philosophers can explain this away, they can also explain away the belief in the objective reality of nature, despite the 'consciousness of mankind'. Does the problem of pain finally count against belief in God? Not so, asserted the next essay, by J. R. Illingworth. Everywhere there is suffering, out of which comes progress. 'The sun is so much the cooler by the heat it daily gives to earth; the plant and tree the weaker by the force that has matured their fruit; the animal generations exhausted in continuing their kind.' Does history contain too many tragedies? Not so, announced Edward Talbot. All history, but specially the history of Israel and Greece as studied in Victorian Oxford, is a preparation for the coming of Christ.

Two essays now claimed that belief in the Incarnation is both the fulfilment of man's reason operating on nature and history, and the basis of all Christian dogma. The four last essays in the book drew out some of the consequences of this belief—in the Church as the continuing Body of Christ and therefore 'an organization for the spiritual life, for holiness'; in the sacraments as the means of grace which Christ appointed to feed this spiritual life; in the application of the Church's moral teaching to democratic politics (and here Westcott was quoted with the dictum that 'a national Church alone can consecrate the whole life of a people'); and in the application of the moral law laid down in the Bible to the individual's problems in attaining holiness.

All these essays presented themes on which Gore himself was to write, and conclusions from which he moved little, although the war of 1914 was to challenge, if not confound, the cosmic optimism involved—and although Gore used to describe himself as a pessimist by temperament. These essays were generous and world-embracing in a way which was welcome after the negative tone of much orthodox theology, but they were not the essays which seemed most unusual at the end of the 1880s. In *Lux Mundi*, Gore handled the one theme which then appeared explosive: the challenge of biblical criticism. Westcott, Lightfoot, and Hort were commonly believed to have rescued the New Testament from the German professors, but knowledge about the Old Testament had been made available by German scholars who (conveniently summed up by Professor S. R. Driver of Oxford) were now beginning to be accepted in the English universities. Gore accepted this knowledge, and knew that it affected the New Testament, for it challenged the traditional idea that Jesus was infallible when he ascribed a particular law to Moses or a particular psalm to David, or when he repeated the story of Jonah and the whale.

Even before the publication of the essay in which he accepted this challenge, Gore was very nervous. Should he withdraw? Dean Church advised him to go ahead—but warned him that the disagreement on this matter between the older and younger Anglo-Catholics 'may mark the beginning of a severance which is like the little crack in the glacier, and may open out into a great crevasse'. The problem arose because Jesus Christ was believed to be both God and Man; the Second Person of the eternal Trinity had assumed human nature. Christians had also believed that God the Son, while incarnate, retained divine attributes including omniscience or at least infallibility; exactly how, had been a question confusing even Athanasius. Yet a well-informed theologian such as Gore now had to recognize about Christ, on the crucial page 360:

He shows no signs at all of transcending the science of His age. Equally he shows no signs of transcending the history of His age. He does not reveal His eternity by statements as to what had happened in the past, or was to happen in the future, outside the ken of existing history. His true Godhead is shewn in His attitude towards men and things about Him, in His moral and spiritual claim, in His expressed relation to God, not in any miraculous exemptions of Himself from the conditions of natural knowledge in its own proper province.

These four sentences were intended to say 'how much may legitimately and without real loss be conceded', as the next page stated; but they seemed to many to deny the divinity of Christ, a noteworthy impression if left by the Principal of Pusey House. When *Lux Mundi* was reprinted in a fourth impression, Gore hastened to correct this impression by adding *Corrigenda* after the Contents. He announced that he had not intended to imply that Christ 'surrendered his human nature to fallibility'. Accordingly, Gore wished to substitute for the sentences just quoted: 'He willed to restrain the beams of Deity so as to observe the limits of the science and historical knowledge of His age. . . . He chose to reveal His true Godhead by His attitude. . . .' The 'willed' and 'chose' in this note of correction were Gore's concessions to the outcry raised by the orthodox. They implied that the divine omniscience was merely restrained, not abandoned, by the incarnate Son; and Gore himself later used this very phrase. The question for us is whether they were legitimate concessions, made without real loss to a theologian's integrity.

Gore gave the Bampton Lectures for 1891 on *The Incarnation of the Son of God*, and wrote a sequel.[2] He attempted to defend himself by developing the 'Kenotic' theory of the Incarnation. He had already hinted at it in *Lux Mundi*, a footnote to that fatal page 360. 'This "self-emptying" of God in the Incarnation is, we must always remember, no failure of power, but a continuous act of Self-sacrifice: cf. 2 Cor. viii, 9 and Phil. ii, 7.' He appealed to Scripture here, but since the problem of Old Testament criticism had not occurred to the authors of Scripture all that he could quote was these two incidental, although also revealing, remarks in the letters of St. Paul.[3] Such re-

---

[2] *Dissertations on Subjects Connected with the Incarnation* (John Murray, 1895).

[3] The first remark was made in support of a charitable collection, and may be quoted from the New English Bible. 'For you know how generous our Lord Jesus Christ has been: he was rich, yet for your sake he became poor, so that through his poverty you might become rich.' The second remark was made in

marks were not enough to sustain the weight of philosophy which Gore attempted to place on them, and many of his fellow-theologians displayed both fervour and skill in demolishing his theory. Some of these critics, such as Liddon, protested because the theory was not in the Fathers. Others, however, including liberal theologians such as Hastings Rashdall and William Temple, attacked Gore because the theory seemed an implausible way of defending a Christology essentially patristic. These critics pointed out that Gore wished to maintain the Fathers' faith that the incarnate Lord was God the Son by conceding that his human nature was (to some extent and in some way) liable to ignorance and error; yet the concession which he made raised more problems than it solved. How could we know about the continuity between this fallible Christ and the omniscient, eternal Son? How could the Second Person of the Trinity, who had thus temporarily abandoned or restrained his divine power, at the same time continue to play his role in creating and upholding the universe? Was Gore really saying that Jesus 'had been God but now was a man', as Donald Baillie was to put it? Gore struggled to answer criticisms, although he could not get at one with Liddon: Liddon was dead. And eighty years after *Lux Mundi*, his answers had still not silenced critics, the general verdict being perhaps that Gore had set himself an impossible task by attempting to introduce *one* modern element, our knowledge of the intellectual limitations of anyone alive in the first century A.D., into the Christology of the Councils held in the fourth and fifth centuries.[4]

This was Gore's most original contribution to theology, and it often seemed to have been an intellectual mistake as well as an emotional agony. But the mistake showed his nature. He had surrendered his will to the Christ of the historic Church; he once confessed that he found it 'difficult to imagine how a good man really doubts our Lord's Godhead', although he liked to describe himself as a rationalist and a free thinker. He had made this surrender because, as he used to say, it seemed the only alternative to believing that the ultimate reality was

---

support of an appeal for humility. 'For the divine nature was his from the first; yet he did not think to snatch at equality with God, but made himself nothing, assuming the nature of a slave. Bearing the human likeness, revealed in human shape, he humbled himself, and in obedience accepted even death—death on a cross. Therefore God raised him to the heights and bestowed on him the name above all names . . .' Many scholars believe that in the second passage St. Paul was quoting from a Christian hymn based on the picture in Isaiah 53 of the servant of God who 'poured out' his soul in death.

[4] A useful survey by a Reformed theologian is the doctoral dissertation by Lewis B. Smedes, *The Incarnation: Trends in Modern Anglican Thought* (J. H. Kok N.V., Kampen, 1953). See also Donald Baillie, *God Was in Christ* (Faber & Faber, 1948).

revealed in Nero. But the Christ to whom he had surrendered was not a Christ who had chosen to reveal his Godhead by displaying omniscience. Christ's claim was spiritual and moral.

3

Four years after the publication of *Lux Mundi*, its editor became a parish priest. To some extent Gore's withdrawal from Oxford recalled Newman's; and no priest since Newman had been given such a position among undergraduates. He wished to work in peace, surrounded by a religious community. But he went to the village of Radley, five miles away, where the Community of the Resurrection (as the 'Society' had become) shared the vicarage with him. In his care to get everything and everyone in his parish right, he wrote a long letter asking for the advice of his bishop, William Stubbs. He received this reply:

> My dear Gore,
> Don't be a bore.

The truth was that, like Hort, Gore was made wretched by responsibility for average human life in a parish; and he was greatly relieved when at the end of 1894 Lord Salisbury, the Prime Minister, summoned him to Westminster. As a canon of the Abbey he secured the institution of the daily Eucharist and the setting aside of St. Faith's Chapel for private prayer, preached the *Lux Mundi* vision, and presided over exciting discussions in his austerely furnished home. Henson maintained that Gore advocated the disestablishment of the Church of England in order to make a narrowed Church more definitely Catholic, and it was a shrewd remark up to a point—but it missed the vision. The Sermon on the Mount was expounded as the law of Christ for his disciples. Keenly, publicly, and continuously, Gore embraced the threefold bulwark provided for the defence of Catholic doctrine by the creeds (Apostles' and Nicene), the canon (of Scripture), and the episcopate (in England, Anglican not Roman); but in *The Sermon on the Mount* he once again stressed as supreme the moral challenge of discipleship in the Church.

The Church of England [he said], in order to maintain the ideal of a national church, has in result allowed almost all the power of spiritual discipline, which she should have kept in her own hand, to be surrendered to a Parliament which is in the loosest possible relation to Christianity of any kind. . . . We must set to work to let men understand that, as the Church has a creed which she cannot let go, and a ministry and sacraments which are committed to her to exercise and to dispense, so she has a moral standard, which if she is not to fall under the curse of barrenness, she must re-erect and be true to. Only when men have come to understand what the Christian moral standard is—in marriage and in the home, in commerce and in politics—and to understand that it can no more be dispensed with than the creed or the sacraments, is there any prospect of a healthy revival of Church life.[5]

In his book of 1901 on *The Body of Christ*, which also arose out of Westminster preaching, he advanced a doctrine of the Eucharist ahead of almost all Roman Catholic and of most Anglican teaching of the time.[6] He saw Holy Communion as a sacrifice rather than a mere memorial; but there could be no possibility that a dead Christ in the bread was sacrificed afresh to the Father by the priest at the altar, although this was the implication of many devotionally 'Catholic' commentaries on the Mass. Gore believed in the Holy Communion as a 'living' and 'reasonable' sacrifice. The Christ who was really present in it was the living Lord who gave himself to feed his people. Responding and participating in faith, the congregation counted as well as the priest; through the sacrament, it became the Body of Christ entering the twentieth century. Here were the essential insights which were to be developed—often, of course, without reference to Gore's book, despite its popularity among students of English theology—as the liturgical movement progressed during the century throughout the Christian world.

He was well aware that the Church of England was no model embodiment of such a conception of the nature of Christ's Church, and he edited a volume of *Essays in Aid of the Reform of the Church*. He pulled the book together by an essay pleading for a body of clergy and laity to represent the Church in each parish, diocese, and province and to be the constitutional instrument of reform. He was in many ways a radical when compared with conventional ecclesiastics, but there were significant differences between the Church Self-Government Association which tended to support the position outlined in this essay and the later Life and Liberty Movement of the enthusiasts under William Temple. The men gathering around Gore were theological at heart; and theirs was Catholic theology. Although interested in far more than administrative change in the Church, they were not interested in more freedom for the clergy to be 'modern' in their teaching. On the contrary, Gore hoped that more doctrinal discipline would be imposed on the clergy. And although interested in the national character of the mission of the Church of England, they were not interested in a 'broad' basis for the Church. On the contrary,

[5] Charles Gore, *The Sermon on the Mount* (John Murray, 1896), pp. 49–50. Gore also published Abbey lecture-sermons on Romans and Ephesians.

[6] See E. L. Mascall, 'The Eucharistic Theology of Charles Gore', in *Corpus Christi* (Longmans, Green, 1953).

Gore maintained that the right to elect the representative bodies of the Church should be confined to communicants.

Lord Salisbury had, however, kept his eye on him, and at the end of 1901 offered him the bishopric of Worcester. It meant promoting the most vocal of the younger generation of High Churchmen, and one with a sympathy, however guarded, with 'Ritualism' and 'Socialism'; Gore had just publicly protested against the Government's treatment of the Boers. On Gore's side, to become Bishop of Worcester would mean virtually leaving the Community of the Resurrection, which had just acquired its mother house at Mirfield in Yorkshire. It meant abandoning theological scholarship and a prophet's freedom. It meant accepting 'restraints' which (as Archbishop Lang commented on reading the biography) 'brought out all his testiness and petulance'.

In the end Gore accepted, but he immediately served notice on his brother bishops that he was not going to abandon his theological principles. He refused to be consecrated as a bishop until the objections of Protestant fanatics had been fully answered. He also refused to live in Hartlebury Castle, and hastened the creation of an independent diocese of Birmingham, to the endowment of which he gave the £10,000 which he had inherited from his mother. While Bishop of Worcester he denounced a vicar for disbelieving in the Virgin Birth (the vicar resigned), and threatened to prohibit the new *English Hymnal* because it contained hymns invoking the prayers of the saints (a separate edition of the *Hymnal* was issued for use by worried priests). He also attacked the 'new theology' of the Congregationalist heretic, R. J. Campbell (*The New Theology and the Old Religion*, 1907); Campbell joined the Church of England, was received into communion by Gore in 1915, and died a Canon of Chichester.

Gore became the first Bishop of Birmingham in 1905, and his radical zeal in politics combined with his prophetic moralism to win the respect of the (then largely Nonconformist) city. He was assiduous in teaching the clergy and people, in befriending those who needed his friendship in any problem, in confirming the young (his addresses to them were models), in speaking for civic and national causes (he supported the People's Budget and other Liberal radicalism), and in stirring up the social conscience of churchmen. His six years as Bishop of Birmingham were thus one of the glories of a period which men would view in retrospect as the golden age of the Anglican parish and diocese. His statue, erected by public subscription outside his cathedral, remains as a memorial to the time—like the great cathedral now begun in Liverpool or like the *English Hymnal* itself. It was inevitable that such a vigorous Church should burst the seams of a law which compelled men to argue endlessly about what had been the legal ornaments in English churches during the second year of the reign of

Edward VI, 1548–9.[7] But, aware that his ideals were contrary to the whole conservatism of the English ecclesiastical machine ('an ingeniously devised instrumentality for defeating the objects which it is supposed to promote'), Gore himself was restless. When the India Office asked him to suggest names for the vacant Bishopric of Bombay, he half-seriously suggested himself. In the end, he foolishly accepted a call to be Bishop of Oxford.

He became almost as unhappy as he had been at Radley. The slow ways of country folk again dismayed his ardent intelligence, and too often now his wit was used to express complaints. The diocese which Samuel Wilberforce had created was too large for a bishop without Wilberforce's obsessive energy or superficial rhetoric. It was Gore's conviction that no diocese ought to contain more than two hundred parishes or three hundred priests, and Oxford contained three times as many. He never felt himself to be master of all these parishes—although he did create the Diocesan Board of Finance, and (what mattered infinitely more to him) he did infuse a religious vigour into a diocese which had gone to sleep since Wilberforce's departure. If at Birmingham he had overworked, at Oxford (or, rather, in Cuddesdon Palace) he overworried.

He was depressed because Henson, rather than he, represented the spirit of the best educated clergy and laity in his diocese. They tended to be conservative in secular and ecclesiastical politics, and they refused to untie their purse strings for a bishop with a passion for reform. They aso tended to be liberal in theology, and rejoiced in the limitations on the legal powers of Gore as a disciplinarian. They had little of Gore's sense that the clauses of the creeds stood or fell together.[8] William Sanday, the most respected among the Oxford theological professors, let it be known that as a result of his constant reading of new books from Germany he was losing belief in the miraculous elements in the old version of Christianity. B. H. Streeter, the editor of the Oxford volume *Foundations* (1912), wrote an essay which went far beyond any heresy approached by Gore in *Lux Mundi*, for Streeter seemed to think it probable that the resurrection of Christ had not taken place in a physical manner. Where Sanday and Streeter trod

---

[7] Percy Dearmer, who edited the words of the *English Hymnal*, made his church in London (St. Mary's, Primrose Hill) a place where the 'English use' could be seen in practice as an ordered worship full of colour, music and movement. This 'English use' appealed to the most scholarly interpretation of the Ornaments Rubric referred to above, and could be dubbed by its critics antiquarian, a 'British Museum religion'. Percy Dearmer himself moved away from it in a modernist direction. See his *Life* by his widow, Nan Dearmer (Jonathan Cape, 1940).

[8] A later Bishop of Oxford, Kenneth Kirk, lectured on *The Coherence of Christian Doctrine* in memory of Gore (SPCK, 1950).

cautiously, some lesser men rushed in with public attacks on orthodoxy. And some of the Anglo-Catholic priests who were orthodox in
doctrine were as undisciplined as the liberal theologians in practice,
for they imitated Rome. Such rebels seemed to have created a crisis
similar to that in the second century when the episcopate had emerged
as the guardian of the scriptures and the creeds.[9] Gore set himself to
fight back. If modernizing or Romanizing priests would not do the
right thing, which was to resign their Anglican Orders, he tried to
make life in the Church of England uncomfortable for them. He
poured out his wrath in a booklet of 1914, *The Basis of Anglican
Fellowship in Faith and Organization: An Open Letter to the Clergy
of the Diocese of Oxford.*

Such definite limitation of the theological basis of Anglican fellowship, excluding the 'disloyal' to the Left or the Right, showed Gore's
masterfulness; but it was a futile masterfulness. The modernists answered back, the Romanizers carried on, and Davidson at Lambeth
temporized. When Gore came down the front steps of Lambeth Palace,
having been manœuvered out of some demand for discipline, he would
say to himself (he helplessly told friends), 'Now, Charles, you never
meant to agree to that'. Once, walking back over Lambeth Bridge, he
turned and impotently shook his fist towards the wily archbishop's
study. He cared little about Davidson's struggle to preserve the legal
basis of the Established Church; indeed, he brought fresh trouble on
his head by agreeing with the Liberals that Anglicanism in Wales
ought to be disestablished. Part of Gore's trouble was that inwardly
he felt uneasy about this role as a disciplinarian, in the company of
bishops so spineless, against scholars whose intelligence he respected
(and whose arguments he did not have the leisure to answer properly),
and against ritualists whose rites—for example, devotions to the Reserved Sacrament—he personally enjoyed. As his biographer was to
put it, he was utterly weary of fighting like a hired gladiator.

After preaching a mission to Oxford undergraduates in February
1914, and giving many of them Communion at the end, he broke
down with uncontrollable sobs in the vestry of St. Mary's. The world
tragedy which began six months later seemed a hideous enactment on
a larger scale of the confusion which he saw in the mind of England.
He confessed to a friend that he thought he had made a muddle of his
life.

I suppose I shall never know in this world how far it is my fault. I do not *see*
that it is, though I want to see. But I remain embracing with all my conviction an ideal of Liberal Catholicism which, it appears, no one is willing to
listen to, neither 'Catholics' nor 'Liberals' nor the man in the street, nor any-

[9] As expounded in Charles Gore, *Orders and Unity* (John Murray, 1909).

body else except a very few old ladies and gentlemen. I suppose God has other purposes for the world and the Church. The only thing is to keep a good conscience and do one's best.

In March 1919, he finally told Davidson that he must resign. He refused a canonry back in Westminster and professorships at Oxford and London. He decided not to live with his own Community of the Resurrection; while he had been a bishop, it had developed at Mirfield under the direction of Walter Frere, who in addition to being a more advanced Anglo-Catholic was a Cambridge man. He refused to attend the Lambeth Conference of bishops. At the age of sixty-six he must be free.

4

He lived for thirteen more years, and they were his greatest period. Based on London, with part-time duties as a lecturer and preacher, and refreshing himself by travel, his sense of fun and his sensitivity to people returned. Occasionally he lost his temper, or would be found alone in despondent gloom; but such occasions mainly served to emphasize the victory over his demons. 'He seemed to me at the end rather a pathetic figure', wrote Henson in 1932, 'for his disciples had gone to the right, and to the left, and he was alone. . . . Probably this is the fate which overtakes every leader who has outlived his greatness, but in his case, it seemed to be emphasized by his tireless industry.' But what Henson was not to know in 1932 was that his own old age would be more bitter and lonely. Although Gore lectured the Anglo-Catholics about the folly of their un-English ways and about the moral grandeur of the Old Testament prophets, he abandoned none of his own 'Church principles', and weakened his hold on life by a trip to India in 1931 in order to investigate among many other things the scheme for the reunion of Anglicans with Protestants in a Church of South India. He still saw it as an essential function of the episcopate to uphold righteousness in society, and issued an indignant pamphlet about the bishops' concessions on contraceptives. And he wrote much more.

'The Christian creed, which I stand here to profess, is a purged or reconstructed creed, which in the truest sense can be called "catholic".' So Gore said in his Gifford Lectures delivered in the university of St. Andrews in the winter of 1929–30.

But I am not appealing to the authority of the Church, or of any church, on its behalf. That is an appeal which Lord Gifford barred. I am standing before you simply as one rational being speaking to other rational beings, and giving my reasons for holding that the Christian view of the world is the most rational view which we men can entertain.

In these lectures, on *The Philosophy of the Good Life*, he gave his final version of the Plato on whose idealism he had admiringly lectured in nineteenth-century Oxford. He once again extolled the ordered beauty of nature, and once again quoted James Mozley's phrase: 'Nature . . . in the very act of labouring as a machine is also sleeping as a picture.' But the centre of Gore's 'natural' theology was the fact which to him was the centre of history, in preparation for Christ: the prophetic vision of an Absolute Goodness above nature. He paid tribute to the Persian prophet Zoroaster, but reserved his best eloquence for the uniqueness of the prophetic tradition in Israel. Forty years before, how mistaken an undergraduate had been to make that remark to Dr. Liddon over dinner! 'Have you heard that Gore is bringing out a new book, in which he throws over the Old Testament altogether?'[10]

Gore rated the religion of India low in comparison with Israel's. Hinduism seemed not to distinguish between good and evil; Buddhism seemed against all life. Although as a Gifford Lecturer he was expected to avoid appealing to any alleged revelation, the best chapter in *The Philosophy of the Good Life* was, of course, on Jesus Christ as 'the supreme teacher of the way of life for man'. This chapter included the inevitable remarks that Christianity 'came into the world as a life to be lived by a community' which believed in the miracle of Christ's resurrection; and it concluded with a sentence which echoed Scott Holland in *Lux Mundi*. 'The primary adventure of faith is always the acceptance of the claim of the Life.'

He covered much of this ground in other writing also: in his book for the Home University Library on *Jesus of Nazareth*, in his lectures on *Christ and Society*, in his contributions to a large *New Commentary on Holy Scripture* which he jointly edited, and in many printed sermons and lesser publications dating from this highly productive retirement. Most of the main ideas of a lifetime were gathered into his three volumes on *The Reconstruction of Belief* (1921–4), and into a militant answer to his critics (*Can We Then Believe?*, 1926); and his *Reconstruction* was his greatest plea for a decision. He once said that it was better to decide wrongly than not to decide at all, and here he wrote: 'There are famous instances of protests by great thinkers that the search for truth was to be preferred to the finding of it, but I believe that, at bottom, this state of mind represents a disease of the intellect.' In over a thousand pages he did his best to give reasons in defence of the decisions which he had made during his first year in Oxford.

It is reason in me which demands goodness in God [he wrote]. If I am

[10] 'You should have seen the old boy sweat' was the undergraduate's comment when he told a friend. Harold Anson, *Looking Forward* (Heinemann, 1938), p. 124.

rationally sure of anything, it is that I find impressed upon my inmost conscious being the obligation of goodness—the sense that I exist in order to be
good. And I am wholly unable to interpret this purpose of goodness, which
I cannot doubt to be real, except in terms of the goodness of God.

Scientists and philosophers of the day were quoted against materialism,
or against the natural selection of chance variations as accounting for
the organization of life. After 170 pages the reader was already in the
midst of a discussion of 'The Historical Religion', and was being
reassured about the historical worth of the New Testament: 'The only
book of the New Testament which it seems to me the evidence shows
to be pseudonymous is the Second Epistle of Peter.' Eye witnesses such
as St. John had recorded the miracles and teachings of Jesus Christ.
Christianity depended on belief in those miracles and on obedience to
those teachings, for the miracles had shown that it was true as Jesus
Christ taught—God is 'the transcendent Creator, under whose hands
nature is plastic'. 'There can be no doubt', declared Gore, 'that one
who holds the prophetic doctrine of God the Creator can find no *a
priori* difficulty about the miracles of the Bible.' The Lord of nature
could do anything, and it was clear enough what he had done. 'The
fact of the empty tomb seems to me as indisputable as any fact of
history.' Jesus Christ was neither (as Harnack assumed) a teacher of a
simple Gospel about the Fatherhood of God and the brotherhood of
man, nor (as Schweitzer claimed) a deluded prophet sharing first-
century follies; he was the Christ who came from eternity to save us
from sin, the Christ who founded and legislated for the Church, the
Christ who was rightly described in the Church's developed doctrine
of the Trinity.

When the thesis of *The Reconstruction of Belief* is summed up in
that manner, it is seen to rest on a series of dogmatic assertions. ('I
could see his mind was an awfully jolly merry-go-round', a student
said, 'but it never stopped where I was, so I could get on.') Yet these
assertions were defended in a charitable and learned spirit, and Gore
showed that he was abreast of modern literature even while he did not
hesitate to reject its conclusions in favour of the faith which he had
received. Far better than in the days when he had tried to wield episcopal authority, he thus vindicated by the quality of his teaching what
he called 'the episcopal succession as the link of connexion and continuity in the Catholic body'; and far better than in the attacks which
he made on his fellow-churchmen who differed from him, he illustrated
in his own person what he wrote at the end of his *Reconstruction*
about the Church of England.

I find that her history in many of its aspects and characteristics makes me feel
ashamed and depressed. But if there is in history the stamp of a divine providence on any society, it is set on the Anglican Church. It was marked out in

the sixteenth century to hold together the ancient Catholic tradition both in creed and order with the appeal of the Reformation to the open Bible as the final court of reference for Christians; and so to present a type of Catholicism which the world had forgotten, which should have priests but not be priest-ridden, and should accept the Catholic tradition but keep it purged by the free use of reason and an all-pervading scripturalness.

He caught pneumonia in January 1932. As he lay semi-conscious, Archbishop Lang heard him say 'transcendent glory'. William Temple assessed him after his death. 'Though I have had many tutors in Christ, he was perhaps above all others my father; and so far as I can picture Jesus Christ, I picture Him as not unlike the father whom I have lost.'

5

The life of Herbert Hensley Henson began in circumstances very different from Gore's. He was born to a Nonconformist ex-businessman in his fifties, who lived in a *bourgeois* retirement beyond his real means and who was obsessed with an Evangelical pietism; and his mother died when he was aged six. At odds with his home, the boy became a keen Anglican communicant and often slipped into churches. He was sent to an inefficient private school in Broadstairs on the Kent coast (where they lived), was miserable, and ran away. In 1881 he found his way to Oxford, where he was too poor to belong to any college; nevertheless he secured a First in history as an 'unattached student'.

Three years later life really began for him, when by examination he won a fellowship at All Souls College. Founded in 1436, All Souls had retained the original character of many medieval colleges or halls and had virtually no undergraduates. The fellows had been an aristocratic, idle lot in the years of the glory of Oriel and Balliol, and they still included those whose achievements were not academic, but when Henson was elected the aim was intellectual as well as worldly distinction. The college provided what his life had lacked: a stability and sense of ease, a warmth of friendship, an assured tolerance of the High Church extremes to which the young man was running, a conversation embracing the culture and politics of England. Throughout his life Henson—like his clerical colleague and rival, Cosmo Lang—loved All Souls as his second home.

His desire to be ordained, formed during lonely visits to churches in Kent as a boy, now wavered. He taught history in the university; he organized a Laymen's League for the defence of the establishment of the National Church; he thought of becoming a barrister. When his vocation reasserted itself, Gore at Pusey House was the first who heard the solemn news. But he was desperately immature, seeing himself as a kind of St. Francis among the poor. He was ordained as a deacon at Cuddesdon in 1887, and he made in his journal a boyish entry which shows, how, despite his debt to Gore, he was now on the move.

I wrote a letter to Raleigh thanking him for the help he had given me by his example and counsel to shake off the chains of the pseudo-Catholic theory. . . . Then I walked into the meadows beyond the Church and sat on a style to meditate. And as I thought the desire came over me to pledge myself to God, there and then; which I forthwith did, bareheaded under the open heaven, promising to be loyal to the Truth, wherever I found it, wheresoever it should call me to seek after it.

Twelve years later he copied out that entry for the benefit of another Fellow of All Souls who was being ordained, Cyril Alington, and he added:

The Church of England has little to offer in the present, and less to promise in the future, and the time may come to you, as it has come to me, when the pressure of a yoke which is irremovable is almost more than flesh can bear. It would not be true to say that I have ever regretted taking Orders; but it is true that I cannot imagine myself—seeing things as I now see them and realizing the bearing of all the issues of Ordination as I do now—having the courage to offer myself for the Ministry now.[11]

The misery behind that heart's cry resulted from the two great mistakes on the part of the advisers of this self-tormenting intellectual. A month after becoming a deacon, he was appointed Head of Oxford House in Bethnal Green, a centre for social work in the East End of London. The young Henson hated the squalor around him, but disbelieved in Socialism as its cure. He also disbelieved in the High Church glamour of this mission which operated on a shoe-string, but he had no alternative to offer as a means of reaching the hearts of the poor. Understandably he accepted the first offer of alternative employment, but it was an appointment by All Souls as Vicar of Barking, a parish of over twelve thousand on the sordid outskirts of London.

At Barking he prayed, he preached, he led his curates, and he opened the garden of his over-large vicarage to his rough parishioners; but he was near to a nervous breakdown. Craving affection, with his don's tongue he managed to insult many of the somewhat puzzled people around him. A born debater, he felt it his duty to try to be a pastor. Wanting to be a scholar, he spent the years of *Lux Mundi* in dockland, immersed in local arguments and in parochial labours for which he had had no training and little inclination. But what he saved from the near-wreckage of his life was perhaps enough. It was an ineffaceable sense of the clergyman's duty. When as a bishop he looked

[11] C. A. Alington, *A Dean's Apology* (Faber & Faber, 1952), pp. 45–7.

back to his early years and addressed the young men whom he was about to ordain, memory did its usual trick of glamourizing the past; but there was enough in the truth about Barking to let this trick be played.

Nearly fifty years have passed since I was myself ordained [he said in 1936]. How little I guessed what lay before me! The immense failures which would overtake my too-ardent beginnings; the disappointments which would shadow my later course; the growing sense of inadequacy which would become a settled resident in my mind. The happiest years in my ministry were those in which, as the vicar of a great industrial parish, I was nearest to the people. Faces look out at me from the past—toil-worn faces, radiant with love and confidence. Nothing of what men foolishly call success is worth comparison with the experiences which those faces recall.[12]

He was rescued from the strain of Barking by Lord Salisbury, who had been a Fellow of All Souls and who had been alarmed by the collapse of Henson's health. The peer was patron of a little almshouse, St. Mary's Hospital, Ilford, where the chaplain (or 'incumbent') had just accepted the Pope's verdict on Anglican Orders by resigning. Lord Salisbury appointed Henson to this post, thus enabling him to spend much more time at All Souls as a fellow with a small stipend. Henson's first book belongs to these years: *Apostolic Christianity*, a discussion of St. Paul's government of the Church in Corinth. But he could not secure any post in the university world, and he could not afford to marry. Then after seven more years, in 1900, Lord Salisbury came to the rescue again. He nominated Henson to the Westminster canonry to which was annexed the rectory of St. Margaret's, the parish church of the House of Commons.

The great Victorian Rector of St. Margaret's had been F. W. Farrar, a prince of the pulpit, and the delighted Henson at the age of thirty-seven set himself to revive that tradition by addressing his sermons there and in the Abbey to the basic questions of the time. As he now saw it, there were three foes to fight. The first was immorality in public life; here he was at one with Gore. The second was any attempt to stifle the freedom of Christian theologians to be loyal 'to the Truth', wherever they found it; here he made Gore very uneasy. The third was any attempt to fasten 'the chains of the pseudo-Catholic theory' on the Church of England. The Church ought, rather, to be enlarged on a definitely Protestant basis in order to be more clearly the 'Great National Church of the English people'; and here, he faced a collision with Gore. Amid these fights, there was one positive Gospel to proclaim, and he had kept his hold on this through the years of misery now closing.

[12] H. H. Henson, *Ad Clerum* (Hodder & Stoughton, 1937), p. 210.

I don't think any outsider can understand how much passion of soul is involved in the Ministry [he had written to Alington the year before]. There is suffering quite unique in nature and intensity wrapped up in this self-surrender to the Service of Souls. One's own faults come home to one with such cruel insistence, and, as the years pass, failures add their dead weight to the heart. One has dark hours, God knows, when the worth of the Ministry, the genuineness of that vast system of Religion, which the Ministry symbolises and interprets, are wrapped in doubt. Everything seems to go for a while, and one has a new anguish. It is not the common distress of mind which every thinking Christian must have experience of at some time or other, but a far more terrible trouble. You are the priest: you face your fellows on the basis of their confidence in your firm conviction: and you are not sure, you do not know, you are not what you seem. I think these troubles will increase. . . . Still, after twelve years of fault and failure and sorrow, I think of Ordination as having *essentially* little to do with subscriptions and formulae—being in reality the answer to Christ's personal vocation, an answer which one must make. . . . In Ordination I see nothing less than that supreme acceptance of Christ's proposal. The poor little temporal and local incidents are just our secular uniform, which counts for little, and is always counting for less. Only that remains. 'Jesus Christ is the Same, yesterday, and to-day, yea for ever.' Everything else fails us: He alone remains. One is untrue to oneself: He is true to us always.

Henson had been in a wilderness unknown to most of the critics or defenders of the 'vast system of Religion'.

6

At Westminster, where he enjoyed a good income for the first time in his life, he married a Scotswoman, Isabella Caroline Dennistoun. In his own words, 'her presence mitigated the resentments which my personal idiosyncrasies and frequent controversies could not but provoke', but the marriage was childless. She was neither his intellectual equal nor very practical, and she grew increasingly deaf, so that writing up his journal (with references to 'the dear lady') gradually became his substitute for conversation with her. Despite his loyalty to her, Henson's solitariness was not really changed; and as he wrote, 'lonely men are apt to become horribly interested in themselves'. Nor did his combativeness grow less, and he argued so persistently with the Dean of Westminster, Armitage Robinson, that this was one of the factors persuading Robinson to exchange Westminster for the quieter Deanery of Wells.

As a preacher in Westminster he found his vocation, and in 1908 he refused the Prime Minister's offer to appoint him to the Professorship of Ecclesiastical History at Oxford. The Prime Minister (Asquith) took the layman's vew: 'the waters are somewhat stagnant, and it is time that they should be moved'. Henson, on the other hand, knew that it was now too late for him to become another Creighton. 'If I had become Professor, the most I could have dared to hope for would have been the kind and measure of success which Stanley obtained', he explained to Davidson; but 'the literary and pictorial historian has been replaced by the patient and infinitely laborious researcher.' Davidson wanted Henson to return to the academic society of Oxford, and as the years went by, when overwhelmed by loneliness or by ecclesiastical duties, Henson would often ask himself whether the Archbishop had not been right.

Fortunately for the history of the Church of England, he remained a preacher and did not hesitate to pronounce on public issues when morality seemed to be involved. For example, he pilloried a British company which was exploiting native labour in Peru. The company's directors threatened legal action, only to see the following reply to their solicitor's letter:

I differ so completely from your clients in their view of what is befitting a clergyman, a gentleman, and a man, that you will not be surprised to learn that I think nothing is required from me in any of those characters which would abate anything of the severity of the censure which I conceived myself called upon to pass on the directors of the Peruvian Amazon Company.

In other utterances which attracted publicity, he vigorously expressed his Protestant conception of the National Church. In 1909 Gore, now Bishop of Birmingham, issued a formal 'inhibition' against Henson's acceptance of an invitation to preach in the Institute attached to the historic Congregational church in Birmingham, Carr's Lane. Henson hoped that, when he disobeyed this episcopal order, Gore would prosecute him in the courts and so give him an opportunity of demonstrating the illegality of the inhibition; but on reflection Gore allowed the incident to pass. In his Westminster pulpits Henson repeatedly urged intercommunion and eventual reunion between the Church of England and his wife's Church of Scotland, and between Anglicans and Nonconformists despite the bitter political quarrels of the time—quarrels on which he often commented in self-consciously independent journalism.

His favourite role was, however, that of the interpreter of biblical scholarship. He brought into the pulpit of St. Margaret's scholars such as J. M. Thompson who were in his view unjustly treated by the ecclesiastical authorities. His own sermons, exactly pondered and elaborately written, attracted much serious interest. What he said seemed to amount to a claim that belief in miracles such as the Virgin Birth of Jesus was optional, and this caused a mild sensation at the time; but time and again he preached the merits of the traditional alliance of Church and State, and above all he preached the divinity of the Redeemer. In later years his sermons tended to be too often absorbed in the description of an historical scene or in the analysis of an ecclesiastical problem, much in the style of Stanley; but criticism to this effect made him uneasy, and it is certainly true that he never preached more effectively than when at the beginning of the twentieth century he was expounding the biblical message week by week to thoughtful Westminster congregations.

In his characteristically truculent Preface to *Apostolic Christianity*, Henson had noted that when estimating modern clergymen 'a knowledge of athletics and theatricals outweighs habits of intellectual industry and a solemn sense of the awfulness of religion'. He had also noted that many laymen had grown to distrust the honesty of preachers, and that this contempt of the clergy was becoming part of unbelief in the towns, for 'urban life not only stimulates a passion for amusement, it also directly ministers to the cynical, sceptical disposition, which, no less than frivolity, obstructs the way of religion'. He had concluded: 'The most urgent necessity of the present juncture seems to be the recovery of public confidence in the clergy.' At the heart of London under Edward VII, as a frivolous society relaxed in the years between Victoria and the great war, Henson did recover the confidence of many in the pulpit he was occupying. One such was a boy of fifteen from a Baptist home in Tooting.

In his sermon he referred to Jeremy Taylor. . . . I remember the musical tincture of the voice as the easy antique English name came out. . . . I was here made vaguely conscious of a spirit of high churchmanship of which I had never dreamed, a spirit of religion which had always attracted me, here at last, pure, learned and English.[13]

When he was made Dean of Durham in 1912, 'the old ambition to be a student which I had laid aside when I left Oxford for Bethnal Green in 1887 . . . resumed something of its former authority in my mind.' But like Tait in Carlisle, he was temperamentally unable to give himself to the quietness of a learned dean.

He was speaking all over the diocese even before the war came with its summons to patriotic oratory. In pre-war Anglican controversies, near or far it was (in his own words) 'apparent from the first that I could not stand outside the conflict'. When the war produced the National Mission of Repentance and Hope, he did stand outside what he regarded as a very mistaken enterprise—and he did so in a belligerently public manner. When the story was spread that at Mons

[13] Eric Bligh, *Tooting Corner* (Secker & Warburg, 1946), p. 206. This quotation is derived from Canon Charles Smyth, whose history of St. Margaret's, *Church and Parish* (SPCK, 1955), is a model in the combination of local with national history.

the British troops had been assisted by angels, he scornfully preached his scepticism. When George V and Davidson appealed for total abstinence from alcohol during the war, he wrote to *The Times* that 'Total Abstinence is no part of morality'. When the Life and Liberty Movement was launched as an Anglican ginger group by what Henson called 'the casuistic facility and untiring eloquence of William Temple', he voted in a minority of one at the enthusiastic meeting in the Queen's Hall, London. He declared that he was voting against a resolution which claimed that 'the present conditions under which the Church lives and works constitute an intolerable hindrance to its spiritual activity.' But perhaps a deeper objection to Life and Liberty was revealed in a sentence of the witty report which he sent to Davidson (on his own initiative): 'The Bishop of Oxford's name was greeted with applause, but then the meeting was "Gore's crowd".'

When Lloyd George nominated him as Bishop of Hereford at the end of 1917, it was natural that Gore and Gore's crowd should explode in protest, for Henson had lost few opportunities of taunting them and of befriending their enemies (apart from the Evangelicals). It was also natural that the more conservative Evangelicals, aroused by old Dean Wace from Canterbury, should counter-attack; and it was natural, too, that many ordinary churchpeople would be ready to believe the worst about a preacher who seemed so much in love with the sound of his own voice expressing his independence. Henson was, in a word, arrogant, and his attitude to those who now objected to his consecration was, in the mild Davidson's phrase, 'venomous'. Lang and Gore may have been right, from their points of view, to absent themselves from the consecration of such a man—although Henson, who was sensitive as many angry controversialists are, never really forgave them.

Nevertheless, Lloyd George may be seen to have been right to force the appointment through, and Davidson was right to make it possible. For Henson was humbled by being made a bishop, and saved for what he had called 'the Service of Souls'. He was humbled to realize the extent of the hostility he had aroused, and he was deeply hurt. Ten years later, he still thought of himself as isolated. He told Davidson:

It has been my misfortune in the course of my life to disappoint every person who has followed me, and every party that has allowed itself to build hopes on me. . . . A kind of Quixotic honesty, a fatal trick of lucid speech, and a temperamental indifference to the impressions I make, may perhaps explain the embodied paradox I seem to be.

If he really was indifferent to the hostility he had aroused, why did his journal contain so many passages of introspection and so many expressions of delight when men praised him?

With his half-hidden sensitivity, he was also humbled by the gravity

Frederick and Beatrice Temple

William Temple

H. H. Henson

of the episcopal office itself. It sobered him to be among the figureheads rather than the critics, the gamekeepers rather than the poachers. It was true, as he wrote in his journal: 'The real "H. H. Hereford" is a very different being from that which hatred and bigotry have imagined—a man full of fears as to himself, and mainly anxious to "do out the duty".' And although he never faced up to the fact with full 'candour' (a favourite word), he was also humbled by having to compromise his much-advertised conscience in order to persuade Davidson to consecrate him a bishop in the face of Gore's opposition.

For 'compromise' does seem to be the just word to use about the document which Davidson wrote for Henson's signature at Lambeth Palace on 17 January 1918. The document was in the form of a reply to a letter from the Archbishop. Davidson's letter to Henson ran:

I am receiving communications from many earnest men of different schools who are disquieted by what they have been led to suppose to be your disbelief in the Apostles' Creed, and especially in the clauses relating to Our Lord's Birth and Resurrection. I reply to them that they are misinformed, and I am persuaded that when you repeat the words of the Creed you do so *ex animo* and without any desire to change them. I think I understand your reluctance to make at this moment a statement the motives of which might be misconstrued, and it is only because you would relieve many good people from real distress that I ask you to let me publish this letter with a word of reassurance from yourself.

Davidson also wrote, and made Henson sign, a two-sentence reply; it was the only way of silencing Gore. 'I do not like to leave any letters of yours unanswered. It is strange that it should be thought by anyone to be necessary that I should give such an assurance as you mention, but of course what you say is absolutely true.' To the end Henson blustered, and he got the Archbishop to take down a third sentence at his dictation. 'I am indeed astonished that any candid reader of my published books, or anyone acquainted with my public Ministry of thirty years, could entertain a suggestion so dishonourable to me as a man and as a clergyman.' As an echo of his rebuke to the directors of the Peruvian Amazon Company, this was out of place; for Henson, in order to go to Hereford, was willing to state that he accepted *ex animo* (sincerely), and had no desire to change, the credal statements that Jesus was conceived by the Holy Ghost and born of the Virgin Mary, and that on the third day he rose again. But in Westminster he had preached the view which he held to the end of his life: that belief in the Virgin Birth and Physical Resurrection was both optional and probably wrong.[14]

We cannot wonder that his critics thought that Henson had now

[14] See, e.g., his letter of 1947 in *Letters of Herbert Hensley Henson*, ed. E. F. Braley (SPCK, 1951), pp. 208–9.

retracted his heresies because he wanted to be a bishop, but it is not necessary to blame Henson for bowing to the Archbishop's insistence. His belief in Jesus Christ was what mattered supremely to him, and he accepted not a mere teacher but the Incarnate God and the Risen Lord, of 'yesterday' as well as 'today'. The Apostles' Creed was the only existing symbol of the faith of the community which thus worshipped Jesus Christ. If the question were put as it was in 1917, he had to answer that it would be false to 'disbelieve' in such a creed, and presumptuous to wish to change it. He had bared his heart to Alington in 1899 (and Alington now sent that letter on to Gore). 'Everything else fails us: He alone remains. One is untrue to oneself: He is true to us always.'

7

Bishop Henson surprised his critics. He won the respect and even the affection of many of the laity, and even of most of the clergy, in two very different dioceses which he governed. He never allowed himself to be immersed in minor duties or pleasantries. He never admitted a telephone to the house (but would send out his chaplain with a pile of coins for use in the public kiosk), and normally spent his mornings reading and writing in his study unless he was in London. He ruled by sermon, article, or letter, writing out what he had to teach with a care for his prose which added to the distinctive and memorable quality of his mind. His wit could still hurt, and his love of controversy could still lead him into debates where he was in the minority because in the wrong, but as a pastoral bishop he was surprisingly tender. He had set great store by the unity of spirit and service among those who served Westminster Abbey or Durham Cathedral, and when he became the bishop of a diocese he built up a pride in it. Young men were attracted to work under such leadership. Many people already in the diocese gave him their hearts, and then his own inner nature responded. He took these duties in his own diocese far more seriously than his speeches in the provincial or national assemblies of the Church, although he enjoyed debates. When William Temple attended a meeting of bishops in York in 1921 he found that Henson 'spoke many times' but always refused to serve on committees. Archbishop Lang in the chair observed: 'My dear Bishop of Durham, if you think you can get out of doing the solid work of committees merely by making fantastic speeches, we shall have to prove that you are mistaken.'

When Lloyd George transferred him to Durham in 1920, the move was accompanied by almost universal regret in Herefordshire and an almost universal welcome back to the great Northern see ('The Bishop-

rick' as he liked to call it). When he resigned from Durham at the beginning of 1939, the tribute signed by all the clergy and lay officials in
the diocese praised a 'great and generous episcopate'. His success was
all the more striking because his historical and critical eye was quick
to see how the conditions of his work were far different from those of
the great divines whom he admired. The Victorian preachers had commanded attentive and intelligent congregations, and what they said
had quite often got into the newspapers; but Henson came to think
that he had spent too much time on the preparation of sermons. In the
twentieth century, sermons seemed to count for little. The Victorian
prelates had entertained the gentry and mediated in industrial disputes.
Henson now consorted with 'the County' and warned the miners that
Labour would ruin the country. Yet a bishop, even a Bishop of Durham, was no longer a 'great national officer', despite Henson's nostalgic
claim.

He constantly pictured himself as a man condemned to live in an
age of decline. He inspected, without admiring, the age of democracy.
He did not believe in conferences—and specially not in those which
William Temple convened. 'I admire his industry and envy his various
ability', Henson once confessed, 'but I distrust his judgment, dislike
his company, and dissent from his reading of ecclesiastical duty.'[15] He
did not believe in movements, and specially not in Moral Rearmament,
the American emotionalism under F. D. Buchman which many softer-
centred church leaders wished to bless, but which Henson cursed eloquently. He did not believe in any simple panacea to cure the Church's
alienation from the people. But he 'did out the duty', and he urged
his clergy that if they were to be respected they, too, must work. He
was never popular with the miners, but he was not mobbed by them
as seemed likely. (They threw a Dean of Durham into the river; some
said that they thought that the Dean was the Bishop.) 'Now gentlemen',
he ended on one occasion when his car had been surrounded by an
angry crowd, 'I am not unemployed as unfortunately you are. I have
much to do: and I must therefore bid you good-night.' These were not
the words of another Westcott, but the unemployed broke into cheers.

The second surprise produced by Henson's twenty-two years as a
bishop was his conversion from the eloquent defence of the Church of
England 'by law established' to the eloquent recognition of disestablishment as inevitable if the Church's worship was not to be dictated by
the secularized House of Commons. He hated to be called inconsistent,
and there was indeed a basic consistency of conviction through his life,

[15] This was, however, in September 1942, when 'I am trying to reconcile myself to solitude born of self-conscious obsoleteness'. He could claim less than two
months later: 'I like and admire Temple, but I regard his ceaseless pronounce-
ments with deepening anxiety.' *Letters of H. H. Henson*, pp. 136–8.

apart from the consistency of clarity, vigour, and acumen in all that he wrote or said. In his early twenties, when he had organized the Laymen's League in Oxford, he had been backing up Archbishop Benson's view of the nation's continuing history; in his forties, when he had preached the glorious comprehensiveness of the National Church, he had done so in a Westminster where Parliament, the Abbey, and St. Margaret's seemed good neighbours; and in his fifties, when he had owed his positions in the Church to two Liberal Prime Ministers, he had been convinced that statesmen and public alike wished the Church well under the right leadership. His ability to produce theological arguments or rhetoric in defence of the alliance of Church and State had always depended on a belief that it was a genuine alliance, with obligations acknowledged on both sides. When he became a bishop, the legal bent of his mind meant that it was like changing from being an advocate to being a judge. He regarded the episcopate as an institution for the government of the Church. The 'lawlessness' of the clergy distressed Henson as it distressed Gore—and he did not think it relevant that in the past he had often defied bishops himself, for the Anglo-Catholic lawlessness of the 1920s seemed to be directed against the Protestant nature of the National Church. The authority of the episcopate could not be restored, he believed, unless Parliament authorized a Prayer Book which the bishops could enforce 'inexorably' (his word to Davidson in 1923). When in 1927–8 the House of Commons refused to do this, Henson saw no honourable alternative to breaking up the Establishment. He had argued against Gore, for he had suspected that Gore favoured disestablishment in order to fasten a clerical and Anglo-Catholic control on the Church; but now he, too, would 'mend or end'.

In January 1928, between the Prayer Books, he discussed Church and State in a university sermon at Cambridge, taking as his text: 'Can two walk together, except they be agreed?' He announced his conversion to the view that the spiritual freedom of the Church was now paramount. In the summer he would like to have been offered York when Cosmo Lang went to Canterbury, but he knew that to the end he had been too controversial. William Temple was appointed, a man for whose confused sentimentality Henson nursed a suspicion exceeded only by his contempt for the glamour surrounding each 'sonorous platitude' from Archbishop Lang. 'The knowledge that I can have no other sphere of work than the diocese of Durham must have considerable effect on my performance of duty, and the effect ought to be wholesome', he wrote. But it was inevitable that he should continue to express independent opinions about Church and State, demanding a clarification in the relationship between Parliament and the Church Assembly; and it says much about where his heart lay that the Church's confusion following the insult from the House of Commons troubled him so deeply. We can compare Henson's lectures cn *Anglicanism* at Uppsala in 1920 with his book on *The Church of England* in 1939, and note that the two volumes, while both being superb discussions of the Anglican system in the light of English history, reached opposite conclusions. In 1920 disestablishment would be like pulling down Westminster Abbey in order to improve the aspect of the surrounding buildings, but in 1939 the Establishment was morally indefensible. 'A faithful picture of an Effete Establishment' was how Henson himself described the latter book to Archbishop Lang, who had sent him a long and worried protest against its pessimism. On the other hand, the mind of the Church of England as a whole was neither so clear nor so legal as the mind of Hensley Henson, and in retrospect it may be seen that those who considered other things more important than Prayer Book revision understood the Church better than he did. Davidson, Lang, and Temple all certainly believed that they had a deeper understanding, and that the over-clever Henson was flawed by a love of extremes.

Moreover, the Englishman, whether in church or out of it, is essentially practical (as Henson himself often stressed); and for all the astuteness of his analysis of the system and its crisis, Henson was seldom constructive or even realistic in his contributions to the debate about the immediate issues. To the creation of the Church Assembly, which on any showing held the key to Anglican independence and self-respect, he had contributed little except carping criticism, because he had thought the Church Assembly 'anti-national'; and when the Archbishops appointed a commission to examine the relations of Church and State, he refused to send to it any comment except his certainty that it was wasting its time unless it advocated a complete revolution in the relationship.

In 1934 an episode showed how Henson regarded the spiritual crisis of the decade. A Unitarian minister was invited to preach in the new Anglican cathedral in Liverpool. It was Henson who led the protests against this apparent compliance with the denial of the divinity of Christ. For some years now he had grown increasingly uneasy about a lack of reverence for the person of Christ in some of the utterances associated with the Modern Churchmen's Union. He had refused to join that body, and he seized the opportunity presented by the controversy about Unitarians in a cathedral pulpit to demonstrate clearly that he regarded the worship of the divine Christ as the heart of historical Christianity and as the essence of the teaching of the Church of England.[16]

[16] His friend Ralph Inge, the Dean of St. Paul's, looking back in 1951, complained that Henson 'ceased to be a *thinker*, and so became a yes-man among the bishops'. But a month later Inge was recording the nature of his own thought:

The Gifford Lectures which Henson published under the title *Christian Morality: Natural, Developing, Final* (1936), were of no permanent importance, but they emphasized that the wide diffusion of a Christian spirit in the conduct of men and nations depended on the definite discipleship of the minority which fully submitted to the full claim of Christ. Over his large collection of history books he placed the figure of the One whom he regarded as the Judge of it all, on a crucifix. As he watched the societies of Stalin and Hitler, and the sensuality and 'puerile superstitions' of the secularized West, he saw the fulfilment of his warning in his Gifford Lectures that 'Christianity carries the fortunes of mankind, and that its failure would mean nothing less calamitous than the spiritual suicide of humanity'.

He retired at the age of seventy-six to Hintlesham, near Ipswich, just before the outbreak of the war; he sold off all the furniture he did not need, as if wanting to emphasize that the glory had departed from the empty rooms, cold floors, and peeling paint of Auckland Castle. In 1940 Winston Churchill dramatically reinstated him as a canon of Westminster, believing that his gallant preaching would arouse England; but cataract was now damaging his eyes and he had to resign. He lived, fighting blindness and despair, until 1947. Almost until his last day he wrote up the indiscreet journal which is now under lock and key in the library of Durham Cathedral, not far from his grave.[17] On these confessions he based three volumes of autobiography, under the curious title *Retrospect of an Unimportant Life*. The title seemed to continue, or to pick, a quarrel with the world, yet congratulations poured in when some of the sparkling treasures of the journal were thus revealed. Another volume was made up of articles from his diocesan magazine, *Bishoprick Papers* (1946).

Cyril Alington, to whom Henson had written on his ordination in 1899, became Headmaster of Eton and, in 1933, Dean of Durham. Some lines which Alington wrote about Henson in *The Times* are recorded above the grave.

> By nature gifted with the grace to shine
> As statesman, scholar, orator, divine,
> He waged, as led by some peculiar star,
> With power and prejudice a truceless war;
> While craven souls the big battalions seek,

'George Tyrrell once said that some day nothing might be left of Christianity except Pauline Christ-mysticism and the law of love—I have been moving in the same direction . . . what happened 2,000 years ago cannot matter to us now, and there has been no revelation of the future.' Adam Fox, *Dean Inge* (John Murray, 1960), pp. 263–4.

[17] I am grateful to the Dean and Chapter of Durham for permission to consult this.

He pledged his sword to service of the weak,
And, self-consistent to a long life's end,
Forgave no folly and forgot no friend.

It was not the deepest truth about Henson. Alington, who was a happy man, would himself confess that he never really understood the emotion behind the account of the call of Christ in the letter of 1899. Nor could the privileged Alington understand why Henson, with his half-buried and largely ineffective sensitivity to the conditions of the poor, should be shocked at the elegance and comfort with which the Deanery at Durham was furnished in the 1930s. ('The fleshpots of Eton' was one of Bishop Henson's comments to his dean.) Alington was an Insider, and Henson stood beyond his circle. But the poem over the grave in Durham shows something. It shows why, when Charles Gore saw the Church as the Body of Christ, the genius of the Church of England demanded that there should arise an equally dedicated preacher and bishop to point out that the eternal Christ might sometimes disagree with his Body on earth.

FOR FURTHER READING

Gore's executors asked G. L. Prestige, an Oxford scholar who was later editor of the *Church Times*, to compile *The Life of Charles Gore: A Great Englishman* (Heinemann, 1935). The book was well written, but surprisingly did not discuss Gore's theology at any length, or contain a single footnote. Both these defects were put right by James Carpenter, *Gore: A Study in Liberal Catholic Thought* (Faith Press, 1960). Gore Memorial Lectures have been established at Westminster Abbey; they have included G. L. Prestige, *The Soul of a Prophet* (SPCK, 1948), and A. R. Vidler, 'Charles Gore and Liberal Catholicism', in *Essays in Liberality* (SCM Press, 1957). The development of Anglican theology from *Lux Mundi* in 1889 to 1939 was summarized with a masterly clarity by A. M. Ramsey, *From Gore to Temple* (Longmans, Green, 1960).

Henson's own *Retrospect of an Unimportant Life* was published in three volumes (Oxford University Press, 1942–50). *Letters of Herbert Hensley Henson* and *More Letters* were edited by E. F. Braley (SPCK, 1951–4).

1821-1902. *1881-1944*

Frederick and William Temple

1

Anything more hostile to the New Testament than our modern English religion is difficult to conceive. Well, I believe that the only thing that can save us is a vigorous attack from within the Church on the existing conceptions of religion. . . . If I lived 700 years before Christ, I should call it the word of the Lord. I don't know whether Amos actually saw things: probably not: but his vision was mine—'I saw the Lord standing above the altar' (His own altar it was) 'and He said unto me, SMITE!'

It was a very undergraduate letter. Its author was William Temple, and he wrote it in 1901, in the palace at Canterbury which his father, Archbishop Frederick Temple, had recently caused to be built. Forty-one years after writing it, he became Archbishop of Canterbury, the first son to follow his father in the post. But he did not 'smite'. Instead, he followed his father 'within the Church'. When he died in 1944, he was eighteen years younger than his father had been at the time of his death in 1902. But although his life was cut short, at the time of William Temple's death there were many who voiced the conviction that he had proved himself among the noblest figures in the story of Christianity. Even his critic Hensley Henson agreed that he was 'the most variously distinguished of the 32 Archbishops of Canterbury since the Reformation'.

William Temple was very much his father's son; in Henson's words, 'he was magnificently endowed by Nature, and all the circumstances of his life favoured him'. The security of a youth spent in Victorian episcopal palaces, and in the school and college where his father had been headmaster and tutor, never left him. Both father and son were self-confident and, while in theory they were democrats, in practice they relied little on the views of colleagues and cared even less about the attacks of critics. Both had the rare endowment of a photographic memory. Over a considerable period of time they could recall exactly what they had read or whom they had met. Both shared wide and keen interests in the history of thought and in current problems, with an ability to pronounce on many matters where lesser contemporaries would have pleaded ignorance or modesty. William would recall that his father had been reluctant to reveal his opinions, lest the son should agree with them too readily. When he delivered his Gifford Lectures he repeated the essential arguments of his father's Bampton Lectures half a century before, and he described a father's relations with his children.

He gave them being; to a great extent he shapes their circumstances; perhaps his influence over them is so great that they will never knowingly act against his wishes; yet they are free to respect his wishes or not; if they do so, it is because it appears to them good to do so; when he controls them, he does not coerce them, because his control is effective through their wills and not either apart from or against their wills.[1]

Frederick Temple was always so formidable, and could be so boorishly rude, that we might expect a clever and sensitive son to rebel against him—as, say, Matthew rebelled against Thomas Arnold. But the guidance of Frederick always appeared good to William's will. This temperamental affinity between father and son probably owed much to the fact that the father was in his sixties, and beginning to mellow, when he had two sons, of whom William (the younger, born at Exeter in 1881) was the brighter. An old man's delight that his name would be carried on may account for the gentleness with which he handled the boys; it was a delight which never came to the childless William. A glimpse survives of Frederick Temple coming out of daily prayers in the chapel of Fulham Palace, his arms around his two sons' shoulders. But in Frederick Temple's case, a special factor contributed to this normal happiness, for his pride in William was not only the pride of a father who had expected to be barren. It was also the pride of one now immersed in ecclesiastical administration, who had been happiest when teaching boys. Frederick Temple was the greatest schoolmaster of his day, and on no pupil was his educational skill lavished more freely than on William. His many letters to William at Rugby and Balliol thus preserved the liberal Anglican intellectual tradition from the 1840s to the 1940s.

For all their closeness and love, however, the father and the son had minds which were bent differently. Frederick Temple had a high mathematical capacity, was really interested in science, and made a formidable administrator. He was fortunate that it was his lot to administer admiring schoolboys and subservient schoolmasters and clergymen, for in most walks of life his essential self-dependence, his brusque speech, and his frequent verbal brutalities would have crippled his work. 'To us, I think', Scott Holland remembered, 'he always appeared like a great ship, furrowing its way alone through the seas'.[2]

William was in many ways the softer man. He would say that his

---

[1] William Temple, Nature, Man and God (Macmillan, 1934), p. 442.
[2] A Bundle of Memories, p. 166.

ignorance of science was so immense as to be distinguished, and his critics added that his style in making appointments, in administering discipline, or in accepting engagements (for example, to write Prefaces to inferior books) revealed little shrewdness about ordinary human nature. He did not possess the physique of his father, hardened by a boyhood on a Devon farm; he was overweight from boyhood. He also suffered from gout from the age of two (although he never touched alcohol or tobacco). It cannot be said that he showed his father's toughness in adversity, for he had no opportunity to do so: although he supported reform in the Church and Socialism in the State, and made sacrifices in such causes, throughout his life he was surrounded by an admiring affection. His approach was always genial. He found it easy to reconcile apparently incompatible intellectual positions in a formula which dazzled men who already loved him for his friendliness and tranquillity. He was a great ecumenical figure among Christians, for although he embodied the highest Anglican assurance and defended the standard Anglican positions he did so without causing the slightest personal offence. In those human relations which are carried on at a deeper level than argument, he constantly communicated an unbreakable love for, and a basic agreement with, everyone. In a shrewd summary recalled by Henson in 1946, Randall Davidson observed that 'the worst fault of Willie is that he is so kind-hearted that he can say no to nobody'.

The whole contribution of Frederick and William Temple to Church and State sprang from the former's education on the Ionian islands of Santa Maura and Corfu at the hands of his mother. Mrs. Dorcas Temple was a straightforward Cornishwoman who understood very little of the Latin and arithmetic which, day by day, she made her son memorize. The family's bungalow was called Government House and its standards were strictly middle-class, but they were too poor to have butter on their bread. Frederick Temple looked after his mother with great devotion until she died in 1866, and did not marry until ten years later. His choice fell on the aristocratic Beatrice Lascelles, who lived until 1915, making her home with William. Frederick Temple used to say wonderingly that every peer now seemed to be a cousin, and William Temple shared his father's deep respect for this great lady; he would repeat his mother's remark that, while he knew more than her, she knew better. It was only after her death that William felt free to marry. He chose Frances Anson, who revealed her qualities by freeing him from all domestic cares while he lived, by accepting his self-sacrifice which brought problems to the first ten years of their married life, and by unobtrusive but deeply appreciated work as a prison-visitor in Winchester during a long widowhood. The two archbishops owed much to these three exceptional and very different women.

2

Frederick Temple was born in 1821 on a small Mediterranean island because—as we saw in connection with Gladstone—the Ionian Islands were virtually British colonies (after 1815). Major Octavius Temple was 'Resident' in Santa Maura, and then for a brief period held a post on Corfu, before he found that he had saved enough to buy an inferior farm in Devon, at Axon near Culmstock. The family helped him to clear the land and to make a home out of the isolated house. But he became unpopular with his neighbours because of his criticisms of the conditions of British agriculture and of the Corn Laws which protected farmers. Never willing to control his tongue, he grew passionately angry with his children over trifles and got involved in some bitter quarrels. Neighbouring farmers denounced him as a radical. Worse, he could not make the farm pay—and he was overcome by the problem of educating the eight of his fifteen children who had survived infancy, specially the two sons then at home, Frederick and John (who became a colonel). There was a tradition of culture in the family, despite their present poverty; Octavius Temple's father had been a scholarly country clergyman. If the boys were to be sent to school, there seemed no alternative but their father's return to the colonial service. Octavius Temple, who had been too outspoken to be popular with his superiors, had to accept the Lieutenant-Governorship of the notoriously unhealthy Sierra Leone, leaving his family behind. Within ten months of his acceptance of the post, he was dead.

The family struggled on under the severe guidance of the mother. Until the age of twelve, Frederick Temple had no education except two hours a day which she supervised. Most of his time he spent as a farm boy. When he became a schoolmaster he still loved to climb trees, and to recall his skill at ploughing and threshing; when he visited a Chartist meeting and all who entered had to show their hands to prove that they were working-class, his hands were horny enough. To the end of his days he retained the marks of this childhood: a rough accent, no small talk, clarity and directness of mind and speech, an unwearying strength which made light of the burden of incessant labour despite heart trouble and failing eyesight.

These basic endowments were supplemented by an education at Blundell's School, Tiverton. It was a small grammar school, but Frederick Temple's five years there raised his level in classics and mathematics sufficiently for him to be nominated by the trustees of the school to a scholarship confined to Blundell's boys at Balliol College. He was entirely shaped by his mother's insistence that he should win by working and conforming. Poor as he was, he was a strong Tory in his youth, and no revolutionary when he grew up. One of the trustees met him in a country lane after the meeting, and said: 'Temple, I cannot say what you are going to be, but this I am sure of, that if you live long enough, you will be one of the greatest men in England.' Frederick walked home on air.

And so he walked through Oxford, in clothes and shoes which had to be patched. He could not afford to drink any wine, or to light a fire, or to use his oil-lamp in the evenings. Night after night he would sit on the staircase in Balliol, at his books under the public light. But his mind stirred. He enjoyed the metaphysics of Kant and Coleridge, and the cleverness of his Balliol tutors, Tait and Ward. He was awakened to the new biblical criticism, explaining to his mother that the Bible which she accepted literally was the Word of God to her because it appealed to her conscience. He was thrilled by Newman's power to convey the reality of the unseen world in continuity with the apostles. But when he reported his excitements to his mother he received wise advice for a young man so poor, and obeyed it: 'Freddy, don't argue.' He secured the highest honours in classics and mathematics, with a fellowship at Balliol in 1842, and was ordained by Samuel Wilberforce. Although other Blundell's Scholars had been despised, he had become a popular undergraduate in a college which respected his integrity, and which enjoyed his high spirits amid bleak poverty; and he now made a popular tutor also.

Tait invited him to join the Rugby staff, but Temple wanted to give his life to the education of boys in the 'workhouses', the rejects of Victorian society. He wanted to give them his practical sense, for he did not mind rolling up his sleeves or making sure that they were washed and combed; and he wanted to awaken their minds. From 1848 to 1857 he was, therefore, in the service of the newly formed Committee of the Privy Council on Education. For a year he worked as an examiner in the Education Office, but then the scheme which really interested him was launched. An estate near Twickenham, formerly owned by Sir Godfrey Kneller the painter, had been bought by the Government in order that a small college might be built for training schoolmasters to teach workhouse boys. In 1849 Kneller Hall Training College was opened. Frederick Temple was Principal, with the future compiler of the *Golden Treasury* of English poetry, Francis Palgrave, as Vice-Principal. He began with the highest enthusiasm.

But it soon became clear that the experiment would fail. Temple's fellow-clergymen worried about whether the new school was ecclesiastical enough. The pupils were few and mostly stupid, and the paternalist scheme for workhouse schools foundered. Temple made no secret of the problems as he saw them, and successive governments made no secret of their unwillingness to produce more money. The Principal tried browbeating the ministers; the ministers brushed him off, although they noted his abilities. At the end of 1855 Temple resigned from Kneller Hall, and employment was found for him as an Inspector of Training Colleges. He was a competent civil servant in the honourable work of the Education Office, and he had to his credit the fruitful suggestion that Oxford and Cambridge should sponsor examinations in the schools. But fifteen years after taking his degree, his outstanding energy and intelligence had not yet found adequate expression. He had hoped in vain to be elected Master of Balliol in 1854. Frustrated in his work, and unmarried while his mother lived, he was so miserable that he would read the obituaries in envy of the dead. What he had lost was his naïve idealism (which his son never lost); for after the failure at Kneller Hall his advice to the Education Office was chiefly aimed at strengthening middle class education by closer links between the grammar schools and the universities. The working class, he would suggest, needed only the rudiments. What he had gained was an experience of education at many levels and in many places—that, and a reputation for hard work.

Tait had wanted him as his successor at Rugby, but that had been when he had just begun at Kneller Hall, and he had not been willing to move. Dr. Goulburn, a stately and saintly Etonian, had been appointed. In 1857 Goulburn was leaving the school (which had declined) to be Dean of Norwich and a devotional writer; and Tait, now Bishop of London, again urged Temple on the trustees. This time Temple agreed to be a candidate. Matthew Arnold was not the only one to prophesy that the great days of Rugby would return, and the prophecy turned out right. When he had shocked people by walking from the station carrying his own bag, Temple reorganized a school which had been living too much on the Doctor's legend. Better arrangements were made for appointing and paying the masters, and more emphasis was placed on science and modern languages, which now had specialist teachers. With William Butterfield as architect, much more accommodation was built. The game of Rugby Football was made less barbarous. Temple forced these reforms through, and found that he had less of a battle than he had expected, for trustees and masters alike respected him, while the boys worshipped him. 'A beast, but a just beast' was the famous description given by a boy in a letter home. They hung on his every word, and told anecdotes about his crushing remarks. In their football clothes they crowded into the chapel on a Saturday afternoon to hear their headmaster prepare them for the next day's services. Parents responded almost as warmly as boys. Soon Temple had three times as many applications for places as he could accept.

Frederick Temple's share in *Essays and Reviews* was the only major mistake which he made as a headmaster. He admitted that he had underestimated the furore which the book would cause in the country, as the charge of heretical liberalism which had hung over Rugby since Arnold's time seemed to have been justified. Temple's own contribution was not heretical, or in any deep sense theological. It was simply an address to the boys which had been reworked to form a university sermon at Oxford. He had spent no more than ten hours on it. Its theme was 'The Education of the World', developing the stock comparison between the growth of an individual and the growth of mankind, and indulging in interpretations of biblical texts which did more credit to the author as a preacher than as a scholar.[3] There were some carelessly written passages about the obedience to the law in the Old Testament being replaced by the imitation of the example in the New, and about the imitation being replaced in its turn by an inner religion. These passages were not only echoes of Coleridge and Thomas Arnold; they were based on Frederick Temple's own experience of being liberated at Oxford from the over-simplicity of his mother's religion. William Temple was to restate the truth in them, when he delivered his Gifford Lecture on 'Authority and Experience.' But at the time they seemed sinister, because the orthodox placed them alongside some far more 'extreme' passages in other essays in the volume. The real worry, now as in the days of Thomas Arnold's indiscretions, was lest Rugby parents should be scared off.

When the book was attacked by the bishop who had ordained him, and apparently condemned by his patron Tait, all Temple's obstinacy was aroused. One seed of the idea of *Essays and Reviews* had been a conversation with Jowett at Kneller Hall when he had deplored the reticence of Christians in England over the intellectual challenges to the old orthodoxy; and he was not going to abandon the fight now. Another factor in his mind was that his chivalry forbade him to desert the other essayists by withdrawing his contribution in response to the clamour of the clergy or the cowardice of the bishops. He remained the friend of some of them (he often preached for Jowett at Balliol, and at the end it was he who buried Jowett). He sought to allay criticism not by recanting his share in *Essays and Reviews* but by publishing another book, consisting of sermons exactly as he had preached them at Rugby. This did reassure parents and others. The boys needed little reassurance. 'Dear Mother', wrote a Sixth Former in response to an anxious inquiry from home, 'Temple's all right; but if he turns Mahometan, all the school will turn too.'

Although Temple generally admitted that it had been an indiscretion for a Headmaster of Rugby to get involved in a major religious controversy, he never went back on his conviction that it had been right for

[3] Geoffrey Faber, *Jowett*, p. 235, considered the whole essay 'sad rubbish'.

someone to break the conspiracy of silence; and when the storm blew over, others came to agree that Temple the churchman had not been wrecked by this solitary error on the part of Temple the schoolmaster. Partly because they had come to share a common belief in disestablishment in Ireland, Gladstone was ready to face a storm in order to promote a teacher so earnest in religion and so sensible in politics. When the Deanery of Durham fell vacant he pressed it on Temple, who refused. When the death of old Harry Phillpotts at last released the bishopric of Exeter, and Samuel Wilberforce's move to Winchester also freed Oxford, Gladstone bade Temple choose his bishopric.

Wisely he chose Devon, where he could constantly appeal to his status as a local boy who had risen by industry and self-help. The wrench of leaving Rugby was great, and the storm came. Soon after congratulating him on his appointment, Samuel Wilberforce joined those who urged him to withdraw his essay now. As Temple refused, Shaftesbury and Pusey joined forces to prevent the scandal to the Church. There was an attempt made to block his election by the Greater Chapter of Exeter, but the majority voted to obey the Crown. Another attempt was made to stop the legal ceremony of his 'Confirmation' as a bishop. A sister was summoned to testify whether 'or not he had been born in wedlock, since bastards could not then be bishops. When the day of the consecration, 21 December, arrived, Bishop Wordsworth of Lincoln entered a final protest, although Wordsworth's *protégé* Benson had defended Temple in *The Times*. Jackson of London, who presided in Tait's absence through illness, proceeded with the consecration, but in the crowded and dark Westminster Abbey Temple was white-faced. His anxiety partly excused his harshly arrogant conduct towards his successor at Rugby, a dim schoolmaster brought in by trustees who were exhausted by the Arnold tradition.[4]

3

Three signs marked Frederick Temple's beginning as a bishop. In the middle of the Abbey service a crowd of working men entered. It was their dinner hour; they had come to pay tribute. Second, having

[4] Temple became a member when the governing body of Rugby School was reconstituted. He used this position to pursue his disapproval of his successor, Henry Heyman, who eventually had to be extricated from a disastrous reign by the offer of a rich living in 1874. It was said of Dr. Heyman: 'If a headmaster can't teach and can't preach and can't organize, he ought to be either a scholar or a gentleman.' The school then recovered, and a later headmaster, John Percival, was in the great tradition; William Temple, who was at Rugby under him, wrote his biography. See J. B. Hope Simpson, *Rugby since Arnold* (Macmillan, 1967).

frustrated his enemies, he at last withdrew his contribution to *Essays and Reviews*. Third, he preached at his enthronement in Exeter Cathedral a sermon which showed the worried orthodox what kind of a man had come among them. He had come, he said, to 'pour out before you all that is in my heart of devotion to you and to our common Master, our Lord God, the Son of God, Jesus Christ'.

His rule was all the more necessary because of the slackness in the diocese caused by the extreme Toryism and the long old age of Bishop Phillpotts, who had been reduced to muttering from his large palace on the outskirts of Torquay. In the event, Bishop Temple made his mark not as a liberal theologian (except through his shrewd advice to many young inquirers such as his own son William), but through the manliness of his addresses to working men on the evils of drink and through the vigour of his warnings to the clergy against neglect of duty. No one could call him soapy, but his fifteen years as inspector and teacher of the Church in Devon had an effect for which the best precedent was the episcopate of Samuel Wilberforce at Oxford.

Until his Rugby colleague and constant ally Benson was called to create the diocese of Truro (under his guidance), Temple had to travel over Cornwall as well as Devon. He enjoyed his journeys, particularly since they so often included confirmations of young people. As he watched the dull faces of the boys who knelt before him (he counted them easily, and thus discovered that some of them came to be confirmed twice), he formed a yet stronger resolve. Teachers must be trained; teachers must be sent into the parishes; and the clergy must themselves teach. He broke into the slumbers of Exeter Cathedral by insisting that its canons also must work, and he established himself in a restored palace by the cathedral. He had no assistant bishop, the officials whom he appointed were his creatures, and his Diocesan Conference, summoned amid talk of democracy in the Church, listened to what he wanted.

In 1885, when the gentle Jackson died, the diocese of London needed the touch of an invigorating chief, and Temple was moved from Exeter. At this stage there was no theological outcry. It was not merely that the Church of England had grown somewhat more liberal under Tait. By the age of sixty-four, Temple had also changed. He had come to love more than anything else the response of simple people to his simple preaching. When in reply to Jowett's urging he had agreed to deliver Bampton Lectures at Oxford, the course had contained nothing on which heresy-hunters could fasten. What counted in these lectures— and what gradually filled St. Mary's, after a poor initial attendance— was the rugged honesty of the man. He was, indeed, rather sober and old-fashioned for Oxford. 'I am only working out to its logical conclusion what was said long ago by Bishop Butler in England and by

Kant in Germany. . . . The fact is the doctrine of Evolution does not affect the substance of Paley's argument at all.' But the lectures showed that the Bishop of Exeter had continued to think about science, and to accept its teachings gladly in its proper sphere. The impact of the age of Darwin had of course made him stress that some truths were revealed only in the Bible, not in everyman's conscience or in science. But he clearly had no wish to contradict science; he speculated, for example, that the miracle of the resurrection of Christ would turn out to have been 'not a miracle, but the first instance of the working of a law till the last day quite unknown, but on that last day operative on all that ever lived'. 'It is plain', he concluded, 'that the antagonism between Science and Religion arises much more from a difference of spirit and temper in the students of each than from any inherent opposition between the two.'[5]

In London as in Exeter, Temple concentrated on diocesan duties. The concentration was necessary if he was to deal with his ten thousand letters, five hundred meetings, and seventy confirmations a year, but his sense of duty made him proud of the drudgery involved.

The real student knows perfectly well [he once said], and it is the thing of great importance in practical life, that nine-tenths of all good work, whatever it may be, is what we usually call drudgery, has a mechanical character about it, requires nothing more than orderliness. . . . Nine-tenths of all good work is labour in which those who are engaged cannot feel any conceit at all; . . . and the man of genius is distinguished from others mainly by this, that he sees, all through, what this mechanical drudgery is going to lead to . . .

Such a character repelled many of the sophisticated, as Benson noted this in his diary in 1891.

It is very, very painful to see the Lords always so unappreciative of the Bishop of London—the strongest man nearly in the House, the clearest, the highest toned, the most deeply sympathetic, the clearest in principle—yet because his voice is a little harsh, and his accent a little provincial (though of what province it is hard to say), and his figure square and his hair a little rough, and because all this sets off the idea of his independence, he is not listened to at all by these cold, kindly, worldly wise, gallant landowning powers. Some day his force and goodness *must* carry them.

The same qualities eventually carried the clergy. Their terribly earnest bishop, so overbearing and angular, could move them profoundly when he preached about the cross of Christ, or about righteousness in English life, or about the mission to the world. They knew all about his humble origins. (He had to borrow £5,000 in order to become Bishop of London, and could repay it only because his wife

---

[5] Frederick Temple, *The Relations between Religion and Science* (Macmillan, 1884), pp. 59, 113, 197, 246.

received a legacy.) But they revered him, and they welcomed him as Archbishop of Canterbury in 1896. Amid all the worldliness of imperial London as the Victorian age reached its sunset, Temple's integrity exerted an appeal. Here was a link with the early morning simplicity of an older England. So blind that extra large cards had to be printed showing him his words, Frederick Temple crowned Edward VII (but put the crown on back to front).

He had no general policy for the Church, for he had come to think it 'a young thing' to have a general policy; and 'Freddy, don't argue' was still his motto for particular problems, where he would either decide or keep silent. He had strong principles of morality and piety; these were what the drudgery of church life led to; and these he hammered home. He also had some liberal ideas, for example over divorce. 'The Church', he declared, 'always strongly dissuaded the innocent party from remarrying, but never forbad it.' But his liberalism was very far from being extreme. He told a disappointed General Gordon that even in order to convert Africa the Church could not allow three wives at a time. He told an equally disappointed Mr. Gladstone that Anglicanism in Wales, although a minority, was working hard and did not deserve to be disestablished. He was greeted often by working men, but he made little effort to be their champion. It was characteristic of him that during the great London Dock Strike, when he was on holiday, he returned in order to mediate between the strikers and the employers at the Mansion House alongside Cardinal Manning; but when he thought the strikers were being unreasonable (he said that they were going back on their word in the negotiations), he resumed his holiday, thus giving Manning the glory of ending the dispute. He was the constant adviser of Benson, but his was almost always practical advice; and when he went to Lambeth himself at the age of seventy-six, no one could be surprised that he took no advice.

As Primate he bothered little with affairs which he was too old to begin studying or remedying. When troublesome questions were submitted to him by the colonial bishops, the letters were left unanswered. When invited to Scotland, instead of a vision of the Churches' reunion he gave them sermons on the evils of alcohol. When invited to pronounce on ritual, he pointed to the Book of Common Prayer. The building and equipment of a palace close by the cathedral at Canterbury (as at Exeter) did interest him—and so did the renewal of the drainage and much stonework in Lambeth Palace, and the handing over of the adjacent ten acres to the local authority as a playing field. The money for this work came from the sale of Addington Park to a South African diamond merchant. As an excited undergraduate Frederick Temple had found calm, and as a depressed official in the Education Office he had found relief, in going to as many church services as he could; now as a half-blind archbishop, he delighted to attend worship in Canterbury Cathedral. He would kneel upright, explaining: 'I always do that. My mother taught me.' And there today he kneels upright in effigy, on a monument which recalls the best description of him in the prime of his manhood. He was 'granite on fire'.

4

The young William Temple once asked his father what he thought about Coleridge's speculations on the Trinity. Frederick Temple replied:

I cannot understand him; and I have never been able to feel sure that he understood himself. Nevertheless, I am obliged to confess that from seventeen to five-and-twenty I indulged largely in such speculations. But I felt all along like a swimmer who sees no shore before him after long swimming, and at last allows himself to be picked up by a ship that seems to be going his way. I do not want to check your imaginings. Go on as long as you feel that you get any good at all by doing so. But I rather fancy you will come to the same end as I came to long before you. My passing ship was S. John.

The theological story of William Temple is the story of the truth in his father's prophecy. The metaphysical speculations which he reported home were his chief interest from the time when he read the philosophers in his spare time as a schoolboy at Rugby to the day when he gave up teaching at Oxford in 1910. His later books reflected this interest. During the war he produced a book in the high metaphysical style, finishing it on the night before his wedding (*Mens Creatrix*, 1917), and while Bishop of Manchester he produced another, although this was more theological (*Christus Veritas*, 1924). As Archbishop of York he snatched intervals from his duties in order to conduct a general survey of his own philosophy and other people's in Gifford Lectures (*Nature, Man and God*, 1934).

What he did in this teaching, however, was to reduce the rhetorical conflicts of the metaphysicians to a clear order where every argument was crisply given its place and related to the Christianity of his father. The theologian Emil Brunner gently pointed out to William Temple on a post card that while he called his theology 'natural' it was in fact Christian; and the point was not unwelcome, for Temple stated his attitude frankly in the first of his Gifford Lectures. 'The plain and crude fact is that you can get out of philosophy just what you put into it—rearranged no doubt, set in order and rendered comprehensible; but while the machine may determine the size and shape of the emergent sausage, it cannot determine the ingredients.' In his Preface to that book, Temple acknowledged that his main conclusions were not the result of a conscious analysis of problems. 'All my decisive thinking goes on behind the scenes. . . . Often when teaching I have found my-self expressing rooted convictions which until that moment I had no notion that I held.' And the most deeply rooted of these convictions was that the truth of Christianity was beyond the reach of philosophy. 'The primary assurances of Religion are the ultimate questions of Philosophy', he noted in the second of these lectures. 'Religion finds its fullest expression in absolute surrender to the Object of its worship. But the very existence of that Object is a main theme of philosophical disputation.' It was a synthesis of worship and disputation which many of his contemporaries admired, even if (like some of those who grew up with him at Rugby and Oxford) they privately thought him a bumptious fat boy, or (like a tutor at Balliol) suspected that he some-times thought 'that he had found a solution, when he had found a phrase'.

If Temple had done nothing more than to put the metaphysics of his Oxford into a Christian synthesis, his books might have rated a paragraph in a comprehensive history of English philosophy—but scarcely more, for the whole intellectual tradition of which he was a part and a climax collapsed during his lifetime, as he had the rare courage to acknowledge. While he was delivering his Gifford Lectures in Glasgow, Hitler came to power in Germany. The cosmic optimism of Oxford metaphysics was already under attack from a younger generation of sharper thinkers, and from Englishmen disillusioned by the 1914 war and its squalid aftermath. In the 1930s and 1940s it came to seem implausible, and by 1970 it had been forgotten. The abiding impressiveness of Temple's life lay, however, in the application of an able mind, confident in its philosophical equipment, to the religious questions of the day.

He sensed this destiny when as a tutor of philosophy at Queen's College he confessed that he did not want to spend all his life lecturing in the morning and going to the Common Room in the evening. He was happy during his six years at Queen's—with ample leisure for reading; with duties which amounted to little more than expounding his views on Plato, or personality, or knowledge, or society, to young men who drank it all in; with music and friendship around him in the university; with his mother holding court in her Keble Road house. He used to say that he had to pray long for guidance when eventually a strong call came to leave Oxford. But he was an actor who wanted a larger stage: the Church of England, which he loved and was half-inclined to 'smite'. And more profoundly he was a churchman because, not content with a Platonic idealism, he wanted a word from eternity. His own masters were those who saw Christ standing as the answer. The poems of Browning moved him deeply, and he quoted them throughout his life. In sermons which he repeated on many occasions and finally revised to make his most enduring book, *Readings in St. John's Gospel* (first series 1939, second series 1940), St. John was presented as a Plato for whom the Word had become flesh.

His deliverance from a life of metaphysical swimming and cultured ease came through his inherited sense of duty towards the people's education. The Workers' Educational Association had come into being through the energy of Albert Mansbridge of the Co-operative Wholesale Society. Mansbridge visited Oxford looking for a leader for this movement, a leader who could stir the indifferent who were to be found equally among the university authorities and in the trade unions. He found his man in William Temple, who served as President of the Workers' Educational Association from 1908 to 1924. 'He invented *me*', Temple said later about Mansbridge, the explanation being that Mansbridge introduced him to the working class. He was never as familiar with everyday life as his own father had been, or as any parish priest has to be, and he often tended to believe that trade unionists would be interested in Plato or Browning; but the speaking that he did for the W.E.A., together with his visits to the Oxford Medical Mission in Bermondsey, broadened his horizons beyond the places of privilege where he lived, and were the making of the People's Archbishop of the second world war. Precisely because he was so privileged and secure in his own life, once he began to gain knowledge about the conditions of the people he felt free to conduct propaganda for the Labour movement—as his father had not felt free. (Between the father and the son was the same gap as between Henson and Gore.) Already at the Pan-Anglican Congress in 1908 the voice of William Temple was heard as well as the voice of John Malcolm Ludlow, urging that Christianity must be 'applied to the economic system'.

The Student Christian Movement was another liberating force in William Temple's life, and also received the reward of a lifetime's loyalty as a spokesman and counsellor. The movement had grown out of the Evangelical revival and missionary enthusiasm of the 1870s, but when Temple was a young don at Oxford it was finding its way into a wider world. If the Gospel was to be received by students, and preached by them as their life's work, it must be related to intellectual questions. If it was to be spread through Asia and Africa, the social problems of Asia and Africa must be studied first. And if missionaries were to go out from Britain, there must be some study of Britain's own responsibilities as the world's leading colonial power—and of Britain's own problems as a capitalist state where there was gross inequality. With its summer conferences under canvas, its local missions, its magazine, and its eager Christian Unions in the universities, the movement then specialized in taking students and young dons from conventionally religious homes and making them think about Christianity's whole task in the modern world. William Temple was just such a man, and the General Secretary, Tissington Tatlow, soon spotted him. He became a fluent speaker on all the movement's concerns. His first book, *The Faith and Modern Thought* (1910), grew out of addresses to the London Inter-collegiate Christian Union. In 1910 he attended the World Missionary Conference in Edinburgh as a steward appointed by the S.C.M., and from Edinburgh he went to Australia in order to conduct university missions.

Ever since the nursery (where he had kept a little mitre) he had scarcely allowed any question that one day he would follow his father into the ministry of the Church of England. In 1906, however, he was brave enough to confess to Francis Paget, Bishop of Oxford: 'I am inclined, very tentatively, to accept the doctrine of the Virgin Birth, and with rather more confidence, that of the Bodily Resurrection of our Lord.' Paget, who shared the opinion of his successor Gore that confidence in both doctrines was essential to a priest, replied that he could not take the responsibility of ordaining him. Oxford theologians both Broad (Streeter and Rashdall) and High (Scott Holland and Gore) continued to advise Temple about his lingering doubts, and Randall Davidson refused to regard Paget's refusal as final. After a long talk with Temple in 1908, the Archbishop felt able to tell Bishop Paget that 'I myself regard him as being, *in all essential particulars*, an orthodox believer both in the Virgin Birth of Our Blessed Lord and in His Resurrection'; and he offered to ordain him. Davidson explained to Paget that Temple

has been definitely sharing in Christian and Evangelistic work (both in connection with the Student Christian Movement and otherwise) and he has shewn me, beyond question, that his whole attitude towards the Faith has undergone a change or a 'deepening', and that *credal* things possess now a reality for him which they did not, to anything like the same degree, possess before.

In 1909 William Temple was made a deacon, and in 1910 a priest, in Canterbury Cathedral. Some five years later, during a symphony concert in London, he experienced absolute certainty about the Virgin Birth. Already in *The Faith and Modern Thought* he had declared that reason and experience demanded Christian belief; 'the whole creed is the only hypothesis that meets the facts'. Henceforth his philosophy was tied securely within the framework of the Church's orthodoxy, and he never regretted his abandonment of individualist and intellectualist habits of mind. He had found the real world—indeed, he had found himself—by belonging to the society around him, and in particular to the Church; and with his whole heart he rejected the position of Descartes, 'I think, therefore I am'. 'If I were asked what was the most disastrous moment in the history of Europe', he declared as Gifford Lecturer, 'I should be strongly tempted to answer that it was that period of leisure when René Descartes, having no claims to meet, remained for a whole day "shut up alone in a stove".' That was the day of *je pense, donc je suis*. The basis of his own thought was shown in *Christus Veritas*: 'the self is capable of complete satisfaction in proportion as it is left outside the field of its own attention.' To this sentence on page 29, Temple added a footnote: 'In other words, joy is the fruit of humility.'

5

In a speech to the Oxford Union defending the Liberals' Education Bill of 1906, William Temple had stated his adherence to the tradition of Arnold and Tait and his repudiation of the 'denominational ideal' championed by Gore; the National Church was 'the whole people of England in its religious capacity'. The first post that he accepted as a clergyman was accordingly a public school headmastership. Since Rugby was not vacant, he became headmaster of Repton, with ideas about reforming the public school system. But he found that he was not his father; he simply could not get interested enough in the problems of boys. He preached to them and he talked to them about the Greeks, but he soon knew that he would never make a good schoolmaster.

When the liberal essays called *Foundations* were published under his editorship, his Oxford friend Ronald Knox wrote about the editor:

> A man so broad, to some he seem'd to be
> Not one, but all Mankind in Effigy:
> Who, brisk in Term, a Whirlwind in the Long,
> Did everything by turns, and nothing wrong,
> Bill'd at each Lecture-hall from Thames to Tyne
> As Thinker, Usher, Statesman or Divine.[6]

And when Ronald Knox wrote criticism which was intended to be more serious (a book called *Some Loose Stones*), accusing the contributors to *Foundations* of being obsessed with the question how much of orthodox Christianity a modern 'Jones' could be persuaded to swallow, William Temple gaily replied: 'I am Jones himself, asking what there is to eat.' However, he also made it plain to Knox that, like his father

[6] Ronald Knox, 'Absolute and Abitofhell', reprinted in his *Essays in Satire* (Sheed & Ward, 1928).

before him, he was more orthodox than those pages in the book which had given most offence, and like his father he kept criticism out of the school sermons which he published. Clearly the headmastership had been a false move, but what was he to do?

After two years at Repton he nearly accepted a post as a missionary in India, as Principal of St. John's College, Agra, only to find that Davidson thought his contacts with the mysterious world of Labour in England too valuable for it to be right for him to leave the country. He did accept Henson's post at Westminster, only to find that the offer had to be withdrawn since he had not been ordained long enough to satisfy the Abbey's statutes. This negotiation about St. Margaret's, Westminster, was public knowledge, and in 1914 everyone was relieved when a London pulpit suited to his gifts was offered to him, as Rector of St. James's, Piccadilly.

It was in the pulpit of St. James's that he worked out his exposition of St. John. His educated congregation wanted deep preaching, not a superficial commentary on the war news as supplied by too many other clergy. Temple gave them a Christ who was the incarnation of the love of God in a world of selfishness and tragedy. He presented an attractive Jesus, not a mere symbol in a Catholic or Evangelical scheme, yet the presentation was never sentimental; when his mother died on Good Friday 1915, he kept the news secret until after he had finished preaching about the death of Jesus. He brushed aside critical questions to concentrate on this spiritual meaning of the text. And so he found, for himself and others, a centre which was affirmed when they sang in S. S. Wesley's anthem at his consecration as a bishop in York Minster, and when they inscribed on his grave in the cloister at Canterbury, the text: *Thou wilt keep him in perfect peace whose mind is stayed on Thee.*

When the war broke out so soon after Temple's move to Piccadilly in 1914, it presented him with a crisis to which his profound theology must be made profoundly relevant, and this was the beginning of the influence which he exercised over the mind of the nation during the next thirty years. He used his London church as a base for prolific consultation, speaking, and journalism. He became editor of the recently founded church newspaper, the *Challenge*, urging social and ecclesiastical reform. He became a secretary of the National Mission of Repentance and Hope, and supervised the production of its extensive literature. He was the youngest member of the Archbishops' Commission on Church and State; and when Dick Sheppard of St. Martin-in-the-Fields wanted a 'ginger group' to press for self-government and a radical renewal in the Church, he became chairman of the Life and Liberty Movement. It had the slogan: 'The rising tide of Life within the Church demands Liberty.' While in his mid-thirties he was thus a force of inspiration to the Church of England, and among church leaders he had by now a unique appeal to the intelligent young.[7]

A few, such as Henson, resented this easy success, but during 1917 Temple disarmed jealousy by a brave act. Little more than a year after marrying Frances Anson, he resigned from St. James's. The church brought him a regular congregation which he had grown to love, the architecture of Sir Christopher Wren, a rectory in the heart of the capital, and an income over £2,000 a year. He exchanged all this for a salary of £700, in order to give his whole energy to itinerent propaganda work on behalf of the Life and Liberty Movement, despite the scepticism of Archbishop Davidson and the coolness of the Establishment generally.

The Church Assembly which emerged from the propaganda disappointed idealists such as Temple and Sheppard. The new Parochial Church Councils listened not to the rushing wind of the Spirit but to comparatively minor matters, and no really effective steps were taken in Temple's lifetime to rationalize the deployment of the clergy, to equalize their payments, to reform canon law, or to revise the Prayer Book officially. But the Church of England did acquire an instrument of reform, however irresolute the hands might be which wielded it. And with the Church Assembly it gained one other asset: the knowledge that its best hopes were stored in the capacious figure of William Temple.

How was he to lead the advance? He was supplied with a home and a pulpit at Westminster Abbey as a canon in 1919, and early in 1922 was consecrated Bishop of Manchester (with Dick Sheppard as preacher). Edmund Knox, the last bishop, had been an Evangelical martinet, and the leading laymen were stolidly Conservative. The diocese needed to be divided by the creation of a separate diocese of Blackburn (which was done in 1927)—and even after that, it was still the second largest in England. But such problems were conquered.

In April 1924 he presided over the conference at Birmingham where 1,500 delegates were harangued by Gore and others about the social teachings of Christianity. This 'Conference on Christian Politics, Economics and Citizenship' was the high-water mark of the wartime and post-war reforming tide. No conference in English history had been more thoroughly prepared. After a nation-wide discussion and a careful analysis of questionnaires, twelve volumes were produced in connection with it, advocating many of the reforms which began to be put into effect twenty-one years later. There were those who regarded 'Copec' as a peak moment of English religion, before disillusionment in society

---

[7] Lectures by William Temple to students in 1921 and 1925 were published and reprinted with an essay by J. Eric Fenn, under the title *About Christ* (SCM Press, 1962).

brought a return to ecclesiastical obsessions and to doctrinal rigidity. And there were those who lamented that its oratory was never followed up in a long-term, large-scale organization which might have been a Life and Liberty Movement for the English nation, or at least an adult version of the Student Christian Movement. Instead, the formulation of a moral and social theology was left to the small Anglo-Catholic 'Christendom' group, which threw up some provocative ideas but suffered under the two handicaps of nostalgia for the Middle Ages and ignorance of economics.[8]

Looking back, some have blamed William Temple for not leading the Anglican Establishment more boldly into Socialism, or for not working out more precisely what Christian Socialism involved. Such a verdict, however, would not do justice to the historical situation in which Temple found himself. The Church was still for the most part deeply conservative in theology or in prejudice, in organization or in the lack of it, in politics or in the belief that religion should not get mixed up with the problems of society; and the fat and jolly William Temple owed his platforms to his basic conformity with this Establishment. (Even the leadership of Life and Liberty had not been an exodus into the desert.) Rejecting the intuition of Henson that after the disasters of the Revised Prayer Book a radical change in the relations of Church and State was essential to the Church's self-respect, Temple announced that the votes of the House of Commons had been the will of God.

On the other hand, while happily at work within the Anglican Establishment, Temple was by the standards of his time remarkably courageous and prophetic. It was a dismal time: the England of Ramsay MacDonald and Stanley Baldwin. Successive governments were unable to deal with economic slumps or with the dictators who had arisen in response to the even greater problems of unemployment in other countries. In the Church of England, Davidson and Lang drifted on. Temple was not able to arouse in public, or perhaps in himself, any great conviction that this stagnation could be cured quickly. The monthly magazine, *The Pilgrim: A Review of Christian Politics and Religion,* published by Longmans during seven years from 1920 as a vehicle for Temple and his friends, never paid its way and had to be abandoned, as the weekly *Challenge* had been.[9] He did what he believed he could do; although he was ambitious in the sense of believing that a leader's role in great affairs was his natural lot, he

[8] For a study of social thought in the Church of England 1918–39, see John Oliver, *The Church and Social Order* (Mowbray, 1968).
[9] Many of William Temple's contributions to the *Pilgrim* were collected with some of his addresses as Bishop of Manchester in his *Essays in Christian Politics and Kindred Subjects* (Longmans, Green, 1927).

spoke his mind with little thought about possible damage to his career, with the result that his life was unstained by worldliness or intrigue and even his critics who were irritated by his effortless superiority and tendency to omniscience, or by his personal popularity, admitted his integrity. From 1918 to 1925 he was a card-carrying member of the Labour Party—which was in the eyes of the Anglican Establishment an act of courage. (He resigned over Labour's foreign policy.) He constantly preached civic responsibility in industrial Lancashire where his pastoral duties lay, and although he was out of England, being treated for gout, at the time of the General Strike, with some other churchmen he attempted—rather amateurishly, he later admitted—to mediate between the owners, the miners, and the Government in the Coal Stoppage which followed. This activity in relation to working-class politics revived the tradition of Westcott and Gore, whom Temple always had in mind. Davidson suspected that it contributed to the unpopularity of the bishops' Prayer Book with the politicians; and the indignant Baldwin asked how the bishops would feel if the industrialists proposed to revise the Athanasian Creed. Such pleas to confine himself to ecclesiastical duties left Temple unmoved. When he was enthroned in Manchester Cathedral, he expressed the tone of his ministry in a sermon. It was so similar to, and yet so different from, his father's defiant affirmations in Exeter Cathedral in 1869.

I come as a learner, with no policy to advocate, no plan already formed to follow. But I come with one burning drive; it is that in all our activities, sacred and secular, ecclesiastical and social, we should help each other to fix our eyes on Jesus . . . Pray for me chiefly that I may never let go of the unseen hand of the Lord Jesus and may live in daily fellowship with him.

That explains why William Temple was never rattled. (When interrupted in his writing, he would break off in the middle of a sentence, so that he could resume immediately the piece of business was done.) It explains why he got a good report in a candid and anonymous little book of 1928 about the leaders of the Church. 'He is a modern man in a modern world, eager for social reform, eager for the re-statement of truth, always eager for something . . . No Bishop is more popular in his diocese.'[10] And it explains why Henson's ironic comment in 1920 was in the event wide of the mark:

The new Bishop of Manchester will have a great opportunity for putting his theories to work in his new Diocese. He starts with the advantage of never having had to lose his self-confidence in the school of experience; and is young enough to have a large margin of experimental failure before he too must register himself among the Baffled.[11]

[10] *The Looking-Glass of Lambeth* by 'The Unknown Layman', in fact Sidney Dark (Philip Allan, 1928), p. 50.
[11] *More Letters*, p. 140.

6

'The Way of Renewal' was the title of a campaign for Bible study and prayer in groups, launched by the new leaders of the Church of England after Randall Davidson's resignation. Looking back, we can see that it would have been more renewing for the Church of England had William Temple been made Archbishop of Canterbury at the age of forty-seven. But it seemed impossible to promote anyone over the head of Cosmo Lang, who had been made Archbishop of York in the year when William Temple had been ordained a priest.

Lang, whose ambition came out of the England of Curzon and F. E. Smith, turned out to be the ecclesiastical equivalent of MacDonald or Baldwin. When he got ecclesiastical power, he did not know what to do with it. Part of the problem was that he fell seriously ill immediately after his move, but essentially his was the tragedy of the *arriviste* who arrived. As he signed on real letters the 'Cosmo Cantuar:' which he had practised while still a vicar, he sighed to his chaplain: 'What's the use, when it's all dust and ashes?' It was a characteristic piece of self-dramatization by a man who took care to provide for his biographer both notes of guidance and also plenty of romantic material.[12] He loved to act his part against the background of the palaces and gardens at Bishopthorpe and Lambeth, and in ecclesiastical pageants in York Minster or Canterbury Cathedral, while Temple was embarrassed by the splendour of the Bishopthorpe gardens and became the first Archbishop of Canterbury to open his own front door. When on holiday Lang would spend hours alone in prayer—and would grow introspective, recording his self-condemnation on paper. He had also put on paper while a scholboy an imaginary *Who's Who* entry showing himself as Earl of Norham, Prime Minister, and the father of eight (all to his biographer's delight). In real life Lang the bachelor, the Scot who grew apart from his family, craved the affection of his chaplains and the company of England's grandees; Temple, although childless, was deeply happy as a son and husband, and needed none of the applause which he so often received.

In 1924, the year of Temple's presidency over Copec, a number of friends arranged that a portrait of Lang by Sir William Orpen should be painted to hang at Bishopthorpe. 'They say in that portrait I look proud, prelatical and pompous', Lang remarked in Henson's hearing. Henson interjected: 'And may I ask Your Grace to which of those epithets Your Grace takes exception?' Yet Lang was, like Henson himself, more than a careerist. Archbishop Söderblom of Sweden, when shown the Orpen portrait, said: 'That is what the Devil meant

[12] See J. G. Lockhart, *Cosmo Gordon Lang* (Hodder & Stoughton, 1949).

him to be, but thanks be to God it is not so.' Orpen himself, when the
Archbishop had been sitting for him, made the most profound of this
series of remarks. 'I see seven archbishops. Which of them am I to paint?'

The meteoric rise of Cosmo Lang can be recounted briefly, since in
the event it was less momentous for the Church of England than seemed
likely at the time. He was the son and grandson of ministers of the
Church of Scotland. Born in 1864, he was brought up in Glasgow. As
a student at that university he was intoxicated by the metaphysics of
Edward Caird, then a professor in Glasgow before becoming Master of
Balliol. Walking in the park one day he shouted: 'The Universe is one
and its Unity and Ultimate Reality is God!' (Could there be a better
summary of the philosophy of William Temple?) In the year of Archbishop Tait's death, he entered Balliol. He flourished in the Balliol
atmosphere of hard study and high debate, and after a period of uncertainty, when he struggled to be a barrister without having his heart
in it, he became a Fellow of All Souls two years after Henson. Next
year the thought came to him insistently: 'After all, why shouldn't *you*
be ordained?'

Like Tait and Davidson, this young Scot chose the Church of England and was confirmed. Like Henson, he was ordained in the parish
church at Cuddesdon and worked among the poor (as a curate in
Leeds, having refused an invitation to be Henson's curate). After
returning to Oxford for a short spell as Dean of Divinity at Magdalen
and Vicar of St. Mary's, he became Vicar of Portsea at the age of
thirty-one. He was at the head of fourteen or more curates, all living
celibately in the vicarage and 'working' an artisan parish of about
40,000. He became an eloquent preacher, a tireless parish priest (when
not away), a favourite of Queen Victoria at nearby Osborne—another
young Samuel Wilberforce. In 1901 Winnington-Ingram, who had just
become Bishop of London, arranged that Lang should follow him as
Bishop of Stepney. He soon acquired a national reputation as the
leader of the Church of England Men's Society. He was also a canon
of St. Paul's; the aged Dean Gregory, when installing him, was under
the impression that he was Charles Gore. His vision of the Church was
indeed like Gore's, but more than any of the great churchmen just
mentioned he had a flair for the personal contact, for the common
touch without losing dignity, for an appeal to the imagination. Much
depended on his presence and voice, but something of his magnetism
is preserved in his books. We have the novel about the Jacobite rebels
in the heather, *The Young Clanroy*, based on stories told to the choristers at Magdalen; we have the published sermons about the miracles
and parables of Jesus; we have the lectures at Cambridge on pastoral
work.[13] As he moved from scenes of historic beauty to scenes of

[13] *The Opportunity of the Church of England* (Longmans, Green, 1905).

modern poverty, he could urge the privileged to stoop with him and the poor to rise with him. For others as for himself, life could be the greatest romance.

He was made Archbishop of York at the age of forty-four. Asquith, the Prime Minister, believed that the Church of England deserved young and decisive leadership; and Davidson wanted a fellow-archbishop who would be more actively co-operative than Maclagan, who had just retired from York at the age of eighty-three.[14] His appointment, like Winnington-Ingram's to London or Gore's to Worcester, emphasized that the bishops were not now expected to suppress High Church ceremonial, whatever Frederick Temple might have said about the law of the land. Lang was an ambassador of the High Anglican ethos into the coldly Low province in the North: the ethos of a warm humanity in service based on a dignified beauty in worship. In the diocese and the province alike, he made his mark as a pastor. But at the national level he was in the event far less decisive, because there policy was shaped by the caution of Davidson. For nineteen years Lang played second fiddle to his fellow-Scot at Lambeth.

He played that instrument very gracefully; his was the command of English, and his was the skill as the chairman of the relevant committee, that made the Lambeth Appeal of 1920 so eloquent and so acceptable a plea for reunion. But the oratory did not present a thought-out policy of his own to seize the new opportunities in Church and State. In the conversation with the Free Churches after that Appeal, Lang caused excitement by acknowledging their ministers as 'ministers of Christ's Word and Sacraments within the Universal Church of Christ which is His Body'. But, shrewdly, he had not said that they were ministries *of* the Universal Church—and, when the Free Churchmen pressed him, he showed no enthusiasm to march on to a reconciliation. He also did little to identify the Church of England with the poor, although his maiden speech in the House of Lords was a plea that the peers should pass the People's Budget of the Liberals.

Even in a body so conservative as the Church of England, Lang was beginning to seem like a figure out of the history which he could recount so well. The two most dramatic crises in his life as an archbishop brought him great unpopularity. In 1914, after this first experience of public abuse, most of his hair fell out and the remainder went white, so that he had to try wearing a wig until it got caught in a chandelier. The trouble arose out of a speech in York. Lang remembered how the Kaiser and Edward VII had knelt side by side at the bier of Queen Victoria, and he now declared that he resented 'coarse and

---

[14] In 1860 Maclagan had been chosen by Tait to be the first organizer of the London Diocesan Church Building Society. See F. D. How, *Archbishop Maclagan* (Wells, Gardner, Darton, 1911).

vulgar' attacks on the Kaiser. 'A personal memory of the Emperor, very sacred to him,' made him feel that the Kaiser had got involved in the war 'not without great reluctance'. The British public responded to Lang with even coarser and more vulgar comments. Lang did not really learn his lesson, for when George V died in 1935 the Archbishop again came forward with an unctuous description of the deathbed.

In the Abdication crisis of 1936, there was a similarly disastrous flight of eloquence. During the drama caused by the determination of Queen Victoria's eldest grandson to marry a lady with two husbands still living in the United States, Lang as Archbishop of Canterbury did little more than any man would have felt compelled to do if in the position of chief pastor of the Church of England in the 1930s; for Edward VIII was to be crowned and anointed in Westminster Abbey as King and Supreme Governor of the Church, at a time when that Church was doing its utmost to discourage remarriage after divorce. Lang made the Church's official attitude clear if it was ever in doubt, although he was never forced to declare what he would have done had the King insisted on Mrs. Simpson being crowned as Queen. However, the decisive voice raised against the King's marriage was not the Archbishop's; it was the British public's and Commonwealth's—or at least, it was public opinion as interpreted by Stanley Baldwin.[15]

When Edward had abdicated and gone into exile, Lang made a broadcast, lamenting this 'craving for private happiness'.

Strange and sad it must be that for such a motive, however strongly it pressed upon his heart, he should have disappointed hopes so high and abandoned a trust so great. Even more strange and sad it is that he should have sought his happiness in a manner inconsistent with the Christian principles of marriage, and within a social circle whose standards and ways of life are alien to all the best instincts and traditions of his people . . . How can we forget the high hopes and promise of his youth; his most genuine care for the poor, the suffering, the unemployed; his years of eager service both at home and across the seas? It is the remembrance of these things that wrings from our hearts the cry—'The pity of it, O, the pity of it!' To the infinite mercy and the protecting care of God we commit him now, wherever he may be.

Baldwin congratulated Lang on this sermon: 'it was the voice of Christian England.' Its sentiments were those of many, including Edward's mother Queen Mary. Yet once again Lang's rhetoric had

---

[15] A survey of the evidence by a competent journalist is Brian Inglis, *Abdication* (Hodder & Stoughton, 1966). The storm was unleashed by Bishop Blunt of Bradford's guarded criticism of the King during a diocesan conference. This was meant to be a gentle rebuke of Edward's irregular churchgoing, but was taken by the press as an opportunity to break the silence surrounding Mrs. Simpson. For a biography of this Socialist bishop, see J. S. Peart-Binns, *Blunt* (Mountain Press, Queensby, Yorks., 1969).

brought him to a fall. Many of those who believed that 'the King must go' believed also that the Archbishop should have exercised more restraint when the King had gone. A least one bishop's sermon at that time was a model of restraint without weakness.[16] Perhaps Lang should have confined himself to William Temple's robust comment: 'It has happened to many a man before now to find himself beginning to fall in love with another man's wife.'[17]

Unlike William Temple, Cosmo Lang did not have the moral stature needed to carry off a prophetic rebuke. His whole style of life made it easy for the friends of Edward VIII to express an angry contempt for his snobbery and irrelevance to the times. Such men would, no doubt, have disliked any archbishop.[18] But there were others, more sympathetic, who more sadly remembered the high hopes of his early years, his genuine care for the poor, his eager service, and who regretted that as an archbishop from 1909 to 1942 he found his happiness within an aristocratic circle increasingly alien from the life of the English people. And such people looked away from William Cosmo Gordon Lang (as he had been christened—but the William was too plebeian for use) to William Temple.

7

William Temple seemed to put into unfalteringly copious words, and to embody stoutly among the powerful, an integrity which Lang lacked —and which in lesser men could lead to eccentricity or heartbreak. For there were men of God in England from 1914 onwards who were not 'leaders' in the grand Victorian sense, but who communicated their faith to the man in the street because it was a faith held amid tragedy, as befitted the real situation of the Church in the twentieth century. These prophets impressed because they reminded the Englishman of the crucified Christ.

Had this been a book about prophets rather than leaders, we might have described at greater length the two best-known among them:

[16] Maurice Headlam, *Bishop and Friend: Nugent Hicks, Sixty-fourth Bishop of Lincoln* (Macdonald, 1945), pp. 149–53.

[17] *York Diocesan Leaflet*, January 1937.

[18] Examples of the hatred of Lang are preserved in *Chips: The Diaries of Sir Henry Channon*, ed. R. R. James (Weidenfeld & Nicolson, 1967). When Lang retired, Channon wrote (p. 313): 'This aged prelate has done irreparable damage to the Church of England. His evil face, thin lips, hard, small, terrible eyes are enough to frighten even an adult. Only his voice redeemed him, and his dignity—though it was the dignity of a Grand Inquisitor. Winston loathed him'. But Channon was soon deploring Churchill's appointment of an archbishop who made Socialist speeches, and when Temple died Channon described him as 'a fat fool of 63 with a fuddled, muddled brain who looked more like Queen Victoria than her daughter did' (p. 396).

H. R. L. Sheppard and G. A. Studdert Kennedy. Here we can mention only their common origins in the Established Church (Sheppard was the son of a priest who served in the royal household as Sub-Dean of the Chapels Royal, and Studdert Kennedy was the son of an Irish vicar in Leeds), and we can add only a few words about their revolt. Both were ordained; Sheppard worked in the West End of London and Studdert Kennedy in the back streets of Rugby and Worcester. Both were marked like many other young clergymen by a contempt for conventional ecclesiasticism and by an uncertainty about themselves, but both were distinguished by a rare enthusiasm, eloquence, and charm. Both met their destiny in the war. 'Dick' Sheppard became the Vicar of St. Martin-in-the-Fields, opening his church to troops on leave at all hours of the day and night. Studdert Kennedy became 'Woodbine Willie', the fabulously effective and beloved chaplain to the troops in France. After the war, these two men were the country's best known parsons, and they kept a vast audience. Sheppard became the first regular broadcaster of sermons from St. Martin's; he made that church in Trafalgar Square a pulpit of love and a centre of social service. Studdert Kennedy was a poet and brilliant orator, and he became a travelling missioner sponsored by the Industrial Christian Fellowship. Before many audiences he created a vision of a society obedient to the Sermon on the Mount. But popular as they were, both men were prophets in the grim tradition of Jeremiah. To men with such power of sympathy the war had been like a fresh crucifixion, and had revealed truths which placed them for ever outside the sedate tradition of Anglican respectability. The real God was the God of love, who suffered. The Church was called to this cross of love in a world of hatred. And Christianity was tested by its love. Both men became deeply feeling pacifists. Later, the squalid suffering in the post-war cities broke their hearts. Studdert Kennedy's rough rhymes expressed something of his agony:

> When Jesus came to Birmingham they simply passed him by,
> They never hurt a hair of him, they simply let him die.

Both men were tormented by asthma, a sign of the weariness in their overcrowded lives of listening to others' troubles; a sign, too, of the tension near breaking point in their spirits. Studdert Kennedy died while travelling to speak in 1929. Three years previously Sheppard had had to resign from his vicarage because of his health, and although he lived until 1937, and was for periods Dean of Canterbury and a canon of St. Paul's, he never really recovered either health or happiness. His book *The Impatience of a Parson* (1927) was a plea for a new Archbishop of Canterbury and a new Lambeth Conference to make Anglicanism more Christlike. He did not try to conceal his disappointment when instead of a new St. Francis Cosmo Lang was moved to Canterbury next year, although the Archbishop had been very good to him while 'Dearest Dick' was a confused young man. From disappointment he declined to despair; his misery was increased when his wife left him. There was no one with him when he died, but his funeral in London was a great public occasion.[19]

We might have described Conrad Noel, vicar of the magnificently beautiful church and village of Thaxted in Essex from 1910 to 1942. There he preached Christian Socialism, and added High Church ceremonial to show what the people had lost when the corporate piety and colourful drama of the Mass had been banished from the Church of England. Others offered the same formula—if more mildly, as in Temple's own case; but what was unique in Thaxted was the relevance to the countryside. Craftsmanship to adorn the church, folk song under the inspiration of Gustav Holst, folk dancing on the vicarage lawn— all were put across with an imaginative and rather dotty courage by this priest. The flags of the red revolution and of the Irish Republican Army were displayed in the church. Empire Sunday was denounced from the pulpit: 'help the Catholic Crusade to shatter the British Empire. . . .' As an eccentric, Conrad Noel outclassed even Lady Francis Warwick, the extremely rich Socialist who as its patron had presented him to the parish. His appeal lay to his own congregation, which on the whole accepted him as a good man; to the excited readers of his book about Jesus as a social reformer; and to those fringes of the Church of England and the Labour Party which their critics would call lunatic. The considerable sizes of these fringes did not compensate for his wider failure to seem a serious figure. Conrad Noel is seen as serious only when we reflect on the Church of England's failure to capture the imagination of country folk, despite the Church's great, indeed excessive, resources of men and buildings in rural parishes.[20]

Or we might have made the short journey from Thaxted to Cambridge, to sit under the dramatic, always eloquent, personality of Charles Earle Raven, for many years Professor of Divinity. He had both the equipment and the leisure to explore scholarly interests (which he shared with Temple) such as the seventeenth-century Christians who had reconciled religion with science, or those in the nineteenth century who had reconciled it with Socialism. But he was more conspicuous for his public advocacy of these causes in twentieth-century controversies, and here he went further than Temple. He contrasted the 'Gospel of Jesus' with frozen orthodoxy; he urged a courageous accept-

[19] See R. Ellis Roberts, *H. R. L. Sheppard* (John Murray, 1942), and William Purcell, *Woodbine Willie* (Hodder & Stoughton, 1962).

[20] See Reginald Groves, *Conrad Noel and the Thaxted Movement* (Martin Press, 1967).

ance and baptism of the evolutionary world-view; he wanted the ordination of women and many other modern moves in the Church; he was a pacifist. A man conscious of his own great gifts, he grew embittered about the timidity of the official leadership of the Church, but always made an exception to honour William Temple.[21]

Or we might have gone to London, to meet Basil Jellicoe. His protest against capitalism took the form of an intensely pastoral priesthood in the slums around Euston Station. He cared passionately about housing, and under his inspiration the St. Pancras House Improvement Society built flats and gained nation-wide publicity for this great cause. He died of overwork in 1935, at the age of thirty-six.[22]

It would, however, not be true to say that the housing problem was neglected by the bishops. It was not the bishops' bench that failed; it was public opinion, mesmerized as this was by the post-Gladstonian and pre-Keynesian economic doctrine that public expenditure on such objects as housing was dangerous in times of slump or stagnation. Prominent among the church leaders who took the trouble to master the facts, and to speak out, were two bishops, William Temple and Cyril Garbett of Southwark.[23] More radically than Garbett, Temple put the urgency of rehousing in the setting of a vision of the City of God on earth. Even a parish priest whose experiences were happier than any of the priests just mentioned admired 'Archbishop William Temple, who lives in the future.'[24]

It is easy to see why Temple was preferred above the other bishops by such men who were in revolt against normal church life. But we may ask, without pretending that he was universally popular: what was the secret of his appeal to the more conventional as well as to the rebels?

The clue may be provided by a little incident connecting Temple with Canon Peter Green, the greatest parish priest in twentieth-century England.

Peter Green loved, and was loved by, people of Manchester and Salford among whom he had lived humanely and worked carefully since 1911. His influence was spread as a frequent contributor to the *Manchester Guardian* and as the author of almost forty books. He never married, and was a great trainer of curates. He was a High Churchman

---

[21] F. W. Dillistone has a biography of C. E. Raven in preparation. Raven told the story of his early years in *A Wanderer's Way* (Martin Hopkinson, 1928). He summed up his mature teaching in his Gifford Lectures on *Natural Religion and Christian Theology*, 2 vols. (Cambridge University Press, 1953).

[22] See Kenneth Ingram, *Basil Jellicoe* (Centenary Press, 1936).

[23] Garbett had been, like Lang, Vicar of Portsea. Charles Smyth, *Cyril Foster Garbett* (Hodder & Stoughton, 1959), is the best written of all the episcopal biographies.

[24] Arthur W. Hopkinson, *Pastor's Progress* (Michael Joseph, 1941), p. 31.

(and had fallen out with Bishop Knox because of that), but his church-manship meant self-discipline and steady visiting and teaching rather than anything showy or exclusive. 'My object is first of all to gather a congregation, large, converted, instructed and missionary-hearted', he once wrote, 'and then to set the congregation to work.' It was pater-nalism, and in depressed Lancashire it worked. Perhaps such devotion always would produce results, although it was Green's misfortune to live so long that he found his own mind weakened and his brother-clergy battling without the visible success which had surrounded his own ministry. When he retired in 1951 he summed up his con-ception of the work of a parish priest. 'Leave politics alone but con-centrate on training up of the individual . . . to make the Altar the centre of the Christian life.' He refused four bishoprics: New Guinea, Lincoln, Birmingham, and Blackburn.[25]

As Archbishop of York in 1936, Temple preached at a service of thanksgiving for Peter Green's completion of twenty-five years as Rector of St. Philip's, Salford. Green had always got on with him, and the Archbishop would have been blamed by no one if he had been sentimentally fulsome. Temple had himself found house-to-house visit-ing when a parish priest embarrassing, and had once astonished Green by discussing a book of German philosophy which he had read during the intervals of one of the annual missions to the holiday-makers in Blackpool; so that an easy eloquence in praise of the dedicated parish priest might have been a tempting compensation. (What might not Lang have said?) In fact Temple used as his sermons one of the medita-tions on St. John's gospel which were soon to be published in his book. He expounded the passage in the tenth chapter about the good shep-herd, and thus explained the absence of a eulogy of Green: 'it is not proper that we should speak other than with great restraint in God's presence of his servants.'

On such a basis William Temple could appeal without any trickery both to the rebels and to those who kept the parishes going. He made up for any aloofness because men felt that he habitually dwelt with St. John and the Good Shepherd; that he, no less than Peter Green, was a saint of God.

[25] When offered Lincoln in 1920, Green told Randall Davidson that he felt uneasy about the palaces and incomes of the bishops. Incredulously, the arch-bishop showed him Lambeth Palace, asking: 'Canon, do you really think that all this is wrong?' Green commented politely that such things were lawful, but at least for him not expedient. After a moment's silence Davidson is reported to have said: 'Do you know, such a thought had never occurred to me before!' H. E. Sheen, *Canon Peter Green* (Hodder & Stoughton, 1965), p. 88.

8

As a leader in the movement for Christian reunion, William Temple was in himself the most solid sequel to the 1920 Lambeth Conference's 'Appeal to All Christian People'. A united Church had then been glimpsed as essential to the service of the Kingdom of God, and glowing words had resulted:

The vision which rises before us is that of a Church genuinely Catholic, loyal to all Truth, and gathering into its fellowship all 'who profess and call themselves Christians', within whose visible unity all the treasures of faith and order, bequeathed as a heritage by the past to the present, shall be possessed in common, and made serviceable to the whole Body of Christ. . . . The spiritual leadership of the Catholic Church in the days to come, for which the world is manifestly waiting, depends upon the readiness with which each group is prepared to make sacrifices for the sake of a common fellowship, a common ministry, and a common service to the world.

When the Lambeth Conference met again in 1930, it had to confess that no memorable advance had been made in the conversations with the Free Churches in England. At the conference itself William Temple, who was in charge of the committee on reunion, made one of his rare mistakes by leaving an impression of coldness on the Free Church visitors, but (as the Free Church leaders were the first to acknowledge when Temple later apologized) the lack of warmth in the Anglican atmosphere was far from being his fault. The early 1930s were a time when it was possible to hope that the Victorian Establishment, imperial or ecclesiastical, would last for a while longer; that decade saw the building of new Anglican cathedrals in Delhi and Cairo. And while most churchgoers probably shared the simple religion of the King-Emperor, George V, among the clergy these years were the heyday of Anglo-Catholicism. The influence of Keble, of Gore, and of many other spiritual teachers had won the hearts of many. The High Church party was confident during Lang's time at Lambeth; and when Temple feared in the 1940s that he was getting out of touch with the younger generation of theologians, it was to Anglo-Catholics that he turned.[26]

Men who felt that a century after its beginning the Oxford Movement was triumphant were in no mood to make concessions to the Free

[26] Among the many commemorations of the centenary of the Oxford Movement, the English Church Union sponsored a collection of essays under the title *Northern Catholicism*, ed. N. P. Williams and Charles Harris (SPCK, 1933). The short report on *Catholicity* (Dacre Press, 1945) also recorded the enthusiasm of Anglo-Catholics, but included a caricature of Protestantism. The symposium on *The Apostolic Ministry*, ed. K. E. Kirk (Hodder & Stoughton, 1946), attempted to undo the scholarly work of Lightfoot and to present episcopacy as essential to the Church. It was subjected to some devastating replies.

Churches, which after their moment of political power in 1906 were now visibly in decline as religious forces in the nation. Conversations with the Eastern Orthodox churches, designed to develop the good will which Davidson had secured, seemed more important. Even more to the liking of the Anglo-Catholics was the 'Concordat of Bonn' negotiated in 1932 between Anglican representatives and the small Old Catholic body which had broken away from the Roman Catholic Church on the Continent. By this agreement, the Anglicans and Old Catholics established intercommunion without doctrinal or organizational uniformity. Not a single Anglican practice had to be sacrificed. It was otherwise in South India.

The prospect of reunion in South India—a scheme involving four Anglican dioceses, the Methodists, and an existing merger of Congregationalists and Presbyterians—was less congenial to Anglo-Catholic consciences, for it was the first attempt to bridge the gap between episcopal and non-episcopal churches and it did not include any act of reconciliation which might be interpreted as episcopal ordination. The places of the creeds and of the confirmation also seemed insecure. The United Church was, however, to have bishops in the apostolic succession, and gradually these were to ordain new presbyters in South India. (The question of episcopal ordination for incoming missionaries was left unresolved.) It was also relevant that South India was a long way abroad, and that the Anglicans there, although wishing to go forward to reunion with the blessing of the Lambeth Conference, did not insist that the United Church should be reckoned a part of the Anglican Communion. Thus Anglican concessions in the scheme did not seem to jeopardize any essential Anglican principle, or to be precedents for areas where Anglicanism formed a more enthusiastic denomination.

The South India story had gathered momentum at the Tranquebar conference of Indian Christians in 1919, under the saintly Bishop Azariah. 'We face together the titanic task of the winning of India for Christ—one fifth of the human race. Yet confronted by such an overwhelming responsibility, we find ourselves rendered weak by our unhappy divisions, divisions which we did not create and which we do not desire to perpetuate.' The spirit behind that manifesto had appealed to some High Anglicans, among them E. J. Palmer, an Oxford don who had become Bishop of Bombay in 1908 (when Gore had withdrawn). Palmer saw in the reunion movement an opportunity to renew the Church, to make it more truly Catholic, not by bargaining but by self-sacrifice and resurrection, not by making concessions but by uniting convictions, not by human diplomacy but by praying to be told a plan which already existed in the mind of God. It was a conception of Catholicity far more dynamic than the look backwards of a Newman or a Benson (or of C. H. Turner, the Oxford theologian who continued the appeal to Cyprian in the 1920s), yet it was plainly not individualism or congregationalism. As the title of his book put it: *The Great Church Awakes*. 'Jimmy' Palmer greatly influenced the Lambeth Conference of 1920; and the Lambeth Conference of 1930 felt able to offer a guarded blessing to the 1929 scheme for a Church of South India. The bishops, however, then added notes of caution which were among the factors postponing the consummation of the reunion until 1947. Nor did they commit themselves to the precise terms of any future Anglican relationship with the United Church—a subject which caused much heart-burning at the next Lambeth Conference.

The crisis for Temple came in 1943, when the Anglicans in India had asked for further advice about the scheme. Would the Church of England break off communion with them if they allowed four of their dioceses to enter the Church of South India, thus condoning what the Anglo-Catholic organization in England, the Church Union, had roundly called 'an Act of Schism'? Temple led the English bishops in reassuring Anglican India on this point. Would the Church of England refuse to be in communion with the Church of South India because the latter would include some presbyters without episcopal ordination? Temple replied in terms which were not entirely clear; intercommunion would exist but would not be unrestricted. This was a departure from the normal Anglican line, to which Temple had usually adhered, that intercommunion should be regarded as the fruit of a unity established on a clearly episcopal basis. Temple had taken that line because he saw how intercommunion between the Free Churches had not led them to a fuller union; it seemed that the very pain of not being able to receive the Lord's Supper together might be needed as a spur to organic unity. Indeed, so sure was Temple about the place of episcopacy in reunion that he was pleased when the Anglicans in South India revived the idea of a service to reconcile the episcopal and non-episcopal ministries at the inauguration of the proposed Church. However, this idea had been abandoned in 1929 because High Churchmen such as Lang had objected to its ambiguity—and it was now abandoned again, this time because non-Anglicans suspected that it concealed a demand for episcopal ordination. So Temple and the Church of South India's other Anglican supporters had to envisage some intercommunion with a Church not wholly episcopalian.

Behind the confusion in this reply lay much pressure on Temple from Anglo-Catholic quarters, specially from the superiors of the religious orders. T. S. Eliot wrote a pamphlet, *Reunion by Destruction*, and there were many threats of an exodus from the Church of England— precisely what Davidson had feared. And Temple in the midst of the war was (like the Davidson whom he had goaded into Life and Liberty) preoccupied and tired. One thing he was determined to avoid:

a full-dress debate by the English Convocations. When asked to arrange this by Anglo-Catholics who wished to probe the scheme in great theological detail, he replied that the discussion at the Lambeth Conference in 1930 had been enough to assist the English bishops in replying to the limited requests for practical advice which reached them from their brethren in South India. He was thus willing to face criticism in order to help the scheme through—but his tactics, by depriving the clergy of their debate, stored up bitterness which exploded when the reunion had come in 1947, still without a full English investigation. When the Lambeth Conference met in 1948, 134 of the bishops of the Anglican Communion voted that the bishops, presbyters, and deacons of the Church of South India were bishops, priests, and deacons of the Church of God; but 94 voted against, including Garbett of York. About a hundred bishops abstained or were absent when the vote was taken. The same hesitation marked the resolutions of the Convocation of the clergy in England, and when some of the bishops sponsored an appeal for financial help to the Church of South India, nine of the diocesan bishops refused to sign it.[27] By then Temple was dead, but he would probably have agreed with Bishop Sundkler, the historian of the protracted negotiations in South India, that the real tragedy was the delay. The delay robbed the United Church of the presence of most of those who had conceived the vision. It was inflicted largely by English, rather than by Indian, hesitations.[28]

The South India scheme was by no means the only possible pattern of reunion. Another method, more congenial to many Anglo-Catholics, was to integrate the ministries of the uniting churches from the beginning by a service of reconciliation. Since this service would include the laying on of hands with prayer, it could be interpreted as episcopal ordination, and the hope was held that it would result in a church less untidy than South India. (This alternative was blessed by the Lambeth Conference in 1948, 1958, and 1968 for possible use in North India and Ceylon—and in England itself, for the projected reunion with the Methodist Church.) Gradually, as the hesitations which had surrounded and delayed the birth of the Church of South India were

---

[27] The story is outlined in E. W. Kemp, *The Life and Letters of Kenneth Escott Kirk* (Hodder & Stoughton, 1959). Kirk, who was Bishop of Oxford 1937–54, was the Anglo-Catholic leader. He had done valuable work as an Oxford don before the war, reviving the study of Christian ethics and writing a great and strikingly humane book on *The Vision of God* (Longmans, Green, 1931). His rigorism over the Church of South India extended to remarriage after divorce, but not to new ethical issues such as the use of nuclear weapons.

[28] The story of reunion has been told by Bengt Sundkler, *The Church of South India* (Lutterworth Press, 1954). For a searing comment on the indifference of English churchmen to the realities of the situation in Asia, see A. T. Hanson, *Beyond Anglicanism* (Darton, Longman, & Todd, 1965).

eclipsed by admiration for its worship and work, it was seen that, whether or not the South Indian method was suitable for imitation elsewhere, a similar courage in perseverance to the end was needed in all who accepted the spiritual authority of the ecumenical movement.

This movement, which became the most impressive aspect of twentieth-century Christianity, insisted that Christians must unite, and before that must meet. It was motivated by something very like Thomas Arnold's concern for change in the Church in order to fit the Church better to meet the churchless masses. But it did not make Arnold's mistake of underestimating theology; instead, it went along Newman's path into the whole history of Christendom, back to the apostolic unity, and along Maurice's road into the unifying confession of a faith in Christ as King. In the 1920s it attracted theologians such as Gore into its discussions of faith and order in the divided churches, and by the 1930s it was ready to receive a focus by the formation of a World Council of Churches. It then owed much to William Temple, who had shown his ability to master an international and interdenominational assembly at the Faith and Order Conference in Lausanne in 1927. To the prestige which the leaders of the Church of England then commanded in the Christian world, Temple added his own rare equipment, and he fell into place as the ecumenical movement's most prominent personality.

The institutional problems to be solved under Temple's guidance before a World Council of Churches could be built resulted from the history of the ecumenical movement's inspiration. The movement had attracted support mainly from students and many others interested in the 'Life and Work' angle and therefore inclined to rest content with co-operation. Temple's heart was in theology, and he chaired the Edinburgh 1937 World Conference on Faith and Order which reached an impressive degree of theological unity; at the 'World Conference on Church, Community, and State' held in Oxford immediately before the Edinburgh meeting, he had been almost silent. He was therefore trusted even by those who were worried by warnings, such as those issued by Bishop Headlam of Gloucester, to the effect that 'Faith and Order' was in danger of being swallowed up by a merely social Gospel. Yet Temple's days as Bishop of Manchester had made his social concern widely known, his political views were a great deal more acceptable than Headlam's, and during the discussions of the 1930s he was able to unite the two streams, theoretical and practical, in his flood of eloquence.[29]

[29] Headlam, who in 1937 was still anxious to reach an understanding with Hitler, thought that William Temple and George Bell would secure too good a platform for their anti-Nazi passions if a World Council of Churches was constructed. This scholarly prelate, who also opposed William Temple's policy of

One problem Temple could not solve: the wish of the missionaries to stay outside the churches' control, in the International Missionary Council. This hesitation was inevitable, for the Gospel of many of the missionaries was markedly simpler than the theology of, say, the Eastern Orthodox Churches. But the separation was never complete. For example, J. H. Oldham, Temple's close friend and collaborator, had been the brain behind the World Missionary Conference at Jerusalem in 1924—and went on to run the Oxford Conference thirteen years later, when the main theme was the neopaganism of the European totalitarians. And although the stream which had started from the World Missionary Conference at Edinburgh in 1910 was not brought fully into the World Council of Churches until 1961, the world war, as interpreted by Temple, increased the spiritual unity in this ecumenical movement. When Temple was enthroned at Canterbury in 1942 the most quoted passage in his sermon referred to the ecumenical movement as 'the great new fact of our era'. He had two developments in mind: the missionary expansion which had made Christianity global, and the impetus to unity in the Christian mission which held fast to this world-wide fellowship through the war. The coming of the war frustrated the plan to constitute the World Council of Churches under Temple's chairmanship, but when the council was formed at Amsterdam in 1948 all who knew about its background agreed that he had played as large a role as any man in the expression and embodiment of its spirit—social, theological, and missionary.

Temple did live to see the creation of the British Council of Churches, in 1942. There had been many forms of co-operation between the churches before this date, and in recent years many of them had been under Temple's inspiration, but the council now provided a single forum. As he declared at the council's inauguration in St. Paul's Cathedral: 'In days like these, when the basic principles of Christianity are widely challenged and in many quarters expressly repudiated, the primary need is for clear and united testimony to Christianity itself.'

---

supporting the 1944 Education Act, shared Frederick Temple's bad manners, unflagging industry, and intellectual power, without his common sense. See Ronald Jasper, *Arthur Cayley Headlam: Life and Letters of a Bishop* (Faith Press, 1960). But Headlam contributed to the ecumenical movement by his Bampton Lectures of 1920 on Christian reunion, and by his ability to be friends with Eastern Orthodox churchmen. See Stephen Neill, *The Church and Christian Union* (Oxford University Press, 1968), for Bampton Lectures which pay tribute to Headlam's influence.

9

As a leader of the Church of England, William Temple was at his best when testifying to his vision of God in Christ—as in his Mission to Oxford in 1931, when in Newman's old pulpit he repeated and excelled the spiritual triumph of his father's Bampton Lectures in the same place. 1931 was a year when St. Mary's, for all the energy of its new vicar, seemed a museum to many in Oxford. An historian in the college next door had just published these words about that church:

I know of few buildings where there is more of the bitterness which chills the heart. . . . The building is empty as a nursery when the children have left their home. . . . Now one who reads the Christian Fathers must climb some curious raised beach, dry it matters not how many years, and find only the fossils, the silt, the debris of old fangs: the dust of the beginnings of life. . . . Week in, week out the flame grows fainter; the ashes of the fire are raked and re-raked.[30]

But in 1931 a large and young congregation in St. Mary's, after listening to William Temple, whispered the old words (for Temple had pointed out that hearty singing might be insincere):

> Were the whole realm of nature mine,
> That were an offering far too small;
> Love so amazing, so divine,
> Demands my soul, my life, my all.[31]

That was the spirit in which he took over the chairmanship of the Archbishops' Commission on Doctrine in 1925, and presided over its somewhat leisurely work; and what unity there was in the commission's report in 1938 derived in no small measure from his ability to set the disagreements of the theological parties in the context of that hymn. The report marked the failure of attempts such as Gore's to establish a wider uniformity of doctrine, but did so without too much worry that the Gospel itself was in peril. 'There are some among us who hold that a full belief in the historical Incarnation is more consistent with the supposition that our Lord's birth took place under the normal conditions of human generation. . . . The majority of the Commission are agreed . . . that the tomb was empty because the Lord had risen.' So the great battles of modernism had their echoes. But the positive agreements which had emerged about the nature of the scriptures and the sacraments, and the eirenic spirit of the whole report even when it failed to agree about miracles, were more important than

[30] E. L. Woodward, *The Twelve-Winded Sky* (Constable, 1930), pp. 19–25.
[31] Temple's addresses were published as *Christian Faith and Life*, and last reprinted with a reminiscent Foreword by F. R. Barry (SCM Press, 1963).

these echoes. In his Introduction Temple stressed the agreements and their basis. He could fairly claim that 'it has always been our desire to set forth the truth of the Everlasting Gospel unchanged in substance'; and he could frankly confess that the years since Davidson's appointment of the commission had been years in which the gift of this Gospel of God to sinners had come to be prized more highly than the gift of diversity in Anglican theology. He wrote:

As I review in thought the result of our fourteen years of labour, I am conscious of a certain transition of interest in our minds, as in the minds of theologians all over the world. We were appointed at a time when theologians were engaged in taking up the prosecution of the task which the war had compelled them to lay aside. Their problems were still predominantly set by the interest of 'pre-war' thought. In our country the influence of Westcott reinforced by that of the *Lux Mundi* school had led to the development of a theology of the Incarnation rather than a theology of Redemption. . . . A theology of the Incarnation tends to be Christo-centric metaphysic. And in all ages there is need for the fresh elaboration of such a scheme of thought or map of life as seen in the light of the revelation of Christ. A theology of Redemption (though, of course, Redemption has its great place in the former) tends rather to sound the prophetic note; it is more ready to admit that much in this evil world is irrational and strictly unintelligible; and it looks to the coming of the Kingdom as a necessary preliminary to the full comprehension of much that now is. If the security of the nineteenth century, already shattered in Europe, finally crumbles away in our country, we shall be pressed more and more towards a theology of Redemption. In this we shall be coming closer to the New Testament.

'If we began our work again to-day', Temple wrote in this Introduction, 'its perspectives would be different. But it is not our function to pioneer.' It was no longer *his* function; he felt that he had said what he had to say in philosophical theology, and that a new generation must take up the task in the new conditions. But it was a sign of the greatness of his spirit that at York and Canterbury he scarcely ever failed in sympathy with the struggles of younger theologians, however uncongenial their austerity might be. He backed the appointment as the first General Secretary of the emerging World Council of Churches of a young Dutch theologian whose master was the anti-liberal Karl Barth; and he enthusiastically commended (as supplying 'the principles of missionary policy for our generation') a book which was another Dutch and Barthian onslaught against the recognition of non-Christian religions advocated at the Jerusalem Conference of 1928.[32]

He continued to read and to think theology because he enjoyed it.

[32] Hendrik Kraemer, *The Christian Message in a Non-Christian World*, published for the International Missionary Council before the Tambaram Conference of 1938.

He was, after all, a philosopher, or rather a philosophically minded preacher, and not a practical economist or politician. It was not that he was incapable of performing his duty to handle some secular details. On the contrary, his leadership of the study of unemployment which produced a large book on *Men without Work* (1938) was an outstanding example of ecclesiastical sponsorship for useful research and detailed recommendations in response to an urgent challenge in society.[33] He persuaded the Pilgrim Trust to finance the investigation, and able thinkers to serve on its committee. He enlisted Eleanora Iredale, a great activist, as secretary. When the problem of unemployment was studied closely in six areas, he could use investigators who included many churchmen already interested and active in this concern, and when the development of 'occupational centres' for the instruction of the unemployed was encouraged by these findings, this work also involved many who were already associated with Temple either in church work or in the Workers' Educational Association. As the war approached and raged, J. H. Oldham, assisted by Eleanora Iredale, published the *Christian News-Letter* in order to spread the idea of experts taking counsel together about society's problems in the light of the Christian Gospel. Himself a layman, Oldham envisaged a network of small groups covering the country around the Christian Frontier Council in London. That plan never succeeded fully, partly owing to the failure of the churches to release resources for the service of such groups; but Temple as Archbishop of Canterbury set an example to other churchmen by his eagerness to listen to the well-informed discussions around the small, half-deaf, but always stimulating and fructifying, figure of Oldham. Yet all the time, even when dutifully attending to these investigations and debates in secular terms, Temple knew that the basic problems were spiritual.

His response to the spiritual crisis came out when in 1941 the Industrial Christian Fellowship organized a conference at Malvern which was in some ways the successor to 'Copec'. The aim was 'to consider from the Anglican point of view what are the fundamental facts which are directly relevant to the ordering of the new society that is quite evidently emerging, and how Christian thought can be shaped to play a leading part in the reconstruction after the war is over.' The continuity with 1924 lay in the broad sweep and the optimism, and in the rush and frustration of the conference itself. Above all, it lay in Temple's chairmanship, for he was able to astonish the conference by drafting its agreed conclusions after debates both brief and confused. But it

---

[33] Arthur Marwick, *Britain in the Century of Total War* (Penguin Books, 1970), p. 229, reckons it 'the most complete survey of the life of the unemployed . . . a classic of objectivity and sensitivity'.

was plainly not enough in 1941 to urge particular social reforms without a mastering vision of society. When Sir Richard Acland dominated
the Malvern Conference by his demand that the Church should commit
itself to the public ownership of the principal means of production,
Temple was inclined to agree. However, the exhausted four hundred
at Malvern were not willing to endorse Socialism so wholeheartedly in
a hurry, and diplomats such as Bishop George Bell had to rescue the
situation by a formula that 'private ownership of the main industrial
resources may be a stumbling-block, making it harder for men to live
Christian lives'.

That 'may be' about the Socialist panacea was not accidental. The
speakers at Malvern were mostly concerned with somewhat philosophical attempts to work out 'the Anglican point of view', and came mainly
from the Christendom group of Anglo-Catholics desiring a 'Christian
sociology'. In his little book on *The Idea of a Christian Society* (1938),
T. S. Eliot, who was very far from being a Socialist, had argued that
Christianity was still a live option as the central dynamism in English
life. With an eye on Hitler and Stalin, Eliot had urged that a society's
basic necessity was to find a spiritual creed, and he believed that when
the crisis came most Englishmen would wish to see Christianity as the
creed of England—not compelling doctrinal uniformity but putting the
social pressure behind, instead of against, Christian lives. Now, in 1941,
the crisis had come; and the contribution of the Church must surely be
weightier than any party politics. Churchmen thinking along these
lines naturally relied on Temple more as a theologian than as ex-
member of the Labour Party.

However, neither the detailed discussions of the *Christian News-
Letter* nor the theology of the Malvern conference could be enough.
Some synthesis of the detailed with the general was needed. Temple
supplied this synthesis for many thousands of Christian Englishmen
during the second world war, when the social teaching which he had
begun in the *Challenge* during the Kaiser's war came to its climax in
the publication of his Penguin paperback on *Christianity and Social
Order* in 1942. This was a small, highly compressed, and highly effective book: a book which was authoritative for more reasons than its
author's high office. It attracted publicity by including some practical
suggestions about the reform of the banking system and other controversial matters; and more publicity came as the Archbishop expanded
these ideas in speeches. However, the central thrust of the book was
theological. Its concern was to persuade readers that Christianity *was*
relevant to social order, to the economic and political factors which
so largely conditioned men's lives. There were, Temple claimed, some
'middle axioms' half-way between pure doctrine and detailed politics.
Once these were stated—and Temple, after some thirty years of dis-

cussion, could state them magisterially—then surely men must go with a new vision into the politics of the emerging society, subordinating everything else to morality with its personal values.

Temple believed that a better order would include both state control and enterprise through competition, both public and private ownership, both a corporate spirit and civil liberties, and he stressed these different elements differently at different times of his life, but he did see some clear objectives for a Christian in social policy. He advocated the kind of housing which would provide for family life in privacy and the provision of universal education up to eighteen, as first charges on the economy. He wanted each worker to have a voice in the control of the enterprise for which he worked, a five-day week, and holidays with pay. As illustrations of how such principles might be worked out he was prepared to offer some controversial suggestions—but, as he stressed, as a citizen, not as an archbishop. Could each enterprise devote part of its profits to a fund to maintain wages and dividends in bad times, and part to the provision of amenities for the public? Could the public, rather than private bankers, gain the profit from the creation of credit? Could investors who had recovered in dividend more than the original sum invested be edged out of an enterprise by the withering away of the value of their capital, year by year? Could the land on which cities were built be nationalized, and could the taxation of rural landowners be adjusted in order to reward productivity? And could the costs of production be equalized internationally? Whatever the merits of such bright ideas—and few economists have acknowledged many merits in them—Temple's ingenuity was seldom at a loss before any challenge to be specific. Nor did his courage quail before the consequent indignation of bankers, shareholders, and landlords.[34]

Temple's own major contribution to social progress was, appropriately enough, his share in the passage of the Education Act of 1944. He himself regarded the raising of the school leaving age to sixteen as the most important feature of R. A. Butler's plans for post-war development in the schools, but Butler and the other architects of the great Act relied on him for his leadership in securing church support for the religious provisions.

The essential features of the Butler Act in respect of religion were three. Every school day should begin with an act of worship. Every child, unless withdrawn by parents, should be instructed in the Christian religion according to a syllabus agreed between representatives of the churches and the Local Education Authority. And, third, the Act provided both for the transfer to state control of those schools which the

[34] A 'critical' (in fact, hostile) assessment of *William Temple's Political Legacy* has been supplied by John D. Carmichael and Harold S. Goodwin (Mowbray, 1963). Hensley Henson would have enjoyed this book.

Church of England could no longer afford to maintain and for very large state subsidies to the running and capital costs of the smaller number of church schools and church colleges to train teachers—schools and colleges which the Church could still afford to control as its own distinctive contribution to the education of the people. In short, the Act of 1944 achieved a concordat between Church and State on questions which the Balfour Act of 1902 had been powerless to settle; and it witnessed a unanimity which would have seemed incredible to the contestants in the denominational disputes before 1914. Some idea of an agreement along the lines of the Butler Act had been in the minds of many men concerned with education. Many agreed syllabuses, for example, were already in operation. But the agreement in 1944 would have been far harder to achieve had Temple not been so enthusiastic over educational progress in general, had he not been so well equipped and entitled to answer secularist complaints, had he not enjoyed friendship of Free Church leaders such as the Methodist veteran Dr. Scott Lidgett, had he not outweighed Anglican leaders such as Bishops Headlam and Kirk who wanted the preservation of the Church's own schools given the first priority, and had he not been able to dismiss others such as Henson who wanted the Church's schools to be abandoned.[35]

The Education Act had an immense effect on the life of the people after the second world war. It made provision for over three thousand church schools to be supported largely by the local authorities, and for the Church of England to retain some rights in a further two thousand schools; it also made possible the far more effective educational programme of the Roman Catholic Church. It provided the basic structure of education; and on this basis, it gradually became possible to move nearer to the ideal of the people's awakened mind—the ideal of the Workers' Educational Association. It provided also for the instruction of the people in the basic facts of Christianity. That did not usually lead to active church membership, but nor did it usually lead to an active hostility to religious education or to religion as a whole. The biblical stories and the Christian moral teaching which were imbibed in schooldays could be linked with religious broadcasts and television programmes; and since Christianity was in these ways still kept alive—imperfectly, but to the indignation of some secular humanists—a possibility remained. Here and there among the English people, a man or a woman might understand and enter the spirit of the Christian Church.[36]

[35] A survey of the debate from 1870 to 1944 has been made by Marjorie Cruickshank in *Church and State in English Education* (Macmillan, 1963).
[36] A shrewd estimate was provided in the report of the Durham Commission on religious education in schools, *The Fourth R.* (SPCK, 1970).

In his pastoral duties as Archbishop of Canterbury, Temple was both handicapped and helped by the war. Travel in over-crowded trains and the blackout became exhausting, yet his willingness to speak at large meetings in London and in other cities was essential to the two campaigns 'The Church Looks Forward' (1942) and 'Religion and Life' (1944). The campaigns recalled all the forward-looking vitality of 'Life and Liberty' days, with the added advantages of the prestige of his office and the expectancy of the wartime audiences now that at last an Archbishop of Canterbury had a constructive policy and the courage to advocate it. The work at Lambeth was more anxious than ever, for many correspondents wrote in with questions involving fundamental ethics; yet William Temple pronounced with all his father's decisiveness and with scarcely a trace of his father's gruff brevity. Should soldiers be issued with contraceptives for use in their off-duty hours? Temple protested that 'if men and women would abstain from fornication, the problem confronting the Minister of Health would be reduced to negligible proportions'. Must ladies wear hats in church? Temple decided not, to the relief of the authorities responsible for clothes rationing. May Christians fight? Temple argued against pacifism, but he argued at such a level that he retained the respect of the pacifists. May Britain retaliate against Germany by bombing cities? Temple was reluctant to criticize the British authorities publicly while they were waging war, and he died before the largest R.A.F. raids posed the ethical question in its sharpest form; but he did make some strong, if largely private, interventions against the growing tendency to hate and revenge—as did Davidson in 1914–18. Should Christians pray for victory? Lang, and also Cyril Garbett who succeeded Temple at York, encouraged this patriotism at prayer, but Temple went further than any other Anglican archbishop had ever done in saying that peace according to the will of God, not a national military victory, must be the chief aim.[37]

The Archbishop of Canterbury who was harrassed by so many problems, and left to cope without proper assistance at Lambeth, did not complain—in contrast with his predecessor, who went off to retirement in a self-pitying mood, 'from a somebody to a nobody'. The strain of those years wore down William Temple until a thrombosis following an infection from which he might have recovered in happier days killed him—and Cosmo Lang was moved to find himself on his eightieth birthday, in his last great public ceremony, officiating at his successor's funeral.

[37] His chief addresses as Archbishop of Canterbury were published as *The Church Looks Forward* (Macmillan, 1944), and *Some Lambeth Letters* were edited by William Temple's nephew, Frederick Temple (Oxford University Press, 1963).

These always anxious, and ultimately fatal, war years were William Temple's finest hour. As the American theologian Reinhold Niebuhr wrote: 'The man, the hour and the office stood in a creative relation to each other in a way we are not likely to see again in this generation.' Another American theologian, Joseph Fletcher, quoted in his study of Temple's thought the words of Richard Hooker about the cost of such work: 'Ministers of good things are like torches, a light to others, waste and destruction to themselves.' And this torch did flame; for Temple reached out to touch the imaginations of England and the free world. His politics got him quoted in the newspapers, but political controversy was not the secret of his serious influence. His voice could be heard through millions of wireless sets, continuing to teach about God in Christ. His thought, always clear, burned with its clarity now: with the clarity of his conviction that in the secular world Christians stood for the eternal Kingdom of God.[38] It was not because he had views on politics, but because he saw God reigning over the everyday world, that he won the admiration of President Roosevelt and of many privates in the Army. To the emerging ecumenical movement which was finding the strength of its integrity in Christian Europe's resistance to Hitler he gave the comprehensive life of the Church of England— at a time when the ecumenical movement, later to be really world-wide, was small and European enough to be impressed by that single small, English Church. To the emerging England, he gave the best in Victorian religion—at a time when the democracy was sufficiently conservative, or sufficiently frightened, to welcome the reminder. He said privately that he intended to resign in 1951, at the age of seventy, and to write a book about the Holy Spirit; but had that wish been granted, he might have lived on as a lesser man. He would have survived into a less heroic world and nation, and into a smaller Church of England.

In fact when he died he was still at the height of his influence. 'I think he is *felix opportunitate mortis*', wrote Hensley Henson to Cyril Alington, 'for he has passed away while the streams of opinion in Church and State, of which he became the outstanding symbol and exponent, were at flood, and escaped the experience of their inevitable ebb.' History has shown that this was a fair comment. The Archbishopric of Canterbury involved a crowning mercy to both Frederick and William Temple: to the father, in that he held it at all, as a tribute to his real work as a schoolmaster and diocesan bishop; and to the son, in that he held it so briefly.

[38] Two of his most brilliant utterances, on 'What Christians Stand For in the Secular World' and 'Christianity as an Interpretation of History', were reprinted at the end of William Temple, *Religious Experience*, ed. A. E. Baker (James Clarke, 1958).

10

As a philosophical theologian, William Temple regarded the mind's apprehension of reality as both reliable and supreme. He had no time for those who regarded man's evolution as the product of blind chance in a universe whose only laws were physical. 'That there should emerge in the cosmic process a capacity to apprehend, even in a measure to comprehend, that process', he wrote in *Nature, Man and God*, 'is the most remarkable characteristic of the process itself. . . . That the world should give rise to minds which know the world involves a good deal concerning the nature of the world.' And he did not hesitate to put first the mind's spiritual rather than technical activity, just as he did not hesitate to reject Marxist or Freudian explanations of the economic or psychological causes of the mind's decisions. He did not feel dwarfed by the universe. 'I know the stars are there . . . they do not know that I am here', he told Oxford undergraduates in 1931. 'I beat the stars.' Nor did he ever join Christians who received God's revelation as a sheer miracle from a source wholly other than normal existence. 'Unless all existence is a medium of Revelation, no particular Revelation is possible', he asserted.

He frequently compared the mind's highest work with the appreciation of a Beethoven symphony. Through music, or art, or religion, the mind of man reached out to apprehend and comprehend truthfully the beautiful goodness in the real world. And more: through relations with others, men formed and deepened their ethical values, so that the supreme characteristic of life was its personal nature and the supreme activity of mind was its judgement of rightness. 'Your being is personal; live as a person in fellow-membership with all . . . your fellow-members in the community of persons.' Out of his own experience, out of his father's, out of all that had come to him through Rugby and Oxford, Temple drew the conclusion that all the life of the mind, all the life of fellowship, was a preparation for the revelation of God in Christ. For the mind cried out for an explanation of the universe, and 'if we ask for an explanation of the universe as a whole we are bound to formulate the answer in terms of Will'. And the mind cried out for the eternity of this beautiful goodness. 'Arising out of flux, and itself in origin an episode of the flux out of which it arises, mind declares its own nature by demanding permanence.' So the mind attained the conviction that the will of the eternal God was the origin of all that was valuable in the world; mind reached Mind. As Temple claimed:

The more we study the activity of God immanent, the more we become aware of God transcendent. The Truth that strikes awe in the scientist is awful because it is His thought; the Beauty that holds spell-bound the artist is potent because it is His glory; the Goodness that pilots us to the assured apprehension of Reality can do this because it is His character; and the freedom whereby man is lifted above all other nature, even to the possibility of defying it, is fellowship with Him.

Since 'the fullest revelation of truth is of persons to persons', personal worship of God was the heart of William Temple's religion. It was the only cure which he could see for the disease which he diagnosed in *Nature, Man and God:* 'It is the spirit which is evil; it is reason which is perverted; it is aspiration itself which is corrupt. . . . So long as the self retains initiative it can only fix itself upon itself as centre. Its hope of deliverance is to be uprooted from that centre and drawn to find its centre in God, the Spirit of the Whole.' When he came to comment on the woman of Samaria in his *St. John,* he wrote: 'Worship is the submission of all our nature to God. It is the quickening of conscience by His holiness; the nourishment of mind with His truth; the purifying of imagination by His beauty; the opening of the heart to His love; the surrender of the will to His purpose—and all this gathered up in adoration. . . .'

Worship thus understood was based by Temple on a foundation which did not involve the dogmatism of Newman (or the dogmatism of Shaftesbury); here he stood firmly in the tradition of Maurice. In *Foundations* he permitted himself to pronounce that the Council of Chalcedon's definition of orthodox Christology had declared the 'bankruptcy of Greek patristic theology', but in *Christus Veritas* he modified this phrase, claiming that the formula of Chalcedon 'did exactly what an authoritative formula ought to do: it stated the fact'. However, he never believed that the acceptance of Jesus as 'God living a human life', as the Second Person of the Trinity adding this human life to his divine attributes, necessarily involved the acceptance of any philosophical formula of the past. 'It would be disastrous', he wrote, 'if there were an official Church explanation of the Incarnation.' He also moved, as we have seen, towards a more conservative use of the Bible. But he insisted that God's revelation of himself was chiefly through *events,* supremely the event of Jesus Christ—not through propositions. He taught that

there are truths of revelation, . . . propositions which express the results of correct thinking concerning revelation; but they are not themselves directly revealed. On the other hand, this does not involve the result that there need be anything vague or indefinite about revelation itself. . . . What is offered to man's apprehension in any specific revelation is not truth concerning God but the living God Himself.

Religious experience was, he declared, 'the whole experience of religious persons'. He greatly valued the Church's sacraments, but in a sacramental universe; and he called Christianity 'the most avowedly materialistic of all the great religions'. He was clear that God did not depend on the world (he used the equation: 'God – world = God'), but he was also clear that God had chosen to create a world through which his love might be known; when he expounded his doctrine of God the divine love, shown in the divine humility of the cross, was always at the centre. His understanding of the Atonement was exemplarist, but with a profound difference from shallow theories about Christ the example. Here as everywhere else, Temple began his thinking with the vision of God. He wrote in *Christus Veritas:* 'We must first realize Him as exalted in unapproachable Holiness, so that our only fitting attitude before Him is one of abject self-abasement, if we are to feel the stupendous marvel of the Love which led Him, so high and lifted up, to take His place beside us in our insignificance and squalor that He might unite us with Himself.' The crucified Christ revealed to men the divine self-sacrifice. The cross showed what it cost God to enter all suffering, and to take away the self-centredness which was the cause of all sin. It cost a broken body, a broken heart. The love of God for the world, the purpose of God to spread his Kingdom of love in all the world: these were the basic lessons which William Temple learned from the teaching and death of Jesus.

The specific propositions which he taught were, as we have seen, his response to the society around him and to the events in his lifetime. He was accordingly not so infallible as his admirers tended to believe, and after his death he soon went out of fashion, as the intellectuals grew absorbed in secularism and the rest in money. From Cambridge a flood of new thinking spread out to drown the world where Temple was at home as a philosopher or amateur economist; whatever was valuable in his ideas would have to be restated by those who, unlike him, had taken full account of Wittgenstein and Keynes. Yet even after such revolutions, his stature as a true prophet might still emerge, like the spire of a church seen across the Fens around Cambridge. Essentially, his life illustrated his theory about Israel's prophets; what he did by his writing and speaking was to show how the mind of a man of God could be related to the life of the world, and to the events where God was at work in the world. He demonstrated that, precisely because of loyalty to its own theological principles, the Church of England could seek to be the Church of the whole nation, with a mission pursued mainly by quiet pastoral work and by the provision of opportunities to worship in beauty and grace. Such work and worship interested Temple more than any controversy in which he was engaged. This general approach which was the essence of his prophetic mission could, one might suppose, be adopted in a different world. The most difficult question to answer was whether men with anything like the necessary stature and confidence would appear in the future. Or did Frederick Temple's son stand at the end of an era? He died on the same morning, 26 October 1944, as Princess Beatrice, the last surviving child of Queen Victoria.

FOR FURTHER READING

Frederick Temple asked that no biography should be written, but his disciple E. G. Sandford, Archdeacon of Exeter, edited *Memoirs of Archbishop Temple by Seven Friends* in two large volumes (Macmillan, 1906). There were also some ephemeral memoirs.

William Temple, Archbishop of Canterbury: his Life and Letters was compiled by F. A. Iremonger, then Dean of Lichfield but formerly associated with Temple in the Life and Liberty movement and as Head of Religious Broadcasting (Oxford University Press, 1948). It was rather a breathless chronicle. Joseph Fletcher, *William Temple: Twentieth Century Christian* (Seabury Press, New York, 1963), was a more analytical assessment by an American scholar, who also added some factual details. For further analysis, see Owen C. Thomas, *William Temple: Philosophy of Religion* (SPCK, 1961), and Robert Craig, *Social Concern in the Thought of William Temple* (Gollancz, 1963). Canon A. E. Baker, a disciple, contributed with others to *William Temple: An Estimate and an Appreciation* (James Clarke, 1948), edited short extracts to illustrate *William Temple's Teaching* (James Clarke, 1949), and collected some longer essays and addresses under the title *Religious Experience* (James Clarke, 1958).

Epilogue

1

These men had many limitations, to be accounted for partly by their loyalty to the Church of England. Even the intellectuals among them were reluctant to rebel against their inheritance. The radical German theologians used to complain that such English theology as they knew about—which was not much—suggested that it had been written to the sound of church bells. And, preferring to do their work in order to meet the demand of an occasion in the life of the Church or the nation, English theologians were reluctant to be systematic in the German style. William Temple was typical here. None of them disciplined himself in order to write books of doctrine which would be placed among the chief treasures of Christendom, although the posthumous reputation of Newman has shown what a gap he might have filled in the Catholic world and although Maurice may have had it in him to be the English equivalent of Karl Barth (many of whose themes were to resemble his). Academic figures abandoned the quiet suited to their gifts in order to work as churchmen. Even Hort had to pretend that he preferred life to libraries. Taken together, they looked like a race of giants not because they were independent thinkers but because they were the official or intellectual leaders of English religion.

These men might falter, as when both Thomas Arnold and William Temple hesitated to accept the yoke of the priesthood. Of the two who felt most, Matthew Arnold faltered most in the path of orthodoxy and John Henry Newman had to take the most heroic steps to save himself from falling. But all that was really no more than the price which they paid for being sensitive men who had undertaken responsibility for England's religion at such a time. They were identified with 'that vast system of Religion which the Ministry symbolizes and interprets', as Henson wrote, confessing 'faults . . . failures . . . dark hours'. But such moods of introspective doubt were eclipsed by the control which they habitually exercised over their own emotions, and by the command which they held over many other men's minds.

A whole complex of privileges combined to give them this assurance. However impoverished or unhappy some of them were as boys, they were all the sons of Christian homes, with their basic values clear from the beginning. Most of them were educated at schools which in the spirit of Thomas Arnold combined sound learning with the Anglican religion and also with social status. (When Bishop Gore shook his fist towards Archbishop Davidson's study, was it not one Harrovian greeting another?) They almost all received high honours at Oxford or Cambridge. They all had loyal wives, apart from the natural celibates. Their domestic circumstances were almost always easy; they had servants even while they were parish priests or schoolmasters. They worked with the assumption that they had been called and trained to teach the truth to the nation. Those who were pastors expected their parishioners to be obedient, and those who taught in school flogged or preached without qualms. Those who were intellectuals talked confidently over a wide field; beginning with Abraham, like Stanley, or with Adam before his Fall, like Maurice. Those who were ecclesiastical statesmen were often respected as men who had passed a mysterious examination, and who possessed some at least of the qualities which Mr. Gladstone desired to see in a bishop; and on their side they expected a welcome into the ruling elite. Many of them were both scholars and administrators, the philosopher-kings of their well-defined world.

Before the first world war there were already signs that the supply of such men, to arrest the ebb of the Sea of Faith, was dwindling. In August 1913, on his first holiday as Dean of St. Paul's, Ralph Inge went north. In Scotland he much enjoyed hearing some friends' comments, such as this on Archbishop Lang: 'There are two men in Lang—a canny Scot, and a narrow-minded man at that, who is on the lookout for what he can get, and a sentimental Highlander.' The Inges also stayed with the Hensons at the Deanery in Durham. There they discussed Archbishop Davidson. 'I have no patience with a man who is a coward', observed the Dean of Durham, who also declared: 'I no longer have the pleasure I once had in speaking to him.' But Henson added a more thought-provoking comment in the course of their gossip. 'I think one of the most impressive prophecies that have come true was that by Bishop Westcott, who was speaking about the second-rate stuff that was taking Holy Orders. We do not notice it now, but the next generation will have no men to put in high places.'[1]

Whether or not such an assessment was justified at that time, the situation became such that Winston Churchill was widely reported to have observed that among the bishops William Temple, although a Socialist, was 'a sixpenny article in a penny bazaar'; and the quarter-century after William Temple's death did definitely destroy the aristocratic style of leadership in the Church, as in the nation. The trend was now against tradition. Among the young all institutions were

[1] W. R. Inge, *The Diary of a Dean* (Hutchinson, 1949), pp. 22–3.

questioned, and religious institutions were specially unpopular. The whole emphasis of the time was on the new, on the informal, on the spontaneous, and on the physical. The deviant, the rebel, or the 'anti-hero' became the key figure in serious literature and drama. Naturally such a decay of the ancestral virtues surprised and dismayed those who had hoped that the idealism of the war years would flow on under their guidance: men such as the austere Labour statesman Sir Stafford Cripps, in his maturity a devout Anglican, or Christopher Chavasse, the Bishop of Rochester, a firm leader who presided over a commission on evangelism.[2] This commission produced in 1945 a report dedicated to the memory of William Temple and entitled *Towards the Conversion of England*. It called for a confident advance, including an advertising campaign. After much acclaim, little resulted.

The new conditions had no doubt many merits, but they discouraged the emergence of successors to the ecclesiastics whose books were beginning to gather dust in the libraries. The conventions of the Christian family were shaken by many new freedoms. The public and grammar schools wavered, notably in their historic connections with the Church of England.[3] In the more democratic, technical, and rebellious universities, theology could not expect to reign. When able young men graduated, a hundred professions now competed for their skills, each offering cosier rewards than the priesthood. By 1970 only about two hundred graduates a year were being ordained in the Church of England. There were about six thousand fewer clergy in 1970 than in 1901, in a population larger by fifteen millions. Non-graduates could be recruited (over half the men being ordained in the Church of England were now in this category), and older men might predominate (55 became the average age of the clergy), but whether clever or simple, young or old, the clergyman appeared to be the odd man out. Usually ill paid, often overworked, sometimes underworked, but all too often uncertain about what his proper work should be, he was told that he had thrown away his life into a religious machine which was outdated. Not a few of the more promising of the younger clergy migrated to

---

[2] See Colin Cooke, *The Life of Richard Stafford Cripps* (Hodder & Stoughton, 1957), and Selwyn Gummer, *The Chavasse Twins* (Hodder & Stoughton, 1963). Christopher's twin, Noel, was killed in 1917 and awarded the V.C. and Bar. They were the sons of F. J. Chavasse, Bishop of Liverpool.

[3] For the tradition, see, for example, F. D. How, *Six Great Schoolmasters* (Methuen, 1904). Spencer Leeson, who resigned the Headmastership of Winchester in 1946 in order to become a parish priest in the bomb-ravaged dockland of Southampton, and who killed himself by overwork as Bishop of Peterborough, was an enthusiastic embodiment of the old values in the midst of 'the thickening fog of secular ways of thought, a heavy stifling climate, in which on ordinary days and at ordinary times God and man's kinship to him are not denied, but simply left out of account'. A memoir was compiled by some of his friends of *Spencer Leeson: Shepherd, Teacher, Friend* (SPCK, 1958).

work outside the parochial system. The clergy's status in the group which Coleridge called the 'clerisy'—the cultivators and diffusers of civilization—was now insecure, if not denied. Whereas Keble had thwacked village boys who did not salute him, the visiting vicar now often found it hard to get the television turned off. And the basic cause of this decline in status was simple. It was the decline of belief in Coleridge's maxim that 'not without celestial observations can even terrestrial charts be accurately constructed'. Keble's successors, whose lives only made sense on the premise of the reality of the Christians' heaven, now often found themselves figures of ridicule, compassion, or indifference.[4]

Who, then, was to lead the nation's religion? In the universities, theologians increasingly concentrated on their academic specialisms. Bishops devoted themselves to the improvement of the ecclesiastical organization in discreet ways, and above all to the pastoral encouragement of clergy and laity who were easily depressed. Theologians, bishops, and other officials worked conscientiously, but evidently few found the time or the inclination to think widely and few attempted to provide for the public a religious vision of the kind that had come from the eminent Victorians.[5] The charisma of the apostle or the prophet, authoritarian and often controversial, had mostly been replaced by the common sense of a committee absorbed in routine labours. Those who were disappointed by the lack of a creative initiative coming from such leadership could blame it on to the anachronistic appointments system, by which the Prime Minister still assumed responsibility for the most important nominations, and three commissions were appointed to mull over this problem in the post-war Church of England. But it was difficult to imagine that a different appointments system in the Church would easily transform the consequences of secularization.

2

The new climate was recorded by two events, or non-events, at the beginning and the end of the quarter-century after William Temple. The first was the decision not to appoint George Bell to one of the prominent bishoprics.

In much the same way as Randall Davidson was the heir of Archi-

---

[4] Some of the problems involved were explored by Leslie Paul, *The Deployment and Payment of the Clergy* (Church Information Office, 1964), and Peter F. Rudge, *Ministry and Management* (Tavistock Publications, 1968).

[5] An exception was the philosophical and liberal theologian W. R. Matthews, Dean of St. Paul's 1934–67. His autobiography was *Memories and Meanings* (Hodder & Stoughton, 1969).

bald Tait, George Bell seemed to have been destined to follow Davidson as Archbishop of Canterbury. Dean Inge went so far as to hope that he might succeed Davidson immediately in 1928; 'everybody except Cosmo would be delighted'. This was a characteristic piece of un-wisdom on Inge's part, but it was reasonable to think that Bell was the only bishop approaching William Temple in stature.[6]

After a brief spell as a don at Oxford, Bell (a parson's son) had gone as a chaplain at Lambeth, his first job being to edit prayers for use when war broke out in 1914. Ten years later he had begun a short but creative spell as Dean of Canterbury, and since 1929 he had been Bishop of Chichester, somehow finding time to write his massive bio-graphy of Davidson—a better book than Davidson on Tait—and to busy himself with many national and international concerns, as his master had done. He was anxious to see the Church as the patron of dramatists and artists, as the protector of refugees, as the prophet against all debasements of life and politics; and his fame spread in circles where the fact that Archbishop Davidson had trusted him com-pletely counted for little. For example, he was 'Uncle George' to some of the most remarkable of the German and other European churchmen who stood against Hitler. When the World Council of Churches was formed, it was inevitable that he should be, for all his soft-speaking modesty, one of its leaders. Justly praised as a champion of the oppressed and as a tireless worker for Christian unity, George Bell's name will always belong to the story of the ecumenical movement.

His was a figure in the tradition of the great men who have appeared in this book, and in at least one respect he excelled William Temple himself. While Temple was often remote from the routine of parish life, Bell was a first-class pastor and administrator of the Church in the large county of Sussex, despite difficulties far greater than those facing any of the Victorians who have been praised as diocesan bishops. The obvious charge to make against such a man was that he neglected local details because his mind was on the world's tragedies, but in his case the charge was inaccurate. It can also be said that he was neither witty nor original; but the success of Tait and Davidson can be quoted against any such complaints. He tended to lecture or to preach, even in the House of Lords, when his hearers would have preferred a joke; but so did Frederick and William Temple.

He remained Bishop of Chichester until he retired in 1957. As one

[6] Mervyn Haigh, who had succeeded Bell as Davidson's senior chaplain, and who had become Bishop of Coventry and of Winchester, also seems to have been considered for the Primacy on the death of William Temple, most of whose opinions he shared. But he was a highly strung artist by temperament, and could be indecisive or negative. His health collapsed so that he had to retire at the age of sixty-one, in 1952. See F. R. Barry, *Mervyn Haigh* (SPCK, 1964).

who had played such a prominent role in ecclesiastical affairs and in the application of religious insights to daily life, he was entitled to feel disappointed that no fresh sphere of leadership was ever offered to him—and he was entitled to say so to his journal and his intimates, although he seldom gave the impression of being embittered. He seems to have felt, and to have felt rightly, that the way in which he had been passed over for promotion was connected with his public conduct more than with any personal defects. He apparently committed two sins in the eyes of the small group of men—politicians, civil servants, and those consulted by them—responsible for advising the Crown about the Church of England's senior appointments.

The first sin was his activity in pressing for a reform of the relationship of Church and State in England in the 1930s. He wanted something to be done, when Lang, Temple, and most others preferred things to drift on. Bell's second and even greater sin was to denounce what he regarded as moral errors in his own government's conduct of the second world war. Through his friendship with Dietrich Bonhoeffer he was involved in the effort by anti-Nazi Germans to persuade the Churchill government to indicate, however briefly, that if Nazis were removed from power the German people would still have some dignified prospects in the peace. Churchill and Roosevelt preferred to demand the Germans' unconditional surrender—with the result that, when it became necessary to rebuild and rearm West Germany, that nation had been deprived of much of the flower of its potential leadership, executed by the Nazis after the failure of the 1944 plot. Above all, Bell spoke out against the policy of deliberate 'obliteration bombing' of German civilians in cities and towns. This policy—which was, incidentally, of questionable value from the military point of view—seemed contrary to the limitations imposed by the traditional theory of the just war; and Bell, who was no pacifist, could not help recalling that according to the traditional doctrine a war must be 'just', in methods as well as aims, if it was to be tolerable in the Christian conscience. He incurred great unpopularity among those who accused him of trying to weaken the British war effort. His own dean at Chichester Cathedral was specially indignant. For years to come, statesmen would complain that he seemed to be more interested in the World Council of Churches than in the British Empire.[7]

[7] Some of George Bell's wartime addresses were collected under the title *The Church and Humanity* (Longmans, Green, 1946). William Wand, who did some excellent work as a bishop appointed by Churchill to Bath and Wells in 1943 and to London in 1945, has written an entertaining account of the casual manner of these Churchillian appointments. It appears that the attention of Churchill's bishop-making assistant, Brendan Bracken, was attracted to him as the author of a patriotic pamphlet about the war which he had written while Archbishop of Brisbane. See his autobiography, *Changeful Page* (Hodder & Stoughton,

These were political problems, and they can be argued over by authorities who assess differently either the situation as it existed or the relevance of Christian integrity to it. What cannot be disputed is that George Bell spoke as his conscience told him: a conscience informed by many years of handling the complexities of Church and State. Nor can it be supposed that Bell was ignorant that, when he spoke as he did, he was sacrificing his career. When in later years he vainly hoped to move to Canterbury, York, or London, he was treading (or rather, staying put) in the steps of Samuel Wilberforce; but the causes which moved Bell to renounce higher honours were causes rather more significant, and more honourable, than the Hampden or Gorham squalls on the Victorian ecclesiastical ocean. And the lessons to be learned from his life are graver than those taught by the life of Bishop Wilberforce.

One of the rules of the game which these churchmen played, from Wilberforce to Bell, was that a politician had the right not to promote a priest whose politics he disliked; or as the future Lord Shaftesbury said to Lord John Russell in 1846, 'if *caeteris paribus* he have a fit man on his side of politics he may, for the sake of peace, advance such a person'. But the example of Bishop Bell pointed to a change in the audience for the game and in the nature of the game itself. In Victorian times there was an unwritten compact between Church and State, as the leaders of the Church of England and the politicians in London made adjustments to each other within the solid structure of the ruling class in a Christian society. The Queen's withdrawal of her indiscreet Highland journal in response to the respectful pleadings of the young Dean Davidson was not an isolated concession; nor was the exclusion of divorced people from the royal presence an isolated discipline. There was a framework of moral conventions, generally acknowledged however hypocritically. That framework was, however, disintegrating while George Bell was associated with Archbishop Davidson, as both Gore and Henson had the insight to see; and the bombs on Dresden and Hiroshima exploded the myth that Britain and its allies adhered to the old morality, the old faith, and 'Christian civilization'. Bell survived, an eminent Victorian, into an age of great violence, physical and psychological. It was the time which Newman had foreseen: 'a time of widespread infidelity . . . when only the tops of the mountains will be seen like islands in the waste of waters.' In that context the decline in the applause which Bishop Bell received in England seems both inevitable and, in itself, trivial. His lack of luck in the gamble of promotion would scarcely be worth mentioning (for being the senior clergyman in Sussex

---

1965), pp. 155–77. Bishop Wand also wrote many useful books of history and theology, among them *Anglicanism in History and Today* (Weidenfeld & Nicolson, 1961).

cannot be martyrdom), had not this teacher of Dietrich Bonhoeffer been also the disciple of Randall Davidson, thoroughly aware of England's established conventions—and rewards. It is the measure of his courage in the 1940s that a gossip writer in 1928 could thus describe him: 'He is bustling, eager, almost too obviously ambitious, and entirely self-assured. He is the author of a book pleasant in tone and superficial in knowledge. He is diplomatic, courteous, and the inheritor of the tradition of comprehensiveness and peace at any price.'[8]

The second significant event or non-event in the post-Temple period occurred on 8 July 1969, when the Convocations of the clergy failed to approve a scheme for Anglican–Methodist reunion by a sufficient majority. Sixty-nine per cent voted in favour, but it had been agreed that a majority of three-quarters would be necessary. It was a poignant occasion, which had been hailed in advance as the most important day in English church history for three or four hundred years. The majority in the Church of England now clearly believed that there was no long future for a separated Anglicanism. What was needed was the opening of a new chapter, although of course much of the old story could and should be remembered and continued. But this majority was now seen to be powerless to turn the page. Further poignancy was added by the approval of the scheme on the same day in the Methodist Conference by a majority of seventy-seven per cent (an approval renewed in the following year), and by the warning which the Archbishop of Canterbury, Dr. Michael Ramsey, gave in the course of the Convocations' debate about the likely consequences of Anglican hesitation.

The Archbishop recalled the controversies which had surrounded the nomination of Frederick Temple as Bishop of Exeter and the plans for the Church of South India in William Temple's time.

The inferences to be drawn from such episodes are of course limited, but I believe them to be relevant today. First, it is wrong and dangerous for us to allow our decisions to be decided by cries of 'wolf, wolf'. There have been cries of 'wolf, wolf' a few times too often. Secondly, crises of division can be healed in a shorter time than might be expected as soon as fear ceases to be the dominant thought. Thirdly, moral courage has had its place in the leadership of our Church in years past, and still can if we let it. In the present decision we are making there is also this positive factor—that throughout our Church there is ample evidence of a majority conviction. Majorities can have consciences too; and legislation must have a conscience of majorities. . . . When I soberly try to judge the probabilities, I believe that the division in

8 'The Unknown Layman', *The Looking-Glass of Lambeth*, p. 74. The man who grew from that is portrayed in Ronald Jasper, *George Bell, Bishop of Chichester* (Oxford University Press, 1967). Eberhard Bethge records in his *Dietrich Bonhoeffer* (Collins, 1970), p. 49, that 'the only personalities to whom he granted real authority over him were Karl Barth and Dr. Bell, the Bishop of Chichester'.

our Church will be far deeper and more intractable if we don't go forward
than if we do. . . . It is hard to see where leadership will be found. . . . I
wonder whether it will be easy to have any coherent ecumenical policy. . .
A pause will not bring us any new theological light; it will only see a pro-
longing of the miseries of Church politics.

After the debate, Dr. Ramsey commented: 'There will be bitterness,
anger, and cynicism—especially among those on the fringe of the
Church of England who are going to have reason for being disillusioned
about institutional religion. They will say: "Look at these Churches—
how much they share, yet how they disagree." ' Despite such warnings
from the Archbishop and other advocates, the scheme foundered.

It foundered because of opposition from the heirs of the Anglo-
Catholics who had been suspicious of the Church of South India, plus
opposition from those on the Evangelical wing who were indignant
that the South India method of reunion had not been adopted in
England. Largely in order to satisfy Anglo-Catholic consciences, the
scheme defeated in 1969 provided that clergy and ministers should
all go through a service of reconciliation which could be interpreted
as episcopal ordination. Methodist bishops would be consecrated at
this first stage, but for some time there would be two parallel churches.
Some such opposition was inevitable, both from those who disliked the
idea of an eventual Anglican merger with a Protestant body such as
the Methodists and from those who objected to all the formalities of
ecclesiastical diplomacy when all that mattered was the existing union
of hearts. But arguments against this particular scheme might not be
expected to be specially passionate, since the scheme was promoted
by a number of theologians with an Anglo-Catholic background and
supported by the overwhelming majority of the leaders of the largest
of the English Free Churches. The strength of the opposition or indifference in 1969 was revealed in a referendum of the clergy and in a
confused vote in the House of Laity of the Church Assembly, as well
as in the Convocations. It can be attributed in large measure to the
disintegration of leadership, vision, and courage which was the theme
of the Archbishop's warning, and which seemed likely to be a continuing
problem even if that warning were to be heeded in the adoption of a
scheme for Anglican–Methodist reunion in the near future.

The story of the Church of England's talks with the Presbyterians
was equally inconclusive. The small Presbyterian body in England was
always more likely to join forces with the Congregationalists than with
the Anglicans, but there was much to be said for an ecclesiastical reconciliation, if not for full reunion, between the Church of England and
the Church of Scotland. In 1957 a report was issued by a joint commission which advocated a new style of constitutional episcopacy
('bishops in presbytery'); the report's courage ensured its rejection in a

Scotland which had not forgotten bishops or forgiven them. It also advocated the introduction of 'elders' as lay leaders in the Church of England, a proposal which aroused little interest. Conversations were resumed with the aim of mutual understanding, actual negotiations for reunion having been postponed indefinitely.

Underlying these difficulties was the reluctance of all the Churches to accept radical changes. Archbishop Fisher, who in retirement played an uninhibited part in opposing his successor's hopes for the Anglican–Methodist scheme, shared and voiced the generally conservative attitude, declaring in a Cambridge university sermon in 1946 that 'we are not yet ready for organic or constitutional union'. He gave two particular reasons for believing that the Church of England must get on with its own life without the complications which would result from being too ecumenical. The first was that the traditional relationship with the State must be preserved. In his words, 'the Free Churches would certainly not accept our establishment as it is, and the process of extricating the Church of England from what it was not desired to retain, and of accomplishing its transfer to a newly devised constitution, would be a work of even greater magnitude and difficulty than the scheme of reunion itself.' The second reason was that the Church of England must find its own unity first. 'There are tensions within the Church of England itself which are not yet resolved. It has its own problems of recovering its own spiritual authority over itself and of ordering its own life. But when it is thus engaged in a delicate task, it is unwise at the same time to involve it in questions of constitutional affiliation to other denominations.'

That sermon of 1946 was, therefore, the reopening of negotiations which Fisher himself thought should lead to collaboration and intercommunion between the Churches, but not to a complete merger. It was doubtful whether this was psychologically possible. After the 1920 Lambeth Appeal it could be seen that the Churches would either stay as they were (which the Church of Scotland, for one, was content to do); or they would move towards marriage and procreation. For the Church of England in the 1960s, the trouble about staying as it was arose from a growing feeling of impotence. As secularization advanced, the Church felt itself to be in disarray.

3

It would, however, be wrong, because inaccurate, to end on a note of complete gloom in our summary of the Church of England since 1944. One danger in letting the mind dwell too much among books, reports, debates, and leaders is that one may forget that nine tenths of the life of the Church consists of a hidden routine of worship, friendship, and service. That routine is difficult for the historian to grasp or to describe, but it is always there. Indeed, it is usually more attractive than affairs at the so-called 'centre', and it is always the main source of such strength or beauty or happiness as may exist in the Church.[9] In 1939 Archbishop Garbett implied a shrewd assessment of the Church when he remarked, on reading Hensley Henson's 'able' book in 'perfect prose', that the Church of England was not worth preserving if it was what Henson thought it was.[10] But in fact Henson did himself an injustice when he seemed to be obsessed by his eloquence as a Cassandra in ecclesiastical controversies, and Archbishop Ramsey was right to suggest that his influence was due in large part to 'his belief in straightforward pastoral duty as the key to the Church's life'.[11]

In some ways the 1960s were a repetition of the 1820s when the young Gladstone overheard a conversation between two privates of the Guards on top of the London–Eton coach. 'Come now, what is the Church of England?' 'It is a damned large building with an organ in it.' In the midst of a post-war society absorbed in making money and seeking pleasure, the Established Church found its organization in disarray and its message uncertain, and the progress of dechristianization seemed to be taking another great leap forward into a world where the death of God would be finally acknowledged. There were, however, some crucial differences between the periods at the beginning and end of our story. One difference was that the men in power did not now think they needed the Church as a bulwark against the Revolution. The Church of England in 1970 was therefore less official, less wealthy, less respectable, and less worldly than the Church of Regency England. On the other hand, churchmen in 1970 enjoyed an asset which was less noticeable in the ecclesiastics adorning the pages of Jane Austen or Anthony Trollope: humility. The country parsons to whom Thomas Arnold and John Henry Newman addressed their different appeals were a proud, although a worried, set of men. Less pride could be found in the disordered ranks of the Church of England a quarter-century after William Temple's death, although there was some dogged obstinacy and much impressive self-discipline.[12]

[9] A biography may remind us of this. Such a book, full of humour, is *Father Algy*, about the leading figure among the Anglican Franciscans, by Father Denis (Hodder & Stoughton, 1964). Others include the autobiography of the Rector of Liverpool, Edwyn Young, *No Fun Like Work* (Mowbray, 1970), and the book of essays about *John Groser, East London Priest*, ed. Kenneth Brill (Mowbray, 1971). Or a book may recapture some of the flavour of life in a well-loved parish church. Such a book is *You Owe Me Five Fathin's: An Adventure with St. Martin-in-the-Fields* by George Fearon (Skeffington, 1961).
[10] Charles Smyth, *C. F. Garbett*, p. 412.
[11] A. M. Ramsey, *Canterbury Essays and Addresses* (SPCK, 1964), p. 123.
[12] Some interesting reflections about the Church of England's 'loss of nerve'

The administrative reconstruction of the Church was tackled first, as it had been by Charles James Blomfield and the men around him in the 1830s. The successor to Blomfield as the manager of reconstruction (while retaining conservative views on wider problems) was a man who had been, like him, Bishop of Chester and of London: Geoffrey Francis Fisher. His father, grandfather, and great-grandfather had all been parsons in the same village in Leicestershire. Fisher had first made his reputation by his success when he had followed William Temple as Headmaster of Repton, at the age of twenty-seven. He had thrown his genial energy, efficiency and shrewdness into the tasks which the more intellectual Temple had neglected. Boys and masters had been disciplined. Made Bishop of Chester in 1932, he had become the obvious man to succeed Winnington-Ingram as Bishop of London. There he had resumed Creighton's effort to discipline the diocese, and he had achieved a greater success than Creighton, partly because the smoke arising from the bombing of London in the second world war made the old insistence on the use of incense in church seem luxurious. When on the day after William Temple's funeral Cosmo Lang talked with a visiting Frenchman, 'his own preference was for the Bishop of London, Dr. Fisher. He believed that he possessed better judgment than Temple, in whom he saw primarily a prophet.' This was the man who was appointed Archbishop of Canterbury by Winston Churchill in 1945.[13]

The basic questions undermining the Church's influence were, however, ethical and doctrinal. There might well be hope here—hope, for example, of a growth in true religion through the new compassion for the poor and the odd—but if so Christianity's spokesmen would have to vindicate doctrine as well as ethics.[14] In 1962 a group of Cambridge theologians put together a volume of essays designed to take account of some of the new challenges to doctrine, and the first essay was entitled: 'Beginning All Over Again'. The editor of the book, Dr. Alec Vidler, recalled *Essays and Reviews* which had opened up a doctrinal debate in 1860, and also the happier work of the *Lux Mundi* group around Gore. Dr. Vidler believed that

---

come at the end of an autobiography by a bishop who touched the Church's life at many points: F. R. Barry, *Period of My Life* (Hodder & Stoughton, 1970). Others are suggested by the autobiography of the less intellectual, and Anglo-Catholic, Bishop Walter Carey, *Farewell to my Generation* (Mowbray, 1952).

[13] Marc Boegner, *The Long Road to Unity* (Collins, 1970), p. 198. An interim biography is William Purcell, *Fisher of Lambeth* (Hodder & Stoughton, 1969).

[14] A prophet arose in the person of Trevor Huddleston of the Community of the Resurrection, who worked heroically in Africa and returned to face even more daunting tasks as Bishop of Stepney. See his *Naught for Your Comfort* (Collins, 1956). The Community's work has been described by Nicholas Mosley in *The Life of Raymond Raynes* (Faith Press, 1961).

it is not only obtuseness or incompetence that prevents us from adumbrating a re-interpretation of the Christian faith comparable with that so courageously and confidently essayed by the authors of *Lux Mundi*. We consider our situation to be more analogous to that which prompted the publication of *Essays and Reviews*. That is to say, we believe that these are very important questions which theologians are now being called to face, and which are not yet being faced with the necessary seriousness and determination. We do not profess yet to see our way through them: and we do not want to have to reproach ourselves with looking for a way round them.[15]

When that book, *Soundings*, was published, Geoffrey Fisher had retired from Canterbury, claiming that he left the Church of England 'in good heart' (in 1961). In 1963 an explosion was caused by a little paperback by a Cambridge theologian who had gone to do a spell in South London as a suffragan bishop: *Honest to God* by Dr. John Robinson.[16] Fortunately the next Archbishop of Canterbury had been Regius Professor of Divinity at Cambridge (and, incidentally, a boy at Repton during Fisher's headmastership). Dr. Michael Ramsey had the sensitivity to see that the doctrinal crisis had been concealed, but not averted, by the tone adopted in the Church under his predecessor. As he wrote in a pamphlet commenting on *Honest to God*:

As a Church we need to be grappling with the questions and trials of belief in the modern world. Since the War our Church has been too inclined to be concerned with the organising of its own life, perhaps assuming too easily that the faith may be taken for granted and needs only to be stated and commended. But we state and commend the faith only in so far as we go out and put ourselves with loving sympathy inside the doubts of the doubting, the questions of the questioners, and the loneliness of those who have lost their way.

One who had put himself 'inside the doubts of the doubting', we may recall, was Bishop E. W. Barnes of Birmingham, a Cambridge mathematician and a Fellow of the Royal Society. His modernism had already given much offence to conservatives and great trouble to Archbishop Davidson.[17] In 1947 he published the fruits of his wartime reading in a book on *The Rise of Christianity*. It was wide open (as *Honest to God* was to be) to criticism by experts, and it scarcely touched on the

[15] *Soundings*, ed. A. R. Vidler (Cambridge University Press, 1962), p. xi. Dr. Vidler looked back over the theological fashions of his lifetime in his little book on *Twentieth Century Defenders of the Faith* (SCM Press, 1965).

[16] See *The Honest to God Debate*, ed. David L. Edwards (SCM Press, 1963), and R. J. Page, *New Directions in Anglican Theology: A Survey from Temple to Robinson* (Mowbray, 1967).

[17] Barnes made his defence in *Should Such a Faith Offend?* (Hodder & Stoughton, 1927).

more fundamental problems of belief in God (problems brought home to Robinson by the philosophical theology of the Germans, Bultmann and Tillich). But it did echo many plain men's questions about the literal truth of the biblical narratives. An outcry followed in the Church. Archbishop Garbett wrote: 'I do not think that in the whole course of my ministry anything has happened in the C. of E. more likely to injure the work and influence of the Church than this miserable book'. Archbishop Fisher was equally uncomprehending; if he held such views, he announced, he would not be a bishop. What, then, were these views? They were put forward with a humourless air of superiority to the conventional Church, with a frequent stress on the intellectual inferiority of the early Christians, and with little feeling for the poetry of the great biblical myths. To Barnes, religion was primarily a matter of intellectual and spiritual insight; it was not primarily the sinner's response to the saving acts of God, or participation in the community of sinners being saved. The prophets of Israel, Jesus himself, and the early Christians were all presented in this light. Barnes concluded his book with a strong affirmation that this pure religion was superior to the Christian past and adequate as a faith for the future. But what really gave most offence was this kind of short, clear sentence: 'Belief in the virgin birth of Jesus arose from a mistranslation in the Greek version of a scripture passage in Isaiah, 7.4.' The physical resurrection of Jesus was also dismissed. The spokesmen of the Church of England in the 1940s and 1950s took a firm line towards such denials of the miraculous, as firm a line as Gore had taken in the early years of the century. They might or might not be right theologically, but what they were not doing was to put themselves inside the doubts of the doubting. They thought that the biblical message could be stated and commended by a modern translation, such as the new versions of the New Testament by J. B. Phillips (completed in 1959) or by the New English Bible committee (1961; the whole Bible was published in 1970). It was not enough.

How would the urgently necessary restatement of Christian behaviour and belief come? At the beginning of the 1970s no clear answer was in sight. Naturally, at a time when an awareness of the problems seemed to have destroyed the nerve of many potential leaders there was a reaction among many of the most devoted Christians, in the shape of a return to conservative Evangelicalism. By sheer integrity and industry and by the frequent repetition of its simple message, this group became an effective pressure group within the Church. But it had no influence in society comparable with the days of William Wilberforce; and it failed to communicate its enthusiasm to outsiders or even to the bulk of the Church, because it failed to convince them that its teachings, most of which Lord Shaftesbury would have found congenial, were

EPILOGUE 347

true. Here might be the beginnings of a revival, but the prospect remained uncertain.[18]

All that could be said in 1970 was that the Church of England was humbler than it had been since the beginning of the nineteenth century. It was less insistent on old formularies; the Athanasian Creed was almost never heard, and it seemed probable that the terms of the clergy's assent to the Thirty-nine Articles would soon be relaxed still further. It was more convinced that a love of living people was true religion. It was more ready to listen to contemporary critics who might convey the voice of God. It was more concerned to support 'secular' causes which might reflect the will of God. Its own membership was consulted more patiently, and it was more ready to accept other Churches as fully Christian and to work with them. Groups or parties within it were far less rude to each other, and its parishes were less exclusively parochial. There was widespread support for the revision and modernization of its Prayer Book through experiments. These were signs of hope in a generally discouraging situation.[19]

The hundredth Archbishop of Canterbury, with a background of Anglo-Catholic churchmanship and biblical theology behind him, was prominent among those who sympathized critically with the new stirring of thought produced by the desire for a vision of God in the age of science, industry, and democracy. He was also prominent among those who stressed the primacy of the personal life of the spirit, in submission and waiting, in prayer amid the confusion. In 1960 his thought had still been marked by some complacency about the Anglican tradition. He wrote then in his survey of Anglican thought from Gore's Liberal Catholicism to Temple's growth into orthodoxy:

Certain factors of Anglican continuity have seldom been absent. . . . The Platonist strain has been characteristic of Anglican divinity since the sixteenth century. . . . There is the Anglican sensitivity to the significance of spirituality, the life of prayer, for theology. . . . There is the constant Anglican devotion to Scripture and the Fathers, and some of this appeared in our era with a detachment from the flux of current tendencies. There is the constant Anglican care for the *Via Media* . . . These influences made for integrity and depth at a time when facile and shallow syntheses were too easy.

Dr. Ramsey then added that the 'conscious influence of continental theologians was small' for English churchmen.[20] By the end of the

18 See John C. King, *The Evangelicals* (Hodder & Stoughton, 1969).

19 As one Anglican's attempt to survey the religious situation, David L. Edwards, *Religion and Change* (Hodder & Stoughton, 1969), is available.

20 A. M. Ramsey, *From Gore to Temple*, pp. 162–6. Dr. Ramsey's background may be seen in his book, *The Gospel and the Catholic Church* (Longmans, Green, 1936).

1960s, however, he had presided over a remarkably modest Lambeth Conference of bishops, and had published a number of small books which showed how the search for integrity and depth might take an English churchman into unfamiliar places, partly under the influence of continental theologians. His mind had moved—in the opposite direction to William Temple's.

The stance which Dr. Michael Ramsey adopted while Archbishop of Canterbury was less obviously confident than had been the tradition of his predecessors, who were accustomed to speak as teachers enjoying an untroubled authority.[21] But it was a position which seemed honest and, in its integrity, courageous. For once more, as when Thomas Arnold had prophesied in the 1830s, no human power seemed likely to save the Church of England as it stood. Once more it needed courage to wait for the revival of the tradition: for the heavenly spark and the kindly light, leading perhaps into a new period of widespread religion, or at least into a reaction against the dominance of cynicism and sensuality.

Why did anyone now wait? Refreshingly, some Englishmen in 1970 combined a belief in the essentials of Christianity with an impatience with the past; and the radicalism of such Christians healthily emphasized that, whatever might be the future of English religion, the dead and buried Victorian age would never revive. Any revival that might be on its way would be new life. But for many, an important factor was that they had been impressed by their predecessors, and preferred some of the values held by their predecessors to the prevailing standards of their own day. Towards the last quarter of the twentieth century, many kinds of Victoriana possessed the appeal of a more dignified, and in many spheres more happily creative, past. Even those who were unable to accept any of the Victorian theologies could find something to admire in some of the Victorian Christians.

It was so in the Victorian age itself, when reverence for the Christian dead could form part of agnostic's creed.

> And through thee I believe
> In the noble and great who are gone . . .

That belief, at any rate, was a reality to Matthew Arnold. Another Oxford aesthete, who also could not share the confident doctrines of the churchmen, paid a wistful tribute to the early days of Christianity —days which, as he recognized, had to some extent been matched by the vitality and power of religion in Victorian England. At the end of

---

[21] See, for example, A. M. Ramsey, *God, Christ and the World* (SCM Press, 1969). Contrast, for example, G. F. Fisher, *The Archbishop Speaks*, ed. E. F. Carpenter (Evans, 1958).

Marius the Epicurean (1885), Walter Pater wrote that in Christianity 'there had been a permanent protest established in the world, a plea, a perpetual afterthought, which humanity would ever possess in reserve against any wholly mechanical and disheartening theory of itself and its conditions'.

FOR FURTHER READING

The literature is plentiful, perhaps more plentiful than the life. Of special interest are books which show how the Church of England looked to a veteran bishop, to an experienced archdeacon, to a sharp-eyed journalist, to a group of clergy with a concern for local work, to a priest with a flair for description of the spiritual climate, and to a progressive dean. See Cyril Garbett, *The Claims of the Church of England* (Hodder & Stoughton, 1947); Guy Mayfield, *The Church of England: Its Members and its Business* (Oxford University Press, 1958); Paul Ferris, *The Church of England* (Victor Gollancz, 1962); *The English Church: A New Look*, ed. L. S. Hunter (Penguin Books, 1964); Roger Lloyd, *The Church of England, 1900–1965* (SCM Press, 1966); and Edward Patey, *Look Out for the Church* (Lutterworth Press, 1970).

Index